THE ASHGATE RESEARCH COMPANION TO CORPORATE SOCIAL RESPONSIBILITY

ASHGATE
RESEARCH
COMPANION

The *Ashgate Research Companions* are designed to offer scholars and graduate students a comprehensive and authoritative state-of-the-art review of current research in a particular area. The companion's editors bring together a team of respected and experienced experts to write chapters on the key issues in their speciality, providing a comprehensive reference to the field.

The Ashgate Research Companion to Corporate Social Responsibility

Edited by

DAVID CROWTHER
De Montfort University, UK

NICHOLAS CAPALDI
Loyola University New Orleans, USA

ASHGATE

Published by
Ashgate Publishing Limited
Gower House
Croft Road
Aldershot
Hampshire GU11 3HR
England

Ashgate Publishing Company
Suite 420
101 Cherry Street
Burlington, VT 05401-4405
USA

www.ashgate.com

British Library Cataloguing in Publication Data
The Ashgate research companion to corporate social
    responsibility. - (Corporate social responsibility series)
    1. Social responsibility of business 2. Business ethics
    I. Crowther, David II. Capaldi, Nicholas
    658.4'08

Library of Congress Cataloging-in-Publication Data
The Ashgate research companion to corporate social responsibility / edited by
David Crowther and Nicholas Capaldi.
        p. cm. -- (Corporate social responsibility series)
    Includes index.
    ISBN 978-0-7546-4777-5
    1. Social responsibility of business. 2. Social responsibility of business--Case studies.
3. Business ethics. 4. Business ethics--Case studies. I. Crowther, David. II. Capaldi,
Nicholas. III. Title: Corporate social responsibility.

    HD60.S84 2008
    658.4'08--dc22

2007037044

ISBN 978 0 7546 4777 5

Mixed Sources
Product group from well-managed
forests and other controlled sources
www.fsc.org Cert no. SA-COC-1565
© 1996 Forest Stewardship Council
FSC

Printed and bound in Great Britain by
MPG Books Ltd, Bodmin, Cornwall.

Contents

List of Figures

List of Tables

Author Biographies

Rute Abreu is Adjunct Professor in the Business Department at the Escola Superior de Tecnologia e Gestão, Polytechnic Institute of Guarda, Portugal. Her research and teaching interests include corporate social responsibility, corporate finance, investment appraisal, firm valuation, accounting and physics. She is also the coordinator of the Student Employment Office where she collaborates with students and the School on the ongoing implementation of sustainability models, practices and jobs. Her research has been published in journals such as the *Social Responsibility Journal* and *Corporate Governance: An International Journal*.

Güler Aras is Professor of Finance and Dean of the Graduate School at Yildiz Technical University, Istanbul, Turkey. She received a PhD degree in banking and economics with high honours and previously obtained her MBA and bachelor degrees, also with first rank. Güler has taught a number of courses in the area of corporate finance at undergraduate, graduate and doctorate level. She serves as visiting professor at different universities and as adviser to a number of government bodies. She is the recipient of an award for best scientific work from the Association of Institutional Investors Board in Turkey and is a founder and member of various associations and research centres. She is also a member of a number of international editorial and advisory boards. She is the author of six books and has contributed over 100 articles to academic, business and professional journals and magazines and to edited book collections. She has also spoken extensively at conferences and seminars and has acted as a consultant to a wide range of government and commercial organisations. Her research is into financial economy and financial markets with particular emphasis on the relationship between corporate social responsibility and a firm's financial performance.

Nicole Renée Baptiste is a Doctoral Researcher/Associate Lecturer at Manchester Metropolitan University Graduate Business School, UK, attached to the Human Resource Management/Organisational Behaviour Research Group. She is a licentiate member of the Chartered Institute of Personnel and Development (CIPD). She also lectures at Manchester Metropolitan University Business School and City College Manchester (Business Studies Department). Her research interest is interdisciplinary in the areas of human resource management, employee well-being, organisational studies, management and corporate social responsibility. These can all be considered concerns of people management practices and its effects on worker attitudes and behaviours. Her first degree was in business administration from the University of

Lincolnshire, followed by an MBA from London Metropolitan University. She later attained an MSc in research methods from Manchester Metropolitan University and a postgraduate certificate in academic practice (PGC-AP) and is nearing completion of a PhD. Prior to joining Manchester Metropolitan University Business School, she worked as an HRM professional, responsible for recruitment and selection, training and development of employees, which impelled her initial interest in this research area.

Dominique Bessire is Professeur des universités at the Université d'Orléans (France). She started her career as an auditor with KPMG and then spent six years as a controller with Darty, the leading French firm in retail of household equipment. She entered an academic career at the beginning of the 1980s, later gaining a PhD in management science at the Université Paris I Panthéon-Sorbonne in 1993. Her teaching and research fields cover management control, organisation theory, epistemology, corporate governance, corporate social responsibility and ethics. She has published articles in leading French and anglophone academic journals (*Comptabilité Contrôle Audit, Finance Contrôle Stratégie, Sciences de Gestion, Revue Française de Gestion, Critical Perspectives on Accounting, International Journal of Social Economics*) and has presented papers to numerous international conferences. She is the chair of the Laboratoire Orléanais de Gestion, which regroups all the scholars in management science of Orléans University.

Kiymet Tunca Çalıyurt, PhD, CPA, CFE, was born in Istanbul, Turkey, in 1969. She graduated from the Business School of Marmara University, followed by master's and PhD degrees in accounting. She had a period of postdoctoral study in 2004 with Professor David Crowther at London Metropolitan University, examining social responsibility in accounting. Her second PhD is in fiscal law. She has published several national and international books, and many articles and research papers on social responsibility, fraud, corporate governance and ethics in accounting, finance and taxation, as well as making many presentations on these topics.

Nicholas Capaldi is Legendre-Soulé Distinguished Chair in Business Ethics at Loyola University, New Orleans, USA. He also serves as Director of the National Center for Business Ethics. He taught previously at: the University of Tulsa where he was McFarlin Research Professor of Law; Columbia University; Queens College, City University of New York; The United States Military Academy at West Point; and the National University of Singapore. He received his BA from the University of Pennsylvania and his PhD from Columbia University. His principal research and teaching interest is in public policy and its intersection with political science, philosophy, law, religion and economics. He is the author of seven books and over 80 articles, and has edited six anthologies. He is a member of the editorial board of six journals and has served most recently as editor of *Public Affairs Quarterly*. He is an internationally recognised scholar and a domestic public policy specialist on such issues as higher education, bio-ethics, business ethics, affirmative action and immigration. His recent publications include articles on corporate social responsibility, the ethics of free market societies, and an intellectual biography of John Stuart Mill in connection with which he was recently interviewed on C-SPAN's *Booknotes*.

David Crowther is Professor of Corporate Social Responsibility at De Montfort University in the UK, and Visiting Professor of Corporate Social Responsibility at the Yildiz Technical University, Turkey. His career also includes service as general manager, consultant and accountant in a wide range of organisational settings. He is the author or editor of 20 books and has published more than 200 papers on various aspects of organisational behaviour, knowledge management, environmentalism, corporate reporting and social accounting. He is also a founding member of the Association for Integrity in Accounting. His research interests cover a wide area but are primarily concerned with issues surrounding the accountability of organisations to their wider stakeholder community. He is the founding editor of *Social Responsibility Journal* and also on the editorial boards of several journals and has organised a number of conferences and symposia in a variety of areas.

Fátima David is Adjunct Professor in the Business Department at the Escola Superior de Tecnologia e Gestão, Polytechnic Institute of Guarda, Portugal. She earned her PhD from the Universidad de Salamanca in Spain in 2007. Her research and teaching interests include accounting, corporate finance, investment appraisal and corporate social responsibility.

Ana-Maria Davila-Gomez is a professor in the Department of Administrative Sciences at the Université du Québec en Outaouais (UQO), Canada, where she teaches management and organisational change and conducts researches on the managerial challenges towards more social responsible organisations. She holds a PhD from the Ecole des Hautes Etudes Commerciales de Montréal, and an MBA and an industrial engineering degree from the Universidad del Valle, Colombia. For seven years she worked at various private and public organisations in Colombia (*Emcali* – governmental service; *Unitel* – telecommunications; *Lloreda* – processed food manufacturing), supporting and implementing information technology (IT) and business process re-engineering projects. Her recent doctoral research examined the human implications of IT in management education.

Jelena Debeljak is a teaching assistant in the 'Business Ethics and Corporate Social Responsibility' and 'Introduction to Philosophy' courses at Zagreb School of Economics and Management, Croatia. Having graduated from the university in 2006 in philosophy and religious sciences, she is preparing for a master's degree in business. Since 2003 she has been working actively in the Business Ethics Centre of the Faculty of Philosophy of the Society of Jesus in Zagreb. Her interests relate to the broad area of (human) relations phenomena manifested in public and private life, specifically business in its encounters with multiculturalism and the management of the process of positive change.

Ananda Das Gupta, PhD, has been teaching for the last 18 years in the areas of human resource management, entrepreneurship, corporate ethics, etc. His early career was associated with two central universities: North Eastern Hill University (NEHU) and Indira Gandhi National Open University (IGNOU) as Head of the Department of Commerce at Aizawl and Academic Counsellor respectively, prior to joining the Indian Institute of Plantation Management, a national-level institute in Bangalore, India, in 1999 as head of the HRD area. With a number of publications to his credit, he has successfully guided two doctoral scholars, and two others are currently busy doing their doctorates. He was Project Director of a national-level research project funded by the Indian Ministry of Labour, and he is the Associate Professor (HRD Area) and Programme Co-ordinator of both MBA and PGD-ABPM courses. Recently, the book which he edited, *Human Values in Management*, has been published by Ashgate (UK) and a second one is under consideration from Cambridge Scholars Publishing (UK). In the meantime, his other two books are reaching the point of publication: *Ethics in Business: Concept, Cases and Context* by Rawat Publishers, Jaipur, and *Organizational Development and the Human Dimensions in Management* by Pearson, Singapore.

Kumba Jallow is a principal lecturer at the Leicester Business School, De Montfort University, UK. Her research interests include accounting for sustainability and corporate social responsibility, and she has published papers on these subjects in international journals. She has collaborated in research with colleagues from DMU and from other academic and industrial organisations. These subjects are also reflected in her teaching, which is to both undergraduates and postgraduates. She is also editor of *The Journal of Applied Accounting Research*. Kumba has been a trustee of an environmental organisation, and is currently vice-chair of an international development charity. She has a particular interest in African affairs and the role of business in poverty alleviation.

Alexey Kim graduated from Leeds University (UK) with an MA in economics and finance with distinction in 2003. Soon after that he was employed as a lecturer at Westminster International University in Tashkent, Uzbekistan. Currently, he is a senior lecturer and holds the position of Subject Area Leader in Finance and Accounting. Alexey participated as a trainer in several training programmes in statistical methods and presentation skills. He is also a course leader for the university's young entrepreneurs training course, aimed at developing participants' skills and knowledge to be successful entrepreneurs.

Kristijan Krkač is Professor of Business Ethics and Corporate Social Responsibility, Zagreb School of Economics and Management, and Professor of Analytical Philosophy at the Jesuit College in Zagreb, Croatia. He is the author of three books and more then 50 papers on the topic of Wittgenstein and European pragmatism in the fields of religion, epistemology, ontology and ethics. In the area of CSR he is co-editor of *Business Ethics and Corporate Social Responsibility* (2006), and editor of a textbook on the same subjects in Croatian. His interests cover Wittgenstein, pragmatism, normative ethics, business ethics and CSR. In the last few years his interest has extended to the influence of local European cultures on business and vice versa, especially regarding the principal relation of these phenomena, and also regarding particular cultural and business activities. He has co-organised philosophical symposia, also symposia and scientific colloquia on CSR, and he is administrator of the journal *Disputatio Philosophica*.

Geetanjali Kwatra is a lecturer, Arya Kanya Mahavidyala, Shahbad, District of Kurukshetra, India.

Sonia Meza-Cuadra is a Peruvian economist with graduate studies in the Sorbonne University (Paris I), Johns Hopkins University and London Metropolitan University. During the last 20 years, she has lived in Guatemala, France, Peru, the US and the UK, where she has had a professional career and academic studies that combine business and social development. Her last two jobs were for international organisations: the Organization of American States in Washington DC and Oxfam GB in London. She has made two researches into the mining sector in Peru. The first was for her bachelor's degree at the Universidad del Pacifico, Lima, Peru, in 1982. The second, titled 'Setting a framework for sustainable development in the corporate social responsibility strategy for the Peruvian mining industry: a multi-stakeholder perspective', was for her MA in corporate social responsibility from London Metropolitan University, in January 2007.

Lobar G. Mukhamedova has master's degrees in business computing (University of Westminster) and international tourism (Tashkent State Economy University) and is currently Course Leader for business computing at Westminster International University in Tashkent, Uzbekistan. She also works closely with final-year students in developing their research projects, and has been coordinating the production of a multimedia guide to CSR for SMEs in Uzbekistan, as well as developing curricula for the teaching of CSR in the universities of Uzbekistan.

Malika Mukimova is Course Leader for the BA in commercial law at Westminster International University in Tashkent (WIUT), Uzbekistan. She graduated from Tashkent State University in 1994, obtaining a bachelor's degree in international economic relations. She also has a bachelor's degree in international law obtained from the University of World Economy and Diplomacy and a postgraduate diploma in law received on completion of her studies at the College of Law of England and Wales in London, UK. She is currently a registered PhD student at the University of World Economy and Diplomacy. Her main interests lie in the areas of regulation of international labour migration, tort law, family law and comparative law. She is a member of the CSR research project management team which developed and conducted research on CSR practices in Uzbekistan.

Atakan Öngen was born in Samsun, Turkey, in 1978. He is an environmental engineer, having gained his bachelor's degree at Yildiz Technical University in the Department of Environmental Engineering in 2000 and then gaining his master's degree from Istanbul Technical University's Department of Environmental Engineering in 2002. Currently he is a PhD candidate in Istanbul University's Department of Environmental Engineering. He has been working at Namık

Kemal University, Turkey, since 2001 as a research assistant in the Department of Environmental Engineering, where he is working on industrial pollution control and hazardous waste management. He has three publications (two in Turkish, one in English) to his credit, and has made a number of presentations at scientific conferences and symposia. He has been a member of the Chamber of Environmental Engineering as an Administration Committee Member, representing Corlu county for three years.

Ioanna Papasolomou is Associate Professor in the Department of Marketing, School of Business Administration, at Intercollege, Cyprus. She has teaching and research experience in the UK where she worked as a lecturer in marketing at the Department of Management at Keele University and at Chester Business School. She holds a BA (Hons) in business studies from Philip's College in Cyprus, and an MBA, an MPhil in management, a postgraduate certificate in teaching and learning in higher education and a PhD in management from Keele University. Dr Papasolomou has contributed papers to such journals as the *International Journal of Corporate Communications, International Journal of Bank Marketing, Journal of Marketing Management, European Journal of Business Education, Marketing Intelligence and Planning, Journal of Brand Management, Journal of Product and Brand Management* and the *Journal of Marketing Communications*. She has also contributed chapters and case studies to several academic books as well as published papers in conference proceedings. She was also the Chair for the 10th International Conference on Corporate and Marketing Communications that was hosted by Intercollege in April 2005. She is an associate editor for the *EuroMed Journal of Business* and a member of the editorial board for *Social Responsibility Journal* as well as being a reviewer for a number of journals.

Mary Phillips is a lecturer in the Department of Management, University of Bristol, UK. She has published on matters relating to professionals and professionalism, such as continuing professional development and ethics, on green and social enterprise and on gendered representations in current and historical organisations and organisers. Her work is underpinned by the application of literary and critical theory to organisation studies. She has a developing interest in business tycoons – as well as the article in this book, she is currently working on self-representations in tycoon autobiography.

Tejinder Sharma, PhD, is a lecturer in the Department of Commerce at Kurukshetra University, Kurukshetra, India.

Daniel Stevens holds a BSc (Econ.) and MSc in political science from the London School of Economics and a PhD in development studies from the School of Oriental and African Studies, University of London. He is currently Head of Research and Consultancy at Westminster International University in Tashkent, Uzbekistan, and works with both students and staff in developing their research capacity. He is also Course Leader for the MA in international business and management. His own research interests include issues related to the development of civil society in Uzbekistan, particularly the way in which government, international donors and business relate to it. He has been coordinating the project on corporate social responsibility and SMEs at the university.

R. Şeminur Topal is a professor in the Biology Department within the Science Faculty of Yildiz Technical University, Turkey. Mainly educated as an agricultural engineer, her MSc degree is in dairy technology, and her MPhil is from the Department of Agricultural Microbiology of Ankara University. Her PhD is from Istanbul University Health Science Institute's Veterinary Faculty, gained in 1987. She has produced over 130 publications (19 in English and one in German), eight books, four book chapters in Turkish and three book chapters in English. She has been a member of many Turkish governmental advisory committees. She is an Honorary Member of the Academic Advisory Council of Ansted University and was awarded an honorary doctoral degree by Ansted University in 2002.

Wim Vandekerckhove is based at the Center for Ethics and Value Inquiry, Ghent University, Belgium.

Stella Vettori is Associate Professor at the University of Pretoria, South Africa. She specialises in labour law, social security law and the law of negotiable instruments. She is responsible for the creation and design of three postgraduate courses at that university. In 2005 she completed her doctoral thesis, entitled 'Alternative means to protect legitimate employee interests in the changing world of work'. She has more than ten years' practical experience in labour law. She advises numerous companies on labour law issues such as retrenchments and dismissals, affirmative action policies and various codes of conduct. She has published extensively, both locally and abroad. She has also presented at numerous international conferences. She recently published a book entitled *The Contract of Employment and the Changed World of Work* (Ashgate). Her current project is the publication of an international book concerning the effects of ageing populations on the labour market and labour laws.

Rowan E. Wagner is currently a senior lecturer and Subject Area Leader of Management Studies in the Department of Business Administrative Studies at Westminster International University in Tashkent, Uzbekistan. In addition to this job he frequently works as a consultant for community capacity development, social marketing, behaviour change communication and health project/programme development and implementation in Central and South Asia. Rowan has worked in the past as the Project HOPE TB Program Manager in Uzbekistan, the Central Asia Regional Health Delegate for the American Red Cross and the IFRC, and as Technical Adviser for an Abt. Associates/AIHA/MOH Kazakhstan/Uzbekistan health system reform project in Kazakhstan and Uzbekistan, which involved the development and implementation of family practice primary health centres.

Gülsevim Yumuk was born in Tekirdağ, Turkey. She has a bachelor's degree from the Business Administration Faculty of Istanbul University. Her master's degree studies were completed in the Business Administration Department of Trakya University. Her PhD thesis subject is 'The quality cost system approach of manufacturing industry in the Trakya region of Turkey'. Her interests concern the quality cost of total quality management, social responsibility and cost accounting. She teaches subjects related to business administration in Trakya University, Turkey.

Abbreviations and Acronyms

CalPERS	California Public Employees' Retirement System (US)
CIPD	Chartered Institute of Personnel Development
CMB	Capital Markets Board (of Turkey)
CSR	corporate social responsibility
ECOSOC	Economic and Social Council (of the UN)
EMAS	European Eco-Management and Audit Scheme
EU	European Union
GCGF	Global Corporate Governance Forum
GRI	Global Reporting Initiative
HDI	Human Development Index (of the UN)
HRM	human resource management
IFF	Intergovernmental Forum on Forests
ILO	International Labour Organization
MA	Millennium Ecosystem Assessment
MEM	Ministry of Mining and Energy (Peru)
NGO	non-governmental organisation
OAS	Organization of American States
ODS	ozone-depleting substances
OECD	Organization for Economic Cooperation and Development
SD	sustainable development
SR	social responsibility
TIAA-CREF	Teachers' Insurance and Annuity Association – College Retirement Equities Fund (US)
UN	United Nations
UNCBD	United Nation Convention on Biological Diversity
UNED	United Nations Conference on Environment and Development, Rio de Janeiro, June 1992
UNEP	United Nations Environment Programme
UNFF	United Nations Forum on Forests
WERS	Workplace Employment Relations Survey
WCED	World Commission on Environment and Development

Introduction:
An Agenda for Research

David Crowther and Nicholas Capaldi

In recent years the term corporate social responsibility (CSR) has gained prominence, both in business and in the press, to such an extent that it seems to have become ubiquitous. There are probably many reasons for the attention given to this phenomenon not least of which are the corporate excesses witnessed in recent years. For many people the various examples of this kind of behaviour – ranging from BCCI to Enron to Union Carbide to the collapse of Arthur Andersen – will have left an indelible impression among people that all is not well with the corporate world and that there are problems which need to be addressed (Crowther and Rayman-Bacchus 2004). For others the problems arise from the increasingly globalised world with the elimination of borders as barriers and the rise in power of the transnational corporation (Dasgupta 2006).

One of the implications of the current concern with corporate misbehaviour, however, is that this is a new phenomenon – one which has not been of concern previously. Issues of socially responsible behaviour are not, of course, new and examples can be found from throughout the world and at least from the earliest days of the Industrial Revolution and the concomitant founding of large business entities (Crowther 2002) and the divorce between ownership and management – or the divorcing of risk from rewards (Crowther 2004). Thus, for example in the UK (where the Industrial Revolution started), Robert Owen (1816) demonstrated dissatisfaction with the assumption that only the internal effects of actions need be considered and the external environment was a free resource to be exploited at will. Furthermore he put his beliefs into practice through the inclusion within his sphere of industrial operations the provision of housing for his workers at New Lanark, Scotland. Others went further still; for example, in Belper,[1] Jedediah Strutt and his sons provided farms to ensure that their workers received an adequate supply of milk, as well as building accommodation for their workforce which was of such high standard that these dwellings remain highly desirable in the present day. Similarly, the Gregs of Quarry

---

[1]   Belper is a small town in the centre of England.

Bank[2] provided education as well as housing for their workforce. Indeed, Salt went further and attempted to provide a complete ecosphere for his workers. Thus there is evidence from throughout the history of modernity that the self-centred approach towards organisational activity was not universally acceptable and was unable to satisfactorily provide a basis for human activity.

Since that time there has been a concern for the socially responsible behaviour of organisations which has gained prominence at certain times while being considered of minor importance at others. Thus, during the 1970s, for example, there was a resurgence of interest in socially responsible behaviour. This concern was encapsulated by Ackerman (1975) who argued that big business was recognising the need to adapt to a new social climate of community accountability but that the orientation of business to financial results was inhibiting social responsiveness. McDonald and Puxty (1979), on the other hand, maintained that companies are no longer the instruments of shareholders alone but exist within society and so therefore have responsibilities to that society, and that there is therefore a shift towards the greater accountability of companies to all participants.

It was as long ago as 1967 that Marshall McLuhan first stated that we now live in a global village and that technology was connecting everyone together. Much has changed since then in terms of technology and now with access to the Internet available to everyone we truly do live in a global village in which anyone can interact with anyone else, wherever they are living and whatever time zone they are residing in. The Internet has changed the world as never before and this is having profound consequences for people everywhere.

Marshall McLuhan was prophetic in some of the things which he had to say. When he was talking about this global village he also said that war would continue to be a feature of the world but that there would be an increasing emphasis upon economic war rather than physical war. Well, physical war has not gone away but it might be argued that the reasons for wars in the present are to do with economic reasons at least as much as they are to do with imperialistic or ideological reasons – at least as far as governments and countries are concerned. But governments, as the epitome of the nation state, are becoming less important. Particularly in Europe, but also in other parts of the world, we have seen a number of new nation states becoming established. But this is beside the point, because what is becoming more important than governments and nation states is the multinational company, operating in a global environment. Some of these multinationals are very large indeed – larger than many nation states and a good deal more powerful. Arguably it is here that the economic war for the global village is taking place.

The philosophical foundations of capitalism

There are thus many reasons for the current interest in CSR; it is a topic which is considered to be of particular importance at the present time and definitions of

---

2   Quarry Bank is another industrial location near the centre of the UK.

corporate social responsibility are many and diverse: one which has been created by the European Commission is:

> CSR is a concept whereby companies integrate social and environmental concerns in their business operations and in their interaction with their stakeholders on a voluntary basis. ... every large corporation should be thought of as a social enterprise; that is an entity whose existence and decisions can be justified insofar as they serve public or social purposes.

Corporate social responsibility (CSR) has been one of the most debated management issues, with both academics and practitioners trying to give proper meaning to the concept and justifying why corporations should adopt ethical and socially responsible behaviour, yet there is lack of consensus on what the concept means, what it entails, why it should be embraced, how it should be operationalised, what its roles are in achieving organisational effectiveness or performance and many other issues bordering on the concept. At the same time the development of a theoretical underpinning for CSR has been given increased priority, with a critique of utilitarianism and its antecedent, classical liberalism, featuring prominently.

Classical liberal philosophy[3] is considered by many to be the philosophy which underpins the capitalist economic system. Its adoption, as utilitarianism, provides the legitimation for the free market philosophy of the Anglo-Saxon world. This is based upon one of the main principles of utilitarianism, as expounded by John Stuart Mill (1863), that the maximising of individual benefits would lead to the maximisation of organisational benefits and also societal benefits because outcomes are all that matter to the philosophy in order to determine the net benefit which could be derived summatively. This, of course, leads to the situation whereby a large benefit accruing to one person would outweigh small disutilities accruing to a large number of people because the summative effect is positive and therefore deemed to be desirable – remembering, of course, that the philosophy is only concerned with outcomes: ends rather than means. Effectively, this of course provides a legitimation of exploitation by the powerful of the relatively disadvantaged. By extension this allows corporations to exploit their stakeholders without too much concern for effects, especially as traditional accounting conveniently failed to account for much of this exploitation (Crowther 2004b). Classical liberal economic theory extended the individualistic view of society to include organisations as entities in their own right with the freedom to pursue their own ends.

The seeds were therefore set for the acceptance of selfish behaviour and the abuses of corporate power which we have seen culminating in such things as the Enron debacle. But this was not sufficient to satisfy the wants of corporate magnates – the playing field was still too level! So limited liability was also necessary. The concept of limited liability was first introduced in order to enable large-scale investment to take place. With the separation of investment in a business from the

---

3   See Barnett and Crowther (1998) for a more detailed consideration and critique of classical liberalism.

management of that business there was considered to be a need for the protection of the investors, who were often individuals with a relatively small amount of capital, from the possible fraudulent actions of the managers of the business. Similarly, agency theory was developed to attempt to explain and to align the interests of those managers with the investors through the development of suitable mechanisms. This paved the way for the attraction of many more investors, thereby enabling the growth in size of business enterprises, with those investors secure in the knowledge that they were protected from any loss greater than the sum they had invested in the enterprise. Thus, for relatively small levels of risk they were able to expect potentially great rewards and thereby escape from some of the consequences of the actions of the enterprise. Further actions have been taken since to alleviate corporations (and hence shareholders) from the risk associated with their investments. Buckminster Fuller (1981) describes lucidly the actions of successive US governments[4] during the twentieth century which had the effects of transferring all risk to society in general through taxation, reduced regulation and through acting to bail out failed enterprises.

Thus, by the start of the twentieth century it had been accepted that firms had a corporate identity which was distinct from that of their owners and that such firms embodied a presumption of immortality (Hein 1978). In legal terms a company therefore is a person with the power to contract like any other individual,[5] although the reality is that this power is vested in the managers of the company. The effect of this is that managers can enter into transactions for which they have no liability for non-fulfilment. Effectively, by the introduction of this concept of limited liability risk was transferred away from the legal owners of a business and onto those with whom that business transacted. Equally, the ability of managers to engage in those transactions on behalf of the business, without any necessary evidence of ownership – merely delegated responsibility – meant that most risk was thereby transferred away from the business. The potential rewards from owning a business became divorced from any commensurate risk – effectively separating the risk/reward relationship upon which finance theory is based.

Still these changes have not been sufficient and so recent concern has been with the free market as a mediating mechanism. The argument, of course, is that unregulated transacting will benefit everyone but this is only true in a situation of perfect competition;[6] with the power inequalities which exist this only justifies exploitation by the powerful (aka corporations). This then creates an environment in which CSR is needed.

---

4   These changes have, of course, been paralleled in the actions of all other governments of the Western world.
5   *Wenlock (Baroness) v River Dee Co, 1887.*
6   One of the first assumptions of economics is that of perfect competition – readily acknowledged to be an unrealistic set of assumptions which are quickly relaxed in theory. This of course never gets a mention by the free marketers – or even their critics!

The effects of technological development

Perhaps of more importance at this point is to return to Marshall McLuhan and the way in which technology is bringing about the global village – and I am referring now to the Internet. The increasing availability of access to the Internet has been widely discussed and its effects suggested, upon both corporations and upon individual members of society (Rushkoff 1997). For corporations much has been promulgated concerning the opportunities presented through the ability to reach a global audience and to engage in electronic retailing; much less has been said about the effects of the change in accountability provided by this medium. Much of what has been said is based upon an expectation that the Internet and the World Wide Web will have a beneficial impact upon the way in which society operates (see for example Holmes and Grieco 1999). Thus Sobchack (1996) argues that this technology will be more liberating, participatory and interactive than previous cultural forms while Axford (1995) argues that it will lead to increasing globalisation of politics, culture and social systems. Much of this discourse is concerned at a societal level with the effects of Internet technology upon society, and only by implication upon individuals within society. It is, however, only at the level of the individual that these changes can take place. Indeed access to the Internet, and the ability to communicate via this technology to other individuals, without regard to time and place, can be considered to be a revolutionary redistribution of power (Russell 1975) – a redistribution in favour of us all as individuals. Moreover, the disciplinary practices of society (Foucault 1977) break down when the Internet is used because of the lack of spatial contiguity between communicants and because of the effective anonymity of the communication which prevents the normalising surveillance mechanisms of society (Clegg 1989) to intercede in that communication. Thus the Internet provides a space for resistance to foment (Robins 1995).

Of particular interest, however, is the way in which access to the technology to use the Internet can redefine the corporate landscape and change the power relationship between large corporations and individuals. In this respect the changes in these power relationships can be profound and even revolutionary. The technology provides a potential challenge to legitimacy and can give individuals the ability to confront large corporations and to have their voice heard with equal volume within the discourse facilitated by cyberspace. In this respect the power imbalance is being equalised and we are moving from a global marketplace to a truly global village.

The performance dialectic

According to Crowther (2002), although organisational performance is normally presented as a dialectical performance along the two incompatible dimensions of financial performance and social/environmental performance, this is in fact a false dialectic. Although the annual reporting of organisations presents it as such, empirical evidence demonstrates that organisations actually perform equally well along both dimensions. Thus, that dialectic is a construction inherent in annual reports which is created and maintained through the semiotic of these reports, to such an extent that the perception of the dialectic as extant is generally accepted within the discourse of both corporate reporting and of accounting theory. Thus the dialectic appears in a form which is believed so absolutely that an alternative becomes inconceivable; it has therefore assumed the mantel of a myth (Cassirer 1946; Miller 1992). Indeed the proponents of environmental accounting and reporting found their analysis upon the existence of this dialectic. It therefore becomes necessary to consider why, if this dialectic does not in fact exist, it is created through the semiotic of the corporate annual reporting mechanism.

If the dialectic does not exist in corporate performance itself then its creation in the annual report must be undertaken by either the authors of the script of that report or by the readers of that reporting script. Although it has been argued that the semiotic is created by the reader of the report based upon his or her understanding of the contents of that report, the implication of this is that each person produces an interpretation based upon the linguistic, social and environmental experiences which underpin any understanding. Thus each person creates an individual semiotic (Habermas 1971) from the information available to him/her but moreover seeks to create a semiotic understanding based upon the intentions of the group which holds power (Lakoff 1975). That group is, of course, the authors of the script who are at the same time the managers of the organisation.[7] For that semiotic to be created, however, in such a way that the dialectic between the internal (or traditional accounting) and the external (or social) perspectives upon corporate performance is understood to exist, it is of course necessary that sufficient signals are created within the text for the semiotic to be extracted as a general interpretation. It is in this method that the author's meaning is reinstated in the text (Gadamer 1975). The only people with the power to achieve this are, of course, the authors of the text. Hence it must be concluded that the dialectic of corporate reporting is both created and maintained by the managers of the organisation. It therefore becomes necessary to consider why this might be so.

The management of an organisation tends to be treated as a discrete entity[8] but it is important to remember that this entity actually comprises a set of individuals with their own drives, motivations and desires. Thus every individual has a desire to fulfil his/her needs and one of these is self-actualisation (Maslow 1954). This need is the one at the top of Maslow's hierarchy of needs and consequently perhaps the one most considered in terms of motivation. The next two most important needs – the need for esteem (as reflected in self-respect and the respect of others) and the need for love and belonging (as reflected in the need for being an integral part of a community) – are, however, more important for the understanding of the behaviour of the members of the dominant coalition of management within an organisation. These two needs help to explain why managers, in common with

---

7   More specifically it is the dominant coalition of managers.
8   Or rather a coalition which acts in unison.

other individuals, need to feel important, skilled and essential to organisational performance.

One view of good environmental performance is that of stewardship and thus, just as the management of an organisation is concerned with the stewardship of the financial resources of the organisation, so too would management of the organisation be concerned with the stewardship of environmental resources. The difference, however, is that environmental resources are mostly located externally to the organisation. Stewardship in this context therefore is concerned with the resources of society as well as the resources of the organisation. As far as stewardship of external environmental resources is concerned then the central tenet of such stewardship is that of ensuring sustainability. Sustainability is focused on the future and is concerned with ensuring that the choices of resource utilisation in the future are not constrained by decisions taken in the present. This necessarily implies such concepts as generating and utilising renewable resources, minimising pollution and using new techniques of manufacture and distribution. It also implies the acceptance of any costs involved in the present as an investment for the future.

Not only does such sustainable activity, however, impact upon society in the future; it also impacts upon the organisation itself in the future. Thus, good environmental performance by an organisation in the present is in reality an investment in the future of the organisation itself. This is achieved through the ensuring of supplies and production techniques which will enable the organisation to operate in the future in a similar way to its operations in the present and so to undertake value creation activity in the future much as it does in the present. Financial management also, however, is concerned with the management of the organisation's resources in the present so that management will be possible in a value-creation way in the future. Thus the internal management of the firm, from a financial perspective, and its external environmental management coincide in this common concern for management for the future. Good performance in the financial dimension leads to good future performance in the environmental dimension and vice versa. Thus there is no dichotomy between environmental performance and financial performance and the two concepts conflate into one concern. This concern is, of course, the management of the future as far as the firm is concerned.[9] The role of social and environmental accounting and reporting and the role of financial accounting and reporting therefore can be seen to be coincidental. Thus the work required needs be concerned not with arguments about resource distribution but rather with the development of measures which truly reflect the activities of the organisation upon its environment. These techniques of measurement, and consequently of reporting, are a necessary precursor to the concern with the management for the future.

Similarly the creation of value within the firm is followed by the distribution of value to the stakeholders of that firm, whether these stakeholders are shareholders

---

9   Financial reporting is, of course, premised upon the continuing of the company – the going concern principle.

or others. Value, however, must be taken in its widest definition to include more than economic value as it is possible that economic value can be created at the expense of other constituent components of welfare such as spiritual or emotional welfare.[10] This creation of value by the firm adds to welfare for society at large, although this welfare is targeted at particular members of society rather than treating all as equals. This has led to arguments by Tinker (1988), Herremans et al. (1992) and Gray (1992), amongst others, concerning the distribution of value created and to whether value is created for one set of stakeholders at the expense of others. Nevertheless if, when summed, value is created then this adds to welfare for society at large, however distributed. Similarly, good environmental performance leads to increased welfare for society at large, although this will tend to be expressed in emotional and community terms rather than being capable of being expressed in quantitative terms. This will be expressed in a feeling of well-being, which will, of course, lead to increased motivation. Such increased motivation will inevitably lead to increased productivity, some of which will benefit the organisations, and also a desire to maintain the pleasant environment which will in turn lead to a further enhanced environment, a further increase in welfare and the reduction of destructive aspects of societal engagement by individuals.

Thus increased welfare leads to its own self-perpetuation. In the context of welfare also, therefore, financial performance and environmental performance conflate into a general concern with an increase in welfare. It can therefore be argued that environmental performance and financial performance are not different dimensions of performance which must inevitably be in opposition to each other. Rather they are both facets of the same dimension of concern for the future. The conflation of financial performance and environmental performance into the same concept does not, of course, mean that environmental accounting becomes irrelevant. Rather it raises the profile of such accounting and places it at the centre of organisational accounting alongside management accounting. Furthermore it means that more work is needed to develop the embryonic concepts of environmental accounting and make the quantification of environmental effect more effective, meaningful and comparative. Thus it becomes apparent that more work is needed in the area of environmental accounting but, moreover, it becomes apparent that this is work which is vital for the understanding of corporate performance and the future of that performance. Thus, environmental accounting and performance must inevitable become the concern of corporate management.

Conclusion

This introduction has covered a number of seemingly unrelated issues and this is deliberate, as the intention has been to highlight a number of issues which are currently being debated within the discourse of CSR. The purpose of this book is

10   See, for example, Mishan (1967), Ormerod (1994) and Crowther et al. (1998). This can be equated to the concept of utility from the discourse of classical liberalism.

to take this exploration further by looking at more varied aspects of CSR. So all the contribution in this book are concerned with different aspects of CSR but are united through their concern with the effect of corporate activity upon the various stakeholders to that corporation, although all of the contributors consider this issue through differing theoretical lenses and are concerned with different stakeholder groupings. Part of our intention is to show the diversity of concerns which fall within the umbrella term of corporate social responsibility. It is equally part of the objective of this book to show that a concern with corporate social responsibility is a worldwide issue which is being addressed by scholars in many countries. Thus the contributors to this book come from a number of different countries. Our aim is to present a spectrum of approaches from a variety of scholars from different countries and from different disciplines in order to show the diversity of the debate and the diversity of contributors. In doing so we hope to both broaden the debate and make it more inclusive by the facilitation of scholars from different countries, disciplines and ontologies in engaging with each other because it is our belief that this is a manner in which progress will be made.

It is necessary to treat the various issues under discussion in separate chapters, each contributed by different experts in various locations throughout the world. One implication of this is that these are discrete topics whereas there is considerable overlap in the topics. Thus many topics will be referred to in the context of various chapters about seemingly diverse subjects. For example, sustainability is such an important concept, and so central to any discussion of corporate social responsibility, that it features extensively in the various contributions to this volume. So too are concepts such as accountability and governance.

It is important also to recognise that this volume is not encyclopaedic in the coverage of corporate social responsibility – such a task would be impossible. There is not as yet – and may never be – any overall consensus concerning what is meant by corporate social responsibility. There are many different definitions which inevitably include (or exclude) certain activities when discussing responsible business practices. Moreover, any analysis of corporate social responsibility is still embryonic; theoretical frameworks, measurement and empirical methods still remain to be resolved. This volume therefore does not seek to do more than to highlight a number of important debates which are taking place in the arena. The choice of topics is, of course, that of the editors; in making this choice we recognise, of course, that many readers will disagree with what has been included or, more significantly, what has been excluded. We recognise this likelihood is a consequence of the choices we have made.

References

Ackerman, R.W. (1975), *The Social Challenge to Business*, Cambridge MA: Harvard University Press.

Axford, B. (1995), *The Global System*, Cambridge: Polity Press.

Barnett, N.J. and Crowther, D. (1998), 'Community identity in the 21st century: a postmodernist evaluation of local government structure', *International Journal of Public Sector Management*, 11 (6/7), 425–39.

Bentham, J. (1789), *An Introduction to the Principles of Morals and Legislation*, many editions.

Buckminster Fuller, R. (1981), *Critical Path*, New York: St Martin's Press.

Cassirer, E. (1946), *Language and Myth*, trans. S.K. Langer, New York: Dover.

Clegg, S.R. (1989), *Frameworks of Power*, London: Sage.

Crowther, D. (2004), 'Limited liability or limited responsibility', in D. Crowther and L. Rayman-Bacchus (eds), *Perspectives on Corporate Social Responsibility*, Aldershot: Ashgate, 42–58.

Crowther, D. (2002), *A Social Critique of Corporate Reporting*, Aldershot: Ashgate.

Crowther, D., Davies, M. and Cooper, S. (1998), 'Evaluating corporate performance: a critique of economic value added', *Journal of Applied Accounting Research*, 4 (3), 2–34.

Crowther, D. and Rayman-Bacchus, L, (2004), 'Perspectives on corporate social responsibility', in D. Crowther and L. Rayman-Bacchus (eds), *Perspectives on Corporate Social Responsibility*, Aldershot: Ashgate, pp1–17.

Dasgupta, S. (2006), 'Globalization and its future shock', in S. Dasgupta and R. Kiely (eds), *Globalization and After*, New Delhi: Sage, pp143–83.

European Commission (2002), *Corporate Social Responsibility: A Business Contribution to Sustainable Development*, Brussels: EC.

Foucault, M. (1977), *Discipline and Punish*, trans. A. Sheridan, Harmondsworth: Penguin.

Gadamer, H.G. (1975), *Truth and Method*, trans. G. Bardent and J. Cumming, London: Sheed & Ward.

Gray, R. (1992), 'Accounting and environmentalism: an exploration of the challenge of gently accounting for accountability, transparency and sustainability', *Accounting, Organizations & Society*, 17 (5), 399–425.

Habermas, J. (1971), *Knowledge and Human Interests*, trans. J.J. Shapiro, Boston MA: Beacon.

Hein, L.W. (1978), *The British Companies Acts and the Practice of Accountancy 1844–1962*, New York: Arno Press.

Herremans, I.M., Akathaparn, P. and McInnes, M. (1992), 'An investigation of corporate social responsibility, reputation and economic performance', *Accounting, Organizations & Society*, 18 (7/8), 587–604.

Holmes, L. and Grieco, M. (1999), 'The power of transparency: the Internet, e-mail and the Malaysian political crisis', paper presented to Asian Management in Crisis Conference, Association of South East Asian Studies, University of North London, June 1999.

Lakoff, R. (1975), *Language and Woman's Place*, Cambridge: Harper & Row.

McDonald, D. and Puxty, A.G. (1979), 'An inducement – contribution approach to corporate financial reporting', *Accounting, Organizations & Society*, 4 (1/2), 53–65.

McLuhan, M. and Fiore, Q. (1968), *War and Peace in the Global Village*, San Francisco: Hardwired.

Maslow, A.H. (1954), *Motivation and Personality*, New York: Harper & Row.

Mill, J.S. (1863), *Utilitarianism, Liberty and Representative Government*, many editions.

Miller, D.F. (1992), *The Reason of Metaphor*, London: Sage.

Mishan, E.J. (1967), *The Costs of Economic Growth*, Harmondsworth: Pelican.

Ormerod, P. (1994), *The Death of Economics*, London: Faber & Faber.

Owen, R. (1816 [1991]), A New View of Society and other writings, London: Penguin.

Robins, K. (1995), 'Cyberspace and the world we live in', in M. Featherstone and R. Burrows (eds), *Cyberspace/Cyberbodies/Cyberpunk*, London: Sage.

Rushkoff, D. (1997), *Children of Chaos*, London: HarperCollins.

Russell, B. (1975), *Power*, London: Routledge.

Sobchack, V. (1996), 'Democratic franchise and the electronic frontier', in Z. Sardar and J.R. Ravetz (eds), *Cyberfutures*, London: Pluto.

Tinker, T. (1988), 'Panglossian accounting theories: the science of apologising in style', *Accounting, Organizations & Society*, 13 (2), 165–89.

PART I

THEORETICAL DEVELOPMENTS

Overview of Part I

Although much has been written about CSR, in the main it has been descriptive and evaluative. Much less attention has been paid to the development of a coherent body of theory to explain the development of the phenomenon. The attempts which have been made primarily attempt to develop the theory in the context of political economy theory or social contract theory, although other approaches exist. The contributors in this part do not, however, seek to develop an overall theory of CSR; rather they look at particular aspects of CSR and theorise those aspects. Thus there is a depth and breadth to the overall contribution of this section which makes a considerable contribution towards extending the discourse.

Thus, in the first chapter, Crowther situates CSR activity as a developmental process which changes its emphasis as a business matures in its approach to CSR. He argues that a wide variety of activities have been classed as representing CSR, ranging from altruism to triple bottom-line reporting and different approaches have been adopted in different countries, in different industries and even in different but similar corporations. Significantly however, for him, the socially responsible activity of corporations shows a developmental process of increasing maturity over time. Thus the purpose of this chapter is firstly to develop a typology of such activity and then to show evidence for convergence towards a commonality which has universal application. He argues that the voluntary approach taken by the European Community is effective without the need to develop any imposed standards.

This term, sustainability, has become ubiquitous both within the discourse of globalisation and within the discourse of corporate performance, and this is the concern of Jallow in the next chapter. Sustainability is, of course, a controversial issue and there are many definitions of what is meant by the term. At the broadest definitions, sustainability is concerned with the effect which action taken in the present has upon the options available in the future. If resources are utilised in the present then they are no longer available for use in the future; consequently there is a need to tread lightly on the earth and remember the legacy that we owe to our children to leave the world as we found it. Sustainability is a controversial topic because it means different things to different people. There is a further confusion surrounding the concept of sustainability because for the purist sustainability implies nothing more than stasis – the ability to continue in an unchanged manner – but often it is taken to imply development in a sustainable manner and the terms 'sustainability' and 'sustainable development' are for many viewed as synonymous.

For Jallow this confusion and controversy provides a challenge to CSR research which needs to be recognised and accommodated.

According to Crowther, stakeholder theory is based upon the notion of the social contract between an organisation and society and is premised in the notion that if the organisation affects any stakeholder then it also has a concomitant responsibility towards that stakeholder. He considers the various definitions of stakeholders in this context and the way in which they interact with the corporation and with each other. He argues that corporations have recognised the importance of all stakeholders to their current and future performance and have acted to take into account their needs. Thus, for him, there has come about both a recognition that corporations are accountable to their stakeholders and a consequent development of the principles upon which this demonstration of accountability should be based. This reflects a recognition that the organisation is an integral part of society, rather than a self-contained entity which has only an indirect relationship with society at large. This self-containment has been the traditional view taken by most organisations as far as their relationship with society at large is concerned, with interaction being only by means of resource acquisition and sales of finished products or services. Recognition of this closely intertwined relationship of mutual interdependency between the organisation and society at large, when reflected in the accounting of the organisation, can help bring about a closer, and possibly more harmonious, relationship between the organisation and society.

Bessire is interested in the concept of transparency – a concept which is central to the discourse of corporate social responsibility. She argues that transparency is assumed to be necessary but its meaning in practice is never questioned. In this chapter, therefore, she traces the origins of the concept and tries to uncover the theoretical connections with managerial, economic and even philosophical literature, before considering the adverse effects of discourses on transparency: the dissimulation of a struggle for power, the expression of a disciplinary power and more generally the exclusion of ethics. Then she argues for the need to break away from the anti-humanist assumptions on which economic science has developed and which underpin most discourses on transparency. For her it is necessary to rebuild management science on a radically different basis, with a stronger emphasis on the concept of trust and the necessity of promoting pluralist democracy.

Transparency is, of course, an integral aspect of corporate governance and it is with governance that Aras is concerned in the next chapter. She outlines the four major principles on which good governance needs to be based and also investigates the relationship between a firm's performance and shareholders' returns. Her main focus, however, is upon governance and financial markets, where problems lead to such phenomena as insider trading and situations of conflicts of interest which are also known as the private benefits of control. For her these problems are situated within the agency problem, which has been subject to much analysis and investigation in terms of conflicts of interest. But, significantly, the role of trust in the agency relationship is significantly missing from the analysis – an omission which she aims to remedy.

Ananda Das Gupta is also concerned with both governance and sustainable development. For him sustainable development seems to be something like motherhood and apple pie – everyone finds it a good thing, and there is almost universal appreciation. At first sight, this is highly positive, as this could signal the entrance of a holistic and responsible thinking into the world of politics and society. But as it often happens with other catch phrases that suddenly come into vogue, like 'empowerment' and 'participation', it might not be more than a rhetoric which fails to translate into practice; this all the more so because sustainable development can be given several different interpretations. He argues that many companies are choosing to make an explicit commitment to corporate social responsibility in their mission, vision and values statements. Such statements frequently extend beyond profit maximisation to include an acknowledgement of a company's responsibilities to a broad range of stakeholders, including employees, customers, communities and the environment. This strategy, by which a company's core values – independent of specific strategic goals – serve as the guiding force in determining a company's mission and vision, as well as its day-to-day policies and practices, is often described as a 'values-based business approach'.

For Topal and Ongen the environment is the most important aspect of social responsibility. For them, the environment is in a kind of trust for anyone with children and who therefore has a stake in future generations and the ability of the ecosphere to support life in the future. Thus they, too, have a concern with sustainability but in an environmental context. But they are concerned with more than this as they continue to argue that environmental good practice is also about business efficiency. They elucidate this within the context of business behaviour and environmental conservation, as well as considering the stakeholder community and the ethics of environmental protection in their wide-ranging chapter. Their concern extends beyond business behaviour into the way in which science can be applied for the protection of the environment against further degradation.

A number of issues feature prominently in this section, and will be referred to again in the other sections of this book. Some, such as sustainability and/or sustainable development or the effects of the environment, have been dealt with through chapters devoted to these topics. Other concepts are equally important but are not dealt with in individual chapters; examples of such concepts include governance, trust and the social contract between business and society. Whether or not they have been treated as subjects in individual chapters, these concepts are all central to any discussions about corporate social responsibility. Thus they inevitably permeate the various chapters in this book, and therefore serve to underlined the inter-relatedness of the various topics selected for inclusion.

The Maturing of Corporate Social Responsibility: A Developmental Process

David Crowther

Introduction: developing standards for reporting

There has been considerable change in the emphasis of corporate reporting of corporate social responsibility (CSR) activity in recent years. This change is not just in terms of the extent of such reporting, which has become more or less ubiquitous throughout the world, but also in terms of style and content. When researching into corporate activity and the reporting of that activity in the 1990s it was necessary to acknowledge (Crowther 2002) that no measures of social or environmental performance existed which had gained universal acceptability. Good social or environmental performance was subjectively based upon the perspective of the evaluator and the mores of the temporal horizon of reporting. Consequently, any reporting concerning such performance could not easily be made which would allow a comparative evaluation between corporations to be undertaken. This was regarded as helpful to the image-creation activity of the corporate entities who were reporting, as the authors of the script were therefore able to create an image which could not be refuted through quantificatory comparative evaluation. Instead, such images could be created through the use of linguistic and non-linguistic means. Thus each company was able to select measures which created the semiotic of social concern and environmental responsibility and of continual progress, through the selective use of measures which supported these myths. As a consequence of the individual selection of measures to be reported upon, a spatial evaluation of performance, through a comparison of the performance with other companies, was not possible and a temporal evaluation was all that remained. This temporal evaluation was, of course, determined by the authors of the script, through their choice of measures upon which to report, in order to support the myth of continual improvement. Because any measure of such performance did not have universal acceptance as a measurement tool, each company had to determine its own priorities for social and environmental performance and develop appropriate measures for reporting upon impact. It is convenient, however, that companies who were all undertaking very similar operations chose different measures of performance – measures which all show their performance as being not just good but, by implication, the best that can be achieved.

While this research was being undertaken steps were being taken to change this and to develop some kind of standards for reporting. Thus in 1999 the Institute of Social and Ethical Accountability[1] published the AA1000 Assurance Standard with the aim of fostering greater transparency in corporate reporting. AccountAbility, an international, not-for-profit, professional institute has launched the world's first-ever assurance standard for social and sustainability reporting. The AA1000 framework[2] is designed to improve accountability and performance by learning through stakeholder engagement. It was developed to address the need for organisations to integrate their stakeholder engagement processes into daily activities. It has been used worldwide by leading businesses, non-profit organisations and public bodies. The framework is designed to help users to establish a systematic stakeholder engagement process that generates the indicators, targets and reporting systems needed to ensure its effectiveness in overall organisational performance. The principle underpinning AA1000 is inclusivity. The building blocks of the process framework are planning, accounting and auditing and reporting. It does not prescribe what should be reported on but rather the 'how'.

According to AccountAbility the AA1000 Assurance Standard is the first initiative offering a non-proprietary, open-source assurance standard covering the full range of an organisation's disclosure and associated performance (that is, sustainability reporting and performance). It draws from and builds on mainstream financial, environmental and quality-related assurance, and integrates key learning with the emerging practice of sustainability management and accountability, as well as associated reporting and assurance practices.

At about the same time the Global Reporting Initiative (GRI) produced its Sustainability Reporting Guidelines, which have been developed through multi-stakeholder dialogue. The guidelines are claimed to be closely aligned to AA1000, but focus on a specific part of the social and environmental accounting and reporting process, namely reporting. The GRI aims to cover a full range of economic issues, although these are currently at different stages of development. The GRI is an initiative that develops and disseminates voluntary Sustainability Reporting Guidelines. These Guidelines are for voluntary use by organisations for reporting on the economic, environmental, and social dimensions of their activities, products, and services. Although originally started by an NGO, GRI has become accepted as a leading model for how social environmental and economic reporting should take place. It aims to provide a framework that allows comparability between different companies' reports whilst being sufficiently flexible to reflect the different impacts of different business sectors.

---

1   The Institute of Social and Ethical Accountability is probably better known as AccountAbility.

2   See <http://www.accountability.org.uk>.

The GRI incorporates the active participation of representatives from business, accountancy, investment, environmental, human rights, research and labour organisations from around the world. Started in 1997, GRI became independent in 2002, and is an official collaborating centre of the United Nations Environment Programme (UNEP) and works in cooperation with UN Secretary-General Kofi Annan's Global Compact. The Guidelines are under continual development and in January 2006 the draft version of the new Sustainability Reporting Guidelines, named the G3, was produced and made open for feedback. The GRI pursues its mission through the development and continuous improvement of a reporting framework that can be used by any organisation to report on its economic, environmental and social performance. The GRI has become the popular framework for reporting, on a voluntary basis, for several hundred organisations, mostly for-profit corporations. It claims to be the result of a permanent interaction with many people that supposedly represents a wide variety of stakeholders relative to the impact of the activity of business around the world.

GRI and AA1000 provide a set of tools to help organisations manage, measure and communicate their overall sustainability performance: social, environmental and economic. Together, they draw on a wide range of stakeholders and interests to increase the legitimacy of decision-making and improve performance. Individually, each initiative supports the application of the other – at least this is the claim of both organisations concerned; AA1000 provides a rigorous process of stakeholder engagement in support of sustainable development, while GRI provides globally applicable guidelines for reporting on sustainable development that stresses stakeholder engagement in both its development and content. Part of the purpose of this chapter, however, is to question the need for these standards, as all the evidence concerning standard-setting suggests that standards are derived by consensual agreement rather than by the actions of a third party.

The EC approach

The European Union, through its Commission, has concentrated on the enaction of corporate social responsibility (CSR) as an expression of European cohesion. The Green Papers *Promoting a European Framework for Corporate Social Responsibility* (EC 2001) and *Corporate Social Responsibility: A Business Contribution to Sustainable Development* (EC 2002) define the pressure from the European institutions for corporations to recognise and accommodate their responsibilities to their internal and external stakeholder community. The first document (EC 2001: 8) described CSR as '… a concept whereby companies integrate social and environmental concerns in their business operations and in their interaction with their stakeholders on a voluntary basis'. The essential point is that compliance is voluntary rather than mandatory, and this voluntary approach to CSR expresses the reality of enterprises in beginning to take responsibility for their true social impact and recognises the existence of a larger pressure exercised by various stakeholder groupings in addition to the traditional ones of shareholders and investors. Moreover, it reflects the different traditions of business and differing stages of development throughout the Community. Nevertheless, the need for social responsibility is by no means universally accepted but evidence shows that ethical and socially responsible behaviour is being engaged in successfully by a number of large corporations – and this number is increasing all the time. Additionally, there is no evidence that corporations which engage in socially responsible behaviour perform, in terms of profitability and the creation of shareholder value, any worse than do any other corporations. Indeed, there is a growing body of evidence[3] that socially responsible behaviour leads to increased economic performance – at least in the longer term – and consequentially greater welfare and wealth for all involved.

All of this means that a wide variety of activities have been classed as representing CSR, ranging from altruism to triple bottom-line reporting, and different approaches have been adopted in different countries, in different industries and even in different but similar corporations. The purpose of this chapter is firstly to develop a typology of such activity and then to show evidence for convergence towards a commonality – in other words that the voluntary approach of the EC is effective without the need to develop any imposed standards.

Defining CSR

The broadest definition of corporate social responsibility (see Crowther and Rayman-Bacchus 2004) is concerned with what is – or should be – the relationship between global corporations, governments of countries and individual citizens. More locally the definition is concerned with the relationship between a corporation and the local society in which it resides or operates. Another definition is concerned with the relationship between a corporation and its stakeholders. All of these definitions are pertinent and each represents a dimension of the issue. A parallel debate is taking place in the arena of ethics – should corporations be controlled through increased regulation or has the ethical base of citizenship been lost and need to be replaced before socially responsible behaviour will ensue? However this debate is represented it seems that it is concerned with some sort of social contract between corporations and society.

This social contract implies some form of altruistic behaviour – the converse of selfishness (Crowther and Çalıyurt 2004) – whereas the self-interest of classical liberalism connotes selfishness. Self-interest is central to the utilitarian perspective championed by such people as Bentham, Locke and J.S. Mill. The latter, for example, advocated as morally right the pursuit of the greatest happiness for the greatest number. Similarly, Adam Smith's free-market economics is predicated on competing self-interest – recognising what he regarded as inevitable despite his personal concern for ethical behaviour. These influential ideas put interest of the individual above interest of the collective. The central tenet of social responsibility, however, is the social contract between all the stakeholders to society, which is an

---

3   See Crowther 2002 for detailed evidence.

essential requirement of civil society. This is alternatively described as citizenship, but for either term it is important to remember that the social responsibility needs to extend beyond present members of society. Social responsibility also requires a responsibility towards the future and towards future members of society. Subsumed within this is, of course, a responsibility towards the environment because of implications for other members of society both now and in the future.

CSR therefore involves a concern with the various stakeholders to a business but there are several problems in identifying socially responsible behaviour:

- Research shows that the concern is primarily with those stakeholders who have power to influence the organisation. Thus organisations are most concerned with shareholders, less so with customers and employees and very little with society and the environment. CSR would imply that they are all of equal importance.
- The definitions imply that CSR is a voluntary activity rather than enforced though regulation whereas in actual fact it is an approach to decision-making and the voluntary – regulated debate is irrelevant.
- Claiming a concern is very different to actually exhibiting that concern through actions taken (Crowther 2004).

Because of the uncertainty surrounding the nature of CSR activity it is difficult to evaluate any such activity. It is therefore imperative to be able to identify such activity and it is argued that there are three basic principles (see Crowther 2002 and Schaltegger et al. 1996 for the development of these principles) which together comprise all CSR activity. These are:

- sustainability
- accountability
- transparency.

Sustainability is concerned with the effect which action taken in the present has upon the options available in the future. If resources are utilised in the present then they are no longer available for use in the future, and this is of particular concern if the resources are finite in quantity. Thus raw materials of an extractive nature, such as coal, iron or oil, are finite in quantity and once used are not available for future use. At some point in the future, therefore, alternatives will be needed to fulfil the functions currently provided by these resources. This may be at some point in the relatively distant future but of more immediate concern is the fact that as resources become depleted then the cost of acquiring the remaining resources tends to increase, and hence the operational costs of organisations tend to increase. Similarly, once an animal or plant species becomes extinct then the benefits of that species to the environment can no longer be accrued. In view of the fact that many pharmaceuticals are currently being developed from plant species still being discovered this may be significant for the future.

Sustainability therefore implies that society must use no more of a resource than can be regenerated. This can be defined in terms of the carrying capacity of the ecosystem (Hawken 1993) and described with input/output models of resource consumption. Thus the paper industry, for example, has a policy of replanting trees to replace those harvested and this has the effect of retaining costs in the present rather than temporally externalising them. Viewing an organisation as part of a wider social and economic system – which is of course in accordance with the Gaia hypothesis (Lovelock 1979) – implies that these effects must be taken into account, not just for the measurement of costs and value created in the present but also for the future of the business itself. Measures of sustainability would consider the rate at which resources are consumed by the organisation in relation to the rate at which resources can be regenerated. Unsustainable operations can be accommodated for either by developing sustainable operations or by planning for a future lacking in the resources currently required. In practice organisations mostly tend to aim towards less unsustainability by increasing efficiency in the way in which resources are utilised. An example would be an energy efficiency programme.

Accountability is concerned with an organisation recognising that its actions affect the external environment, and therefore assuming responsibility for the effects of its actions. This concept therefore implies a quantification of the effects of actions taken, both internal to the organisation and externally. More specifically the concept implies a reporting of those quantifications to all parties affected by those actions. This implies a reporting to external stakeholders of the effects of actions taken by the organisation and how they are affecting those stakeholders. This concept therefore suggests a recognition that the organisation is part of a wider societal network and has responsibilities to all of that network rather than just to the owners of the organisation. Alongside this acceptance of responsibility, therefore, must be a recognition that those external stakeholders have the power to affect the way in which those actions of the organisation are taken and a role in deciding whether or not such actions can be justified, and if so at what cost to the organisation and to other stakeholders.

Accountability therefore necessitates the development of appropriate measures of environmental performance and the reporting of the actions of the firm. This necessitates costs on the part of the organisation in developing, recording and reporting such performance and to be of value the benefits must exceed the costs. Benefits must be determined by the usefulness of the measures selected for the decision-making process and by the way in which they facilitate resource allocation, both within the organisation and between it and other stakeholders. Such reporting needs to be based upon the following characteristics:

- understandability to all parties concerned
- relevance to the users of the information provided
- reliability in terms of accuracy of measurement, representation of impact and freedom from bias
- comparability, which implies consistency, both over time and between different organisations.

Inevitably, however, such reporting will involve qualitative facts and judgements as well as quantifications. This qualitativeness will inhibit comparability over time and will tend to mean that such impacts are assessed differently by different users of the information, reflecting their individual values and priorities. A lack of precise understanding of effects, coupled with the necessarily judgemental nature of relative impacts, means that few standard measures exist. This in itself restricts the inter-organisation comparison of such information. Although this limitation is problematic for the development of environmental accounting it is in fact useful to the managers of organisations as this limitation of comparability alleviates the need to demonstrate good performance as anything other than a semiotic.

Transparency, as a principle, means that the external impact of the actions of the organisation can be ascertained from that organisation's reporting, and pertinent facts are not disguised within that reporting. Thus all the effects of the actions of the organisation, including external impacts, should be apparent to all from using the information provided by the organisation's reporting mechanisms. Transparency is of particular importance to external users of such information as these users lack the background details and knowledge available to internal users of such information. Transparency, therefore, can be seen to follow from the other two principles and equally can be seen to be a part of the process of recognition of responsibility on the part of the organisation for the external effects of its actions and equally part of the process of transferring power to external stakeholders.

Regulation of standards

Much of the broader debate about corporate social responsibility can be interpreted, however, as an argument between two positions: greater corporate autonomy and the free market economic model versus greater societal intervention and government control of corporate action. There is clear evidence that the free market proponents are winning the argument. They point to the global spread of capitalism, arguing that this reflects recognition that social well-being is dependent on economic growth. Opponents concede this hegemony but see the balance shifting in their favour, through (for example) greater accountability and reporting. Some opponents suspect the corporate team of cheating on their environments, both ecological and social, while others object fundamentally to the idea that a free market economy is beneficial to society.

Resolving these arguments seems intractable if not impossible because they assume divergent philosophical positions in the ethics versus regulation debate as well as in more fundamental understandings of human nature. I do not propose to offer any definitive answers since any attempt to do so would itself involve making value judgements. It is possible, though, to highlight the terrain upon which these arguments roam. Moreover, we can look for evidence of the relationship between economic growth (as manifest through corporate profitability) and socially responsible behaviour in an effort to resolve this seemingly dichotomous position. I have argued elsewhere (for example, Crowther and Jatana 2005) that the creation of shareholder value is often not through the operational activities of the firm but rather through the externalisation of costs, which are passed on to customers, employees and other stakeholders including society at large. Examples of this practice are evidenced elsewhere and it seems that companies adopt a philosophy that any stakeholder does not matter in isolation.

There is, however, a growing body of evidence (for example, Crowther and Çalıyurt 2004) which shows a link between corporate socially responsible behaviour and economic profitability which is reinforced by much of the research into socially responsible investment funds. This evidence, however, suggests that there is a positive relationship between the two if a longer term view of corporate performance is recognised.

Similarly there have been many claims (see Crowther 2000) that the quantification of environmental costs and the inclusion of such costs into business strategies can significantly reduce operating costs by firms; indeed this was one of the main themes of the 1996 Global Environmental Management Initiative Conference. Little evidence exists that this is the case but Pava and Krausz (1996) demonstrate empirically that companies which they define as 'socially responsible' perform in financial terms at least as well as companies which are not socially responsible. It is accepted, however, that different definitions of socially responsible organisations exist and that different definitions lead to different evaluations of performance between those deemed responsible and others. Similarly, in other countries efforts are being made to provide a framework for certification of accountants who wish to be considered as environmental practitioners and auditors. For example, the Canadian Institute of Chartered Accountants is heavily involved in the creation of such a national framework. Azzone et al. (1996), however, suggest that despite the lack of any regulatory framework in this area a degree of standardisation, at least as far as reporting is concerned, is beginning to emerge at an international level, one of the central arguments of this chapter.

Growth in the techniques offered for measuring social impact, and reporting thereon, has continued throughout the last 25 years, during which the concept of this form of accounting has existed. However, the ability to discuss the fact that firms, through their actions, affect their external environment and that this should be accounted for has often exceeded within the discourse any practical suggestions for measuring such impact. At the same time as the technical implementation of social accounting and reporting has been developing, the philosophical basis for such accounting – predicated in the transparency and accountability principles – has also been developed. Thus, some people consider the extent to which accountants should be involved in this accounting and argue that such accounting can be justified by means of the social contract as benefiting society at large. Others have argued that sustainability is the cornerstone of social and environmental accounting and that auditing should be given prominence.

An examination of the external reporting of organisations gives an indication of the extent of socially responsible activity. Such an examination does indeed demonstrate an increasing recognition of the need to include information about this and an increasing number of annual reports of companies include some information in this respect. This trend is gathering momentum as more organisations perceive the importance of providing such information to external stakeholders. It has been suggested, however, that the inclusion of such information does not demonstrate an increasing concern with the environment but rather some benefits – for example tax breaks – to the company itself. One trend which is also apparent in many parts of the world, however, is the tendency of companies to produce separate social and environmental reports. In this context such reports are generally termed CSR reports or sustainability reports, depending upon the development of the corporation concerned. This trend is gathering momentum as more organisations realise that stakeholders are demanding both more information and also accountability for actions undertaken. Equally the more enlightened of these corporations are realising that socially responsible activity makes business sense and actually assists improved economic performance.

This realisation obviates any need for regulation and calls into question the standards suggested by such bodies as AccountAbility. The more progressive corporations have made considerable progress in what they often describe as their journey towards being fully socially responsible. In doing so they have developed an understanding of the priorities for their own business – recognising that CSR has many facets and needs to be interpreted differently for each organisation – and made significant steps towards both appropriate activity and appropriate reporting of such activity. The steps towards CSR can be likened to increasing maturity as all organisations progress towards that maturity by passing through the same stages (see below), although at different paces. The most mature are indeed recognising that nature of globalisation by recognising that the organisational boundary is permeable (see Crowther and Duty 2002) and that they are accountable also for the behaviour of other organisations in their value chain.

Developing a typology of CSR activity

The preceding analysis makes possible the development of a typology of CSR maturity. It would be relatively easy to develop a typology of CSR activity based upon the treatment of the various stakeholders to an organisation but as Cooper et al. (2001) show, all corporations are concerned with their important stakeholders and make efforts to satisfy their expectations. Thus a concern with employees and customers is apparent in all corporations, being merely a reflection of the power of those stakeholder groupings rather than any expression of social responsibility. Similarly, in some organisations a concern for the environment is less a representation of social responsibility and more a concern for avoiding legislation or possibly a reflection of customer concern. Such factors also apply to some expressions of concern for local communities and society at large. It is therefore inappropriate to base any typology of CSR activity upon the treatment of stakeholders as this is often based upon power relationships rather than a concern for social responsibility and it is not realistic to distinguish the motivations.

A different typology is therefore proposed – one which is based upon the three principles of social responsibility outlined earlier. Moreover, it shows the way in which CSR develops in organisations as they become more experienced and more convinced of the benefits of a commitment to this form of corporate activity. The development of this typology is based upon research and interviews with CSR directors and concerned managers in a considerable number of large corporations, many of which are committed to increasing social responsibility. It demonstrates stages of increasing maturity (see Table 1.1).

Table 1.1 Stages of maturity of CSR activity

Stage of development	Dominant feature	Typical activity	Examples
1	Window dressing	Redesigning corporate reporting	Changed wording and sections to reflect CSR language (see Crowther 2004)
2	Cost containment	Re-engineering business processes	Energy efficiency programmes
3	Stakeholder engagement	Balanced scorecard development	Customer/employee satisfaction surveys (see Cooper et al. 2001)
4	Measurement and reporting	Sophisticated tailored measures	CSR reports
5	Sustainability	Defining sustainability: re-engineering processes	Sustainability reporting
6	Transparency	Concern for the supply chain: requiring CSR from suppliers	Human rights enforcement: for example, child labour
7	Accountability	Reconfiguration of the value chain	Relocating high value added activity in developing countries

It is argued in this chapter that the CSR activity of corporations demonstrates increased maturity over time as the actions required are recognised and undertaken. In part this is in response to pressure from stakeholders but in part also it is internally driven as firms increasingly recognise the benefits from socially responsible behaviour.[4]

This can be considered as a developmental process with the leading exponents of CSR only now beginning to address stage 6 and consider stage 7 (see Table 1.1). Less-developed corporations are at lower stages of development. What is significant about this, however, in the context of this chapter, is that agreed standards and regulations are not just unnecessary but also irrelevant. The leaders in the field have recognised the commercial and economic benefits accruing from increased social responsibility. Moreover there is a reasonably open discourse in existence between these companies – and the individuals within them who have responsibility for CSR activity, who incidentally are mostly fairly committed individuals – in which best practice is identified and shared.

References

Azzone, G., Manzini, R. and Noel, G. (1996), 'Evolutionary trends in environmental reporting', *Business Strategy and Environment*, 5 (4), 219–230.

Çalıyurt, K.T. (2004), 'Auditing and financial reporting for non-governmental organisations in Turkey and the European Union: comparisons and recent developments', in D. Crowther and K.T. Çalıyurt (eds), *Stakeholders and Social Responsibility*, Kuala Lumpur: Ansted University Press, pp130–141.

Cooper, S., Crowther, D., Davies, M. and Davis, E.W. (2001), *Shareholder or Stakeholder Value? The Development of Indicators for the Control and Measurement of Performance*, London: CIMA.

Crowther, D. (2004), 'Corporate social reporting: genuine action or window dressing?', in D. Crowther and L. Rayman-Bacchus (eds), *Perspectives on Corporate Social Responsibility*, Aldershot: Ashgate, pp140–160.

Crowther, D. (2002), *A Social Critique of Corporate Reporting*, Aldershot: Ashgate.

Crowther, D. (2000), *Social and Environmental Accounting*, London: FT Prentice Hall.

Crowther, D. and Çalıyurt, K.T. (2004), 'Corporate social responsibility improves profitability', in D. Crowther and K.T. Çalıyurt (eds), *Stakeholders and Social Responsibility*, Penang: Ansted University Press, pp243–66.

Crowther, D. and Duty, D.J. (2002), 'Operational performance in post-modern organisations – towards a framework for including time in the evaluation of performance', *Journal of Applied Finance*, May, 23–46.

Crowther, D. and Jatana, R. (2005), 'Modern epics and corporate well being', in D. Crowther and R. Jatana (eds), *Representations of Social Responsibility*, Hyderabad: ICFAI University Press, pp125–65.

---

4   See Crowther and Çalıyurt (2004) for an evaluation of the financial benefits accruing from this socially responsible behaviour.

Crowther, D. and Rayman-Bacchus, R. (2004), 'Introduction: perspectives on corporate social responsibility', in D. Crowther and L. Rayman-Bacchus (eds), *Perspectives on Corporate Social Responsibility*, Aldershot: Ashgate, pp1–17.

European Commission (EC) (2002), *Corporate Social Responsibility: A Business Contribution to Sustainable Development*, COM (2002) 347 final, Brussels: EC, 2 July.

European Commission (EC) (2001), *Green Paper – Promoting a European Framework for Corporate Social Responsibility*, COM (2001) 366 final, Brussels: EC, 18 July.

Hawken, P. (1993), *The Ecology of Commerce*, London: Weidenfeld & Nicholson.

Lovelock, J. (1979), *Gaia*, Oxford: Oxford University Press.

Pava, M.L. and Krausz, J. (1996), 'The association between corporate social responsibility and financial performance: the paradox of social cost', *Journal of Business Ethics*, 15 (3), 321–57.

Schaltegger, S., Muller, K. and Hindrichsen, H. (1996), *Corporate Environmental Accounting*, Chichester: Wiley.

Sustainability and its Place
in CSR Research

Kumba Jallow

Introduction

Sustainability requires that we tread lightly on the earth – that we remember the legacy that we owe to our children – and theirs – to leave the world as we found it (Gray and Bebbington 2001; WCED 1989); not to live 'as if there were no tomorrow' (Jacobs 1991). This in broad terms indicates responsibility – the responsibility to act in certain ways and to treat the world (and everything/one in it) as we wish to be treated. Hence this chapter brings out the links between sustainability and corporate social responsibility (CSR) to show how researchers in CSR are addressing, explicitly or implicitly, the means by which sustainability may, or may not, be achieved.

It is clear that there is a range of partners in the sustainability project. If sustainability is to be achieved, all of these partners must play a role appropriate to their ability to take us towards it. Corporate social responsibility can be seen as the mechanism by which businesses engage with sustainability by developing strategies which go beyond.

There is some confusion between the terms 'sustainability' and 'sustainable development' and sometimes these are used interchangeably (Bebbington and Gray 2001). This may be a challenge for the researcher, who has to determine whether the terms mean similar or different things and what this may mean to the research being carried out. For the purposes of the discussions presented here, the term 'sustainability' engages with the concepts involved, and 'sustainable development' attempts to describe how sustainability may be achieved in practice through mechanisms, tools and processes (which may include the ways in which people think about sustainability). Hence, theoretical approaches in research are, where appropriate, likely to engage with the principles of sustainability, whereas the practical applications of CSR will demonstrate the ways in which sustainable development may be achieved or worked towards.

Sustainability by definition

Sustainability as a broad term has been in use in management circles for many years to signal the ongoing nature of the business process. It has traditionally been applied in an economic context; that is, that the business will remain economically active and successful into the future. This creates confusion for many when we begin to develop the term to encompass social and environmental longevity. This is because, in this way, sustainability is a concept that critiques the 'Western' or developed world's development model. The model of development to which the developed world (and to a great extent the developing world) has subscribed to is characterised by:

- a progress which occurs because of the dominance of the natural world
- the priority of economic growth
- human measurement of progress by a standard of living which is an economic measure
- the depletion of natural resources (whilst ignoring the social instability which may flow from this)
- different resource management practices in the developed and developing world (which is not recognised in the former's exploitation of the latter's resources)
- consumption patterns in the developing world which, when replicated across the world would, would be catastrophic
- unlimited economic growth (Baker 2006).

In some senses these ideas have been rejected by certain societies or parts of society for many years, but formally it is only since the 1970s that the principles outlined above have begun to be questioned. An increase in population but, perhaps more importantly, an increase in economic activity and consumption meant that such unprecedented growth was seen to bring about unprecedented problems which needed to be addressed. For many, the key response was that of the World Commission on Environment and Development (WCED), also known as the Bruntland Report (after its Chair). This set the terms by which sustainability – or more properly sustainable development – could begin to be operationalised. Before and at the time of publication in 1987 the WCED report was considered radical (see, for instance, Redclift's 1987 comments). The key features of the WCED report are shown in Table 2.1.

The WCED report attempted to articulate how sustainability needed to be regarded as the combination of environmental, economic and social factors, where none of these was given priority over the other two. The graphical representation of sustainability in its simplest form is often given as a Venn diagram, where the intersections of each circle (economic, social, environmental) represent sustainability. This may also be shown as a triangle where elements of each aspect may be represented along the sides and where all need to be present for sustainability to exist (see Figure 2.1).

Table 2.1 The WCED and sustainable development

Key terms	Explanation
Sustainable yield	Allowing natural regeneration of resources
Environmental sustainability	Preservation of systems and processes
Sustainable society	Setting of ecological boundaries; social justice
Sustainable development	Maintaining a positive process of social change

Source: after Baker 2006

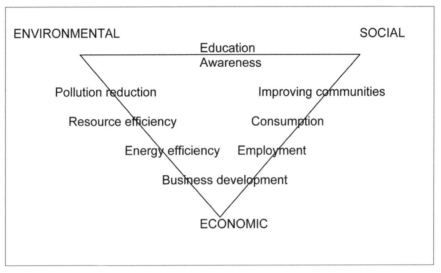

Figure 2.1 Elements of sustainability

Unfortunately the terms used in WCED's report are ambiguous and inconsistent. This was in part deliberate, because the report was designed to promote debate and engagement, and was not intended as a definitive guide to sustainable development. Operationalising sustainable development was considered a matter for negotiation between individuals and institutions; the report was an encouragement for innovation. However, this led to contradictions in practice – whether deliberate or accidental. For instance, technology may be employed to preserve environmental sustainability and provide a sustainable yield, but if environmental assets were removed from a community to provide resources elsewhere, social justice would be challenged.

Hence sustainability is, as a concept, difficult to characterise definitively, and in practice is difficult to operationalise in a unified way. Hence it is contestable (Jacobs 1991) and therefore open to interpretation, abuse and misrepresentation. It is also subject to capture by those who would make it their own. 'Capture' in this sense means that the concept is subsumed into a more generalised business framework where the term may sound the same but where the meaning may be subtly changed so that it appears to follow a consensus but actually fulfils another agenda. Such capture may be explicit – for instance in the use of the word in the World Council on Business and Sustainability's name (hence suggesting that business is the 'guardian' of sustainability), or implicit, as in an organisation's use of the environmental management system ISO 14000 to act as a management tool (in other words integrating the concept into traditional management practices rather than addressing it as a holistic challenge). It may even be unacknowledged that there is capture – businesses who, for instance, pursue a reporting regime which itself determines what is or is not acceptable to report are capturing the concept of sustainability to legitimise their activities or to promote partial accountability without realising that there is more to the concept than environmental management or equal opportunities for employees.

The ways in which sustainability have been described, discussed and analysed have revealed how difficult it is to reach a definition that encapsulates all of the aspects that is sustainability. Any definition must consider the 'three-legged stool' of the environment, the social and the economic; that is, each of these should be considered both separately and in an integrated way. It must also incorporate the eco-justice aspects of intra- and intergenerational human equity – fairness across the globe which extends to those humans yet unborn. This is a very difficult idea in terms of balance – how easily can we reconcile the concept of, say, preserving environmental assets for future generations if this means that some humans alive today (say those in developing countries) are denied access to the same assets in order to preserve them? A further consideration is interspecies equity – fairness towards other species in the way we frame our relationship with them. To take a 'deeper green view' (a more radical environmental position) in this respect would be to extend interspecies equity to being fairness in the relationship between one species and another – whatever the life-form. This would require the conferment of rights and responsibilities to all species. The idea that non-humans should have rights and responsibilities has a long history, emerging from the animal rights campaigns and surfacing in the 1990s argument for gorilla rights akin to human rights. As Eckersley (1992) points out, humans understand this concept and display it in their creation of a limited liability company which, although not human, has the legal position of a human with its own legal rights and responsibilities. However, the counter to this is that any rights violations are presently brought through a human system (courts, human representatives, legal process, etc.), and for non-human forms the outcomes are still decided by humans. It is difficult (but not impossible) to imagine how non-humans might develop a means of settling interspecies equity disputes.

Sustainability must be derived from a firm ethical position (as suggested in the preceding discussion of rights) and it must be capable of explaining both what is happening now, and where we would like to be (often called the sustainability gap – see Gray and Bebbington 2001, for instance). This may be what could be described as almost a synthesis between a positivist and a normative position in methodological terms. Research which embraces sustainability issues must have a clear approach to these ethical and moral issues and must seek to determine where the interface between all the foregoing issues is situated. No wonder, then, that sustainability means whatever you want it to mean!

The role and position of natural capital

Early analysis of what sustainability was incorporated ideas from ecology and economics. The idea that ecological systems provided 'stocks' of ecological goods which need to be maintained and preserved is echoed in the economic analysis that economic capital needs to be maintained to provide a basis for wealth creation. In ecology, the reduction of stock – say, a reduction in biodiversity – affects the ability of the remaining stock to develop, to reproduce or to survive. In economics, a reduction in capital reduces the amount of wealth that can be created from it.

Hence this connection between ecology and economics in terms of the understanding of the need to maintain capital has been a useful way of understanding what sustainability may or may not be.

Capital maintenance within sustainability

There have been wide-ranging debates as to what sustainability means as a theoretical concept, and what place within a general ethical position it should take. Sustainable development (that which could be described as the operationalisation of sustainability) has been in wide currency since WCED and it has been a term criticised as belonging to the neoliberal analysis of economics because, its critics would say, it is a concept that does not radicalise the relationship with nature (that is, nature can be approached as a benefit to humans) and does not question whether there are benefits to 'development', 'profit' and 'growth'.

Interspecies equity moves the sustainability analysis into more radical areas because it requires giving equal consideration to non-humans, whether these be sentient beings, other living organisms or, in some analyses, non-living substances (rocks, the water in streams, the sky, the mountains in Leopold's (1947) view). Non-humans are granted equal consideration as part of the whole of natural capital, and sustainability begins to move away from an anthropocentric (human-centred) position to one that is more ecocentric (although whether a position that is defined by humans can ever be completely free from human bias is debatable). If natural capital is thus comprised, a question is then posed: at what resolution does the equality begin? Do we consider that individuals of a species are granted equity? Does this extend to whole species or should we consider that an ecosystem is the unit of natural capital? If the stock of natural capital is large, presumably there will be more available to occupy by a greater number of species, and the result is biodiversity at its optimum. However, a mature ecosystem may contain only a few dominant species – does this evolutionary process enhance or inhibit interspecies equity? Where such stocks are more limited, environmental pressure may reduce the number of occupying species, and this may result in the need to protect individual species. This protection may actually cause the demise of another species, so equity is not served by such intervention. This is where the position begins to resemble an anthropocentric one, where humans are making the decisions on behalf of other species. The maintenance of such capital, then, in order to preserve a level of equity, itself compromises that equity.

Intragenerational equity requires that we take note of the demands of all humans wherever they are, and have regard for the amount and types of capital available. Jacobs (1991) would argue that this equity is best served by making the distribution of environmental consumption more equal. Pearce (1995) argues that a concern for the environment, and therefore a subsequent attitude towards it, may be determined by where you are and what monetary income you have. There is an elitism among rich environmentalists in the developed world – it may be said that one cannot be concerned about wider environmental issues if one is concerned about day-to-day survival. Similarly if a majority-world dweller is faced with the choice of fuel wood or forest preservation, the survival instinct would make the immediate choice – actions about the future are less important. Compare this situation with the poor in a developed country whose backyard is a dumping ground for toxic chemicals (environmental 'bads' often finding themselves sited in poor neighbourhoods). Here the environmental concern is less global and theoretical than local and actual.

There is a conflict between intra- and intergenerational equity, often faced by those who can least afford to delay their environmental concern. Being fair to the future will require reducing one's own impacts; survival may dictate that future generations are not granted consideration, and that there is a trade-off between current and future generations. Hence the maintenance of capital for the future may be compromised by the needs of today.

Jacobs (1991) has taken the requirement for intergenerational equity as the basis for sustainability. His basis for this is that sustainability equates with environmental management and protection, which takes place over time, and therefore over generations. He also links sustainability with environmental consumption, and the capacity and availability of natural capital to allow consumption. Hence his analysis relates to the ability of humans to limit their own environmental consumption so that future generations can enjoy the same levels of environmental consumption, as currently enjoyed. Hence the actions of current generations should recognise the debt owed to future generations – not inheriting from the past but borrowing from the future.

This view is refuted by Gilpin (2000) – an environmental economist – who states that the current generation owes the future nothing. This is because, he argues, the needs of future generations are uncertain and unpredictable and so cannot be appropriately provided for. What future generations do inherit from us are the developments in science and technology which will enable them to apply the solutions generated to live more sustainably. Hence it could be argued that there is no requirement to build up or maintain capital stocks for the future but rather, for the present, to use capital or maintain it for others to use. However, it seems that this approach maintains the short-termism that is evident in much of economic analysis, and assumes that a technocentric approach (O'Riordan's 'almost arrogant ... assumption that man (sic) is supremely able to understand and control events' (1981: 1)) will be sufficient to deliver sustainable development to the future.

The differences in emphasis and definitions have led to typologies which describe sustainability as 'weak' sustainability, 'strong' sustainability (see Jacobs 1991; Pearce 1995; Gray and Bebbington 2001) and even 'absurdly strong' sustainability (Daly 1995; Holland 1997). These are often distinguished by their treatment of the possibility of substitution of capital, and their acceptance (or otherwise) that some types of capital need to be maintained regardless of other substitutions.

The central theme of sustainability addressed in this way is that nature, represented by capital, can be regarded as a commodity and thus traded as such. This has the positive benefit of recognising the effects on nature as an economic 'good' or bad' (how else can humans account for what is done to nature?), but economic rationality, rather than human intuition, will determine how the commodity is used. (It will not be argued here that economic pricing and the valuation of nature are, or are not, the same thing, nor that economics is not equipped to deal with all of the effects upon nature.) This leads to the concept of *offset*, so that an aspect of capital, priced or weighted economically, can be substituted for another of similar price or weighting. Here the weak and strong 'split' comes into play. In 'weak' sustainability, offset is possible in all cases of capital, as long as an economic advantage is gained from the substitution and, as Beckerman (1994) analyses it, as long as there is no decline in human welfare. In Jacobs' (1991) analysis (because his begins with intergenerational equity) weak sustainability means that future generations should not be faced with environmental catastrophe, and that present generations have a duty to prevent this, but anything less than this is allowable. Hence this allows not only for offsets, but for an amount of depletion in natural capital.

In 'strong' sustainability, the offset has limits. Here, critical natural capital (that for which there is no human-made substitute – examples may be the ozone layer or an individual species) should be maintained regardless of what is happening to other forms of capital. Hence, there may be substitution between, say, a standing forest, felled to provide building materials, and the subsequent dwellings so constructed, but if this threatened the existence of a species or an ecosystem, then no substitution is allowable. If we base this in consumption terms (Jacobs 1991) then 'strong' sustainability will be served if future generations have the opportunity to experience the same capital consumption as the current generation has been allowed. This implies that future generations will determine their own ethical position – the current generation has no place in issuing a moral imperative to the future in regard to the current levels of environmental consumption. This position also implies that if future generations are to inherit the same capacity to consume the environment, then it is the total stock that matters, and therefore substitutability is possible regardless of the types of capital involved. However, Jacobs (ibid.) argues that sustainability based upon intergenerational equity is essentially an ecocentric approach because it requires environmental protection of species and of ecosystems, and aesthetic preservation.

Holland (1997) argues that there are flaws in the division between the weak and strong approaches, and that, in effect, they are the same. In the strong form of sustainability, critical capital has to be maintained because there is no human-made form to be substituted. However, if this action were to be contemplated under a weak sustainability paradigm, a decline in (any) capital would lessen human welfare and would therefore not be tolerated. Hence non-substitutable capital cannot be eroded in either paradigm. This is supported by Jacobs (1991) who uses the terms 'minimal' (for weak sustainability) and 'maximal' (for strong sustainability). These terms reflect the level of environmental capacity passed on to the future. Because of the current level of today's environmental degradation, there may be little difference between the two states (ibid).

One of the assumptions in all of this is that the substitution is between human-made and natural capital, and if this is the case, it raises other issues: for instance, what is the nature of human-made capital? Is there an element of natural capital incorporated at some point within human-made capital, and if so, is all capital not essentially natural? Conversely, as economic 'progress' has exploited, or will exploit, the natural capital it needs to increase human welfare, is not all capital human-made?

Similarly, taking the prominence of intergenerational equity as our starting point, future generations will require a total stock passed to them which will include human and social capital, some of which – technology, for example – which will help to preserve natural capital (as Gilpin proposes). Hence, current generations have a duty to pass on different types of capital, and this again raises the issue of whether there is substitutability between human-made and natural capital: is total substitution allowed (so that, for instance, technological advances in energy will compensate for the reduction in fossil fuel availability)? Therefore does it matter whether we can distinguish between human and natural capital, in this type of analysis?

Instead of dividing capital between human-made and natural, perhaps the analysis should be between exhaustible and reproducible capital, in which case either of the former can be included in either of the latter. This will then define what can and cannot be substituted, but there still remains the problem that whether we take a strong or a weak position; the decline of exhaustible capital is not allowable in the framework of sustainability.

Linking the capitals model with CSR

However, natural capital is not the only element of sustainability. Examining the maintenance of natural capital gives it undeserved priority and, although it redresses the balance away from economic prioritising, it implies that nature and economy are our main considerations. But sustainability is more than environment and economy – the social aspects need to be included. At one level it could be felt that nature encompasses social concerns; however, these need to be made explicit rather than being subsumed elsewhere.

How may this be done without undoing our understanding of sustainability as developed in the previous section? This may be achieved by extending the concept of capital. Hence, the sustainability of a project or a set of activities can be assessed using the four capitals model developed by Ekins et al. (1992). This explains the types of capital available for human activity so that an analysis of capital consumption or preservation can be carried out. The four types of capital are:

- Ecological or natural capital – the sources and sinks available from the natural world. This would include natural resources (in this case water) and their availability for and manner of abstraction; the absorption of waste through natural processes and the availability of waste receivers, such as rivers and seas; the services provided by ecology, such as climate regulation; other aspects such as scenery, amenity and aesthetics.
- Human capital – individual labour, as economically defined; 'brains, energy and ambition' (Alan Gilmour, EFC, Ford Motor Co., as quoted in Ekins et al. 1992: 104); the availability and the uptake of fulfilling work; health; adequate education and appropriate training; experience; creativity, intuition and individual spirituality.
- Social capital – the organisational and institutional boundaries around human capital, and the collective experiences of society; the relationships formed at home, in the community and at work.
- Physical and financial capital – the products of human use of other capitals – the physical and financial infrastructure created by humans. This is also known as manufactured capital, and includes technology and research and development.

The model allows the constraints of sustainability to be revealed, if we assume constant or increasing stocks. Thus:

- All resources going into the economic process cannot exceed the sum of new environmental resources created by investment (both renewable, such as the sun, or non-renewable, such as new discoveries or technologies which act as substitutes for exhaustible resources).
- Waste emissions cannot exceed the absorption capacities. Waste will include those which impact on the capital stocks which produce environmental services (for instance, emissions which cause climate change) and those

39

which impact on the environmental services themselves (for instance, the emission of smoke particles affecting air quality). The perceived effect on humans of these two types of waste may be the same, but the effect on capital stocks, although less easily affected, may be more serious. This is because it is likely that fewer emissions are needed to damage the environmental services because these will have a more direct effect on the absorption capacities of such services. This, however, does rely on the cleaning capacity of the environmental service itself; it may be that today's environmental damage is sufficient enough to damage both the environmental service and the capital stocks.

However, any model of sustainability has to be examined against current practice. Many large companies are expressing a desire to be more responsible in their operations and to be actors in the debate about sustainability and the sustainability gap. Yet these approaches need to be reviewed in the light of our discussion about what we consider sustainability to be. In many cases business takes the role of protecting the environment by mechanisms of *eco-efficiency*; that is, the more efficient use of natural resources (often through technological advances) which allow production to use less material, to use less energy and/or produce less waste. Indeed it is encouraged to take this approach by the development of environmental management systems such as ISO 14000 and the European Eco-Management and Audit Scheme (EMAS). This approach is known as 'eco-modernity' (see, for instance, Welford 1997). The approach demands that business examine the environment (as it defines it – usually as a loose definition of the natural world as available to be exploited) and its appropriation of it. In traditional economic activity, much of the environment (the air breathed or polluted, the landscape from which resources are drawn, the contribution of other species) is treated as an externality – an expense dealt with elsewhere. This approach has been modified and now business begins to recognise its role in environmental protection, but this initially is regarded as a cost to be borne by the business and therefore it has an effect on the bottom line. The environment needs to be managed in order to mitigate its costly effect on profits. There is no radical system change needed here – technological innovations, capital and management techniques will all make a contribution (Blair and Hitchcock 1997). Hence environmental improvements can be made which eventually are recognised to improve profits – energy efficiency saves money as well as producing less climate change emissions; resources are used more efficiently so producing less waste (a double saving as waste processing costs are also reduced) and so on.

Business also takes a role in policy development in this approach, as partnerships are formed between business and government to design and implement policy. An example of this would be the development of the 'polluter pays' principle and its incorporation into legislation. Business agrees to develop mechanisms that will reduce pollution (process rather than end-of-pipe solutions) and governments monitor this through regulation. Hence there is a cooperative rather than an adversarial approach to policy, which ensures its successful implementation.

How does this sit with the earlier discussion of what sustainability is and how this approach may affect capital? Proponents of the eco-modernity model cite the WCED report as support for this, stating that it flows directly from the recommendations that WCED put forward. Hence business is delivering sustainable development. However, the ways in which this is happening must be examined. Certainly if we consider that sustainability is concerned with the ways in which capital is utilised, developing a more efficient approach would seem to suffice. However, this cannot incorporate *eco-effectiveness* or *eco-justice*. Efficiency has its roots in traditional economic models of optimum allocation of resources, and these can be any type of capital, substitutable or critical. Indeed this has been taken further by such proponents as Weizsacker et al. (1997) who argue that by being more resource-efficient, wealth can be increased. However, the question remains: wealth increases for whom? At what cost to those left behind? In order to increase wealth, demand must be maintained or even increased, and so limits to growth have to be set aside. It is a model that suits the 'developed' or rich world very well, but ignores the needs of large parts of society to protect their own environment. It also has little if nothing to say about environmental justice (for instance, the right to use resources in different ways as appropriate to the needs of different parts of society) and it says nothing about social justice at all. If one takes the simplest model of sustainability – a combination of economic, environmental and social factors, eco-modernity addresses the first to the largest extent, the second to some extent and the third not al all. Eco-modernity will address some of the issues around the use, appropriation and substitution of *environmental* capital but cannot begin to (indeed ignores) the issues of *social* capital.

Hence, a more inclusively *sustainable* model is needed if business is really to become a partner with society in delivering sustainable development. One of the challenges for researchers in this area is to assess what alternatives are available, possible and acceptable. Another challenge is to engage with business to assess how far business is able or willing to go; a more radical research agenda may examine whether (rather than how) business is likely to deliver sustainable development. Consider Table 2.2 with this in mind.

Table 2.2 CSR and the five capitals model: case study at Wessex Water

Wessex Water (WW) is a water treatment and supply company in the south of England and, as such, is a direct user of a natural resource. In order to manage its activities and to provide transparent reports of this management, WW developed, in partnership with Forum for the Future, a model that incorporated the idea of capital maintenance. WW began to apply this model to its activities and in 1998 identified which elements of its business consumed or affected which category of capital (see table below). This model was further expanded to allow the company to focus on five areas, and in 2000 the model was renamed 'the five capitals model' (Wessex Water 2000: 1). The reports became more specific about the types of capital employed and used the categories of capital to form the basis of the structure of the report. It is interesting to note that the manufactured/financial/infrastructural capital category is used increasingly as the reports progressed; the importance of financial or commercial considerations was emphasised in 1999 when the report contained an extract from the financial pages of the annual report (Wessex Water 1999: 34). This integration is completed in 2001 when the annual report is used as the place to disclose the environmental accounts, although the reporting process is split across three sites: the website, the paper summary and the annual report. The reporting process now continues to 2005.

Capital	Elements included in 1998	Elements included 1999–2005
Ecological – 'Our environment'	Water, energy, transport, biodiversity	Water, transport, greenhouse gas emissions, biodiversity
Manufactured – 'Our infrastructure' or 'Our finances'*	No specific mention	Capital and maintenance programmes Annual and green accounts
Human – 'Our employees'	Employees	Employees
Social – 'Customers and community'	Customers and community	Customers and community

*This is the 'fifth' capital in 2001.

External relations and engagement with social capital
The Chairman's statement is used to discuss the external influences which impact upon the water industry and the business of WW. Such influences come from, inter alia, the UK government, the regulator Ofwat, the European Union and the Environment Agency. The Chairman has used this section to engage with social capital actors to raise awareness of what the company considers to be the main issues that need to be addressed. For instance, WW has challenged what it sees as the UK government's interest in sustainable development as being too economic in focus, and has argued that Ofwat's requirement for water prices to be reduced conflicts with the larger goals of sustainability by preventing investment in longer-term aims. The report also acknowledges that

customers can recognise the conflict between short-term price reductions and long-term environmental solutions, and are often supportive of those broader aims.

Issues where capital categories are integrated

WW has made connections between different categories of capital. Thus climate change can be identified as having an impact on environmental and economic capital; and the effect of managing water extraction can be seen to be increasing human and economic capital, but potentially decreasing environmental capital. This thus invokes the arguments of substitutability, and is recognised as a potential conflict within WW. The issue of affordability, for instance, is raised as one which the company shares responsibility with elements of its social capital (the government) towards its customers (as communities, also part of its social capital).

The statement defines its commitment to sustainability by its approach to energy usage, recognising that energy use may need to increase if standards in water delivery are required to be raised. Hence this will adversely affect the natural capital. WW is attempting to mitigate this effect by examining sustainable energy sources, thus alluding to the principle of renewable and exhaustible resources.

In 1999 the capitals were again clearly identified, with manufactured capital being split between infrastructure and financial capital. The statement saw a discussion of the conflicts between natural and manufactured capitals, seeming to return to the prominence of manufactured capital through the emphasis on finance and business issues. However, in the following year there is a refocusing on natural capital and a reduction of emphasis on manufactured capital.

In 2001 a substitution issue appears: pollution decreases are achieved only with higher energy usage. There is therefore an implicit understanding of the substitution arguments. Pollution as waste emission may affect capital stocks or environmental services (that is, the absorption sinks); energy may be from renewable or exhaustible sources. WW once more explored the use of renewable energy sources to replace its exhaustible supplies, which is a practical demonstration of the replacement of one form of natural capital with another. Engagement with social capital in terms of government criticism and pricing mechanisms continues in this statement.

Finally, in 2005 there is explicit reference for the first time to 'corporate social responsibility', bringing WW to the point where we might see a connection between CSR and the capitals model.

Sustainability, CSR and corporate citizenship

If businesses are to play their part in delivering sustainable development, how can we determine their role? How will businesses shape their organisations so that they can contribute to a more sustainable future? Where are the partnerships likely to arise?

To attempt to answer these questions one needs to establish the role of business in society and assess how or whether that role includes an involvement in a society which is moving towards sustainability. There are differing views of the responsibility of business to society, from the traditional neoclassical view that a business has a responsibility only to its owners – to stay in business and generate rewards for the provision of capital by the owners – through to the view that a responsible business has rights and responsibilities as a responsible citizen. This progression follows the following lines:

- Businesses recognise that there are a range of responsibilities – ethical, legal, economic, philanthropic – that are mutually accepted both by the business and by society.
- Businesses need to maintain behaviour established by mandatory and voluntary codes.
- There is a greater recognition of the public role of private business entities, so that such organisations are citizens of society and this is a valid way to understand CSR (McIntosh et al. 2003).

For some writers (for instance, McIntosh et al.) the term 'corporate citizenship' is more inclusive than 'corporate social responsibility' because it makes more explicit the role of business in society, as an active member of society. CSR may be regarded as something a business does (or does not do) to or for society. For others (for instance, Andriof and McIntosh 2001) the terms are interchangeable. The term 'corporate social responsibility' is useful in that it can incorporate the social aspects of sustainability; this then requires environmental aspects to be incorporated into the social. The disadvantage with this term is that, whilst it suggests strongly that business has a responsibility to society, it implies that responsibility is not owed to other organic or non-organic entities. This would create a conflict with the more radical views of what sustainability might mean. The concept of citizenship may be more usefully linked to sustainability as it implies partnership, responsibility, active participation (perhaps) and equality (in that business is not separate from other citizens in society). It remains an anthropomorphic idea – business as 'human' citizen – but does allow us to make the demand that business be responsible for all its activities, whatever these affect. The partnership aspect may be particularly pertinent as business can be encouraged to build relationships with other members of society to determine how sustainability may be achieved.

Table 2.3 attempts to link the stages of citizenship with the ideas of capital maintenance and degrees of sustainability (weak to strong). This typology is capable of development and may act as an indicator of the position of an organisation being researched. It may also act as a prompt to link ideas of CSR and citizenship with the concept of sustainability through the framework of the capitals model.

Table 2.3 Modes of corporate citizenship and categories of capital

Mode of citizenship	Type of activity	Position regarding capital
Avoidance of all imperatives (informal economy)	Market activity – creating profit and private property	No regard for capital: substitution not even recognised as a factor
Compliance with legal framework – usually smaller, local businesses	Market activity	Would regard all capital as substitutable
Discretionary – business 'does no harm'	Enterprise – as above but also public and non-financial wealth creation	Would recognise different types of capital but would regard complete substitution compatible with business aims
Pro-active businesses who see themselves as agents of social change	Enterprise	Would regard some capital as non-substitutable, for example those companies who engage in biodiversity action plans
'Third-generation' businesses who have progressed through a range of CSR processes to become citizens	Livelihood businesses contributing to their communities	Potentially models of 'strong' sustainability recognising the need to maintain critical capital

(*Source*: adopted from McIntosh et al. 2003)

Conclusion

The concept of sustainability is complex and difficult to assimilate. Welford (1997) has attempted to configure it as a three-dimensional model as a means of capturing each of the aspects and demonstrating their inter-relationship. These dimensions are crucial to our understanding of sustainability and are ignored at our peril. And yet their very complexity makes any analysis fraught; it is easier to reduce the analysis into its component parts – by examining each separately, a limited understanding may be achieved. However, sustainability is more than the sum of its parts and cannot be comprehended as such. The challenge for CSR researchers is to accept this complexity and incorporate it into their research process.

References

Andriof, J. and McIntosh, M. (2001), *Perspectives in Corporate Citizenship*, Sheffield: Greenleaf.

Baker, S. (2006), *Sustainable Development*, London: Routledge.

Bebbington, J. and Gray, R. (2001), 'An account of sustainability: failure, success and a reconceptualization', *Critical Perspectives on Accounting*, 12, 557–87.

Beckerman, W. (1994), 'Sustainable development: is it a useful concept', *Environmental Values*, 3 (3), 191–209.

Blair, A. and Hitchcock, D. (1997), *Environment and Business*, London: Routledge.

Daley, H.E. (1995), 'On Wilfred Beckerman's critique of sustainable development', *Environmental Values*, 4 (1), 49–70.

Eckersley, R. (1992), *Environmentalism and Political Theory*, London: UCL Press.

Ekins, P., Hillman, M. and Hutchison, R. (1992), *Wealth beyond Measure*, London: Gaia.

Gilpin, R. (2000), *The Challenge of Global Capitalism: The World Economy in the 21st Century*, Princeton NJ: Princeton University Press.

Gray, R. and Bebbington, J. (2001), *Accounting for the Environment*, 2nd edn, London: Sage.

Holland, A. (1997), 'Substitutability, or why strong sustainability is weak and absurdly strong sustainability is not absurd', in J. Foster (ed.), *Valuing Nature*, London: Routledge.

Jacobs, M. (1991), *The Green Economy – Environment, Sustainable Development and the Politics of the Future*, London: Pluto.

Leopold, A. (1947), *A Sand County Almanac*, Oxford: Oxford University Press.

McIntosh, M., Thomas, R., Leipziger, D. and Coleman, G. (eds) (2003), *Living Corporate Citizenship: Strategic Routes to Socially Responsible Business*, London: FT Prentice Hall.

O'Riordan, T. (1981), *Environmentalism*, London: Pion.

Pearce, D. (1995), *Blueprint 4*, London: Earthscan.

Redclift, M. (1987), *Sustainable Development: Exploring the Contradictions*, London: Routledge.

Weizsacker, E. von, Lovins, A. and Lovins, L. (1997), *Factor Four: Doubling Wealth, Halving Resource Use*, London: Earthscan.

Welford, R. (1997), *Hijacking Environmentalism – Corporate Responses to Sustainable Development*, London: Earthscan.

Wessex Water (2000), *Striking the Balance*, report, Wessex Water.

Wessex Water (1999), *Striking the Balance*, report, Wessex Water.

World Council on Environment and Development (WCED) (1989), *Our Common Future*, Oxford: Oxford University Press.

Stakeholder Perspectives on Social Responsibility

David Crowther

Stakeholders

The standard definition of a stakeholder is that this is any person who has an interest in the activity of an organisation, although it is normally considered to be a person who is actually affected by that activity. So owners, investors, employees, customers and suppliers are all stakeholders – but so too would be citizens living around the location of the organisation's operations and the government at national and local levels. Bodies such as trades unions, consumer associations and civic societies would also be considered to be stakeholders because the norm is to consider stakeholders as groups rather than as individuals. From this understanding of stakeholders, stakeholder theory has been developed as a way of managing an organisation. Within this theory attempts have been made to provide frameworks by which the relevant stakeholders of an organisation can be identified on the basis that a stakeholder is relevant if they have invested something in the organisation and are therefore subject to some risk from that organisation's activities. A useful approach is to separate stakeholders into two groups (Cooper 2004): the voluntary stakeholders, who choose to deal with an organisation, and the involuntary stakeholders, who do not choose to enter into – nor can they withdraw from – a relationship with the organisation.

From a radical perspective all the standard definitions of stakeholders are, however, deficient as they assume that only humans can be stakeholders. These people claim that the natural environment is affected by the actions of an organisation and is therefore a stakeholder to that organisation (Crowther 2002a). As environmental impact becomes of increasing concern to society as a whole then this notion is gaining recognition. A few theorists go further and claim that activities in the present have potentially significant implications for possibilities in the future and that therefore the future is also an important stakeholder. An increasing concern with sustainability is bringing this into general acceptance, although still very few would recognise the future as a stakeholder.

Stakeholder theory is based upon the notion of the social contract between an organisation and society and is premised in the notion that if the organisation affects any stakeholder then it also has a concomitant responsibility towards that stakeholder. A fundamental aspect of stakeholder theory, therefore, is that it attempts to identify different groupings within society to whom an organisation has some responsibility. Stakeholder theory provides the critical vocabulary for connecting a wide variety of values and interests to the firm. Discourse is no longer confined to the firm's abstract duties to 'society' but can be about the firm's duty to specific customers, suppliers, investors, and employees and others.

Stakeholder language rejects the categorical split of the world into the two opposing forces of 'business or economic interests' and 'social or moral interests'. Such an approach leaves business and ethics separated whereas stakeholder language provides a way to sidestep the separation of the economic and the moral and offers managers a way to see business and ethics as going together. According to stakeholder theory, even economic claims are moral claims and cannot be separated from other issues. This focus on values, both economic and moral, pushes managers to be explicit about their goals and how they want to do business, and especially about what kinds of relationships they want and need to create with their stakeholders in order to manage their organisation.

A stakeholder management approach can be considered to exist when the managers of an organisation consider the impact of its operations on its stakeholders before making any decision. Due to the diverse nature and conflicting needs of the various stakeholders it is necessary for this type of management to involve some form of trade-off. This balancing act is in sharp contrast to shareholder management approaches which claim as their advantage the fact that they reduce the number of conflicting objectives by providing a clear and single aim for organisations. A further step is taken by some stakeholder theorists in suggesting that an essential premise of stakeholder theory is that the interest of all stakeholders have intrinsic value, and no set of interests is assumed to dominate the others. This premise that the various stakeholder groups are considered equal, in that none of them dominates any other, does not receive universal support within stakeholder theory, however, and some have rejected this as being naïve and idealistic. In fact when stakeholder theory is used as a managerial tool it is specifically concerned with identifying which stakeholders are more important and as a result should receive a greater proportion of management's time – which of course equates to the most powerful. So it can be considered that stakeholder theory is about power, just like other approaches to organisational management, and that the main difference is in recognising different power relations. Thus frameworks have been developed for identifying and ranking stakeholders in terms of their power, legitimacy and urgency: if a stakeholder is powerful, legitimate and urgent then its needs will require immediate attention and be given primacy.

Such frameworks are, of course, essentially managerial and cause obvious problems in that some stakeholders will always be less powerful than others and therefore receive less consideration. More worrying, however, is that a stakeholder such as the environment has no power and must rely on a proxy, such as an environmental pressure group, in order to bring its claims to prominence. Stakeholder theory, therefore, is deficient and relies upon ethics to compensate, as well as adopting concepts such as sustainability and accountability from CSR theory to develop in response to this criticism. It can be argued that such theoretical developments are necessitated by observation of practice because stakeholder activism – whether of small shareholders, consumers, environmental campaigners or the anti-globalisation movement – is an increasingly powerful feature of society which is forcing changes to organisational management practice as well as to theory. Such development can be expected to continue.

Stakeholder perspectives on organisational performance

While few would argue with the claim that a business is an entity insofar as it is perceived to act as a whole towards the fulfilment of the particular objectives which it has, it is in reality a composite entity which consists of an association of individuals, each working towards a commonalty of shared purpose. The actuality is different from this in that the common purpose is often not clearly identified and articulated and that the individuals are not necessarily working totally towards that common purpose, particularly when this purpose conflicts with or diverges from their individual motivations and objectives. This is particularly apparent when these individuals are considered within the context of the stakeholder community because the different stakeholder groupings have different desires and different motivations, which are often in conflict with those of other stakeholders (Crowther and Rayman-Bacchus 2004a). These conflicts need to be resolved in some fashion in order for the business to function and it is obvious that, as businesses do actually function, that they end up being resolved by some means.

Just as the functioning of an organisation, however, can be seen to be a composite of its various constituents, so too does this reflect upon the performance of the business and the multiple facets of that performance (Crowther 2002a). It is clear that the determination of good performance is dependent upon the perspective from which that performance is being considered and that what one stakeholder grouping might consider to be good performance may very well be considered by another grouping to be poor performance (Child 1984). The evaluation of performance, therefore, for a business depends not just upon the identification of adequate means of measuring that performance but also upon the determination of what good performance actually consists of. Just as the determination of standards of performance depends upon the perspective from which it is being evaluated, so too does the measurement of that performance, which needs suitably relevant measures to evaluate performance, not absolutely as this has no meaning, but within the context in which it is being evaluated. From an external perspective, therefore, a very different evaluation of performance might arise.

The measurement of stakeholder performance is perhaps even more problematic than the measurement of financial performance. Objective measures of stakeholder performance are in the main not reported in the annual reports of companies and so it is necessary to look elsewhere. For example, in the UK such measures are included within the 'Britain's Most Admired Companies' surveys annually published in *Management Today*. These measures provide a reputation rating, as gathered from rivals' perceptions, in nine categories and these measures are added up to provide a total score. The nine categories are:

- quality of management
- quality of goods and services
- capacity to innovate
- quality of marketing
- ability to retain top talent
- community and environmental responsibility
- financial soundness
- value as long-term investment
- use of corporate assets.

These ratings have previously been used by academics, especially in the environmental field (see Çalıyurt and Crowther 2004). The 'Britain's Most Admired Companies' articles report on the ratings of 260 large UK companies in 26 different sectors each year. Due to the subjective nature of the scoring it is difficult to predict whether there would be an industry effect although it would appear that this is less likely. Also, it is only the largest 260 companies that are included in these surveys and therefore no separate size effect test has been undertaken. The companies reported on are not necessarily the same for each year although there is a lot of overlap.

In considering the various stakeholders it is important to recognise that determining performance for each is problematic because there is not the certainty of financial information to measure performance. It is necessary, therefore, to use proxy measures which can be considered to give a representative indication of performance. Companies will tend to develop their own proxy measures of factors which they believe are important for their own stakeholders. Examples include:

- quality of goods and services as a proxy measure of customer performance
- the ability to retain top talent as a measure of employee performance
- community and environmental responsibility for environmental performance.

One additional factor is of concern to many companies and that is the capacity to innovate. Although it cannot strictly be considered as representing a concern with stakeholders we will consider it here because it is not subject to financial measurement. Let us look at the most important stakeholders in greater detail.

Customers

The quality of goods and services that a company produces has can be considered as a proxy for customer performance. What this measure appears to neglect is any reference to price or value for money but it will still provide information on an important and significant component of customer satisfaction.

Employees

The ability to retain top talent can be considered as a proxy for employee satisfaction, which relates back to our consideration of reward systems in the preceding chapter. Again this measure is not a perfect match and only considers 'top talent' rather than the whole workforce, although it is potentially true that the companies that score well in this respect have a different attitude to employees. Possibly for some companies such measures as days lost due to industrial action might be more important. Others might consider health and safety measures to be more important.

The environment

The environment, although not considered important by as many companies as consumers and employees, has been identified as important by a significant number of companies. This practitioner interest is certainly reflected by a very considerable academic interest over the last 20 years.

The capacity to innovate

It was decided to consider this rating here because of the importance placed upon innovation in Kaplan and Norton's 'Balanced Scorecard'. They suggest that managers need to define a complete internal process value chain that starts with the innovation process (Kaplan and Norton 1996). This is not to say that innovation is the whole of the internal process rather only the start.

The implications for corporate social responsibility

The acceptance of a stakeholder approach to organisations[1] and the existence of multiple perspectives upon the objectives of an organisation inevitably imply a rejection of a monistic view of organisations. Thus there can be no one single view of the objectives of the organisation and consequently no one single evaluation of the performance of that organisation. It is therefore inevitable within this paradigm that if monism is rejected as a view of organisations then this implies that the economic

---

1   See Freeman (1984) for details of this discourse.

rationality view of organisations and their behaviour must also be rejected.[2] This rejection is based upon a reconsideration of classical liberal economics.

Classical liberal philosophy places an emphasis upon rationality and reason, with society being an artificial creation resulting from an aggregation of individual self-interest, and with organisations being an inevitable result of such aggregations for business purposes. Thus Locke (1690) viewed societies as existing in order to protect innate natural private rights while Bentham (1789) and J.S. Mill (1863) emphasised the pursuit of human need. Of paramount importance to all was the freedom of the individual to pursue his[3] own ends, with a tacit assumption that maximising individual benefits would lead to the maximisation of organisational benefits and also societal benefits. In other words societal benefits can be determined by a simple summation of all individual benefits. Classical liberal economic theory extended this view of society to the treatment of organisations as entities in their own right with the freedom to pursue their own ends. Such theory requires little restriction of organisational activity because of the assumption that the market, when completely free from regulation, will act as a mediating mechanism which will ensure that, by and large, the interests of all stakeholders of the organisation will be attended to by the need to meet these free market requirements. This view however resulted in a dilemma in reconciling collective needs with individual freedom. De Tocqueville (1840) reconciled these aims by suggesting that government institutions, as regulating agencies, were both inevitable and necessary in order to allow freedom to individuals and to protect those freedoms.[4]

Thus classical liberal arguments recognise a limitation in the freedom of an organisation to follow its own ends without any form of regulation. Similarly Fukuyama (1992) argued that liberalism is not in itself sufficient for continuity and that traditional organisations have a tendency to atomise in the pursuance of the ends of the individuals who have aggregated for the purpose for which the organisation was formed to fulfil. He argued that liberal economic principles

---

2   Economic rationality presupposes that organisations, and the people within those organisations, behave in a rational manner in terms of maximising utility, and the underlying assumption of such rationality is that the organisation is attempting to maximise utility for its owners, or shareholders. It is assumed also that there exists a single (or at most two) utility-maximising course of action. Under economic rationality this utility is presumed to be synonymous with wealth, perhaps because such wealth can be quantified in accounting terms and thereby become subject to mathematical analysis. It is also assumed unquestioningly in the discourse of economic rationality that what benefits the shareholders of a business will also benefit the other stakeholders to the organisation as well as society at large. Thus the monistic viewpoint of economic rationality is based upon a stance within the discourse of modernity and accepts the philosophy of classical liberal economics. Indeed, this view also accepts the tenets of classical liberalism in general.

3   The use of the term *his* here is deliberate as these writers were only concerned with a certain section of society, who were of course all male.

4   See Barnett and Crowther (1998) for a more detailed consideration and critique of classical liberalism.

provide no support for the traditional concept of an organisation as a community of common interest which is only sustainable if individuals within that community give up some of their rights to the community as an entity and accept a certain degree of intolerance. On the other hand Fukuyama considered the triumph of liberal democracy as the final state of history, citing evidence of the break-up of the Eastern bloc as symbolising the triumph of classical liberalism.[5]

Although this classical liberal/economic rationality view of organisations can be viewed as one paradigm representing the structure and behaviour of organisations, with consequent implications for the evaluating and reporting of performance within such an organisation, it is by no means the only such paradigm. Indeed it is one which is specifically rejected within the analysis of this chapter. An alternative paradigm, predicated in the stakeholder view of organisations and the dynamic disequilibrium existing within organisations, and brought about by the conflicting needs of the various stakeholders, is a pluralistic paradigm.[6] Such a paradigm views organisations not as entities acting for a particular purpose but rather as a coalition of various interest groups acting in concert, through the resolution or subsumption of their convergent interests, for a particular purpose at a particular point in time. This purpose changes over time as the power of the various stakeholders changes and as various stakeholders join, and influence, the dominant coalition while other stakeholders leave that coalition.

Corporate social responsibility

In recent years the concept of corporate social responsibility (CSR) has gained prominence to such an extent that it seems ubiquitous, both in the popular media and among academics from a wide range of disciplines. There are probably many reasons for the attention given to this phenomenon, not least of which is the corporate excesses witnessed in recent years. For many people the various examples of this kind of behaviour – ranging from BCCI to Enron to Union Carbide to the collapse of Arthur Andersen – will have left an indelible impression among people that all is not well with the corporate world and that there are problems which need to be addressed (Crowther and Rayman-Bacchus 2004a).

Issues of socially responsible behaviour are not, of course, new: examples can be found from throughout the world and at least from the earliest days of the Industrial Revolution, despite the concomitant founding of large business entities (Crowther 2002a) and the divorce between ownership and management – or the divorcing of risk from rewards (Crowther 2004a). But corporate social responsibility is back

---

5   Fukuyama presents these arguments as the end of history, which he does not celebrate. In actual fact it is his critique of classical liberalism which is the most significant contribution of his work. This aspect of his work is almost universally ignored in favour of his end-of-history argument.

6   Pluralism was of course one of the strands of classical liberalism which was written out of the discourse of liberalism during the late nineteenth century.

on the agenda of corporations, governments and individual citizens throughout the world. The term 'corporate social responsibility' is in vogue at the moment but as a concept it is vague and means different things to different people. For example, Topal and Crowther (2004) are concerned with bioengineering and its effects upon biodiversity and therefore upon the future of the planet. On the other hand Castells (1996) and Mraovich (2004) are concerned with the consequences of the networked society, while Rayman-Bacchus (2004) is more concerned with trust in, and legitimacy of, corporate behaviour and the constant tension between economic wealth and social wellbeing.

> This raises the question as to what exactly can be considered to be corporate social responsibility. According to the EU Commission (2002: 347 final: 5), '… CSR is a concept whereby companies integrate social and environmental concerns in their business operations and in their interaction with their stakeholders on a voluntary basis'. This is not a new definition and has resonance with earlier idea such as those of Dahl (1972) who stated, '… every large corporation should be thought of as a social enterprise; that is an entity whose existence and decisions can be justified insofar as they serve public or social purposes'.

A concern for stakeholders

All definitions seem to be based upon a concern with more than profitability and returns to shareholders. Indeed, involving other stakeholders and considering them in decision-making is a central platform of CSR. Stakeholder management is based upon a consideration of all stakeholders. Numerous definitions of a stakeholder have been provided within the literature and Sternberg (1997) demonstrates that Freeman (1984)[7] has used multiple definitions and cites the following two as examples: 'those groups without whose support the organization would cease to exist' (Freeman 1984: 31) and 'any group or individual who can affect or is affected by the achievement of the organization's objectives' (ibid.: 46).

The stakeholder management approach can be considered to exist when the management of an organisation considers the impact of its operations on its stakeholders before making any decision. Due to the diverse nature and conflicting needs of the relevant stakeholders it is necessary for this type of management to involve some form of trade-off. This balancing act is in sharp contrast to value-based management (VBM) (Cooper et al. 2001) that claims as one of its advantages the fact that it reduces the number of conflicting objectives by providing a clear and single aim for organisations. A further step is taken by some stakeholder theorists in suggesting that an essential premise (Jones and Wicks 1999) of stakeholder

---

7   This work is very often referred to as the seminal work in the area of stakeholder management.

theory is that the interest of all (legitimate) stakeholders have intrinsic value, and no set of interests is assumed to dominate the others (Clarkson 1995; Donaldson and Preston 1995). This premise that the various stakeholder groups are considered equal, in that none of them dominates any other, does not receive universal support within stakeholder theory, and Gioia (1999) suggests this portrayal 'to be not only misleading but hopelessly idealistic'. In fact when stakeholder theory is used as a managerial tool it is specifically concerned with identifying which stakeholders are more important and as a result should receive a greater proportion of management's time. It would seem therefore that the consensus which is exists is only that there are multiple stakeholders who have a stake in an organisation.

Donaldson and Preston (1995) suggest that there are three arguments for stakeholder theory. The first is that it is an accurate description of how management works. This implies that all management is a form of stakeholder management where the interests of different stakeholders are actually considered. The other two arguments could be considered to be conflicting views as to why stakeholder management is appropriate. The first view holds that it is more morally and ethically correct for organisations to consider wider needs than purely concentrating on the needs of one group, usually taken to be shareholders. Thus by adopting a stakeholder approach the objective of the firm is to be become a more ethical and more socially responsible organisation. The second view suggests that the reason for managing your stakeholders is to create shareholder wealth. This view suggests that shareholder wealth can be created through the correct management of the other stakeholders and in this respect it is considered to have instrumental power. Evan and Freeman (1988), drawing upon the work of Kant, have criticised this argument as they believe it is unethical to use the other stakeholders merely as means to achieve the end of shareholder wealth. Both of these views suggest that stakeholder management is a way of achieving an organisation's objective; the dispute is more over whether this should in terms of financial performance or social performance.

The link between stakeholder performance and financial performance, its instrumental power, has been argued to exist for a number of reasons. Firstly, Shankman (1999) suggests that a balance between the different stakeholder groups' interests is essential in ensuring that the organisation continues to be viable and achieves other performance goals. Jones (1995) suggests that stakeholder management is a source of competitive advantage as contracts between organisations and stakeholders will be on the basis of trust and cooperation and therefore less expense will be required in monitoring and enforcing such contracts. In a similar vein there have been numerous empirical studies performed which attempt to find links between corporate social responsibility and financial performance (in these studies financial performance has been defined in terms of both accounting and market-based measures). Waddock and Graves (1997) report on the evidence to that date and suggest that the results have been mixed with some research finding a positive relationship whilst others find 'an ambiguous or negative relationship'. More specific stakeholder evidence was provided in the UK by Greenley and Foxall (1997), who found 'some support to the proposition that orientation to multiple stakeholders is positively associated with performance, such associations are contingent on the external environment'.

An underlying assumption which is not always explicitly recognised in these studies is that the firm should be operating for shareholders; that is, they should be concerned with shareholder wealth maximising. Therefore stakeholder management, or corporate social responsibility, is not an end in itself but is simply seen as a means for improving economic performance. This assumption is often implicit although it is clearly stated by Atkinson et al. (1997) and is actually inconsistent with the ethical reasons for adopting stakeholder theory. Instead of stakeholder management improving economic or financial performance therefore, it is argued that a broader aim of corporate social performance should be used (Jones and Wicks 1999). Furthermore, Jones and Wicks note that certain ethicists need no instrumental justification as moral behaviour 'is, and must be, its own reward'. Waddock and Graves (1997) consider whether stakeholder management enhances corporate social performance, as opposed to financial performance, and they find a positive relationship.

A fundamental aspect of stakeholder theory, in any of its aspects, is that it attempts to identify numerous different factions within a society to whom an organisation may have some responsibility. It has been criticised for failing to identify these factions (Argenti 1993) although some attempts have been made. Indeed Sternberg (1997) suggests that the second of Freeman's definitions of stakeholder (see above), which is now the more commonly used, has increased the number of stakeholders to be considered by management adopting a stakeholder approach; in fact this definition includes virtually everything, whether alive or not. However, attempts have been made by stakeholder theorists to provide frameworks by which the relevant stakeholders of an organisation can be identified. Clarkson (1995) suggests that a stakeholder is relevant if they have invested something in the organisation and are therefore subject to some risk from that organisation's activities. He separates these into two groups: the voluntary stakeholders, who choose to deal with an organisation, and the involuntary stakeholders, who do not choose to enter into – nor can they withdraw from – a relationship with the organisation. Mitchell et al. (1997) develop a framework for identifying and ranking stakeholders in terms of their power, legitimacy and urgency. If a stakeholder is powerful, legitimate and urgent then its needs will require immediate attention and given primacy.

Irrespective of which model is used, it is not controversial to suggest that there are some generic stakeholder groups that will be relevant to most organisations. Clarkson (1995) suggests that the voluntary stakeholders include shareholders, investors, employees, managers, customers and suppliers and they will require some value added, otherwise they can withdraw their stake and choose not to invest in that organisation again. It is argued that involuntary stakeholders such as individuals, communities, ecological environments or future generations do not choose to deal with the organisation and therefore may need some form of protection, perhaps through government legislation or regulation. Other more specific interest groups may be relevant for certain industries due to the nature of the industry or the specific activities of the organisation. For example, utility industries in the UK have been regulated by a government-appointed regulator since privatisation and thus the regulator is a stakeholder of these organisations. Similarly certain industries are more environmentally, politically or socially sensitive than others and therefore attract more attention from these stakeholder groups; again the water or nuclear industries provide examples here.

Stakeholder management has significant informational needs. It is extremely difficult to manage for a variety of stakeholders if there is no measurement of how the organisation has performed for those stakeholders. Thus for each stakeholder identified it is necessary to have a performance measure by which the stakeholder performance can be considered. Due to the nature of the stakeholders and their relationship with the organisation this will not necessarily be easy nor will it necessarily be possible in monetary terms. Therefore non-financial measures will be of great importance but this information is often considered more subjective than financial information. Therefore measures of customer satisfaction are sometimes based on surveys and sometimes on statistical performance measures such as numbers of complaints or returns, or market share or customer retention.

A stakeholder-managed organisation attempts to consider the diverse and conflicting interests of its stakeholders and balance these interests equitably. The motivations for organisations to use stakeholder management may be in order to improve financial performance or social or ethical performance, howsoever these may be measured. In order to be able to adequately manage stakeholder interests it is necessary to measure the organisation's performance to these stakeholders and this can prove complicated and time-consuming. Recently the Centre for Business Performance, Cranfield University, has set up a 'Catalogue of measures' related to their Performance Prism that contains measures of each of the 'dimensions of performance' – stakeholder satisfaction; strategies; processes; capabilities; stakeholder contributions. The stakeholders identified were customer, employee, investor, regulator, community and suppliers, and in total the catalogue includes over 200 relevant measures. This shows the vast number of stakeholder measures that could be used in any organisation although it is not expected that all of these will be relevant for an individual organisation. This again highlights the potential complexity of measuring performance for stakeholders as these numerous measures will provide conflicting evidence on performance that somehow must be reconciled. In comparison, VBM techniques that propose the use of a single metric to measure performance as well as set objectives and reward executives appear far simpler.

Stakeholder concern

All companies, however, claim to be concerned with a variety of stakeholders and take their needs into considering in strategic decision-making. For example, research by Cooper et al. (2001) conducted in the UK shows that certain stakeholders are considered by all organisations. These are shareholders, customers and employees, with suppliers and society and the environment also being considered important by the majority of companies.

Although CSR involves a concern with the various stakeholders to a business there are several problems with this research in identifying socially responsible behaviour:

- The research shows that the concern is primarily with those stakeholders who have power to influence the organisation. Thus organisations are most concerned with shareholders, less so with customers and employees and very little with society and the environment.
- The research does not indicate the extent to which any action is taken and the extent to which this is voluntary.
- Claiming a concern is very different to actually exhibiting that concern through actions taken (Crowther 2004b).

The broadest definition of corporate social responsibility is concerned with what is – or should be – the relationship between the global corporation, governments of countries and individual citizens. More locally the definition is concerned with the relationship between a corporation and the local society in which it resides or operates. Another definition is concerned with the relationship between a corporation and its stakeholders. For us, all of these definitions are pertinent and represent a dimension of the issue. A parallel debate is taking place in the arena of ethics – should corporations be controlled through increased regulation or has the ethical base of citizenship been lost and needs replacing before socially responsible behaviour will ensue? In the UK at the present the government seems to believe that citizenship needs to be taught to our schoolchildren, presumably in the belief that this will manifest itself in the behaviour of corporations in the future. However this debate is represented it seems that it is concerned with some sort of social contract between corporations and society.

The social contract

This social contract implies some form of altruistic behaviour – the converse of selfishness. Self-interest connotes selfishness, and since the Middle Ages it has informed a number of important philosophical, political and economic propositions. Among these is Hobbes's world where unfettered self-interest is expected to lead to social devastation. A high degree of regulation is prescribed in order to avoid such a disastrous outcome, but in the process we sacrifice our rights. Self-interest again raises its head in the utilitarian perspective as championed by Bentham, Locke and J.S. Mill. The last, for example, advocated as morally right the pursuit of the greatest happiness for the greatest number. Similarly Adam Smith's free-market economics is predicated on competing self-interest. These influential ideas put interest of the individual above interest of the collective. Indeed from this perspective, collective interests are best served through self-interest. At the same time this corporate self-interest has come to draw disapproval in modern times, as reflected in many of the arguments within this book. The moral value of individualism has all but vanished.

While governments and consumers alike look to business to continue delivering economic and social benefits, many observers remain concerned about corporate self-interest; a self-interest that is synonymous with those of the managers. Managerial self-interest is unavoidably driven by a combination of shareholder interests (backed up by markets for corporate control and managerial talent) and occupational rewards and career opportunity. The public interest is easily sacrificed on the altar of these managerial motivators (or constraints). Moreover, public interest is not homogeneous and therefore cannot be simply represented. Public interest has become factionalised into constituencies and stakeholder groupings, each concerned with its particular interests. Consider for example the 'not-in-my-back-yard' protests over the building of recycling plants and mobile telephone masts, yet opinion polls support the former and sales of mobile phones demand more of the latter.

It has often been noted, from a global perspective, that corporate self-interest seems to be associated with an unequal distribution of economic and social benefits. However, it seems unfair to lay the responsibility for such inequality solely at the door of the corporation. National and regional politics, religious conviction and differentiated moral values all play an immeasurable role in shaping a nation's life chances. Nevertheless there is worldwide suspicion that corporate egoism is a significant (if not the most important) influence on economic and social development. There are, however, many examples of corporations behaving altruistically, from the paternalism of nineteenth- and twentieth-century industrialists, to modern-day donations to charities and the ad hoc secondment of managers to community projects. However, the perceived value of such giving is tainted by suspicions that many such acts seem self-serving. For example, there is room to ask whether Microsoft is giving away computers out of altruism or as part of an aim to reinforce its brand name. Many modern projects of altruism are tied to the purchase of products from the giving corporation; for example, the Tesco supermarket chain. Other initiatives are clearly pushing at the boundaries of acceptable corporate behaviour, such as donations to political parties. These examples show that corporate altruism covers a wide range of socially acceptable behaviour, from selfless giving to self-interested giving.

Perhaps one reason for corporate self-interest being such a mixed blessing is that we are overly reliant on evaluating the consequences of corporate action, especially apparent in the fixation with the bottom line. Nothing concentrates the managerial mind like performance targets and outcomes. However, as Wilbur (1992) argues, self-interest encompasses not just consequences and results, but also requires freedom of choice and consistency. From this perspective the pursuit of corporate (self-interested) activity should be guided by structured alternatives and consistency, in order to ensure that the self-interest of others is not undermined by selfish action. Sensing that we cannot rely on corporate altruism we the public are demanding that our governments initiate more legislation and tighter regulation.

However, even this move has shown important weaknesses. Many of the politicians and policy-makers are in the pockets of business. Self-interest is even here, and it is not acceptable to us. These arguments casts doubt on the extent to which we are able to arrange our economic and political institutions in order to harness self-interest to the benefit of society. The functioning of a civilised society includes putting the interests of others before self-interest. As Baron et al. (1992) and Mansbridge (1990) observed, altruism is part of social, political and economic life. However, the exploitative nature of capitalism sits uncomfortably with Kant's (1785) ideal of mutual respect for the interests of others, and even less with Rawls's (1971) desire to see a strong form of egalitarian liberalism. These tensions (between capitalism and liberalism, and between meeting unconditional social obligations and the pursuit of economic value) drive the need for constant vigilance of corporate activity. Since we are unlikely to abandon capitalism, nor escape from the fixation on performance measurement, managerial commitment to upholding the interests of others could straightforwardly be included in the managerial performance appraisal (Crowther and Rayman-Bacchus 2004b).

Crowther and Rayman-Bacchus (2004a) have argued that the corporate excesses, which are starting to become disclosed and which are affecting large numbers of people, have raised an awareness of the asocial behaviours of corporations. This is one reason why the issue of corporate social responsibility has become a much more prominent feature of the corporate landscape. There are other factors which have helped raise this issue to prominence and Topal and Crowther (2004) argue that a concern with the effects of bioengineering and genetic modifications of nature is also an issue which is arising general concern. At a different level of analysis Crowther (2000; 2002b; 2002c) has argued that the availability of the World Wide Web has facilitated the dissemination of information and has enabled more pressure to be brought upon corporations by their various stakeholders.

Alongside this recognition that corporations are accountable to their stakeholders has come a development of the principles upon which this demonstration of accountability should be based. Inevitably this is predicated in accounting as a mechanism by which such action can be measured and reported. In generic terms this has come to be called either social or environmental accounting.[8] The objective of environmental accounting is to measure the effects of the actions of the organisation upon the environment and to report upon those effects. In other words the objective is to incorporate the effect of the activities of the firm upon externalities and to view the firm as a network which extends beyond just the internal environment to include the whole environment (see Crowther 2000; 2002a). In this view of the organisation the accounting for the firm does not stop at the organisational boundary but extends beyond to include not just the business environment in which it operates but also the whole social environment. Environmental accounting therefore adds

---

8   Although among academics the terms 'social accounting' and 'environmental accounting' are deemed to denote different aspects of responsible accounting, among practitioners the terms tend to be treated as synonymous and generally called 'environmental accounting'. This approach has been followed here.

a new dimension to the role of accounting for an organisation because of its emphasis upon accounting for external effects of the organisation's activities. In doing so this provides a recognition that the organisation is an integral part of society, rather than a self-contained entity which has only an indirect relationship with society at large. This self-containment has been the traditional view taken by an organisation as far as their relationship with society at large is concerned, with interaction being only by means of resource acquisition and sales of finished products or services. Recognition of this closely intertwined relationship of mutual interdependency between the organisation and society at large, when reflected in the accounting of the organisation, can help bring about a closer, and possibly more harmonious, relationship between the organisation and society. Given that the managers and workers of an organisation are also stakeholders in that society in other capacities, such as consumers, citizens and inhabitants, this reinforces the mutual interdependency.

References

Argenti, J. (1993), *Your Organization: What is it For?*, London: McGraw-Hill.

Atkinson, A.A., Waterhouse, J.H. and Wells, R.B. (1997), 'A stakeholder approach to strategic performance management', *Sloan Management Review*, 38 (3), 25–37.

Barnett, N.J. and Crowther, D. (1998), 'Community identity in the 21st century: a postmodernist evaluation of local government structure', *International Journal of Public Sector Management*, 11 (6/7), 425–39.

Baron, L., Blum, L., Krebs, D., Oliner, P., Oliner, S. and Smolenska, M.Z. (1992), *Embracing the Other: Philosophical, Psychological, and Historical Perspectives on Altruism*, New York: New York University Press.

Bentham, J. (1789), *An Introduction to the Principles of Morals and Legislation*, many editions.

Çalıyurt, K.T. and Crowther, D. (2004), 'Social responsibility towards stakeholders', in D. Crowther and K.T. Çalıyurt (eds), *Stakeholders and Social Responsibility*, Penang: Ansted University Press, pp 1–18.

Castells, M. (1996), *The Rise of the Network Society*, Oxford: Blackwell.

Child, J. (1984), *Organisation: A Guide to Problems and Practice*, London: Harper & Row.

Clarkson, M.E. (1995), 'A stakeholder framework for analysing and evaluating corporate social performance', *Academy of Management Review*, 20 (1), 92–117.

Cooper, S. (2004), *Corporate Social Performance: A Stakeholder Approach*, Aldershot: Ashgate.

Cooper, S., Crowther, D., Davies, M. and Davis, E.W. (2001), *Shareholder or Stakeholder Value*, London: CIMA.

Crowther, D. (2004a), 'Limited liability or limited responsibility', in D. Crowther and L. Rayman-Bacchus (eds), *Perspectives on Corporate Social Responsibility*, Aldershot: Ashgate, pp 42–58.

Crowther, D. (2004b), 'Corporate social reporting: genuine action or window dressing?', in D. Crowther and L. Rayman-Bacchus (eds), *Perspectives on Corporate Social Responsibility*, Aldershot: Ashgate, pp 140–160.

Crowther, D. (2002a), *A Social Critique of Corporate Reporting*, Aldershot: Ashgate.

Crowther, D. (2002b), 'Psychoanalysis and auditing', in S. Clegg (ed.), *Paradoxical New Directions in Management and Organization Theory*, Amsterdam: J. Benjamins, pp 227–46.

Crowther, D. (2002c), 'The psychoanalysis of on-line reporting', in L. Holmes, M. Grieco and D. Hosking (eds), *Distributed Technology, Distributed Leadership, Distributed Identity, Distributed Discourse: Organising in an Information Age*, Aldershot: Ashgate, pp 130–148.

Crowther, D. (2000), *Social and Environmental Accounting*, London: FT Prentice Hall.

Crowther, D. and Rayman-Bacchus, L. (2004a), 'Perspectives on corporate social responsibility', in D. Crowther and L. Rayman-Bacchus (eds), *Perspectives on Corporate Social Responsibility*, Aldershot: Ashgate, pp 1–17.

Crowther, D. and Rayman-Bacchus, L. (2004b), 'The future of corporate social responsibility', in D. Crowther and L. Rayman-Bacchus (eds), *Perspectives on Corporate Social Responsibility*, Aldershot: Ashgate, pp 229–49.

Dahl, R.A. (1972), 'A prelude to corporate reform', *Business & Society Review*, Spring, 17–23.

Donaldson, T. and Preston, L.E. (1995), 'The stakeholder theory of the corporations: concepts, evidence and implications', *Academy of Management Review*, 20 (1), 65–91.

EU Commission (2002), *Corporate Social Responsibility: A Business Contribution to Sustainable Development*, Brussels: EC.

Evan, W.M. and Freeman, R.E. (1988), 'A stakeholder theory of the modern corporation: Kantian capitalism', in T. Beauchamp and N. Bowie (eds), *Ethical Theory and Business*, Englewood Cliffs NJ: Prentice Hall, pp 75–93.

Freeman, R.E. (1984), *Strategic Management: A Stakeholder Approach*, Boston MA: Pitman.

Fukuyama, F. (1992), *The End of History and the Last Man*, New York: Free Press.

Gioia, D.A. (1999), 'Practicability, paradigms, and problems in stakeholder theorizing', *Academy of Management Review*, 24 (2), 228–32.

Greenley, G.E. and Foxall, G.R. (1997), 'Multiple stakeholder orientation in UK companies and the implications for company performance', *Journal of Management Studies*, 34 (2), 259–84.

Jones, T.M. (1995), 'Instrumental stakeholder theory: a synthesis of ethics and economics', *Academy of Management Review*, 20 (2), 404–37.

Jones, T.M. and Wicks, A.C. (1999), 'Convergent stakeholder theory', *Academy of Management Review*, 24 (2), 206–21.

Kant, I. (1785), *Groundwork of the Metaphysics of Morals*, many editions.

Kaplan, R.S. and Norton, D.P. (1996), 'Using the balanced scorecard as a strategic management system', *Harvard Business Review*, January/February, 75–85.

Locke, J. (1690), *Two Treatises of Government*, many editions.

Mansbridge, J. (1990), *Beyond Self-Interest*, Chicago: University of Chicago Press.

Mill, J.S. (1863), *Utilitarianism, Liberty and Representative Government*, many editions.

Mitchell, R.K., Agle, B.R. and Wood, D.J. (1997), 'Towards a theory of stakeholder identification and salience: defining the principle of who really counts', *The Academy of Management Review*, October, 853–86.

Mraovich, B. (2004), 'The power of networks: organising vs. organisation', in D. Crowther and L Rayman-Bacchus (eds), *Perspectives on Corporate Social Responsibility*, Aldershot: Ashgate, pp 59–82.

Rawls, J. (1971), *A Theory of Justice*, Cambridge MA: Harvard University Press.

Rayman-Bacchus, L. (2004), 'Assessing trust in, and legitimacy of, the corporate', in D. Crowther and L. Rayman-Bacchus (eds), *Perspectives on Corporate Social Responsibility*, Aldershot: Ashgate, pp 21–41.

Shankman, N.A. (1999), 'Reframing the debate between agency and stakeholder theories of the firm', *Journal of Business Ethics*, 19 (4), 319–334.

Sternberg, E. (1997), 'The defects of stakeholder theory', *Corporate Governance: An International Review*, 5 (1), 3–10.

Tocqueville, A. de (1840), *Democracy in America*, many editions.

Topal, R.S. and Crowther, D. (2004), 'Bioengineering and corporate social responsibility', in D. Crowther and L. Rayman-Bacchus (eds), *Perspectives on Corporate Social Responsibility*, Aldershot: Ashgate, pp 186–201.

Waddock, S.A. and Graves, S.B. (1997), 'Quality of management and quality of stakeholder relations', *Business and Society*, 36 (3), 250–279.

Wilbur, J.B. (1992), *The Moral Foundations of Business Practice*, Lanham MD: University Press of America.

Corporate Social Responsibility: From Transparency to 'Constructive Conflict'

Dominique Bessire

Introduction

For some decades, the word 'transparency' has been used very extensively, in situations related to day-to-day life as well as in the managerial area. Two domains put a specific emphasis on this concept: corporate governance and corporate social responsibility. In both domains, the necessity for transparency is taken for granted and is very seldom questioned. The connection between corporate governance and social responsibility via the concept of transparency has intrigued us and the consensus on its necessity has roused our suspicion. Our chapter therefore aims to answer the two following questions: why do discourses on corporate governance and on corporate social responsibility make use of the word 'transparency', and what do these unanimist discourses hide? The first section of the chapter tracks the origins of the concept and tries to uncover the theoretical connections with managerial, economic and even philosophical literature. The second section concentrates on the adverse effects of discourses on transparency: the dissimulation of a struggle for power, the expression of a disciplinary power and more generally the exclusion of ethics. The third section points to the necessity of breaking away from the anti-humanist assumptions on which economic science has developed and which underpin most discourses on transparency. It suggests rebuilding management science on radically different bases, notably by a stronger emphasis on the concept of trust and the necessity of promoting pluralist democracy.

Transparency: an instrument to discipline managers

For about two decades, the word 'transparency' has invaded a large range of discourses. It has been especially and almost exclusively abundant in two domains:

first in the debate on corporate governance, and second in discourses on corporate social responsibility (CSR). To understand what is at stake with this selective and extensive use of the term 'transparency', we have to explore the theoretical – social, economic and philosophical – roots of the concept.

An emerging aesthetic

In the middle of the 1980s, Mikhail Gorbachev associated his political and economic reform with the word *glasnost* which in Russian means 'transparency'. We do not think that the word owes its popularity to the Russian president; we rather are convinced that Gorbachev was in tune with a phenomenon originating in the depth of our society (Benaïm 1989). Whatever the interpretation is, we should notice that transparency has nowadays invaded even the most insignificant aspects of our life: the iMac computer is protected by a translucent cover; in fashionable bakeries, customers can see people at work behind a transparent window; the TV, day after day, provides spectators with reality shows; in modern buildings, glass has replaced bricks and mortar; transparency of cosmetic products, such as Neutrogena, is supposed to guarantee their purity. Our readers will doubtless be able to add a long list of other examples to ours and will easily see by themselves how frequent the use of the word 'transparency' has become.

The demand for transparency in business life is nothing new. Since at least the end of the nineteenth century, a lot of legal devices have been designed in order to improve transparency (Garaud 1995; Guyon 1994). But for about two decades, the pressure has been severely intensified, and transparency has taken over the most important current management science debates.

A key concept in discourses on corporate governance and on CSR

It is notably pointed out as the best means to achieve better corporate governance. This concern is highly emphasised in and concretised through a variety of codes of best practices, principles and guidelines. Most of them have been elaborated by committees related to a business, industry, investor or directors' association; see, for instance, in the UK the Cadbury Report (1992); in the US CalPERS's Core Principles and Corporate Governance Guidelines and TIAA-CREF's Policy Statement on Corporate Governance; in France, the *Viénot I* (1995) and *Viénot II* (1999) *Reports*. A few of them have been conceived by governmental or intergovernmental organisations; see, for instance, the OECD corporate governance principles endorsed by OECD ministers in 1999 and revised in 2004. Many of their elements have been later enforced through laws which have been usually only passed after huge scandals; see, for instance, in Germany the KonTraG law (*Gesetz zur Kontrolle und Transparenz in Unternehmensbereich*); in England the law for control and transparency in companies (1999) (Azan 2002); in the US the Sarbanes-Oxley Act (2002); in France the *loi sur la sécurité financière* (law on financial security) (2003).

A similar phenomenon can today be observed in the field of CSR: a variety of voluntary initiatives have been launched which all put a specific emphasis on the need for transparency.

The Global Reporting Initiative (GRI) is backed by the United Nations Environment Programme and it relies on the support of NGOs and more especially of companies. It is usually presented as the most advanced initiative for the promotion of sustainability reporting. The 2002 Sustainability Reporting Guidelines 'represent the foundation upon which all other GRI reporting documents are based' (<http://www.globalreporting.org/guidelines/2002.asp>). In this document it said that 'the principles of transparency and inclusiveness represent the starting point for the reporting process and are woven into the fabric of all the other principles' (p 23), but in Figure 3 (Reporting Principles, p 23), transparency comes above all other principles including inclusiveness. It again insists on the following page on the importance of transparency: 'transparency is an overarching principle and is the centrepiece of accountability. ... Transparency is central to any type of reporting or disclosure.' The European multi-stakeholder forum was launched in 2002 by the European Commission. The final report was established on the basis of the presentations and discussions carried out in four thematic round tables: one of them was entitled 'Diversity, convergence and *transparency* [underlined by the Commission] of CSR practices and tools'; the final report was simply entitled 'Transparency'. This forum indeed 'aimed to promote innovation, transparency and convergence of CSR practices and instruments' (see <http://ec.europa.eu/enterprise/csr/index_forum.htm>). In a few cases the law has enforced this perspective: in France article 116 of the NRE (*Nouvelles régulations économiques* or New Economic Regulations) law requires all French corporations listed on the *premier marché* (those with the largest market capitalisations) to report annually on the social and environmental impact of their activities, commencing with their 2003 annual reports. Although the devices included in this law could be considered as heterogeneous, including a lot of heterogeneous devices, they are all, according to most jurists, underpinned by a common purpose: an increase in transparency (see Athlan website).

Indeed, this common emphasis in the field of corporate governance and of CSR has not come by chance: instruments in latter domain have been and are still inspired by instruments used in the former one. In its home page, under the section entitled 'What is GRI?', the following sentence appears: 'GRI's vision is that reporting on economic, environmental, and social performance by all organizations is as routine and comparable as financial reporting'. The 2002 guidelines themselves insist on this parallelism:

> In the case of financial reporting, over many decades governments and other organisations have created, and continue to enhance, disclosure rules affecting financial reports to increase the transparency of the reporting process. ... GRI seeks to move reporting on economic, environmental, and social performance in a similar direction by creating a generally accepted framework for economic, environmental, and social performance disclosure (Global Reporting Initiative 2006: 24).

This parallelism is widely admitted and appears in the vocabulary: social reporting (versus financial reporting), social rating (versus financial rating) …

Therefore to understand what is at stake when transparency is mentioned in the field of CSR, it is necessary to track its origins in the domain of corporate governance. The word 'transparency' does not actually belong to the scientific vocabulary of economics or of management science. It points, however, to a very important concept which has been developed in the context of the new economic theories. These theories – property rights, transaction costs and agency theories[1] – consider the firm as a nexus of contracts[2] and give a central role to information asymmetry, which is assumed to produce negative effects, since it generates adverse selection and moral hazard, two other key concepts of these theories (Coriat and Weinstein 1995; Charreaux 1997 and 1999; Salanié 1995). In most discourses, improving transparency is assumed to reduce this asymmetry and therefore to prevent agents from adopting opportunistic behaviours. Opportunism is another central, explicit (cost transactions theory) or implicit (agency theory) assumption of the 'new' economic theories. It must be strongly underlined that most (if not all) corporate governance codes are underpinned by these theories (Wirtz 2005); therefore it is not surprising that they grant such an importance to transparency which is assumed to enhance surveillance and control.

The last avatar of panopticism

The obsession with surveillance and control is not new. It reminds us of the Panopticon, the famous architecture conceived by Jeremy Bentham at the end of the eighteenth century. The Panopticon (from the Greek *pan* (all) and *opticon* (seeing)) was proposed as a model of an inspection house by Bentham (2003) in 1787. The philosopher, in a series of letters gathered in a volume, promotes the 'idea of a new principle of construction applicable to any sort of establishment in which persons of any description are to be kept under inspection' (part of the title of Bentham's book). The building is circular. The cells of the inmates occupy the circumference whereas the inspector's lodge occupies the centre. Through ingenious systems of openings and lighting, the inmate is able to be seen at any moment without his knowing if he is actually being observed. The architecture conceived by Bentham functions as a round-the-clock surveillance machine: 'the essence of it consists, then, in the *centrality* of the inspector's situation combined with the well-known and most effectual contrivances for *seeing without being seen*' (Bentham, letter V, his own emphases).

Transparency performs the same functions through two translations (in the proper sense of the word). First, a reification process[3] replaces the verbs 'to see',

---

1   P.Y. Gomez (1996) has demonstrated that, despite slight differences in their approaches, these theories must be considered as a consistent and unique system.

2   For this reason, these theories will be called hereafter 'contractualist theories'.

3   For an insightful analysis of the reification process applied to the concept of 'value creation', but also useful for a critical review of many managerial concepts, see Bourguignon (2005).

'to observe', 'to inspect'… and the substantives which derive from them by an all-including word, 'transparency'. 'To see' implies at least the existence of a subject who may have intentions. The word 'transparency' belongs to the vocabulary of physics; it points to an objective property of materials (for instance, crystal, diamond) and has the appearance of neutrality. Transparency appears to constitute a desirable character (for instance, we prefer to drink transparent water rather than a troubled beverage); in common language, it has usually positive connotations associated with purity. In the second translation, the architecture of bricks and mortar is replaced by a virtual one composed of information systems which are more and more developed.

A common purpose: discipline

Panopticism plays a central role in the extension of discipline. And discipline is a key concept for contractualist theories, notably in the field of corporate governance (Gomez 1996). The analysis of the Panopticon conducted by M. Foucault in *Discipline and Punish, the Birth of the Prison* (1991) will enable us to highlight this convergence.

According to Foucault, 'the exercise of discipline presupposes a mechanism that coerces by means of *observation*, an apparatus in which the techniques that make it possible *to see* induce effects of power and in which, conversely, the means of coercion make those on whom they are applied clearly *visible*' (pp 170–171). He adds a little further on that 'disciplinary power … imposes on those whom it subjects a principle of compulsory *visibility*. In discipline, it is the subjects who have *to be seen*. … It is the fact of *being* constantly *seen*, of being able always *to be seen*, that maintains the disciplined individual in his subjection' (ibid.: 187; in both quotations, emphases are ours).

Discipline is also at the centre of preoccupations in the dominant literature which legitimises the claim for transparency and which notably underpins the so-called principles of corporate governance.

This convergence appears first in the *vocabulary* used both to describe the Panopticon and the literature devoted to corporate governance. The latter indeed seems to concentrate on unique question: 'how *to discipline* managers?' It must be noticed that the question is usually asked in an impersonal mode; it would be hard to find the question expressed in a personal mode, for instance: 'how can *shareholders* discipline managers?' We find the same perspective by Bentham, who never indicates on whose account the surveillance is operated. Impersonal character seems to be an important aspect in both cases: surveillance is not specifically achieved through men of flesh and blood, but is embedded in *mechanisms*. The word *government* itself explicitly appears in Bentham's description of the Panopticon as 'a great and new instrument of *governement*'. It is also worth noting that Bentham links his 'idea of a new *principle* of construction' 'with a plan of *management*' (parts of the title of his book, our emphases); in the literature concentrating on corporate governance, the same articulation between *principles* (*principles* of corporate governance) and *management* methods can be found (notably the so-called value-based management). The analogy culminates in the use of the word '*architecture*'. The expression 'theory of organisational *architecture*' is progressively replacing the former expression 'theory of corporate governance' (Charreaux 1999; 2002). Bentham indeed concludes his text by these words 'all by a simple idea in *architecture*' (our emphasis).

The convergence also appears in the importance given to *normalisation*. According to Foucault (1991: 184), 'the power of the Norm appears through the disciplines. … It has joined other powers – the Law, the Word and the Text, Tradition – imposing new delimitations upon them.' We must admit that in the last few decades, normalisation has accelerated in management science (think, for instance, of the International Financial Reporting Standards or of the various codes of best practices for corporate governance).

The convergence can also be seen in the *concern for detail*. 'This infinitely scrupulous concern with surveillance is expressed in the architecture by innumerable petty mechanisms. These mechanisms can only be seen as unimportant if one forgets the role of this instrumentation, minor but flawless, in the progressive objectification and the ever more subtle partitioning of individual behaviour' (Foucault 1991: 173). In the elaboration of accounting standards, codes of best practices, incentive systems, devices for value-based management, and so on, the same concern for detail appears: accounting standards to be correctly interpreted must be accompanied by hundreds of pages; Stern and Stewart (in Stewart 1991) propose more than 100 adjustments in order to compute the EVA,[4] one of the most popular instruments for measuring the so-called 'value creation'.

Finally, transparency and the Panopticon fulfil the same *economic functions*. According to Foucault (1991: 174), 'as the machinery of production [becomes] larger and more complex, … supervision [becomes] ever more necessary and more difficult. It [becomes] a special function, which [has] nevertheless to form an integrated part of the production process, to run parallel to it throughout its entire length.' Foucault adds a little further on that 'surveillance thus becomes a decisive economic operation both as an internal part of the production machinery and as a specific mechanism in the disciplinary power' (ibid.: 175). He insists on the Panopticon's amplification role: 'its aim is to strengthen the social forces – to increase production, to develop the economy …' (ibid.: 207–8). In most discourses, we can observe that transparency is systematically put into relation with market efficiency.

To summarise, Foucault's words to describe the Panopticon could easily apply to the dominant approach of corporate governance: 'a whole problematic then develops: that of an architecture that [is conceived] to permit an internal articulated and detailed control – to render visible those who are inside it' (ibid.: 172). This approach has a very specific mode of realisation: '"discipline" may be identified neither with an institution nor with an apparatus; it is a type of power, a modality for its exercise, comprising a whole set of instruments, techniques, procedures, levels of application, targets' (ibid.: 215).

---

4   Economic value added – a specific way of calculating residual income.

This convergence does not come by chance. Both mainstream economic perspectives and Bentham describe man as a calculating machine, who is ready for any opportunistic behaviour if profits are higher than losses. Faced with this so-called 'reality', there is only one possible answer: discipline. Moreover, it should not be forgotten that Bentham was the inventor of the concept of utility which constitutes the base on which the whole of 'orthodox' economic science has been erected.

In this perspective, transparency will not only fail to produce the expected effects – an increase in morality – but it may result on the contrary in generalised amorality. The second section of this chapter aims to demonstrate this point.

Transparency against ethics and responsibility

Transparency, as it is currently promoted in most discourses, conceals a contradiction, produces adverse effects and finally leads to an exclusion of ethics.

A concealed contradiction and adverse effects

We have seen in the above section how the concept of transparency has moved from the field of corporate governance to the field of CSR. Most, if not all, codes of corporate governance are underpinned by a theoretical corpus in which the best way to maximise stakeholders' wealth is to maximise shareholders' wealth; or, in other words, 'there is only one social responsibility of business – to use its resources and engage in activities designed to increase profits' (Friedman 1970). Therefore there is a contradiction between the philosophy which underpins codes of corporate governance and which concentrates on the protection of shareholders' wealth, and the philosophy which underpins CSR and, on the contrary, insists on the necessity of taking into account the multiple and differentiated stakeholders' interests. The transposition of a concept of transparency from one field to another which is in complete contradiction with the former is somewhat puzzling.

Still more disturbing are the adverse effects of transparency, namely a door open to manipulation and to a totalitarian approach.

The claim for transparency may be dictated by obscure motives. It may hide bonding manoeuvres by companies and their managers. The agency theory has indeed taken into account this possible behaviour of managers. As everyone knows, it identifies three agency costs: monitoring costs, reinsurance costs and residual loss (Jensen and Meckling 1976). Successful firms are assumed to be able to reduce these costs more than their competitors.

There are many signs which may support this perspective. Many organisations which are supposed to promote CSR are in fact dominated by large companies; incidentally this is the reason why the Global Compact initiative, which presents itself as the world's largest voluntary corporate responsibility initiative, is increasingly coming under criticism and this is also the reason why the latest initiative in this field by the European Commission, the creation of a European Alliance for CSR, has been highly contested, namely by NGOs.

Moreover, transparency produced by companies appears to be very selective: to focus light on defined areas allows others to be left in obscurity and the overabundance of information works almost as efficiently as the lack of it. In this perspective, it is not surprising that the limits to transparency are never mentioned and that its costs are never calculated. However, they do exist. First, transparency comes in opposition to business secrecy which, in spite of continuously increasing restrictions, still remains a juridical principle. Secondly, transparency generates significant costs; for example, institution of regulation authorities; creation of a great variety of committees; capture, diffusion and analysis of a huge quantity of information. The fast increase in the number of pages devoted to CSR in annual reports over the past decade speaks volumes on this point. Last but not least, the actual benefits of transparency are not better defined. However, everyone can observe that the more people talk about transparency, the larger scandals there are, in the field of CSR as well as in the field of corporate governance (Fay 2002; Reverchon 2002).

Moreover, the claim for transparency produces adverse effects. The usual reasoning which justifies it is as follows: individuals are opportunistic; they care only for their self-interest and if they think that profits are higher than costs, they will behave in a reprehensible way. The only means to prevent them from such actions is to exert on them a permanent surveillance; transparency appears as the best device to achieve this control. Reality is, however, more complex.

Transparency is assumed by its advocates to increase morality, but in fact it relies on a conception of man (a calculating and opportunistic individual) which appears in contradiction with this aim. Ghoshal and Moran (1996) have already pointed to the caricatural use of the concept of opportunism; they denounce the confusion between opportunism as an inclination and opportunism as an effective behaviour. They suggest therefore a more complex relation between control and opportunistic behaviour.

At first, disciplinary mechanisms increase the cost of opportunism, but formal control tends to create a negative appreciation which in its turn amplifies opportunistic behaviours. At the end, the theoretical result is unpredictable. Moreover empirical studies tend to show that the actual effects do not correspond with Williamson's predictions (Williamson 1991).

Donaldson (1995) also criticises the regressive character of the opportunistic assumption which justifies, explicitly or implicitly, the claim for transparency. He is convinced that the emphasis on opportunism creates a self-fulfilling prophecy which may undermine any cooperation. According to him, the theory of transaction costs indeed proposes a theory of managerial delinquency. This debate sends us back to the opposition between the X and Y theories developed by McGregor (1960) more than four decades ago.

Another danger of the demand for transparency is seldom mentioned, the totalitarian temptation. The word transparency has very positive connotations (besides delinquents, who would be against transparency?). We should however not forget that it points to generalised surveillance which has always constituted the favourite means of all dictatorships. Foucault makes us aware of this danger: the Panopticon 'is the diagram of power reduced to its ideal form; ... it is in fact a figure of political technology'. In the fictional mode, George Orwell, in *Nineteen Eighty-Four* (2000), immerses us in a world seized by transparency, since 'BIG BROTHER IS WATCHING YOU'.[5] Panopticism has had in the past a lot of applications. Today, the Guantanamo camp (Lelyveld 2002) gives us an illustration of the possible use of transparency. The first camp was named – very symbolically indeed – *X Ray Camp*. The individual cages had their four lateral sides made of grating and were illuminated 24 hours a day. There was no possibility for the inmates to escape the permanent surveillance of their keepers; they were totally deprived of any form of privacy.

Exclusion of ethics?

We hope that in the above section we have demonstrated that the demand for transparency may produce adverse effects. We go a step further: we contend that the question of ethics cannot even be stated within the theories to which this concept refers. Dominant economic and managerial theories which support the demand for transparency indeed push into the foreground individuals who are enslaved by self-interest. To prevent them from reprehensible behaviour, such theories propose to exert on these individuals a sophisticated discipline by the means of flawless surveillance mechanisms, subsumed into the concept of transparency. Individuals are therefore called to become the permanent inmates of a virtual prison. But without freedom, there is neither responsibility, nor ethics.

The ethical intention,[6] according to Ricoeur (2002), demands that human freedom be acknowledged:

> When the subject takes a position of freedom, he breaks away from the course of things, from nature and its laws, from life and its needs. ... The assertion of my freedom may have been called the departure point for ethics, but it does not constitute ethics in itself. ... I indeed enter ethics, when to the assertion of my own freedom, I add the will that the Other's [Ricoeur's emphasis] freedom shall be. ... If I stopped believing in my own freedom, if I thought that I am entirely subject to determinism, I would also stop believing in the Other's freedom; ... I could not expect from the Other any help, and similarly, the Other could not expect from me any responsible action [our emphasis]. [If I take the opposite perspective,] I shall now say that the Other calls upon me and that, through his request, he makes me capable of responsibility [our emphasis] [our free translation].

---

5   The original text uses capital letters.
6   Ricoeur uses the expression 'ethical intention' rather than 'ethics' to stress the constantly projective and dynamic dimension of the concept.

Henriot (2002) expresses a convergent point of view: 'in the syntax of ethics, responsibility goes along with the exercise of the subjective function. When the process which is achieved is totally impersonal, there is no place for a responsibility judgement'. Of course, it is possible to conceive 'a world without subjects, a system where individuals would be only docile executants … but in his world of insects, neither responsibility, nor conscience can be granted any place' (our translation).

In other words, dominant perspectives on transparency, which implicitly refer to panopticism, rely on assumptions – calculating and opportunistic individuals who are alienated from their self-interest – which exclude even the possibility of posing questions of responsibility and of ethics. Therefore, transparency, in this approach, does not contribute to a moralisation of business life, but on the contrary to generalised amorality. It must be underlined that Bentham had to face the same criticisms from his contemporaries on his utilitarian philosophy: they already reproached him in very scathing terms for undermining any morality.

Academics who work in the field of critical finance have come to the same conclusion. According to Rainelli-Le Montagner (2002: 447), the traditional financial theory excludes from its area the ethical question:

> In the classical paradigm …, behaviours have not to be judged according to any morality; they are appreciated only with regard to their conformity with prescriptions which result from its modelisation based on the assumption of agents' rationality … Those who decide not to behave according to its rules will be sanctioned, not for the sake of any ethical demand, but because market remunerates only those who comply with its laws [our free translation].

Put together, all these elements – men as opportunistic and calculating individuals ('insects' in Henriot's words), generalised surveillance, the Panopticon as the perfect means to exert it, negation of human responsibility and freedom and therefore exclusion of the ethical question – point to an epistemological perspective that we can subsume into the word 'anti-humanism' (Viveret 2002). This conclusion urges us to break away from the traditional assumptions of orthodox economic theories and to erect theories on radically different bases in order to make room for ethics. The next section suggests a few tracks to follow.

Towards an alternative theory

To break away from the dominant theories is not an easy task. As Charreaux acknowledges (2002: 58), 'the introduction of an alternative paradigm generates costs which are related to a more precise study of the underpinning theoretical frameworks and to the learning of new investigation methods, which differ from the usual economic modelisation and the traditional statistical tests' (our translation). More generally, this inversion in logic is confronted by all the obstacles which have been noted by Kuhn in the course of scientific revolutions (1970). However, we can rely on some references in the organisational field as well as in the philosophical field. Creativity, trust, participation, inter-subjectivity, community, discussion and finally constructive conflict are some of the concepts that we will employ in order to propose a few tracks.

Creativity, an alternative responsibility for the enterprise[7]

To propose another definition of the enterprise's actual responsibility we can go on with the researches conducted by the French economist Perroux and his disciples (Bloch-Lainé and Perroux 1967 and 1968; Bloch-Lainé 1967; Perroux 1973; de Woot 1968) who were themselves deeply influenced by Schumpeter and by the Roman Catholic Church's social doctrine (inspired by Thomas Aquinas). These theoreticians adopt radically different assumptions regarding the ultimate aim of the enterprise and the nature of man.

In his innovative but today unfortunately forgotten book, *Pour une doctrine de l'entreprise* (1968, *For a Doctrine of the Enterprise*), de Woot proposes an interesting perspective. Instead of concentrating on conflicts between managers and shareholders, he immediately assigns a larger field to the issue of the enterprise's purposes; he relates it to the question of common good and of men's participation in the organisational life. First, he explains that it is not possible to define the enterprise's function by referring exclusively to the peculiar purposes of its members and that it is necessary to find a principle which transcends individual interests. He also demonstrates that it is not possible to define the enterprise's purpose in terms of total submission to the common good: the enterprise obviously plays a role which is not devoid of public concerns; however, its contribution is specific. The enterprise has therefore 'a peculiar purpose which differs both from the specific purposes of the individuals of which it consists and from the common interest which transcends the organisation's ends' (de Woot 1968: 185; the translations below are our own free translations from this book). To contribute to common welfare and to enable people to achieve their own ends demands that the enterprise fulfils its own and specific function.

According to de Woot, the economic *creativity* constitutes the enterprise's peculiar function. With these words, we must understand a value creation which is not only quantitative and static, but quintessentially all qualitative and dynamic. The enterprise exists 'to create, to progress, to produce something better' (ibid.: 189). With this perspective, de Woot breaks away from the purpose usually assigned to the enterprise according to quantitative terms: to maximise shareholders' wealth, to reduce costs, and notably to reduce agency costs. Therefore, 'production and creation in the economic area are a unique reality and it is not possible to achieve

---

7   We purposely use the word 'enterprise' to refer to an alternative theory, since the word 'firm' has too strong juridical and contractual connotations: it comes from the Italian *firma*, which means 'signature'. 'Enterprise', on the contrary, is related to the real essence of this human community, engaged in a project which has been launched by an entrepreneur; McGregor (1960) also uses the word 'enterprise'; the German word *Unternehmen* is constructed in the same way: *unter* = amongst and *nehmen* = take (see also the Schumpeterian 'entrepreneur').

the production and distribution function on a sustainable basis without fulfilling both the renewal and progress function' (ibid.: 191).

The creativity function is the only means to achieve the integration of public and individual interests, which takes place respectively up- and downstream of entrepreneurship (ibid.: 186). Through creativity indeed, the enterprise contributes to common welfare, because creativity 'constitutes the spring of social progress and provides us with the means to carry it out' (ibid.: 192). Creativity also enables man to give satisfaction to his highest aspirations, notably through a sense of achievement, and to give meaning to his work. Creativity indeed 'is the fruit neither of chance nor of fate, but the result of a human action' (ibid.: 191).

To be consistent with his perspective on the enterprise, Woot proposes a vision of the organisational actor which breaks away from the dominant approach: man is not only a calculating individual, in search of materialist welfare or of power, he is also 'a heart and a freedom' (ibid.: 191).

Participation and trust (Allouche and Amman 1998; Bidault 1998; Gomez 1995; Hirigoyen and Pichard-Stamford 1998) constitute two central conditions which enable individuals to develop their full humanity in the context of the enterprise.

Without actual participation, men behave only as passive agents and are not able to complete their function as creators and entrepreneurs. An effective participation, on the contrary, incites them to lay out their capabilities in the enterprise's service. Participation increases both enterprise's creativity and personal development. It allows organisational actors to achieve their own success through that of the enterprise and therefore tends to suppress divergences between the purposes of the enterprise and the individuals (de Woot 1968: 208).

This participation has three dimensions: an objective dimension (the organisational actor offers his resources to the enterprise: financial capital, managerial competencies, labour force ...); a strategic dimension (he recognises himself in his work); and last, but not least, a political dimension (he internalises the enterprise's purposes). The strategic participation demands autonomy and the possibility for him to express himself within and through his work; it is achieved through training, information, team work, sharing of responsibilities, flexibility in structures, and so on (ibid.: 210). Political participation requires being allowed to share power and its control (ibid.: 211).

> Trust is situated at the articulation of the strategic and political dimensions, because 'the success in strategic participation relies on the trust of those to whom it is addressed to and trust depends mainly on political participation' (ibid.: 215).

'Constructive conflict' instead of transparency

In the second section of this chapter, relying on Ricoeur's and Henriot's works, we have pointed to the fact that without recognition of subjectivity, there is no room for responsibility. In the perspective which prevails in discourses on CSR, the proposed subject is a dis-incarnated entity – the corporation. But behind this abstraction, there are actors of flesh and blood, shareholders and/or managers. Moreover, responsibility does not exist for itself; it exists only in relation to the Other (Simon 1993), both 'stakeholders' in the discourses on CSR. One important issue in many studies, whoever their authors may be – scholars, legislators or managers – is to decide which actors should be considered as stakeholders and which not. A lot of efforts are devoted to the construction of sophisticated typologies which are criticised as soon as they are published. Debates on the relevance of these typologies, however, hide the most important fact: they all participate in a logic of exclusion. Moreover, in the usual perspective on CSR, the emphasis is put on the production of reports which give a lot of information, usually quantitative information, but which do not allow stakeholders to express their own point of view. In other words, the so-called stakeholders are considered as infants under tutelage who are unable to speak for themselves and to take in hand their destiny. They are denied any autonomy, any freedom.

We propose another perspective: we consider that CSR can deploy itself only through a multiplicity of subjects, all responsible, each of them in a specific way: shareholders, managers, employees, customers, suppliers, and so on. The prevailing paradigm presents us with three questions which are all expressed in terms of interface: how to construct a link between isolated individuals and the enterprise, between the enterprise and its stakeholders and finally between these stakeholders themselves. These questions are no more relevant if we change the paradigm and if *we define the enterprise,* no longer as an abstract entity which has to deal with the expectations of a variety of stakeholders, but *as a community of actors, all stakeholders in the project which legitimates the existence of this enterprise, and all equally responsible.*

This definition has two main interests. It points to an essential weakness of most of the literature on CSR: managers and shareholders are never considered as stakeholders (we could paraphrase Baumol and say that *Hamlet* is played expurgated of the Prince of Denmark). Moreover, it allows us to escape the obsessive and sterile question of who should be considered – or not considered – as a stakeholder.

The enterprise conceptualised as a community of stakeholders thus becomes the locus where multiple subjectivities have to be progressively and continually integrated, the locus for inter-subjectivity. How can the expression of these multiple and often conflicting subjectivities be enabled?

Husserl 'explains in a text written in 1932 that even an empathy which has been actively experienced by "I" and "Thou" allows nothing more than a mere being-together of subjects', because 'to provoke the emergence of an actual inter-subjectivity, ... we also need ... a project and the will to *communicate*' (our emphasis) (Mutelesi 1998; our free translation). Llapassett (n.d.) also notes that 'without an effective process of *communication* [our emphasis] ... inter-subjectivity would be only fantasy' (our free translation). As communication appears to be central, we have turned our reflections towards discourse ethics and the analyses conducted by Apel and Habermas (in Benhabib and Dallmayr 1992) in order to propose a few pathways. The two philosophers suggest transcending the paradigm of subjectivity by the paradigm of communication. 'Whereas Kant allots to the individual the task of applying the universality principle in order to discover what actually are his obligations ..., discourse ethics gives this determination to practical and actual discussions with all the persons who are affected' (Desjardin 2004, in his comments on K.-O. Apel's writings; our free translation). In so many words, 'as soon as we accept to discuss, we have already tacitly accepted a normative and ethical principle which requires us to submit any disagreement to arguments in order to achieve a consensus' (ibid.).

But the analyses which have been conducted by Apel and Habermas and which have founded the concept of deliberative democracy (as opposed to representative democracy) have been criticised. Mouffe (1994), notably, agrees on the necessity of discussion, but thinks that the two authors, since they put the emphasis on the *polis* (living together), tend to blot out the dimension of *polemos* (antagonism). She suggests that 'the aim of democratic politics is to transform an 'antagonism' into an 'agonism'. She advocates for *pluralist democracy* 'which demands not only consensus on a set of common political principles but also the presence of dissent and institutions through which such divisions can be manifested' (Mouffe 1999).

These philosophical discussions may have tangible applications in the business world. They are consistent with the ideas developed by a pioneer of management, Mary Parker Follett. She asks us to consider conflict 'not as warfare, but the appearance of difference, difference of opinions, of interests' (Follett 1942: 30), as 'a moment in the interacting of desires' (ibid.: 34). She identifies three ways of dealing with conflict: domination, compromise and integration. Domination is 'the victory of one side on the other. This the easiest way of dealing with conflict, the easiest for the moment, but not usually successful in the long run' (ibid.: 31). With compromise 'each side gives up a little', but 'if we get only compromise, the conflict will come up again and again in some other form, for in compromise we give up part of our desire, and because we shall not be content to rest there, sometime we shall try to get the whole of our desire' (ibid.: 35). Integration 'means that a solution has been found in which both desires have found a place' (ibid.: 31). 'Only integration stabilizes. But by stabilization [I do not mean] anything stationary [but] that that particular conflict is settled and the next occurs on a higher level' (ibid.: 35). In this perspective, conflict is no more something to eradicate but something which may be used to make progress.

In order to enhance the development of these 'constructive conflicts', we make some suggestions.

First, the role of qualitative data should be re-evaluated. Bissara denounces 'the illusion that numbers are everything' (2003) and criticises the excessive refinement of accounting norms which only contribute 'to darken our understanding of financial statements'. According to him:

> Financial statements cannot be understood if they are not complemented
> by a description, even succinct, of the enterprise's activity and its main
> characteristics. ... This is why accounting information should not be

dissociated from a more 'literary' information which is provided in the annual report or in the document de référence.[8]

What he says about corporate governance can be applied to CSR.

Then the potentiality of the Internet should be more methodically exploited to generalise contradictory debates and to develop the communicative action and discourse ethics preached by Habermas and Apel. An increasing number of philosophical, sociological and political writers are already making serious efforts to build bridges between the propositions made by the German philosophers and the use of the Internet (for instance, see Kamga and Totschnig 2000; Ess 1996; Mukerji and Simon 1998; Poster 1999; Schneider 1996; Toulouse and Luke 1998; Thornton 1996; and Ward 1997, quoted by Perzynski (at <http://socwww.cwru. edu/~atp5/habermas>, 2005). Kamga and Totschnig (2000: 8, 9) already detect 'potentialities for communicative action' in the self-regulation processes of the Internet. They underline the culture of cooperation which is specific to the Internet and which favours 'consensus to the detriment of power struggles' as well as its 'open and ludic character'. Of course, 'the conditions of access to the Internet do not intrinsically guarantee more democracy. But no other medium contains as great a potential to share the production and diffusion of information as the Internet' (ibid., our translation).

The Internet has also a number of characteristics which are interesting for the deployment of CSR and the relationship between stakeholders. Compared to the traditional mode of information diffusion which puts the emphasis on transparency, it breaks away from spatial borders and it allows a highly decentralised participation to modes of communication – the 'one to many' ... which were till recently restricted to institutional and powerful actors' (ibid.: 1, 2). In this perspective, the whole set of stakeholders is called upon to constitute a virtual community whose borders are not defined in advance but can vary according to situations.

Conclusion

In a period which has seen a multiplication of huge scandals of various kinds: violation of human rights, financial wrongdoings, environmental disasters, etc., the demand for transparency is swelling, notably and almost exclusively in two organisational fields, corporate governance and CSR. It goes along with discourses marked by positive connotations and therefore not easily refutable: who could be against transparency? The concept then becomes an ideal without limits and its attractiveness 'discourages the auditor's resistance' (Bourguignon 2005). However, we have pointed to the adverse effects of extended transparency and, notably, generalised amorality. We have demonstrated that it takes its roots in a very pessimistic conception of the nature of man which reduces him to a calculating

---

8   This document is produced for the *Autorité des marchés financiers* which in France plays a role similar to that of the SEC in the US.

individual, enslaved to his self-interest, a perspective which indeed intrinsically excludes ethics. To break away from such a pernicious conception, which has developed taking as its departure point the concept of utility promoted by Bentham, we have to rebuild management science on alternative assumptions. Political and strategic participation (and not only objective participation) constitute two major conditions, which in their turn require trust. This means trust in the full sense of the word, not the residue of erudite calculations. In this perspective, it is necessary not only to fully recognise a space for subjectivity, but also to enable its transcendence through inter-subjectivity. The concept of pluralist democracy elaborated by Mouffe and the concept of 'constructive conflict' proposed by Follett could be usefully applied to facilitate the expression of these multiple subjectivities instead of concentrating most efforts on the development of so-called transparency.

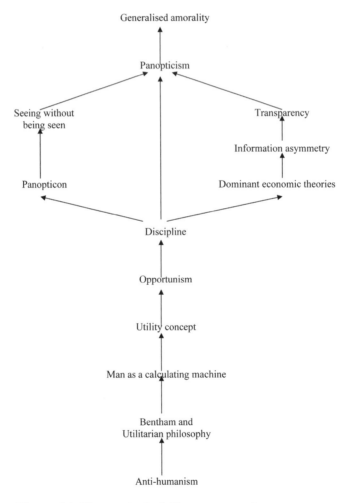

Figure 4.1 The context of discourses on transparency

If you want to get rid of weeds, it is of little use cutting the flowers, the leaves or even the stalk; you have to tear out the roots. At the beginning of this chapter, we had a seductive flower called 'transparency'. We have identified its scientific name – 'information asymmetry' – and we have dug down to its ideological roots – 'utility'. But this kind of plant grows only in a specific kind of soil; we call it anti-humanism. Our chapter aims to set down a few signposts towards radical humanism; it endorses the call of the French philosopher Morin 'to enter a politics of civilisation, a politics of humanism' (in Gibier 2002).

Figures 4.1 and 4.2 compare the two approaches which have been explored: the first one points to the ideological context in which dominant discourses on transparency are embedded with their ultimate consequences; the second one summarises our alternative model.

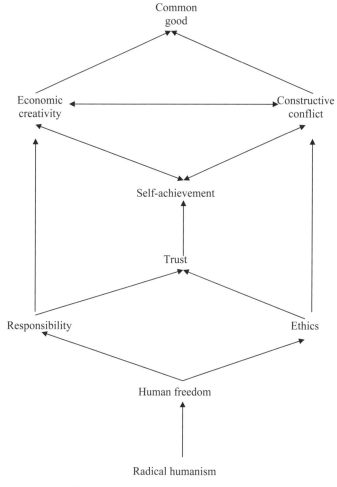

Figure 4.2 An alternative model

References

Allouche, J. and Amann, B. (1998), 'La confiance: une explication des performances des entreprises familiales', *Economies et Sociétés*, série 'Sciences de gestion', numéro spécial XXe anniversaire Confiance et gestion, no. 8–9, pp129–54.

Athlan, L. 'La transparence au travers des principes de la "Corporate Governance" et de la loi NRE', available at <http://www.afje.org/publications/transparence_corporate_governance.htm>.

Azan, W. (2002), 'Evolution des systèmes comptables, contrôle externe et réseaux de culture (KonTraG et NRE)', *Comptabilité Contrôle Audit*, tome 8, vol. 2, novembre, 29–50.

Benaïm, L. (1989), 'Design: l'effet *glasnost*', *Le Monde*, 9 mars 1989.

Benhabib, S. and Dallmayr, F.R. (eds) (1990), *The Communicative Ethics Controversy* (in the series 'Studies in Contemporary German Thought'), Cambridge MA: MIT Press.

Bentham, J. (2003), *Panopticon or the inspection house: containing the idea of a new principle of construction applicable to any sort of establishment, in which persons of any description are to be kept under inspection; and in particular to penitentiary houses, prisons, houses of industry, poor-houses, lazarettos, manufactories, hospitals, mad-houses, and with a plan of management adapted to the principle*: in a series of letters, written in the year 1787, from Crecheff in White Russia to a friend in England, <http://cartome.org/panopticon2.htm>, 36p.

Bidault, F. (1998), 'Comprendre la confiance: la nécessité d'une nouvelle problématique', *Economies et Sociétés*, série 'Sciences de gestion', numéro spécial XXe anniversaire Confiance et gestion, no. 8–9, 33–46.

Bissara, P. (2003), 'L'entreprise française face aux nouvelles normes comptables internationales', conférence prononcée à l'Académie de Comptabilité le 22 avril 2003, *ANSA*, no. 3213 (juillet 2003), at <http://www.ansa.asso.fr/site/3213.asp>.

Bloch-Lainé, F. (1967), *Pour une réforme de l'entreprise*, Paris: Editions du Seuil (1st edn 1963).

Bloch-Lainé, F. and Perroux, F. (eds) (1967 and 1968), *L'entreprise du XXe siècle*, 3 vols, Paris: Presses Universitaires de France.

Bourguignon, A. (2005), 'Management accounting and value creation: the profit and loss of reification', *Critical Perspectives on Accounting*, 16 (4), 353–89.

Cadbury Report – The Committee on the Financial Aspects of Corporate Governance (1992), *Report with Code of Best Practice* [Cadbury Report], London: Gee.

CalPERS, 'Core Principles and Corporate Governance Guidelines', available at <http://www.icann.org/committees/board-governance/board-governance-principles-28mar05.htm>.

Charreaux, G. (2002), 'Variation sur le thème: à la recherche de nouvelles fondations pour la finance et la gouvernance d'entreprise', *Finance Contrôle Stratégie*, 5 (3), septembre, 5–68.

Charreaux, G. (1999), 'La théorie positive de l'agence: lectures et relecture', in G. Koenig (ed.), *De nouvelles théories pour gérer l'entreprise du XXIe siècle*, Paris: Economica, collection 'Gestion', pp61–141.

Charreaux, G. (1997), *Le gouvernement des entreprises, 'Corporate governance', théories et faits*, Paris: Economica, collection 'Recherche en gestion'.

Coriat, B. and Weinstein, O. (1995), *Les nouvelles théories de l'entreprise*, Paris: Le Livre de Poche, collection 'Références'.

Desjardin, A. (2004), 'Karl-Otto Apel, la réponse de l'éthique de la discussion', at <http://www.ac-amiens.fr/academie/pedagogie/philosophie/lectures/Apel.htm>.

Donaldson, L. (1995), *American Anti-Management Theories*, Cambridge: Cambridge University Press.

Ess, C. (ed.) (1996), *Philosophical Perspectives on Computer-Mediated Communication* (in the SUNY series on computer-mediated communication), New York: State University of New York Press.

Fay, S. (2002), 'Aux Etats-Unis, tous étaient touchés', *Le Monde Economie*, Dossier 'L'Europe peut-elle échapper aux scandales financiers?', 17 décembre, pII.

Follett, M.P. (1942), 'Constructive conflict', in H.C. Metcalf and L. Urwick (eds), *Dynamic Administration: The Collected Papers of Mary Parker Follett*, New York: Harper.

Foucault, M. (1991), *Discipline and Punish, the Birth of the Prison*, Harmondsworth: Penguin, trans. from the French, *Surveiller et punir, naissance de la prison*, Paris: Gallimard, collection 'Tel' (first published in 1975).

Friedman, M. (1970), 'The social responsibility of business is to increase its profits', *New York Times Magazine*, 13 September.

Garaud, E. (1995), 'La transparence en matière commerciale', thèse pour le doctorat en droit, Université de Limoges.

Ghoshal, S. and Moran, P. (1996), 'Bad for practice: a critique of the transaction cost theory', *Academy of Management Review*, 21 (1), 13–47.

Gibier, H., propos recueillis par (2002), 'Grand angle avec Edgar Morin, réconcilier l'éthique et l'économie', *Les Echos*, 18 et 19 octobre, 46–7.

Global Reporting Initiative (GRI) (2006), *Sustainability Reporting Guidelines* [Draft], G3 version for public comment, 2 January–31 March 2006.

Gomez, P.Y. (1996), *Le gouvernement de l'entreprise, modèles économiques de l'entreprise et pratiques de gestion*, Paris: InterEditions.

Gomez, P.Y. (1995), 'Agir en confiance', in F. Bidault, P.-Y. Gomez and G. Marion (eds), *Confiance, entreprise et société*, collection 'Essais', Paris: Eska.

Guyon, Y. (1994), '"Les enjeux juridiques"', L'information légale dans les affaires. Quels enjeux? Quelles évolutions?', *La Semaine Juridique*, édition E.I., 387.

Henriot, J. (2002), 'Responsabilité', *Encyclopaedia Universalis*, version 8 (DVD).

Hirigoyen, G. and Pichard-Stamford, J.-P. (1998), 'La confiance, un outil de la finance organisationnelle: une synthèse de la littérature récente', *Economies et Sociétés*, série 'Sciences de gestion', numéro spécial XXe anniversaire Confiance et gestion, no. 8–9, pp219–234.

Husserl, E. (2001), *Sur l'intersubjectivité*, tome I, Paris: Presses Universitaires de France, collection 'Epithémée'. Partial translation of *Zur Phänomenologie der Intersubjectivität*, 3 volumes (I. 1905–20, II. 1921–28, III 1929–35) edited in 1973, La Haye, by Martinus Nijhoff in *Husserlania*, tomes XIII, XIV et XV.

Jensen, M.C. and Meckling, W.H. (1976), 'Theory of the firm: managerial behavior, agency costs and ownership structure', *Journal of Financial Economics*, 3, October, 305–60.

Kamga, O. and Totschnig, M. (2000), 'L'autorégulation de l'Internet et ses répercussions sur le rapport entre les institutions publiques et les citoyens', at <www.er.uqam.ca/nobel/d36410/regulation.pdf>.

Kuhn, T.S. (1970), *The Structure of Scientific Revolutions*, Chicago: University of Chicago Press (first published 1962).

Lelyveld, J. (2002), 'Retour à Guantanamo', *Le Monde*, 9 novembre, 14–15, traduit de l'anglais, © New York Review of Books.

Llapasset, J. (n.d.), 'De l'intersubjectivité et d'internet', chapitre 1, at <http://philagora.net/philo-fac/joseph.htm>.

McGregor, D. (1960), *The Human Side of Enterprise*, New York: McGraw-Hill.

Mouffe, C. (1999), 'For a politics of democratic identity', Globalization and Cultural Differentiation seminar, MACBA-CCCB, March 19–20.

Mouffe, C. (1994), *Le politique et ses enjeux. Pour une démocratie plurielle*, Paris: La Découverte/MAUSS, collection 'Recherches'.

Mukerji, C. and Simon, B. (1998), 'Out of the limelight: discredited communities and informal communication on the Internet', *Sociological Inquiry*, 68 (2), 258–73.

Mutelesi, E. (1998), 'Subjectivité comme auto-organisation. Une étude du constructivisme radical au départ de Husserl', Université Catholique de Louvain, Louvain-La-Neuve, dissertation doctorale à l'Institut Supérieur de Philosophie, at <http:///www.univie.ac.at/constructivism/books/mutelesi/4html>.

Organization for Economic Cooperation and Development (OECD) (2004), *OECD Corporate Governance Principles (2004)*, at <http://www.oecd.org/dataoecd/32/18/31557724.pdf>.

Orwell, G. (2000), *Nineteen Eighty-Four*, Harmondsworth: Penguin (first published 1949).

Perroux, F. (1973), *Pouvoir et économie*, Paris: Bordas, collection 'Bordas études', no. 262.

Rainelli-Le Montagner, H. (2002), 'Des marchés et des hommes', *Sciences de gestion et pratiques managériales*, Paris: Economica-IAE, collection 'Gestion', pp441–9.

Reverchon, A. (2002), 'Etats-Unis et Europe resserrent l'étau juridique', Dossier 'L'Europe peut-elle échapper aux scandales financiers?', *Le Monde Economie*, 17 décembre 2002, III.

Ricoeur, P. (2002), 'Ethique', *Encyclopaedia Universalis*, version 8 (DVD).

Salanié, B. (1995), 'Une nouvelle microéconomie, incitations et théorie des contrats', in *Les nouvelles théories économiques*, *Les Cahiers Français*, no. 272, juillet–septembre, pp. 3-11.

Schneider, S. (1996), 'Creating a democratic public sphere through political discussion', *Social Science Computer Review*, 14 (4), 373–93.

Simon, R. (1993), *Ethique de la responsabilité*, Paris: Les Editions du Cerf.

Stewart, G.B. (1991), *The Quest for Value*, New York: HarperCollins.

Toulouse, C. and Luke, T.W. (eds) (1998), *The Politics of Cyberspace*, New York: Routledge.

Viénot I Report – CNPF et AFEP (1995), Le Conseil d'Administration des Sociétés Cotées.

Viénot II Report – AFEP et MEDEF (1999), Rapport du comité sur le gouvernement d'entreprise.

Viveret, P. (2002), 'Comptabilité et développement : éthique, partage des savoirs, sagesse des modernes', avec la participation d'E. Delesalle, d'E. Arnoult-Brill, S. Diarra, P. Prouvost, P. Viveret, M. Rocard, M. Tudel, R. Gualino et F. Jay, in *Confédération mondiale des experts-comptables sans frontières*, conférence; Petites affiches, no. 211, 22 octobre, pp4–30.

Ward, I. (1997), 'How democratic can we get? The Internet, the public sphere and public discourse', *JAC: Journal of Composition Theory*, 17 (3), 365–79.

Williamson, O.E. (1991), 'The logic of economic organization', in O.E. Williamson and S.G. Winter (eds), *The Nature of the Firm*, Oxford: Oxford University Press.

Wirtz, P. (2005), ' "Meilleures pratiques" de gouvernance et création de valeur: une appréciation des codes de bonne conduite', *Comptabilité Contrôle Audit*, tome 11, vol. 1, 141–59.

Woot, P. de (1968), *Pour une doctrine de l'entreprise*, Paris: Editions du Seuil.

Corporate Governance and the Agency Problem in Financial Markets

Güler Aras

Introduction

It is well known that globalization, together with the ability to transfer knowledge at great speeds, and developments in financial markets have led to an increase in the need for some international rules concerning such things as international financial reporting standards, corporate governance rules, ethics and corporate social responsibility principles. In business activity, these standards have been set forth with a view to minimizing uncertainty and with developing an atmosphere of confidence in a web of emerging complex relations. With the impact of these developments, it is very important for financial markets, and the organizations operating within these markets, to accommodate and implement some rules. The reason for this is the quality of transactions and instruments in the financial sector. This area contains riskier transactions and complex instruments. The uncertainty created by this situation makes it difficult for organizations to create confidence regarding the segments concerned. Obviously, these markets and organizations are successful to the extent that they secure confidence. Legal provisions and the control mechanisms and sanctions introduced by them alone are not sufficient to ensure sound operation of the system and to create confidence. Therefore, the introduction of corporate governance principles aims at increasing compliance with legal provisions and at creating an atmosphere of confidence by giving security to stakeholders and safeguarding the interests of all parties.

The objective of corporate governance in corporations is to maximize shareholders' value in the context of its corporate mission by considering a balance between the achievement of goals and the encouragement of efficient use of resources. Corporate governance helps businesses to meet global challenges while improving organizational competitiveness and safeguarding the interests of all stakeholders. Long-run viability, more efficient resource allocation and elimination of the uncertainties are the other primary benefits of corporate governance.

In this context, our study focuses on the perception, importance and functions of corporate governance and on agency problems in financial markets. Agency problems for the investors and important governance principles are also investigated.

Corporate governance and its principles

One of the main issues which has been exercising the minds of business managers, accountants and auditors, investment managers and government officials – again all over the world – is that of corporate governance. Often a company's main target is to become global – while at the same time remaining sustainable – as a means to gain competitive power. But the most important question is concerned with what will be a firm's route to becoming global and what will be necessary in order to get global competitive power. There is more then one answer to this question and there are a variety of routes for a company to achieve this (Aras and Crowther 2007; 2008).

Probably since the mid-1980s, corporate governance has attracted a great deal of attention. Early impetus was provided by Anglo-American codes (such as the Cadbury Report) of good corporate governance. Stimulated by institutional investors, other countries in the developed world, as well as in the emerging markets, established adapted versions of these codes for their own companies. Supra-national authorities like the OECD and the World Bank did not remain passive and developed their own set of standard principles and recommendations. This type of self-regulation was chosen above a set of legal standards (Van den Berghe 2001). More recently, after the well-publicized big corporate scandals, corporate governance has become central to most companies. It is understandable that investors' protection has become a much more important issue for all financial markets after the tremendous corporate failures and scandals. Investors are demanding that companies implement rigorous corporate governance principles in order to achieve better returns on their investment and to reduce agency costs. Most of the time investors are ready to pay more for companies to have good governance standards (Beiner et al. 2004). Similarly a company's corporate governance report is one of the main tools for investors' decisions. For these reasons companies cannot ignore the pressure for good governance from shareholders, potential investors and other market actors.

Good governance will have a significant impact on a firm's performance and on shareholders returns. In the literature, a number of studies have sought to investigate the relation between corporate governance mechanisms and performance (see, for example, Hermalin and Weisbach 1991; Agrawal and Knober 1996; Loderer and Martin 1997; Dalton et al. 1998; Cho 1998; Bhagat and Black 1999; Coles et al. 2003; Gompers et al. 2001; Patterson 2002; Heracleous 2001; Demsetz and Villalonga 2002; Bhagat and Bernard 2002; Bhagat and Jefferis 2002; Becht et al. 2002; Millstein and MacAvoy 1998; Bøhren and Ødegaard 2006; and Brown and Caylor 2006). These studies do not necessarily report a clear-cut relationship. However, it is clear that corporate governance does matter for a company's performance, market value and credibility, and therefore following corporate governance principles is important for every corporation's benefit.

Since corporate governance can be highly influential for performance, a firm must know what the corporate governance principles are and how it will improve strategy to apply these principles. In practice there are four principles of good corporate governance, which are:

- transparency
- accountability
- responsibility
- fairness.

All these principles are related to the firm's corporate social responsibility. Corporate governance principles, therefore, are important for a firm but the real issue is concerned with what corporate governance actually is.

Conflict of interests in financial markets

In financial markets, there are various areas in which problems related to corporate governance arise. These problems areas include: the agency problem and the subsequent ethical problems that this may lead to; the problems concerning insider trading; manipulation; reporting for the general public; and providing information to investors. These areas are traditional ones for conflicts of interest situations and are also referred as 'private benefits of control' (Baums and Scott 2005).

The general agency problem can be characterized as a situation in which a principal (or group of principals) seeks to establish incentives for an agent (or group of agents) who takes decisions on behalf of the principal and that affect the principal and in which the agent is expected to act in ways that contribute maximally to the principal's own objectives. The difficulties in establishing such an incentive structure arise from either divergence of the objectives of principals and agents or from the asymmetric information between principals and agents (Vickers and Yarrow 1988).

Jensen and Meckling (1976) described the problem more generally as the conflict of interest between 'principals' (shareholders) and their 'agents' (managers). The basic problem is that agents and managers are entrusted by principals and investors with authority over their property and capital, which is supposed to be used to advance the interests of the owners rather than for the personal gain of the agents (Baums and Scott 2005).

As stated by Lambert (2001), agency theory evaluates the impact of the conflict of interest between principals and agents because of such reasons as (1) shirking by the agent; (2) the diversion of resources by the agent for private consumption; (3) the differential time horizon of the agent and the principal; and (4) differential risk aversion of the agent and the principal. Jensen and Meckling (1976) developed agency theory in the context of the conflicts of interest between corporate managers and outside equity and debt-holders. Agency theory starts with the assumption that people act unreservedly in their own narrowly defined self-interest, with (if necessary) guile and deceit. The firm is usually seen as a set of contracts between the various parties involved in the production process, including the owners, managers, workforce and creditors, among others. Agency theory switches the centre of attention from the firm to the set of the contracts that define each firm. It is primarily concerned with the contracts and relationships between principals and the agents under conditions of asymmetric information.

Agency costs are defined as the costs associated with cooperative efforts by human beings. The agency costs within the organization occur when one entity, the principal, hires another, the agent, to act for him or her. According to conventional financial theory, rational shareholders will recognize the incentives facing managers to shirk, to diversify and to under-invest. Therefore, the firm would suffer losses from these decisions, and these losses would represent the agency costs of outside equity financing. Agency costs are defined as the sum of the contracting, monitoring and bonding costs undertaken to reduce the costs due to conflicts of interest plus the 'residual loss' that occurs because it is generally impossible to perfectly identify the agents' interests with that of the principal. Markets are assumed as potent forces to help control agency costs.

Ethical behaviour that is either altruistic (which is concerned for the welfare of others or by the desire to feel good by helping others) or utilitarian (which is concerned with the compliance with rules in the individual's self-interest) is essential for efficient functioning in the economy. It has many implications in agency theory (Noreen 1988). Unwritten agreements, trust and mutual understanding constitute the core of the relationships within the firm. Written contracts which are the fundament of the agency theory 'hit only the high spots of agreements' (McKean 1975: 31). Therefore, if unconstrained opportunism pervades the economy, the contracting, monitoring and bonding costs of principals increase and so do agency costs. On the contrary, 'altruism economizes on the costs of policing and enforcing agreements' (Hirshleifer 1977: 28).

Corporate governance and stakeholders' values in financial markets

The broadest definition of corporate governance is one which encompasses every force which affects corporate decision-making. That would include not only the control rights of shareholders but also the contractual covenants and insolvency powers of debt-holders, the commitments entered into with employees and customers and suppliers, the regulations issued by governmental agencies, and the statutes enacted by parliamentary bodies. And in a still more comprehensive sense, a company's decisions are powerfully affected by competitive conditions in the various markets in which it transacts, and indeed by the social and cultural norms of the society in which it operates (Baums and Scott 2005).

Management can be interpreted as managing a firm for the purpose of creating and maintaining value for shareholders. Corporate governance procedures determine every aspect of the role for management of the firm, seeking to keep in balance and to develop control mechanisms in order to increase both shareholder value and the satisfaction of other stakeholders. In other words corporate governance is concerned with creating a balance between the economic and social goals of a company including such aspects as the efficient use of resources, accountability in the use of its power, and the behaviour of the corporation in its social environment (Aras and Crowther 2008).

The definition and measurement of good corporate governance is still subject to debate. However, good corporate governance will address such points as creating sustainable value, achieving the firm's goals and keeping a balance between economic and social benefits. Also, of course, good governance offers some long-term benefits for a firm, such as reducing risk and attracting new investors, shareholders and more equity (Aras and Crowther 2007c).

For financial organizations, corporate governance is much more important since they produce and provide rather intangible services in the economy. Indeed, the difficulties that such a business would face when it loses its credibility in terms of its relevant circles, number and types of customers, and the losses it would suffer as a result are much higher (Aras and Crowther 2007). Financial organizations are no different from other businesses in terms of their purposes of establishment. Being service providers, financial organizations attempt to reach their targets in two respects. On the other hand, any confidence in management is more important in financial organizations than other businesses. This is indeed because gaining customers, and therefore profitability, in the financial services sector depends on the confidence built up by the organization. Financial organizations need to give more emphasis to ethical values and good governance both as a business and due to the fact that their job often contains riskier and more complex relations (Aras 2006).

When considering corporate governance in financial institutions we are generally confronted with a more complicated field and more problems. The reason for this is concerned with the nature of finance, and therefore of financial services and instruments. These fields contain intangible services and risky instruments and transactions. The fact that characteristics and functions of finance, financial services and these instruments are rather complex, when combined with insufficient information on the part of customers or consumers in these fields and their differentiation in the latter's expectations, leads to scepticism, disappointment and extreme reactions. Often, there are suitable opportunities for abuse for financial service providers under such conditions.[1] When all these combine, customers can readily claim that they are deceived, and this, in turn, contributes to the bad reputation of finance in terms of ethics and ethical behaviour.

---

1   There are many examples of such misbehaviour – in the UK and the US and other countries – which have received high prominence.

These features also imply that the sector of financial services should be governed with serious legal regulations, and should be closely monitored. However, although most people are aware of this requirement, it is rarely fulfilled. This is particularly true in developing countries, since legal regulations have not become established fully or their implementation is not successful, and there are problems in the operation of these markets. Even so it is obvious that one of the reasons for recent financial crises is the operational and regulation problems in these markets. The most typical example of this is the Asian crisis which started in Thailand in 1997 and turned into a global crisis by the contagion effect; as the cause of this crisis, regulations and inspections concerning the banking system in the countries in this region were insufficient, and the standards for determining the credit risk by the banks were not fully established.

On the other hand, apart from such discredit in developing countries, unethical and non-market acts are not at low levels in developed countries either. Although regulations and sanctions are supposedly very strict, these markets are still amenable to abuse. In financial markets and organizations, there may be various areas in which management and governance-related problems arise. These areas include agency problems and corporate governance problems and the costs related to these, reporting and providing information to investors, and functions in which ethical values are given the highest emphasis such as counselling or customer representation.

The interaction of public disclosure, ethical issues and corporate governance can be observed in the Enron case. At the time of Enron's peak market value of $70 billion, some observers have estimated the actual worth of the company as being only about $30 billion (Jensen 2005). Though the business of Enron was a good, viable business and the company was a major innovator, senior managers' efforts to defend $40 billion of excess valuation destroyed the $30 billion core value. If managers could have made contact with the market through public disclosure to help the market to reduce its expectations, probably such a great collapse would have not been realized. However, managers gambled by trying to fool the market through accounting manipulations which led to the inevitable collapse.

Conclusion

In the economy, 'trust' is important. Informal unwritten guarantees are preconditions for all trade and production (Akerlof 1970). On the other hand, international rules and principles may protect investors and stakeholder from the uncertainty in the market.

Corporate governance and agency theory is characterized by conflicts of interests. Businesses attempt to maximize profits as a primary goal on one hand while they face issues of social responsibility and stakeholder rights on the other. Corporate governance is about fair conduct and management by a business and its representatives in all of its relations. In business behaviour, corporate governance principles have been set out with a view to minimizing uncertainty and developing an atmosphere of confidence in a web of emerging complex relations. With the impact of these developments, it is very important for financial markets operating within these countries and markets to accommodate and implement good governance. The reason for this is the quality of transactions and instruments in the financial markets. This area contains riskier transactions and complex instruments. The uncertainty created by this situation makes it difficult for organizations to create confidence in the segments concerned. Legal provisions and control mechanisms and sanctions introduced by them alone are not sufficient to ensure sound operation of the system and create confidence. Therefore, the introduction of corporate governance rules and principles is aimed at increasing compliance with legal provisions and also in creating an atmosphere of confidence by securing the interests of all parties. To achieve its goals, a firm or organization should have (as a whole) governance rules. Corporate governance is not a sacrifice, but a part of the behavioural processes of management and its organization. Corporate governance should not be altered depending on circumstances and countries, but harmonized in accordance with them.

Corporate governance principles help to dissolve any conflict of interest problems by considering a balance between corporate goals. They also help businesses to meet global challenges while improving organizational competitiveness and safeguarding stakeholders' interests. Adhering to corporate governance principles ensures long-run viability, more efficient resource allocation and elimination of the uncertainties facing companies.

References

Agrawal, A. and Knober, C.R. (1996), 'Firm performance and mechanisms to control agency problems between managers and shareholders', *Journal of Financial and Quantitative Analysis*, 31 (3), 377–97.

Akerlof, G.A (1970), 'The market for lemons', *The Quarterly Journal of Economics*, 84, 488–500.

Allen F. (2001), 'Do financial institutions matter?', *Journal of Finance*, 56 (4), 1165–75.

Aras, G. (2006), 'The ethical issues in the finance and financial markets', in *Globalization and Social Responsibility*, eds D. Crowther and K. Çalıyurt, Newcastle upon Tyne: Cambridge Scholars Press.

Aras, G. and Crowther, D. (2008), 'Governance and sustainability: an investigation into the relationship between corporate governance and corporate sustainability', *Management Decision*, 46 (3), 433–448.

Aras, G. and Crowther. D. (2007), 'Is the global economy sustainable?', in S. Barber (ed.), *The Geopolitics of the City*, London: Forum Press, pp 165–194.

Aras, G. and Crowther, D. (2007c), 'Setting standards in harmony: the route to the setting of reporting standards', International Balkans Countries Accounting and Auditing Conference, Edirne, Turkey.

Aras, G. and Muslumov, A. (2005), 'The analysis of factors affecting ethical judgments: the Turkish evidence', in D. Crowther and R. Jatana (eds), *Representations of Social Responsibility*, vol. 1, Hyderabad: ICFAI University Press.

Baums, T. and Scott, K.E. (2005), 'Taking shareholder protection seriously? Corporate governance in the U.S. and Germany', *Journal of Applied Corporate Finance*, 17 (4), Fall, 4–7.

Becht, M., Bolton, P. and Roell, A. (2002), *Corporate Governance and Control*, ECGI Working Paper no. 02/2002, Brussels: ECGI.

Beiner, S., Drobetz, W., Schmid, F. and Zimmermann, H. (2003), *Is Board Size an Independent Corporate Governance Mechanism?*, Working Paper, University of Basel.

Bergmans, A. and Lynne, M.C. (1993), *Insider Trading*, 2nd edn, London: Butterworths Tolley.

Bhagat, S. and Bernard, B. (2002), 'The non-correlation between board independence and long-term firm performance', *Journal of Corporation Law*, 27, 231–74.

Bhagat, S. and Black, B. (1999), 'The uncertain relationship between board composition and firm performance', *The Business Lawyer*, 54 (3), May, 921–63.

Bhagat, S. and Jefferis, R.H. (2002), *The Econometrics of Corporate Governance Studies*, Cambridge MA: MIT Press.

Boatright, J.R. (1999), *Ethics in Finance*, Malden MA: Blackwell.

Bøhren, Ø. and Ødegaard, B.A. (2006), 'Governance and performance revisited', in G. Gregouriu and P.U. Ali (eds), *International Corporate Governance after Sarbanes-Oxley*, Hoboken NJ: Wiley.

Brown, J J L.D. and Caylor, M.L. (2006), 'Corporate Governance and Firm Valuation', *Journal of Public Accounting & Public Policy*, 25 (July–August), 409–34.

Cho, M.H. (1998), 'Ownership structure, investment, and the corporate value: an empirical analysis', *Journal of Financial Economics*, 47 (1), 103–21.

Coles, J.L., Meschke, F. and Lemmon, M. (2003), *Structural Models and Endogeneity in Corporate Finance: the Link between Managerial Ownership and Corporate Performance*, working paper, Arizona State University and University of Utah.

Crowther, D. (2002), *A Social Critique of Corporate Reporting*, Aldershot: Ashgate.

Crowther, D. (2000), 'Corporate reporting, stakeholders and the Internet: mapping the new corporate landscape', *Urban Studies*, 37 (10), 1837–48.

Crowther, D., Davies, M. and Cooper, S. (1998), 'Evaluating corporate performance: a critique of economic value added', *Journal of Applied Accounting Research*, 4 (3), 2–34.

Dalton., D.R., Daily, C.M., Ellstrand, A.E. and Johnson, J.L. (1998), 'Meta-analytic reviews of board composition, leadership structure, and financial performance', *Strategic Management Journal*, 19 (3), March, 269–90.

Demsetz, H. and Villalonga, B. (2002), 'Ownership structure and corporate performance', *Journal of Corporate Finance*, 7, 209–33.

Eisenhardt, K.M. (1989), 'Agency theory: an assessment and review', *Academy of Management Review*, 14 (1), 57–74.

Etzioni, A. (1988), *The Moral Dimension*, New York: Free Press.

Friedman, M. (1970), 'Social responsibility of business is to increase its profits', *New York Times*, Magazine, 13 September, 122–6.

Fulghieri, P. and Suominen, M. (2005), *Does Bad Corporate Governance Lead to too Little Competition? Corporate Governance, Capital Structure and Industry Concentration*, ECGI Working Paper Series in Finance 74, Brussels: ECGI.

Gompers, P.A., Ishii, J.L. and Metrick, A. (2001), *Corporate Governance and Equity Prices*, National Bureau of Economic Research Working Paper 8449, Cambridge MA: NBER.

Jensen, M. (2005), 'Agency costs of overvalued equity', *Financial Management*, Spring, 5–19.

Jensen, M. and Meckling, W. (1976), 'Theory of the firm: managerial behavior, agency costs, and ownership structure', *Journal of Financial Economics*, 3, 305–60.

Jensen, M.J (1989), 'Organization theory and methodology', *The Accounting Review*, LVIII (2), April, 334–5.

Jolls, C., Sunstein, C.R. and Thaler, R.H. (2000), 'Overview and prospects', in C.R. Sunstein (ed.), *Behavioral Law and Economics*, Cambridge: Cambridge University Press, 13–58.

Hausman, D.H. and McPherson, M.S. (1993), 'Taking ethics seriously: economics and contemporary moral philosophy', *Journal of Economic Literature*, 31, 671–731.

Heracleous, L. (2001), 'What is the impact of corporate governance on organizational performance?', *Corporate Governance: An International Review*, 9 (3), 165–73.

Hermalin, B., and Weisbach, M. (1991), 'The effects of board composition and direct incentives on firm performance', *Financial Management*, 20, 101–11.

Hirshleifer, J. (1977), 'Economics from a biological viewpoint', *The Journal of Law and Economics*, 20, 1–52.

Lambert, R.A. (2001), 'Contracting theory and accounting', *Journal of Accounting and Economics*, 32, 1–87.

Loderer, C. and Martin, K. (1997), 'Executive stock ownership and performance – tracking faint traces', *Journal of Financial Economics*, 45, 223–55.

Ma, Y. and Sun, H.L. (1998), 'Where should the line be drawn on insider trading ethics?', *Journal of Business Ethics*, 17(1), 67–75.

McHugh, F.P. (1999), *Ethics in Business Now*, London: Macmillan Education.

McKean, R.N. (1975), 'Economics of trust, altruism, and corporate responsibility', in E.S. Phelps (ed.), *Altruism, Altruism, Morality, and Economic Theory*, New York: Russel Sage Foundations, pp29–44.

Mandel, M.J. (2001), 'Why markets misbehave', *Business Week*, New York, 22 October.

Manne, H.G. (1966), *Insider Trading and the Stock Market*, New York: Free Press.

Martin, D.W. and Peterson, J.H. (1991), 'Insider trading revisited', *Journal of Business Ethics*, 10, 57–61.

Millstein, I.M. and MacAvoy, P.W. (1998), 'The active board of directors and performance of the large publicly traded corporation', *Columbia Law Review*, 8 (5), 1283–1322.

Noreen, E. (1988), 'The economics of ethics: a new perspective on agency theory', *Accounting Organizations and Society*, 13 (4), 359–69.

Patterson, J. (2002),'The Patterson Report: corporate governance and corporate performance research', downloadable at: <http://www.thecorporatelibrary.com/study/patterson.asp>.

Snoeyenbos, M. and Smith, K. (2000), 'Ma and Sun on insider trading ethics', *Journal of Business Ethics*, 28, 361–3.

Stajkovic, A.D. and Luthans, F. (1997), 'Business ethics across cultures: a social cognitive model', *Journal of World Business*, 32 (1), 17–34.

Van den Berghe, L. (2001), 'Beyond corporate governance', *European Business Forum*, Issue 5, Spring.

Van den Berghe, L.A.A. and Levrau, A. (2003), 'Measuring the quality of corporate governance: in search of a tailormade approach?, *Journal of General Management*, 28 (3), Spring, 71–86.

Vickers, J.S. and Yarrow, G.K. (1988), *Privatization*, Cambridge MA: MIT Press.

Werhane, P.H. (1989), 'The ethics of insider trading', *Journal of Business Ethics*, 8, 841–5.

Governance, Sustainable Development and Social Responsibility: Towards Future Mapping

Ananda Das Gupta

Introduction

In the age of globalisation, corporations and business enterprises are no longer confined to the traditional boundaries of the nation state. One of the key characteristics of globalisation is the spread of the market and the change in the mode of production. The centralised mode of production has given way to a highly decentralised mode of production spread across the world.

In the last 20 years, multinational corporations have played a key role in defining markets and influencing the behaviour of a large number of consumers. The rules of corporate governance have changed too. And there have been a range of reactions to this change. On the one hand globalisation and liberalisation have provided a great opportunity for corporations to be globally competitive by expanding their production base and market share. On the other hand, the same situation poses a great challenge to the sustainability and viability of such mega-businesses, particularly in the context of the emerging discontent against multinational corporations in different parts of the world. Labourers, marginalised consumers, environmental activists and social activists have protested against the unprecedented predominance of multinational corporations.

In general, corporate social responsibility (CSR) can be described as an approach by which a company:

- recognises that its activities have a wider impact on the society in which it operates; and that developments in society in turn impact on its ability to pursue its business successfully;
- actively manages the economic, social, environmental and human rights impact of its activities across the world, basing these on principles which

reflect international values, reaping benefits both for its own operations and reputation as well as for the communities in which it operates;

- seeks to achieve these benefits by working closely with other groups and organisations – local communities, civil society, other businesses and home and host governments.

This approach is derived from principles of sustainable development.

Other terms that are used alongside CSR are: corporate responsibility, business responsibility, sustainable development, business ethics, corporate citizenship.

'Governance' and 'good governance' are key words currently being used in development literature. Bad governance is regarded as one of the root causes of all evil within our societies. Major donors and international financial institutions are increasingly basing their aid and loans on the condition that reforms that ensure 'good governance' are undertaken.

So what do 'governance' and 'good governance' actually mean?

The concept of 'governance' is not new. It is as old as human civilisation. It is the process of decision-making and implementation. Governance can be used in several contexts – corporate, international, national and local.

An analysis of governance focuses on the formal and informal actors involved in decision-making, the implementation of decisions made and the formal and informal structures that have been set in place to achieve this.

Good governance

Good governance has eight major characteristics. It is participatory, consensus-oriented, accountable, transparent, responsive, effective and efficient, equitable and inclusive and it follows the rule of law. It assures that corruption is minimised, the views of minorities are taken into account and that the voices of the most vulnerable in society are heard in decision-making. It is also responsive to the present and future needs of society.

Participation by both men and women is a key cornerstone of good governance. Participation can be either direct or through legitimate intermediate institutions or representatives. It is important to point out that representative democracy does not necessarily mean that the concerns of the most vulnerable in society would be taken into consideration in decision-making. Participation needs to be informed and organised. This means freedom of association and expression on the one hand and an organised civil society on the other hand.

Transparency

Transparency means that decisions taken and their enforcement are done in a manner that follows rules and regulations. It also means that information is freely available and directly accessible to those who will be affected by such decisions and their enforcement and that it is provided in easily understandable forms and media.

Responsiveness

Good governance requires that institutions and processes try to serve all stakeholders within a reasonable timeframe.

Consensus orientation

There are large numbers of actors and as many viewpoints in a given society. Good governance requires mediation of the different interests in society to reach a broad consensus in society on what is in the best interest of the whole community and how this can be achieved. It also requires a broad and long-term perspective on what is needed for sustainable human development and how to achieve the goals of such development. This can only result from an understanding of the historical, cultural and social contexts of a given society or community.

Equity and inclusiveness

A society's well-being depends on ensuring that all its members feel that they have a stake in it and do not feel excluded from the mainstream. This requires all groups, but particularly the most vulnerable, to have opportunities to improve or maintain their well-being.

Effectiveness and efficiency

Good governance means that processes and institutions produce results that meet the needs of society while making the best use of resources at their disposal. The concept of efficiency in the context of good governance also covers the sustainable use of natural resources and the protection of the environment.

Accountability

Accountability is a key requirement of good governance. Not only governmental institutions but also the private sector and civil society organisations must be accountable to the public and to their institutional stakeholders. Who is accountable to whom varies depending on whether decisions or actions taken are internal or external to an organisation or institution. In general an organisation or an institution is accountable to those who will be affected by its decisions or actions. Accountability cannot be enforced without transparency and the rule of law.

In the last twenty years, multinational corporations have played a key role in defining markets and influencing the behaviour of a large number of consumers. The rules of corporate governance have changed too. And there has been a range of reactions to this change. On the one hand globalisation and liberalisation have provided a great opportunity for corporations to be globally competitive by expanding their production base and market share. On the other hand, the same situation poses a great challenge to the sustainability and viability of such mega-businesses, particularly in the context of the emerging discontent against multinational corporations in different parts of the world. Labourers, marginalised consumers, environmental activists and social activists have protested against the unprecedented predominance of multinational corporations.

The ongoing revolution in communication technology and the effectiveness of knowledge-based economies has created a new model of business and corporate governance. A growing awareness about the need for ecological sustainability and the new economy framework, with an unprecedented stress on communication and image merchandising, have paved the way for a new generation of business leaders concerned about the responses of the community and the sustainability of the environment. It is in this context that we need to understand the new trends in corporate social responsibility.

The second is an eco-social perspective. The proponents of this perspective are the new generation of corporations and the new economy entrepreneurs who created a tremendous amount of wealth in a relatively short span of time. They recognise the fact that social and environmental stability and sustainability are two important prerequisites for the sustainability of the market in the long run. They also recognise the fact that increasing poverty can lead to social and political instability. Such socio-political instability can, in turn, be detrimental to business, which operates from a variety of socio-political and cultural backgrounds.

The United Nations Conference on the Human Environment, held at Stockholm in 1972, was the first major international discussion of environmental issues. The meeting marked a polarisation between the priorities of economic growth and environmental protection. This polarisation has dominated the debate between rich and poor countries and between interest groups within countries for many years and – given the results of the Kyoto Climate Conference in December 1997 – is still not fully resolved.

There are legitimate reasons for different perceptions of sustainable development and hence political priorities. Although the most significant ecological issues are of truly global importance, industrial and developing countries still have different problems. For the majority of the people affected by environmental problems in developing countries, lack of sanitation and sewage facilities, polluted drinking water, urban air pollution, shrinking water resources, and eroding topsoil are the most pressing problems. In industrial countries, where such problems have mainly been solved, the public focuses instead on issues such as depletion of the ozone layer as well as the accumulating carbon dioxide in the atmosphere and its potential impact on climatic change (WCED 1987: 8).

Sustainable development seems to be something like motherhood and apple pie – everyone finds it a good thing, there is almost universal appreciation. At first sight, this is highly positive, as this could signal the entering of a holistic and responsible thinking into the world of politics and society. But as often happens with other catch phrases that suddenly come into vogue, like 'empowerment' and 'participation', it might not be more than a rhetoric which fails to translate into practice, this all the more so because sustainable development can be given several different interpretations.

The earliest concept emphasised the need for economic development to be compatible with constraints set by the natural environment, one which satisfies the needs of the present generations without putting in jeopardy the satisfaction of needs of the future (Ward and Dubos 1972). More recently, it has also been stressed that economic development should be compatible with political and social institutions. So a holistic concept of sustainable development has emerged in which economic, ecological, social and political factors need to be simultaneously considered. Participation by individuals, particularly at the community level, is seen as an important means for achieving sustainable development and formulating development goals (ibid.).

Those who want to make the point that there has been significant progress over the past 30 years will be able to prove it. They will point to, among other things, the following facts (UNDP 1997).

The social dimension

Average life expectancy (at birth) worldwide has increased by more than a third; today, at least 120 countries with a total population of more than 5 billion have a life expectancy at birth of more than 60 years; the global average is 66 years, compared to only 48 years in 1955. Life expectancy is projected to reach 73 years in 2025 (WHO 1998).

Infant mortality rate fell in the developing countries by more than half (from 149 per thousand live births to 64).

The share of the population in developing countries suffering from chronic undernutrition dropped from about 40 to about 20 per cent.

The population with access to safe water almost doubled, to nearly 70 per cent.

Significant progress has been made in the control of major infectious diseases, such as poliomyelitis, leprosy, guinea-worm, Chagas disease and river blindness.

Net enrolment at the primary school level increased by nearly two-thirds, and adult illiteracy has been reduced by nearly half.

Nearly 60 per cent of the world's salt is now iodised, and millions of children every year are spared mental retardation as a result. Communities are working together to identify their problems, decide on their options and take action, with women emerging to play leadership roles that spark numerous other changes in people's lives (UNICEF 1998).

The economic dimension

In the past 50 years poverty has fallen more than in the previous 500. Real per capita income in the developing world has increased over the past three decades by an average of 3.5 per cent a year. For the first time, long-cherished hopes of eradicating poverty seem attainable, provided that concerted political will is brought to task.

Since 1980 there has been a dramatic surge in economic growth in some 15 countries, bringing rapidly rising incomes to many of their 1.5 billion people, more than a quarter of the world's population.

Determined efforts to implement economic policy reforms have led to substantial improvements in the economic performance of even the least developed nations; as a group, African developing countries experienced improvement in their countries in 1996, with higher output, higher export earnings and lower inflation (UNEP 1997: 2).

The environmental dimension

Legal frameworks, economic instruments, environmentally sound technologies, and cleaner production processes have been developed and applied, particularly in industrialised countries.

The levels of water and air pollution in most industrial countries have declined over the past two decades, and a number of other local environmental indicators have improved as well (UNEP 1997: 2).

Due to the availability of new and better technologies, the rate of environmental degradation in developing countries (atmospheric sulphur dioxide, for example, and soot and smoke) has been slower than that experienced by industrial countries when they were at a similar stage of economic development.

The role of the state has been redefined from a dominating (would-be) engine of development and creator of wealth to a catalytic, enabling facilitator, encouraging and complementing the activities of private businesses and individuals (World Bank 1997).

Demilitarisation continues: after peaking in 1984 at US$1,140 billion, global military expenditures dropped by 39 per cent to US$701 billion in 1996 – the number of armed conflicts came down from 50 (1992) to 24 (1997) (World Bank 1997).

Institutional development is no longer conceived of as a process of strengthening only public institutions (which reinforced the dominance of the state and weakened public accountability) but also the private sector and non-governmental organisations.

Strengthening the role of women in sustainable development efforts is much more widely accepted and more systematically considered in practical work.

A couple of years ago, the United Nations Conference on Environment and Development which was attended by more than 100 heads of state: thousands of political, technological, scientific and private sector delegates also discussed themes touching on the complex, reciprocal relationships between the environment and the economy. Key areas of concern again included massive deforestation, the encroachment of desert zones, acid rain, and the damaged ozone layer of the atmosphere. Also discussed were the endemic poverty of the Third World and the excessive consumption of advanced nations.

Sustainable development is thus generally considered to have economic, environmental and social aspects, with sets of indicators reflecting the evolution within each one as society develops. Less apparent is the ethical component, because sustainable development means linking its practical or material elements to human values. The act of looking at the needs of all the planet's people and considering the needs of future generations is rooted in ethics. The concept that whatever we do must be done for future generations as well as our own is an application of the principle of justice.

The issues

One way of understanding where society is going and the importance of sustainable development is to consider alternative scenarios. The United Nations Environment Program, in collaboration with various research institutes, has produced clusters of such scenarios. One of them is that of 'business as usual'. This scenario assumes that we continue operating as we are and projects what the results of doing so would be 50 years later. It shows the developed world proceeding reasonably well, with the middle class broadening, incomes rising, and businesses generally profiting. Nor does the shorter-term perspective look bad. However, after 50 years, this scenario shows the world reaching significant resource limits as fossil fuels diminish relative to demand and natural resources become depleted. At that point, society reaches fundamental limits. Thereafter the outlook becomes increasingly grim as the economy struggles to deal with the effects of depleted resources all over the planet.

A second scenario, sometimes called 'the fortress scenario', looked somewhat extreme – at least until the terrorist attacks in the US on 11 September 2001. This scenario portrays wealthier countries giving up on the problems of Africa, much of Latin America and Asia. Rather than dealing with them, they withdraw behind their frontiers, keeping everybody else out and trying to achieve internal sustainability. Such an approach may appeal to those who see immigration as the source of their problems and who therefore seek to protect their own countries from the rest of the world. These scenarios suggest a third: a transition to a more sustainable kind of society, conceived on a global scale.

Any effort to improve human relationships, human structures or human institutions must begin by addressing basic values. In a sense, the only central planner for human society is God, who throughout history has been programming humanity by means of a series of religions in how to develop our social interactions. God's work has been to get the rules right at the outset, and He did a good job with physical and biological laws. But we have yet to succeed at the human level: the laws are perfect, but our implementation of them is faulty. We have not learned to 'program them' into ourselves effectively enough to make society work as God intended. That is the really great challenge we face.[1]

Looking from this perspective at our present economic and business systems, our present rules and values are seriously dysfunctional. They are driving us in extremely unsustainable directions, environmentally and socially. They also are unethical. Our underlying values are rooted in 19th-century Darwinian views of species evolving through survival of the fittest. Carried to a logical conclusion, the implications of such values are unacceptable in human terms. In purely economic terms, however, the unemployed and the impaired ought not to be helped because they burden society without contributing to production. Consider the recent example of a report submitted by a tobacco company to the Czech government that said tobacco use should be encouraged because earlier deaths would save

---

1   World Bank (1992), *Governance and Development*, World Bank: Washington DC, p 9f.

considerable sums in pensions and health-care spending. When this report became public, the company apologised and withdrew it, but the episode demonstrates the ethical problems underlying purely economic thought. Another example is the case of the leaked memo drafted by a World Bank official that proposed moving polluting industries from rich, developed countries to poor, developing countries where, it suggested, human life was worth less and so pollution would be less costly to the economy. The fact that the memo's author may have been motivated by a sense of satire does little to lessen the purely economic relevance of such a view.[2]

In short, economic thought cannot ignore the ethical, moral and spiritual dimensions of the world in which it operates. And yet, our society is structured and our institutions are built to function on just such a shortsighted basis. Business corporations are not held accountable for moral values, only for profitability. Their managers are judged only by that very narrow criterion. It is little wonder that they sometimes do extremely damaging things for society as a whole.

The current canvas

Our present society has fundamental structural and institutional problems that we must recognise and manage to resolve. We must change the basic operating principles and values of the structures of our society if we are to move in a more moral, ethical and spiritual direction. For instance, because the economic system only values what is marketed or traded, everything else is considered an externality of no importance to economic analysis. A fundamental problem with economics is that it maintains inadequate accounts. Paying attention only to what has monetary value, economic analysis misses much of what is happening in society. It is like trying to take care of an automobile only by keeping the tank filled and ignoring everything else necessary to keep it running safely. Moreover, society also follows the wrong economic guidelines. Take a measure like gross domestic product. GDP is widely equated with prosperity: higher GDP means greater prosperity. However, GDP also grows because more people are suffering from the health effects of pollution; it grows if more automobile accidents occur requiring repairs, replacements and medical treatment. So GDP is no accurate measure of prosperity and ought not to be used to measure it. The use of monetary measures is similarly inadequate. Too often people say 'more money equals prosperity'. But you cannot eat money. If food runs out, money has no value at all. Neither money nor profit can measure human happiness and well-being.

A related problem is consumerism – the pressure, through advertising and other exhortations to go out and buy, buy, buy to keep the economy going. An American expression, 'When the going gets tough, the tough go shopping', captures this

---

2   US News & World Report (1996), article on the CIA study 'Why do countries fall apart?', 12 February 1996, p 44; and the report by the Woodrow Wilson Center, *Environment and Security Debates: An Introduction* (Washington DC), Spring 1995.

misplaced emphasis. A system that pushes people to buy things they do not need, in a world of limited resources in which people are starving, is a system that has something structurally and fundamentally wrong with it.[3]

The drive for increased productivity is another issue in which the logic of individual decisions has a perverse collective impact on society. Raising productivity is an economic imperative. A company must raise its productivity and reduce its labour costs to increase its profitability. Yet this ignores the fact that employees are also consumers. If the number of people earning wages declines, there are that many fewer consumers to buy products and services. It is a case of sawing off the branch you are sitting on. To benefit the economy in a real sense, why not seek to make everybody a consumer by ensuring total employment. Instead, decision-making in the corporate system moves in the opposite direction. This is encouraged by another structural problem in Western economies: the privatisation of employment and the socialisation of unemployment. In other words, companies reduce their labour costs in the short term by transferring to the government the cost of maintaining the redundant workers. Such a short-sighted system ignores the importance of work as a contribution to society and a spiritual obligation.[4]

Then, of course, the economic system ignores the poor. Since they are not consumers, the poor are excluded or forgotten. Their presence illustrates a series of fundamental failures in present mechanisms for redistributing wealth within society. Any developed society considers extremes of wealth and poverty to be unacceptable. The poor cannot be left to die while the rich walk over their bodies, of course, so at least some effort is made to put the poor out of sight in some way. There is, however, a greater moral principle that requires some level of wealth sharing, and taxation systems are designed to do that. Yet it is possible to escape taxation. With globalisation, wealth creation is increasingly reported not in the countries with strong tax systems, but in the Cayman Islands, Vanuatu and other so-called tax havens. Such avoidance of taxation is logical within a system in which the first priority is to maximise profit. Multinationals increasingly shift their real wealth creation out of places where taxation is heavy, escaping the mechanisms that allow restoration of the social balance. One of the most fundamental crises with globalisation today is the breakdown of the mechanisms for redistributing wealth.

With respect to environmental sustainability, the economic system fails to deal effectively with most environmental problems. It works at the wrong scales in time and space. The economic system is very short-term, while most environmental problems are long-term, planetary, and occur on a very large scale. Businesses only deal with some small fragments of such problems. No mechanism puts together

---

3   Fifty examples in the new Report to the Club of Rome: E.U. von Weizsäcker, A.B. Lovins and L.H. Lovins (1995), *Faktor Vier. Doppelter Wohlstand-halbierter Naturverbrauch. Der neue Bericht an den Club of Rome* (Droemer Knaur, Munich). For criticism of this study, see G. Voss, *Das Leitbild der nachhaltigen Entwicklung – Darstellung und Kritik* (Deutscher Instituts-Verlag (Hrsg.), Beiträge zur Wirtschafts- und Sozialpolitik no. 237 Köln 4/1997), pp 21 ff.

4   Universal House of Justice (1985), *The Promise of World Peace*.

individual forms of corporate behaviour to enable us to look at the larger picture. The result is a fundamental mismatch when it comes to dealing with such large-scale problems as carbon-dioxide accumulation, the ozone hole, persistent organic pollutants, soil and water management, and the like. Too often, the economic system fails to come to grips with the essential issues because it tries to deal with them at the wrong scales in space and time.

Another area of growing concern involves intellectual property. In economic terms, we are witnessing a new 'privatisation' of 'the commons'. Businesses are exploring ways to make money by buying (or privatising) information (the commons) that it can then sell at a profit. Unlike most products, however, the more information is shared, the greater its value to society. Information on good soil management, for example, can be sold as a product only to farmers who can afford it, leaving other farmers to continue destructive agricultural practices. Obviously, there would be greater benefit by making such information available to all who can use it. This brings us to a point where two fundamental value systems collide.[5]

The questions posed by these problems are fundamentally ethical: How do we foster a new moral, ethical and spiritual foundation in business? How do we establish new ground rules for business to help it contribute to a more sustainable society? How can we create a broader legal and institutional framework in which business can work to overcome the problems of fragmentation of responsibility and of inadequate or absent moral and ethical accountability? The root of the problem lies in the way in which economic institutions are structured.

Justice in business

The principle of justice also has applications in business. These applications include the sharing of profits by corporations with all their workers and involving them in decision-making. Justice can apply also to such prosaic things as interest rates. Islam forbade usury, and in early Christianity charging interest was prohibited. That is why Jews, not so restricted by their faith, could make the money that nobody else was allowed to make.

Business also needs to pay more attention to the sustainable management of natural resources. These should be considered as capital accounts. As with managing any other capital account, net losses are to be avoided. Business activity should produce no net loss for any of its capital accounts, be they economic accounts, human accounts or resource accounts. In the same way, businesses should avoid any net transfer of costs, or capital losses, to future generations or other parts of the world. Each generation's accounts should ultimately balance. This, of course, requires new accounting systems to allow us to calculate these various accounts, and that remains a big challenge.

---

5   Prof. Dr Klaus M. Leisinger's lecture given at the 9th Annual Conference of The European Busines Ethics Network, 'Working Across Cultures, Frankfurt, 18–20 September 1996.

Economic activity also must respect the limits of Earth's life-support systems and ecological processes. Because many of those processes are planetary, respecting them will require building new global institutions for managing them at that level. This building of institutions is another major challenge before us.

Businesses need fairness operating on a global basis. They have difficulty dealing with differing regulations, corrupt systems, and so forth. It is therefore in the interest of business to strengthen global mechanisms and establish a level playing field. To achieve that, it would be reasonable for businesses to pay taxes, assuming, of course, that the taxes were applied fairly. As business becomes more enlightened, it will become a leading force to establish effective global institutions, since these institutions will be good for business. Governments hold back for fear of losing power and eroding national sovereignty. So leadership has to come from elsewhere. Businesses are, in many ways, well placed to lead the effort to build the structures all of us need to make this system operate more effectively on a global basis.

Companies increasingly rely on the creativity, entrepreneurship and initiative of all their employees to be successful. As consumer and market needs change more rapidly, and many companies become more decentralised, employees on the front lines must be empowered to make good decisions on their own. A clearly communicated system of values is key to rapid and appropriate decision-making.

The triple bottom-line approach is a proactive answer to questions raised by investors concerned with increased transparency and accountability. Companies that measure their performance according to economic, environmental, and social performance are simply practising cutting-edge risk management.

The Global Reporting Initiative and sustainability

The Global Reporting Initiative (GRI) is an independent global institution that is developing a generally accepted framework for sustainability reporting. The aim of the GRI guidelines is to enable companies and other organisations to prepare comparable 'triple bottom-line' reports. The end goal of the GRI is to make sustainability reporting as routine and credible as financial reporting in terms of comparability, rigour and verifiability.

Industry, accountants, academics, and non-governmental organisations have all been involved in drafting the guidelines. The most recent draft was released during the World Summit on Sustainable Development in Johannesburg earlier this year. Founded by the Coalition for Environmentally Responsible Economies (CERES), the GRI works in close collaboration with the UN and is headquartered in Amsterdam.

Reporting according to a standard such as the GRI will not solve all of a company's problems. Companies are rarely either as virtuous or corrupt as they are portrayed. What people want is a balance of anecdotal and hard data; a frank discussion of challenges as well as a discussion of strengths; a discussion of a company's overarching philosophy on sustainability as well as concrete goals; a discussion of how well prior goals have been achieved; and finally, quantitative performance measures that provide the opportunity to compare a company's performance over time and against other firms.

Reporting does not guarantee social acceptance, but social investors, at least, do tend to consider transparency strength. And companies that are transparent are likely to be treated more fairly by environmental and social activists, as well as the press, than those that hide behind a veil of secrecy or issue glossy green-washing reports with few hard facts.

References

UNICEF (1998), *The State of the World's Children*, UNICEF: New York.

United Nations Development Programme (UNDP) (1997), *Human Development Report 1997*, New York: Oxford University Press.

United Nations Environment Programme (UNEP) (1997), *Global Environment Outlook*, New York: Oxford University Press.

Ward, B. and Dubos, R. (1972), *Only One Earth – the Care and Maintenance of a Small Planet*, London: Deutsch.

World Bank (1997), *World Development Report 1997. The State in a Changing World*, New York: Oxford University Press.

World Commission on Environment and Development (WCED) (1987), *Our Common Future*, New York: Oxford University Press.

World Health Organization (WHO) (1998), *The World Health Report 1998. Life in the 21st Century. A Vision for All*, WHO: Geneva.

The Impact of Social Responsibility on the Environment

R.Ş. Topal and A. Öngen

Introduction

The environment could be said to be a kind of trust on behalf of anyone with children or who has a stake in future generations or who values the ability of the earth to support life. But environmental good practice is also about business efficiency. It is about the best use of valuable raw materials, and feeding the benefits of action straight through to the bottom line. It is tied up in how you source your raw materials and what the impact is upon the environment of their extraction. It is tied up in the quantity of water you use. And it is underlined by the amount of environmental risk you take. If you get it wrong, the costs can be high. The need for global action is increasingly leading governments to begin, through taxation, to price more highly the essential resources which need preserving. Maintain your dependence on these resources too long, and you can find your competitors leaving you behind. A growing body of environmental legislation also threatens to present you with fines and a damaged reputation for any environmental incidents on one of your sites. And in any case, if you have not studied your processes to identify where waste occurs, you are probably losing out on around 1 per cent of your overall turnover that could be switched straight from the trash heap to the bottom line.

- From the aspect of *customer benefit*, customers are becoming increasingly demanding. As awareness of the global scale of environmental problems grows, they are looking for companies to present them with purchasing decisions which can be taken without compromising the future.
- From the aspect of *cost reduction*, there is wasted energy, wasted water, raw materials that are paid for and then thrown away, and the risk of environmental accidents which lead to fines. All these are costing your business money.

People want to optimise their efficiency; meeting this need can be creative while producing an improvement in quality.

- From the aspect of *risk management*, whether or not your business believes it is a responsible one, it can certainly be at risk of falling foul of a growing body of environmental legislation. And being seen as a convicted polluter can have all sorts of impacts in terms of whether you come to be seen as a supplier of choice by your corporate customers, many of whom are now beginning to consider supply chain issues in their own environmental policies.

If we look at environmental issues from a general perspective, the starting point must be our use of raw materials, both non-renewable resources which by definition are not sustainable in the long term and, as importantly, renewable resources which are produced in a fashion which is not currently sustainable. Also, contributions to greenhouse gas emissions through energy use and other parts of our process, plus the potential for environmental accidents and releases of pollutants into air, water or land are other important issues. So, if we have responsibility for strategic management of the business, for safety, health or environment, for product development or for purchasing, we can make a difference in this area. Seeing how we can make a start is important (Anon. 2006a).

Therefore, we must understand that how we operate our process area, stores, distribution centres, wastes and offices affects the environment. We also must know that how we use natural resources, whether for construction, office supplies or marketing materials, has an impact as well. That is why we must strive to promote environmental stewardship throughout our business – from setting expectations with external vendors, to daily business decisions affecting purchasing, merchandising, marketing, store construction and facility management. *Social responsibility is not just a catchphrase or a feel-good initiative. It is a reflection of who we are and how we operate as a company in total.* To us, being socially responsible means striving to embed our values and ethics into everything we do – from how we run our business, to how we treat our employees, to how we impact the communities where we do business. Learning about how we are working to 'conserve energy and resources, construct environmentally sustainable buildings, reduce wastes, improving standards, monitoring conditions, working toward standards improvements, minimising impact on the environment, supporting community giving and employee volunteerism, running responsibly and ethically our business, developing and supporting employees' is very important for production of good environmental conditions (Anon. 2006b).

Sustainable development and corporate social responsibility

'Corporate social responsibility' (CSR) is an expression used to describe what some see as a company's obligation to be sensitive to the needs of all of its stakeholders in its business operations. The principle is closely linked with the imperative of ensuring that these operations are 'sustainable': in other words, it is recognised that it is necessary to take account not only of the financial/economic dimension in decision-making but also the social and environmental consequences (Anon. 2005; Topal 2005).

Sustainable agriculture integrates three main goals; environmental stewardship, farm profitability and prosperous farming communities. These goals have been defined by a variety of philosophies, policies and practices, from the vision of farmers and consumers. *Sustainable development* (SD) demands that we seek ways of living, working and being that enable all people of the world to lead healthy, fulfilling and economically secure lives without destroying the environment and without endangering the future welfare of people and the planet. The precise meaning of SD has been widely debated. Detailed description of 'life on the earth' is very difficult, because of its incredible complex structure. So biologists separate life, in units at hierarchic level, to make the concept workable. The cooperation between international relations and technological developments brought the globalisation concept. So the idea of the 'universal market' spread as a new approach in the intercommunity trade platform, fostered by results of the current combined studies in biotechnology and genetics. A great deal of discussion has arisen, despite some suspicion about the new dimensions of biodiversity. Sustainable development has become a widely used term today and it seems to have become a universal consensus. But this is true only at first sight. A closer investigation reveals that there are many contradictory definitions and that the dissent about a sustainable path to the future is hidden in these definitions. For classification of 'sustainability definitions', an axis of anthropocentricity is proposed along which the different definitions can be located. 'The social systems can only grow to the extent that such growth is backed by greater economic performance' or 'The economic system should be designed in such a way that it promotes personal initiative and subordinates personal interest to public interest'. While the scientific prerequisites for ecological sustainability can be at least roughly defined, this is the case for social, economic and cultural sustainability. But while societal discourses in the social and cultural area can lead to progress, they can have only disastrous consequences in the ecological area. It is fact that ecosystems are not negotiable and nature does not conduct consensus talks. It is essential to have social responsibility applications and to claim protection of sources (Schauer 2002; Topal and Crowther 2003; Topal 2003, 2004, 2005).

Sustainability is a very important and essential rule for the environment, together with CSR. This sustainability offers research and consultancy in the area of CSR: the relationship with corporate sustainability is considered in a schematic model in Figure 7.1 (Anon. 2006c).

Figure 7.1 Compatibility of sustainability with CSR and the management of environmental systems

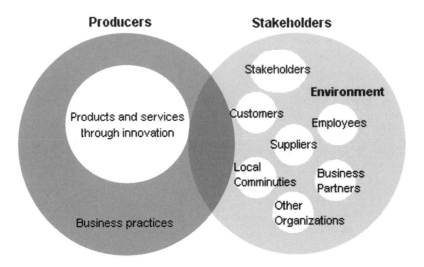

Figure 7.2 A suggested 'sharing ring structure'

There has only been a brief period when sustainable business management and CSR have moved to develop efficient solutions in environmental management. In order to manage CSR, it is worth considering the experiences made so far in environmental management and its environmental accounting instruments as an environmental performance indicator. Since the mid-1990s these projects developed popularly in systematic improvements and mostly company practices have gained considerable contribution to the knowledge available on corporate environmental management. These must be carried out a presumably unique longitudinal analysis on the long-term effects of environmental management systems in companies. The analysis clearly shows 'how and why the initial earthphoria' of many companies has notably reduced. So from the 'producer to consumer' as a 'sharing ring structure' must be established with all stakeholders, as suggested in Figure 7.2 (Anon. 2006c).

A company's stakeholders are all those who are influenced by and/or can influence a company's decisions and actions, both locally and globally. These include (but are not limited to): employees, customers, suppliers, community organisations, subsidiaries and affiliates, joint venture partners, local neighbourhoods, investors, and shareholders or the sole owner. The ethical values of a company are very important in this millennium from the social responsibility and environmental aspects. Some would argue that it is self-evidently 'good' that businesses should seek to minimise any negative social and environmental impact resulting from their economic activity. It can also be beneficial for a company's reputation to publicise (for example) any environmentally beneficial business activities. A company which develops new engine technology to reduce fuel consumption will (if it chooses) be able to promote its CSR credentials as well as increase profits. Some commentators are cynical about corporations' commitment to CSR and SD and say that the idea of an 'ethical company' is an oxymoron. If companies are to achieve 'sustainability,' the first steps must be to learn to think and discuss systemically in terms of levels of consciousness, connectedness and processes. Applied ethics specialists may have lost sight of what traditional ethics was trying to accomplish: a good life for good people over a lifetime in society with others. Ethical integration is essential for all organizations. An independent approach to applied ethics and policy will review the ethics of essential social responsibility, social purpose, organisational life and the environment ecology. CSR's common purpose could be said to be 'creating new possibilities to enhance people's lives by transforming the way the world communicates'. The essence of ideal work is bringing *people together – to connect'*. One of the popular strategic areas of focus over the next five years is the infusion of a *'Winning Environment – Winning Team'* philosophy within most of the global world (Topal 2005).

CSR also has a kind of combined systematic structure, which can be analysed in terms of social audit, as suggested in Figure 7.3 (Social Inclusion 2000). As can be seen from this structure, systematic application of CSR can be involve the control or management of many different factors (van Overwalle 2005).

113

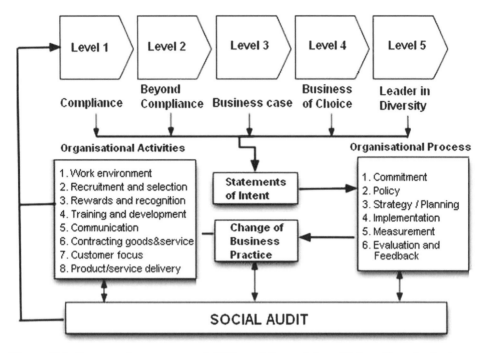

Figure 7.3 Systematic structure of CSR and its social audit functional mission

'CSR is concerned with treating the stakeholders of the firm ethically or in a responsible manner.' 'Ethical or responsible' means treating stakeholders in a manner deemed acceptable in civilised societies. 'Social' includes economic responsibility. Stakeholders exist both within a firm and outside it. The natural environment is a stakeholder. The wider aim of social responsibility is to create higher and higher standards of living, while preserving the profitability of the corporation, for people both within and outside the corporation. Therefore, CSR means the ethical behaviour of business towards its constituencies or stakeholders. Nevertheless, there are a wide variety of concepts and definitions associated with the term CSR, but no general agreement of terms. There is increasing recognition that the current 'system' for achieving good labour and environmental practices in global supply chains through private codes of conduct and monitoring is not working. With a focus on developing nations, it can present recommendations identifying ways the public sector can mobilise its resources and those of others to improve delivery on these important goals. Reputation is built around intangibles such as trust, reliability, quality, consistency, credibility, relationships and transparency, and tangibles such as investment in people, diversity and the environment. All ethics and policy principles and practices are derived from or can be explained by four concepts that lie at the root of applied ethics: *shared purpose, informed choice, responsibility, learning* and *growth*. As a guiding principle, moreover, the first among these four equals is *'shared purpose'*. The challenge to applied ethics is to integrate ethics and policy theory and practice to be consistent with them. The complexity of organisational life demands a direct tie between ethics and policy and rejection of simple formulas or sets of universal values. However, applied ethics has responded by developing increasingly sophisticated, but separate and narrow approaches: *business ethics, government ethics, codes of professional ethics* and *environmental ethics* (Topal 2005).

An offered worldwide environmental policy

All of us are responsible to the communities in which we live and work and to the world community as well as to each other. We must maintain in good order the property we are privileged to use, protecting the environment and natural resources. Most of the important strategy is committed to environmental leadership, instilling the highest environmental values in all employees, utilising the best environmental practices in all we do, and focusing on sustainable growth so that we can produce a statement of 'Environmental Policy'. The main necessities are:

- operating beyond mere compliance with all applicable laws and regulations by uniformly global environmental policies and standards
- honouring environmental management system standards and other voluntary principles to which we subscribe
- maintaining a structure at the corporate and operating company level that assures proper oversight, using environmental accountability as a measure for management performance
- integrating environmental goals into our business strategies and plans while publicly reporting on our progress
- striving for zero waste and 100 per cent resource efficiency, and enhancement of the environment
- utilising innovative technologies and leveraging best practices globally for the greatest environmental gain and continuous improvement
- fostering an environmental ethic among our management, employees, stockholders, customers, suppliers and communities worldwide
- building relationships with regulatory agencies, interest groups, thought leaders and communities to engender collaboration, cooperation and mutual understanding
- enhancing CSR by supporting environmental health and education, conservation and community-based programmes worldwide (Anon. 2006d).

On the other hand, a lot of improvements in environmental performance and the associated management systems have been achieved within companies which are still beneficial. However, the question remains how 'Environmental Management Systems' can be growing up in future, especially at the political level. Also, appropriate accounting instruments for its control are essential for the continuous improvement of corporate environmental performance. The research on the corporate input–output balance and the life cycle assessment were first developed as environmental management accounting instruments. In the 1990s further instruments were developed, including environmental performance indicators (EPI), different approaches to environmental cost accounting and various methods for calculating ecological impact; for example, ecological footprints, impact equivalents – best known for measuring CO_2 emissions (Loew et al. 2002; Anon. 2006c).

Globalisation, if appropriately managed, has the potential to promote SD for all. However, there are increasing concerns that globalisation has led to the marginalisation of a number of developing countries and increased instability in the international economic financial system. Promoting sustainable development in a globalising world requires (related) actions to Agenda 21. Agenda 21 recognised that the implementation of the programmes it called for required a substantially increased effort, both by countries themselves and by the international community, including substantial new and additional financial resources. It also demanded transfer of environmentally sound technologies on concessional and preferential terms, as mutually agreed, and education, capacity-building and development of scientific capabilities. Governance has the most important functions on planning, realising basic strategies and decision-making. So government representatives and bureaucrats have important responsibilities for establishing a sustainable and harmonious planet for the next generations of humankind. They must ensure all people, particularly women, young people, and indigenous peoples, the rights to self-determination, land territories and resources. All countries dedicate their work to the youth of the world, who inspire this process and who will inherit the responsibility of being stewards of this planet (Topal 2005).

Affinity of biodiversity and social responsibility concepts

The approach of evaluating the quality of species communities in agro-ecosystems mainly on the basis of *biodiversity* (in the sense of species richness) must be analysed critically. As Büchs et al. (2003) suggested, evaluation problems consist not of the limitations of the assessment of conventionally managed fields, but in the practical translation into action and application of the procedures within current farming practices, as well as in the control of the success of the measurements. Therefore, biodiversity consists of two components, the diversity component and the expression of dominance structure – with the frequency and percentage of each element within the whole subset considered. So, the same level of biodiversity can be achieved by a considerable richness of different elements or by less richness but a balanced frequency of each element. An exact interpretation is possible using the term 'evenness' (the probability of selecting a certain element taken from a whole subset). However, in common use and mainly by 'secondary users' the 'frequency' component and its interpretation 'evenness' is mostly neglected. So the term 'biodiversity' is actually very often used to express, in an almost diffuse sense, the number of different elements (mostly species) within a subset underlaid by a 'the-more-the-better' interpretation. More recent interpretations of the term biodiversity are not only restricted to 'species richness', but are also related to varieties, races, life forms and genotypes as well as landscape units, habitat types, structural elements (such as shrubs, stone walls, hedgerows, ponds), crop or land use diversity, etc. Finally, the term (bio)diversity is used in areas with only a very indirect relation to the biological component of biodiversity. Hence, the generic term biodiversity forms a hierarchic system relevant for different scale levels sum of elements of a genome, a population, a species community, an ecosystem or a landscape (population, species, biocoenosis, habitat and landscape), compositions and functions. The quality and/or quantity of a component of a higher (scale or hierarchic) level has a direct effect on the quality and/or quantity of components in lower (scale or hierarchic) levels. For example, a change of the landscape pattern (structural component) as a result of a change in land use (functional component) affects the species composition (compositional component) and finally, the processes running in the ecosystems (functional component) (Waldhardt and Otte 2000). However, the interrelations between hierarchic scale levels can also be the other way round, as so-called 'ecosystem engineers' (Jones and Lawton 1995) may influence structures and processes in ecosystems. According to these explanations (Büchs, 2003):

- biodiversity is based upon many interlinked mechanisms which depend on the heterogeneity or 'richness' of their elements in the same way as in the development of functional processes
- the knowledge of rules within and between the components and the hierarchic scale levels is a basic requirement for a sound interpretation of the data recorded, and for the development of advanced concepts on biodiversity management.

The term 'biodiversity', however, became more public only after the signing of the 'Convention for Biodiversity' (UNEP Conference in Nairobi, Kenya, May 1992; 'Earth Summit' in Rio de Janeiro, Brazil, June 1992) by 168 countries. Today biodiversity is a term familiar to many: hardly any research programme with an ecological intention is able to manage without using the term. Similar to the term 'ecology' which was coined more than 30 years ago, the term 'biodiversity' has also been picked up by several groups of society in central Europe with completely different goals. It covers all living things as complementary parts of a big system. This system includes atmosphere, oceans, water resources, rocks and soil, which are thought of as non-living by humanity. According to the II/15 decision of corresponding parties in the FAO's Biodiversity Consensus Committee, 'A possible agricultural biodiversity can affect the natural structure in the future'. These elements which constitute biological diversity for food and agriculture include crop genetic resources, their wild relatives and harvested wild food plants, animal genetic resources, forests, fish and aquatic life, micro-organisms, soil biota, pollinators and predators (FAO 2001a; FAO 2001b; Topal 2003; Topal 2004).

Particularly in applied research, functional aspects of biodiversity and consequently also structural components of agricultural ecosystems are increasingly important. Although there is no doubt about the ethical justifications of maintaining and recovering biodiversity, relatively little is known about whether a certain biodiversity level (higher or lower) or different dominance structures of species communities do influence the functionality of food webs, or whether the quality (and quantity) of the biological control (by natural enemies) of pest organisms in agro-ecosystems is affected. These natural enemies, accompanied by a low abundance level of each species, highlighted three ways in which biodiversity can be viewed (Büchs 2003):

- as a concept (expressed as the 'variety of life'), which is completely abstract and extremely difficult to understand
- as a measurable entity
- as a social/political construct.

Biological diversity is concentrated in areas inhabited by socio-economically marginal and traditional societies, and so it is a key indicator of sustainability and buffering capacity: highly diverse ecosystems are, for instance, more efficient in capturing energy, water, nutrients and sediments than homogenous systems. Thus, the high technical standard of Western societies seems to be a contradiction in the achievement of considerable biodiversity levels. Biodiversity indicators (a) should be holistic, but closely related to the assessment goals; (b) are important to the structure and function of the agro-ecosystem; (c) constitute a response to a range of environmental stresses; (d) can be easily measured, quantified and interpreted; and (e) show an integrative potential in the long term. Also, 'biodiversity indicators have to be common and widespread. They should occur under the different environmental conditions that are of relevance according to the qualities of biodiversity under consideration'. One study where ecosystem features supersede anthropocentric goals has been developed by using soil staphylinid beetle assemblages as an indicator system (Büchs 2003) and thus identifying:

- productive systems (such as arable crops), considering the abundance of beneficial species (predators) only
- self-sustaining ecosystems (such as revegetated mine waste), considering only a selected set of species associated with ecosystems not receiving external nutrient inputs and associated with litter decomposition
- biogeographically characteristic ecosystems (such as calcareous fens), considering species which are of local occurrence and stenotopic (that is, able to withstand only a limited range of variations in environmental conditions).

Biodiversity and its role/function in agro-ecosystems

Increasingly, research suggests that the level of internal regulation of function in agro-ecosystems is largely dependent on the level of plant and animal biodiversity present. In agro-ecosystems, biodiversity performs a variety of ecological services beyond the production of food, including recycling of nutrients, regulation of microclimate and local hydrological processes, suppression of undesirable organisms and detoxification of noxious chemicals. The role of biodiversity in securing crop protection and soil fertility is explored. It is argued that because biodiversity mediates renewal processes and ecological services are largely biological, their persistence depends upon the maintenance of biological integrity and diversity in agro-ecosystems. Various options of agro-ecosystem management and design enhance functional biodiversity in crop fields. In agricultural systems, biodiversity performs ecosystem services beyond production of food, fibre, fuel and income. The net result of biodiversity simplification for agricultural purposes is an artificial ecosystem that requires constant human intervention, whereas in natural ecosystems the internal regulation of function is a product of plant biodiversity through flows of energy and nutrients. This form of control is progressively lost under agricultural intensification. Thus commercial seed-bed preparation and mechanised planting replace natural methods of seed dispersal; chemical pesticides replace natural controls on populations of weeds, insects, and pathogens; and genetic manipulation replaces natural processes of plant evolution and selection. Even decomposition is altered because plant growth is harvested and soil fertility maintained, not through nutrient recycling, but with fertilisers. Thus modern agricultural systems have become productive but only by being highly dependent on external inputs. A growing number of scientists and farmers and many members of the general public fear for the long-term sustainability of such highly input-dependent and ecologically simplified food production systems. Questions are being raised about the growing dependence of modern farming on non-renewable resources, the loss of biodiversity, the loss of land through soil erosion and the heavy reliance on chemical fertilisers and pesticides (Altieri 1999; Saxena et al. 1999).

Farm chemicals are questioned on grounds of cost but their widespread use also has implications for human and animal health, food quality and safety and environmental quality. The commercial agricultural sectors of developing countries suffer from similar problems but the greater challenge for them is to determine new ways to increase small farm productivity that not only benefit the rural poor under marginal agricultural conditions, but also conserve and regenerate the resource base. The development of agro-ecological technologies and systems which emphasise the conservation and regeneration of biodiversity, soil, water and other resources is urgently needed to meet the growing array of socio-economic and environmental challenges. Enhancing functional biodiversity in agro-ecosystems is a key ecological strategy to bring sustainability to production. The roles of biodiversity (predators, parasitoids, antagonists and soil microflora and microfauna) in securing crop protection and soil fertility is explored. Modern agriculture implies the simplification of the structure of the environment over vast areas, replacing nature's diversity with a small number of cultivated plants and domesticated animals. Genetically, modern agriculture is shockingly dependent on a handful of varieties for its major crops. Researchers have repeatedly warned about the extreme vulnerability associated with this genetic uniformity. In contrast, biodiversity is not foreign to traditional farmers in the Third World. In fact, a salient feature of traditional farming systems is their degree of plant diversity in the form of polycultures and/or agroforestry patterns. In fact, the species richness of all biotic components of traditional agro-ecosystems is comparable with that of many natural ecosystems. These systems offer a means of promoting diversity of diet and income, stability of production, minimisation of risk, reduced insect and disease incidence, efficient use of labour, intensification of production with limited resources, and maximisation of returns under low levels of technology. Traditional cropping systems are also genetically diverse, containing numerous varieties of domesticated crop species as well as their wild relatives. Maintaining genetic diversity appears to be of even greater importance as land becomes more marginal and hence farming more risky. The type and abundance of biodiversity in agriculture will differ across agro-ecosystems which differ in age, diversity, structure and management. In fact, there is great variability in basic ecological and agronomic patterns among the various dominant agro-ecosystems. In general, the degree of biodiversity in agro-ecosystems depends on four main characteristics of the agro-ecosystem (Altieri 1999):

1. The diversity of vegetation within and around the agro-ecosystem.
2. The permanence of the various crops within the agro-ecosystem.
3. The intensity of management.
4. The extent of the isolation of the agro-ecosystem from natural vegetation.

The biodiversity components of agro-ecosystems can be classified in relation to the role they play in the functioning of cropping systems. According to this, agricultural biodiversity can be grouped as follows:

• productive biota: crops, trees and animals chosen by farmers which play a determining role in the diversity and complexity of the agroecosystem
• resource biota: organisms that contribute to productivity through pollination, biological control, decomposition, etc.
• destructive biota: weeds, insect pests, microbial pathogens, etc. which farmers aim at reducing through cultural management.

Two distinct components of biodiversity can be recognised in agro-ecosystems. The first component, planned biodiversity, is the biodiversity associated with the crops and livestock purposely included in the agro-ecosystem by the farmer, and which will vary depending on the management inputs and crop spatial/temporal arrangements. The second component, associated biodiversity, includes all soil flora and fauna, herbivores, carnivores, decomposers, etc., that colonise the agro-ecosystem from surrounding environments and that will thrive in the agro-ecosystem depending on its management and structure. The search for self-sustaining, low-input, diversified and energy-efficient agricultural systems is now a major concern of many researchers, farmers and policy-makers worldwide. As given previously in Altieri's results (1994), a key strategy in sustainable agriculture is to restore the functional biodiversity of the agricultural landscape. Biodiversity performs as a key for ecological services and, if correctly assembled in time and space, can lead to agro-ecosystems capable of sponsoring their own soil fertility, crop protection and productivity. Diversity can be enhanced in time through crop rotations and sequences and in space in the form of cover crops, intercropping, agroforestry, crop/livestock mixtures, etc. Correct biodiversification results in pest regulation through restoration of the natural control of insect pests, diseases and nematodes and also produces optimal nutrient recycling and soil conservation by activating soil biota, all factors leading to sustainable yields, energy conservation, and less dependence on external inputs. Diversification can also take place outside the farm, for example in cropfield boundaries with windbreaks, shelterbelts and living fences, which can improve habitat for wildlife and beneficial insects, provide sources of wood, organic matter, resources for pollinating bees, and, in addition, modify wind speed and the microclimate. Such structures can also serve as biological corridors for the circulation of biodiversity across large-scale agricultural landscapes. Agro-ecological design is improved economic and ecological sustainability of the agro-ecosystem, with proposed management systems specifically in tune with the locally available biodiversity and with the existing environmental and socioeconomic conditions (Altieri 1999). Instead of this, some important results show that ecological farming significantly increases biological and landscape diversity and decreases the risk of nutrient leaching and soil erosion. Marginal areas, where low-intensity agriculture creates less pollution load and supports biodiversity, have the most potential for conversion to ecological agriculture. However, owing to the greater impacts of ecological agriculture on biodiversity in intensively managed agricultural areas, ecological farming should be developed within the core areas of intensive agricultural production. Therefore, instead of developing ecological farms on marginal areas, agricultural policy should pay more attention to supporting ecological farming in the heart of intensive production areas (Mander et al. 1999).

Hole et al. (2005) determined four key issues for attention, which we now examine.

1. It remains unclear whether a 'holistic' whole-farm approach (that is, organic) provides greater benefits to biodiversity than carefully targeted prescriptions applied to relatively small areas of cropped and/or non-cropped habitats within conventional agriculture (that is, agri-environment schemes).
2. Many comparative studies encounter methodological problems, limiting their ability to draw quantitative conclusions.
3. Our knowledge of the impacts of organic farming in pastoral and upland agriculture is limited.

4. There remains a pressing need for longitudinal, system-level studies in order to address these issues and to fill in the gaps in our knowledge of the impacts of organic farming, before a full appraisal of its potential role in biodiversity conservation in agro-ecosystems can be made.

Because of these, a new dimension of biodiversity has prompted a discussion about 'hope/satisfaction/suspect' for humans from the current transgenic technology developments. Agricultural biodiversity is a topic which includes all of the corresponding components of agriculture and ecosystem functions. If the agricultural ecosystem functions are thought of together in the case of sustainability, animals, plants and micro-organisms have a key function in a level of 'genetics-practice-ecosystem' for species and diversity. Optimisation and increasing productivity at natural resources, environment and social standards will be obtained basically by well-organised regulation and continuity of current technological developments. But despite these advantages some cases, such as the controlling and monitoring of new products, services and processes, should be guaranteed for social safety and ethics. These are the basic dimensions of production and domestication in agriculture and part of the 'planned agricultural diversity'. All of these are being discussed currently, with the aim of creating new recourses and increasing productivity and disease resistance (Topal 2004).

We need to conserve, sustain and use biological diversity, so that:

- agricultural diversity can provide enough food and safety for basic needs of human beings
- the sustainability of components and managing agricultural diversity can be established (FAO 2001a; Fresco 2000; Topal 2004).

The current dimensions of agricultural biodiversity practices are shown to have widespread applications in developed countries at a farming and marketing level, but also at a consuming level at underdeveloped and Third World countries. The unknown nature of this risk and the unusual method of transmission make it highly alarming to consumers. On the other side it is important for sustainability of the agricultural products from the side of local varieties (Topal 2003; 2004).

Biological diversity is decreasing worldwide drastically. Comprehensive studies show that presently 24 per cent of mammal and 12 per cent of bird species are threatened by extinction. With respect to plants less is known as not all plant species have been described and many of them may be destroyed without even having been discovered. The main reason for the decrease of biological diversity is the destruction of precious biotopes both in developing and in developed countries. One aspect of economic globalisation is the displacement of native plants and animals by invasive species. For example, neophytes are plant species which invade biotopes and change their natural equilibrium. This in itself is neither unusual nor negative. However, the migration of species has increased to such an extent today that the natural equilibrium rate is exceeded. Scientists have moved organisms across all regions of the planet and inevitably some species have travelled as stowaways. Many transported species have unable to adapt to their new conditions: others have succeeded. In the past the formation of international markets for agricultural products had a very negative effect on agricultural biodiversity. International competition forced farmers to cultivate just those species and varieties which returned the highest short-term income. Therefore, regionally cultivated varieties which would have been a very valuable resource for future plant breeding but which have lower yields, have ceased to be cultivated (FAO 2003; Topal 2004). These are other obligations for 'consumer consciousness' work. Precaution to prevent such emergencies have became very important and urgent in the planning procedures of developing countries. All researchers and consumers must be aware of the developments from the wide perspective (Topal 2004).

Global environmental problems

At the dawn of the third millennium, a powerful and complex web of interactions is contributing to unprecedented global trends in environmental degradation. These forces include rapid globalisation and urbanisation, pervasive poverty, unsustainable consumption patterns and population growth. Often serving to compound the effects and intensity of the environmental problems, global environmental challenges require concerted responses on the part of the international community. Global climate change, the depletion of the ozone layer, desertification, deforestation, the loss of the planet's biological diversity and the transboundary movements of hazardous wastes and chemicals are all environmental problems that touch every nation and adversely affect the lives and health of their populations. As with other environment-related challenges, children suffer most from the effects of these global trends and are disproportionately vulnerable. Moreover, all of these global environmental trends have long-term effects on people and societies and are either difficult or impossible to reverse over the period of one generation (UNEP, UNICEF and WHO 2002). The main human activities that lead to extinction of species are listed in Figure 7.4 (Chiras 1991).

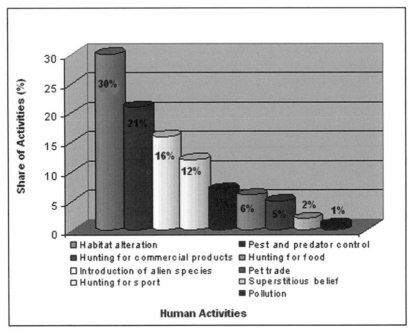

Figure 7.4 An approximate breakdown of the human activities that lead to extinction of species

Note: Often, more than one activity is involved

(*Source*: Chiras 1991)

Climatic changes

It is estimated that this will cause sea levels to rise by between 9 and 80 centimetres by 2100, due to the expansion of warming waters and the melting of polar icecaps and other glaciers, which in turn may produce deadly flooding in many low-lying areas and small island states, displacing millions from their homes. This will increase the number of environmental refugees resulting from weather-related disasters; it will augment the risk of disease migration and disease outbreaks; and will render large areas of the world 'uninsurable' due to the magnitude of property damage from disasters.

It is widely recognised that climate change, by altering local weather patterns and by disturbing life-supporting natural systems and processes, has significant implications for human health. While the range of health effects is diverse, often unpredictable in magnitude, and sometimes slow to emerge, children remain among the most vulnerable to these threats. *Higher temperatures, heavier rainfall* and *changes in climate variability* would encourage vectors of some infectious diseases (such as malaria, schistosomiasis, dengue fever, yellow fever and encephalitis) to multiply and expand into new geographical regions, intensifying the already overwhelming threats to children from such diseases. While heavy rains will become more frequent, there will also be more periods of drought and increased spreading of the deserts. Scientists predict that a lack of rain, warmer temperatures and increases in evaporation could have severe implications in terms of water availability and food security, reducing crop yields in Africa, further compromising child nutrition. There are also numerous health effects, both in terms of disease and injury, associated with extreme weather events, such as heat waves, storms and floods. Extreme weather events can exacerbate health issues such as asthma and respiratory problems due to worsening air pollution, precisely those diseases that most significantly burden children.

Ozone layer depletion

This will produce an increase of ultraviolet radiation reaching the earth's surface, thus posing several health effects:

- increase of melanoma and non-melanoma skin cancers
- cause or acceleration of development of eye cataracts
- reduction of effectiveness of the immune system
- impact on nutrition (for example, reduced plant yield)
- damage to ocean ecosystems and reduction of fish yield (by killing microbial organisms in the ocean).

Skin cancer is the most worrisome health impact of ozone depletion. Overexposure to the sun's harmful ultraviolet (UV) light may damage children's skin. Recent studies indicate that excessive sunburns experienced by children between 10 and 15 years of age increase by threefold the chance of developing malignant melanoma, the most deadly kind of skin cancer, later in life. In Europe, evaluations of UV-related skin cancers suggest that, despite the decline in concentrations of ozone-depleting substances (ODS), skin cancer incidences will not begin to fall until about 2060. Production of the most damaging ozone-depleting substances was eliminated, except for a few critical uses, by 1996 in developed countries and should be phased out by 2010 in developing countries. It is currently estimated the CFC concentration in the ozone layer is expected to recover to pre-1980 levels by the year 2050.

Desertification

Resulting in part from deforestation, desertification is a significant threat to the arid, semi-arid and dry subhumid regions of the world – which account for 40 per cent of the earth's land surface. Throughout the world, drylands still provide much of the world's food in the form of grain and livestock, yet close to 70 per cent of the world's drylands are degraded, thus diminishing the productive land per capita and decreasing food security.

The most common forms of unsustainable land use are over-cultivation, overgrazing, deforestation and poor irrigation practices. More than 250 million people are directly affected by desertification and 1 billion people in more than

100 countries are at risk. These people include many of the world's poorest and most marginalised citizens. In Africa, land degradation is threatening economic and physical survival. Recurrent droughts increase soil degradation problems which, in turn, magnify the effect of drought, both of which enhance the conditions that can cause widespread famines. The consequences of desertification include: malnutrition and famine, increases in water-borne diseases, changes of ecological ranges of infectious diseases, acute and chronic respiratory diseases and burning injuries, decreased agricultural productivity, increased water shortages, increased migration, increased forest and bush burning, loss of biodiversity, increased geographic isolation, increased poverty, altered rainfall, droughts, and major changes in human activities (Menne and Bertollini 2000; UNEP, UNICEF and WHO, 2002).

These issues are addressed in the UN Convention to Combat Desertification in Those Countries Experiencing Serious Drought and/or Desertification, Particularly in Africa (UNCCD), which entered into force in December 1996, and which to date has been ratified by 179 countries. The Kyoto Convention is implemented through action programmes, which at the national level address the underlying causes of desertification and drought and identify measures to prevent and reverse it. It identifies the consequences of desertification as primarily:

- reduction of the land's natural resilience to recover from climatic disturbances
- reduction of soil productivity
- damaged vegetation cover, such that edible plants can be replaced by non-edible ones
- increased downstream flooding, reduced water quality, sedimentation in rivers and lakes and siltation of reservoirs and navigation channels
- aggravated health problems due to wind-blown dust, including eye infections, respiratory illnesses, allergies and mental stress
- undermined food production
- loss of livelihoods compelling affected people to migrate.

Deforestation

This will assume problematic status in the near future, as referred to in the same sources. According to the declaration, more than 110 million hectares of forest, about 11 million hectares a year, disappeared during the 1990s. Most of this loss was in developing countries. About 45 per cent of the world's original forests are gone. Major causes of deforestation and forest degradation lie outside the forest sector and include the need to create agricultural land and to harvest fuel wood for energy. Approximately half of the wood harvested in the world is used as fuel wood and charcoal, mostly in developing countries. In developed countries the main uses are for industrial products. The alarming rates of deforestation and the associated loss of environmental resources, social and cultural traditions – alongside the loss of the economic and productive capacity of forestland – account for the fact that forest preservation is now a major priority on the national, regional and global policy and political agendas. The removal of trees decreases the ability of the soils to absorb and retain water; thus contributing to the depletion of the groundwater aquifers, which supply about one-third of the world's population. Aquifers are the sole source of water for many rural communities worldwide. Cleared lands stripped of their tree cover also are more susceptible to:

- Erosion, which degrades fertile lands and silts waterways, lakes, rivers and coastal waters, thereby degrading water quality for human consumption and disrupting ecosystem processes by choking fish hatcheries, coral reefs, etc.
- Decreased groundwater recharge because the barren soils do not filtrate water as effectively.
- Increased malaria transmission, bearing in mind that 90 per cent of the malaria disease burden is linked with underlying environmental factors (and claiming some 750,000 children under five annually).
- Desertification and drought.
- Loss of biodiversity.

Deforestation is also intrinsically linked to the loss of biodiversity, as original rain forests host numerous species of precious fauna and flora. The significance of protecting rain forests for children cannot be overemphasised. Food security and sustainability of livelihoods as provided by forests are critical to child development. Forests also offer climatic and water resource conservation benefits that directly impact on child health. The rich medicinal resources stored in forests are another link to children's welfare. International efforts in this realm were undertaken through the Intergovernmental Panel on Forests (IPF) and its successor, the Global Environmental Problems Intergovernmental Forum on Forests (IFF). Recently, the international community decided to establish the United Nations Forum on Forests (UNFF), as a new subsidiary body of the United Nations Economic and Social Council (ECOSOC), which is expected to contribute significantly to advancing consensus, building on the many complex issues related to forests. Global environmental problems are schematised in Figure 7.5 (UNEP, UNICEF and WHO 2002).

There is an interesting comment in the same references, that 'One hundred and fifty years ago, the Native American leader, Chief Seattle, is reported to have said "we humans are but a thread in the web of life". He also added whatever we do to the web, "We do to ourselves".' The web is unravelling at an increasing rate. Both plant and animal species have been disappearing at 50 to 100 times the natural rate, due to such factors as the large-scale clearing and burning of forests, over-harvesting of plants and animals, indiscriminate use of pesticides, draining and filling of wetlands, destructive fishing practices, air pollution and the conversion of wild lands to agricultural and urban uses. Recent studies suggest that this high rate of extinction will accelerate even faster, taking an increasing number of living plants and animals away from us forever. This species loss and ecosystem disruption is causing a complex range of circumstances with consequences to human health. In response, governments and communities worldwide are now concerned with the purification of air and water, maintenance of soil fertility, mitigation of floods and droughts, detoxification and decomposition of wastes, maintaining concentrations of vital gases and water vapour in the atmosphere, and controlling infectious agents in the environment. In addition, the loss of biodiversity obstructs the discovery of new medicines to treat various diseases. Another emerging modern health concern is biosafety and the effects of advances in and increased use of biotechnology to genetically modify foods. Biological diversity refers to the variability of biological resources, from genes to ecosystem.

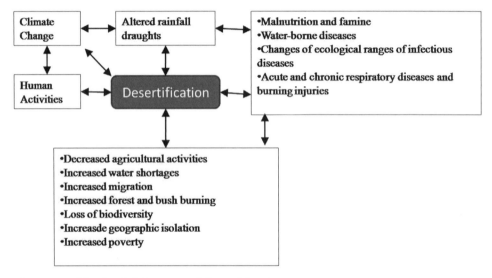

Figure 7.5 The health impact of desertification

Public concern about the health and ecological risks of foods made with biotechnology has intensified in Europe and has spread rapidly to other parts of the world, including the US. Proponents contend that biotechnology could help feed the developing world, cut costs, and reduce the need for pesticides. Detractors say the health risks of the emerging technology are unclear and the environmental hazards potentially alarming. Research is proceeding in order to respond to the many health and environmental questions raised and to guide eventual biotechnology regulations (UNEP, UNICEF and WHO 2002).

The United Nations Convention on Biological Diversity (UNCBD), which was adopted at UNCED in 1992 and has since been ratified by more than 175 countries, establishes three main goals: the conservation of biological diversity, the sustainable use of its components, and the fair and equitable sharing of the benefits from the use of genetic resources. In May 2000, the Convention's Cartagena Protocol on Biosafety was opened for signature. The Protocol seeks to protect the planet's species and ecosystems from the potential risks posed by living modified organisms, commonly referred to as genetically modified organisms, and to establish an advanced informed agreement procedure for ensuring that countries are provided with the information necessary to make informed decisions before agreeing to the import of such organisms. The Protocol has been hailed as a breakthrough from a health and environment perspective in that it is the first global treaty that formally enshrines the 'precautionary approach', as set forth in the 1992 Rio Declaration on Environment and Development, as a principle of international environmental law (UNEP, UNICEF and WHO 2002).

A global monitoring network for biodiversity

Biodiversity is defined in Article 2 of the UNCBD as the 'the variability among living organisms from all sources including, inter alia, terrestrial, marine and other aquatic ecosystems and the ecological complexes of which they are part; this includes diversity within species, between species and of ecosystems'. This is a broad concept with many dimensions. For the purposes of biodiversity monitoring, focus on two scales is suggested: regional and global, and two levels: species and ecosystems. These levels of biodiversity have particular implications at each scale for the delivery of ecosystem services. Current biodiversity monitoring programmes suffer from three main constraints: incomplete taxonomic and spatial coverage; lack of compatibility between data sets owing to different collection methodologies; and insufficient integration at different scales. A pragmatic approach proposed to tackle the global monitoring of biodiversity, with global and regional scale programmes at the species and ecosystem levels, is shown at Figure 7.6 (Pereira and Cooper 2005).

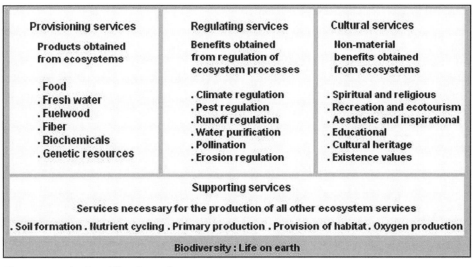

Figure 7.6 A classification of ecosystems

The ecosystem level component can provide information about land cover, the species component and aspects of ecosystem condition. The global scale programmes would emphasise central coordination, whereas the regional scale programmes would follow a bottom-up approach, with an emphasis on regional needs and capabilities. The scientific community would have a major role in designing and implementing the network, including the following: a monitoring programme for the regular global sampling of indicator taxa of terrestrial biodiversity; a global network of regional programmes monitoring indicator populations for terrestrial, freshwater and marine biodiversity; the production of regular and comparable global land-cover maps based on remote sensing; and a global network of regional programmes monitoring habitats that are best monitored, or have particular relevance, at the regional level. Benefits would be obtained from regulation of ecosystem processes for food and fresh water supplies, pest regulation, recreation and ecotourism regulation, education, biochemicals, pollination, genetic resources, erosion regulation, all the way through to cultural heritage and spiritual and aesthetic values. Ecosystem services are the benefits that people obtain from ecosystems, and can be divided into four groups: provisioning services, regulating services, cultural services and supporting services. Generally we only tend to recognise services that have a market value, such as provisioning services and some cultural services, but we benefit from other cultural services (including the existence values that people place on conserving wild biodiversity), and from regulating services, and, indirectly, from supporting services. Each type of ecosystem service depends on particular components of biodiversity. The population abundance of species at the local level is important for ensuring the delivery of regional ecosystem services, such as forest foods and pest control, and is also important for recreational services, such as bird watching (Pereira and Cooper 2005).

The need for biodiversity monitoring

The Convention on Biological Diversity aims 'to achieve by 2010 a significant reduction of the current rate of biodiversity loss at the global, regional and national level as a contribution to poverty alleviation and to the benefit of all life on Earth'. The European Union has set an even more stringent target: to halt biodiversity decline by 2010. Examination of current trends, as well as the exploration of plausible future scenarios, suggests that the CBD 2010 target is unlikely to be achieved unless an unprecedented effort is made, both at the policy and institutional levels, to improve current conservation efforts and to develop new strategies. This would include the implementation of measures targeted at biodiversity conservation inside and outside protected areas and at limiting the causes of biodiversity loss in all economic sectors, from energy production to agriculture. To determine how current conservation efforts can be improved and to guide new strategies, it is crucial that our progress towards the CBD 2010 target and beyond is monitored. How this should be done is now the subject of much debate. Most of the discussion has been directed at what indicators should be used based on existing data. A global monitoring network of biodiversity covers to gather new data for these measures and to integrate current monitoring initiatives (Pereira and Cooper 2005).

Protecting and sharing biodiversity – holders and users of traditional knowledge

In the current debate an important concept is the contribution of traditional knowledge, via its holders and users. Before examining this we need to note thee legal instruments which can serve to protect biodiversity and traditional knowledge and explore the legal tools which can be helpful in sharing their benefits. As given above in the description of biodiversity by CBD; the ecological complex includes diversity within species, between species and of ecosystems. 'Biological resources' include 'genetic resources, organisms or parts thereof, populations, or any other biotic component of ecosystems with actual or potential use or value for humanity'. 'Genetic resources' means 'genetic material of actual or potential value'. While the language of the CBD provides a broad scope for action, CBD discussion documents suggest that the parties are at present focusing on non-human biological materials (NHBMs) and their natural habitats. Those resources thus encompass pharmaceutical as well as natural product resources and crop genetic resources (van Overwalle 2005).

In addition to the semantic discussion on the notion of biodiversity, there has been an interesting debate on the economic nature and value of biodiversity. NHBMs are components of 'common pool resources' and are themselves common pool goods. The question arises as to which extent this economic qualification has/ should have any effect on our thinking on intellectual property concepts in the field of biodiversity. This question calls for further investigation.

Knowledge and importance of traditional knowledge

A key concept in the current debate is traditional knowledge. At present, one interpretation seems to be commonly accepted. The term 'traditional knowledge' is understood to comprise both aesthetic and useful elements, as well as literary, artistic or scientific creations. Consequently, categories of traditional knowledge include, inter alia, expressions of folklore in the form of music, dance, song, handicrafts, designs, stories and artwork; elements of language; agricultural knowledge; and medicinal knowledge. Traditional knowledge thus encompasses a huge amount and efforts have been made to classify the various types of traditional knowledge. According to the World Intellectual Property Organisation (WIPO), traditional knowledge holders are persons who create, originate, develop and practise traditional knowledge in a traditional setting and context. Indigenous communities, peoples and nations are traditional knowledge holders, but not all traditional knowledge holders are indigenous. The CBD talks about users of genetic resources and knowledge. 'Users' of genetic resources or recipients are defined as those individuals or entities that actually import and utilise genetic resources, whether for commercial or purely scientific purposes. By analogy 'users of traditional knowledge' might be defined as individuals or institutions making use of traditional knowledge for commercial or scientific purposes. The search for native micro-organisms or plants harbouring interesting properties has been termed differently: the search and subsequent exploitation is sometimes referred to as 'bioprospecting', or even as biopiracy by gene hunters. Thoughtful observers underline that the word bioprospection mainly refers to legitimate actions carried out in the framework of a law or an agreement, whereas the notion of biopiracy refers to illegal operations. Many countries are both 'holders' or 'providers' and 'users' of genetic resources and traditional knowledge. However, there has been a tendency in the international debate to view developing countries as primarily providers, while more industrialised developed countries have been portrayed as users. The inaccuracy of such generalisations can be seen in the argument that in many cases industrialised countries, such as Australia, are also important providers, while some developing countries, such as Brazil, have highly developed biotechnology and agroindustrial capacities (van Overwalle 2005).

Protected areas in the Convention on Biological Diversity

The Convention on Biological Diversity (CBD) with 188 Parties is the most important international legal instrument for addressing protected areas and for supporting and fostering national and multilateral efforts in a comprehensive manner. The Convention defines a protected area as 'a geographically defined area which is designated or regulated and managed to achieve specific conservation objectives'. Article 8 of the Convention calls for the establishment of a system of protected areas or areas where special measures need to be taken to conserve biological diversity. Accordingly, national protected area systems have been developed and maintained as key elements of national strategies to conserve biological diversity (Gidda and Mulongoy 2004). The government concerned has adopted measures to preserve biodiversity in the area including expanding formally protected areas. Despite these actions, the forested land area is decreasing and fragmenting, and the populations of many species have been reduced. Such erosion of diversity is also evident for agrobiodiversity (Topal 2004).

The Convention recognises protected areas as a tool for *in situ* conservation that must be seen in conjunction with other relevant provisions of the Convention. The Convention has developed guidance on various cross-cutting issues relevant to the establishment and maintenance of protected areas. The important role of protected areas in implementing the objectives of the CBD has been repeatedly emphasised in decisions of the Conference of Parties (COP). Similarly protected areas form a vital element of the various thematic programmes of work involving marine and coastal areas, inland waters, dry and sub-humid lands, and forest and mountain areas. Although at the global level the number and extent of protected areas have been increasing in the past decades, existing systems of protected areas are not representative of all the categories of biodiversity which are important for conservation and sustainable use. This is particularly true for marine areas, of which less than 1 per cent are protected, and with regard to hotspots, in line with the Plan of Implementation of the World Summit on SD. Main discussion points of the Convention include the encouragement of active collaboration on protected areas, and the review of methods and approaches for the planning and management of protected areas, including options for appropriate policies, strategies, and practices consistent with the objectives. Identified ecosystem and bioregional approaches to protected area management and sustainable use of biological diversity, with mechanisms to enhance stakeholder involvement, are the most important characteristics. the Convention identified options and priority actions required for the effective establishment and management of protected areas as well as options for management of transboundary protected areas. Approaches, tools and gaps are discussed in its working programme. The overall purpose of the proposed programme of work is to significantly reduce the loss of biological diversity at the international, national and subnational levels through the implementation of the three main objectives of the Convention, and to contribute to poverty alleviation and SD, thereby supporting the objectives of the Strategic Plan of the Convention, the Plan of Implementation of the World Summit on Sustainable Development and the Millennium Development Goals. It is envisaged that the Convention's work on protected areas should be undertaken in the context of ecosystem approach. The ecosystem approach provides a framework within which the relationship of protected areas to the wider landscape and seascape can be understood, and goods and services delivered by protected areas can be valued (Gidda and Mulongoy 2004).

Key biodiversity issues for protected areas

The CBD's seventh meeting and 12 related programmes of various international organisations provide the first opportunity since the Convention came into force to directly address the Convention's provisions on protected areas in a comprehensive manner. Building on the recent developments, CBD enables Parties, other governments and relevant organisations to effectively implement provisions on *in situ* conservation by channelling efforts and resources in support of an effective global protected area network. The ultimate result of the implementation of the programme of work is the establishment and maintenance of an effectively managed, ecologically representative global system of protected area networks, where human activities are managed to maintain the structure and functioning of the full range of ecosystems, in order to provide benefits to both present and future generations and achieve a significant reduction in the rate of biological diversity loss (Gidda and Mulongoy 2004).

Protected areas and Millenium Ecosystem Assessment (MA)

The MA synthesises information from the scientific literature, datasets and scientific models, and makes use of knowledge held by the private sector, practitioners, local communities and indigenous peoples. All of the MA findings undergo rigorous peer review. The MA is governed by a board comprised of representatives of international conventions, UN agencies, scientific organisations and leaders from the private sector, civil society and indigenous organisations. Assessment panel members are leading social and natural scientists overseeing the technical work of the assessment; they are supported by a secretariat with offices in Europe, North America, Asia, and Africa and coordinated by the United Nations Environment Programme. More than 500 authors are involved in four expert working groups preparing the global assessment and hundreds more are undertaking more than a dozen sub-global assessments (Lucas 2003).

As summarised by Lucas (2003), the first report of the Millennium Ecosystem Assessment describes the conceptual framework that is being used in the MA. It is not a formal assessment of the literature, but rather a scientifically informed presentation of the choices made by the assessment team in structuring the analysis and framing the issues. The conceptual framework elaborated in this report describes the approach and assumptions that will underlie the analysis conducted in the Millennium Ecosystem Assessment. The framework was developed through interactions among the experts involved in the MA as well as stakeholders who will use its findings. It represents one means of examining the linkages 'between ecosystems and human well-being that is both scientifically credible and relevant to decision makers'. This framework for analysis and decision-making should be of use to a wide array of individuals and institutions in government, the private sector and civil society that seek to incorporate considerations of ecosystem services in their assessments, plans and actions. The conceptual framework for the MA places human well-being as the central focus for assessment, while recognising that biodiversity and ecosystems also have intrinsic value and that people take decisions concerning ecosystems based on considerations of well-being as well as intrinsic value (see Figure 7.7, Lucas 2003). As briefly determined by Lucas, the assessment framework developed for the MA offers decision-makers a mechanism to:

- identify options that can better achieve core human development and sustainability goals
- better understand the trade-offs involved – across sectors and stakeholders – in decisions concerning the environment
- align response options with the level of governance where they can be most effective.

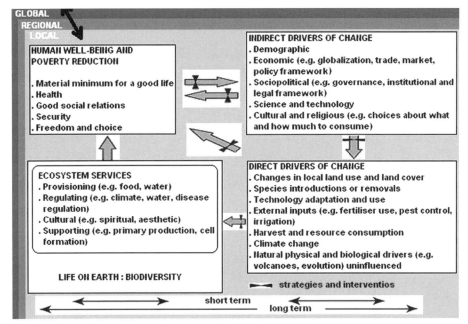

Figure 7.7 **Millennium Ecosystem Assessment conceptual framework**
Note: Black cross bars indicate negative and positive changes characters
(*Source*: Lucas 2003)

With its focus on ecosystem services and human well-being, the MA framework can be useful for decision-makers faced with choices concerning protected areas, and can help countries to assert the important contributions of their protected areas to the global agenda on SD. The MA framework provides the mechanisms needed to assess existing conservation and management strategies for protected areas, and can provide information needed for the design of new plans. The conceptual framework also serves as a useful tool to help identify new areas for protection based on information that it will provide about biodiversity, habitats and ecological processes across multiple scales (Lucas 2003).

As also discussed by Poulsen (2001), biodiversity is related to human activities and natural resources. It affects the species composition and the spatial distribution of plants and animals. Thereby, it affects the availability of natural forest resources, such as non-timber-forest products, to the people who live in, and who are entirely dependent upon, the resources found in forests. People strongly dependent upon local forest resources will be more affected by a changing spatial and temporal distribution in forest resources than people who are less dependent on those resources. Indigenous people living in the interior parts of the forest away from developed infrastructure, and hence often having few or no alternative income sources/options, are therefore more sensitive to (that is, more likely to be affected by) changes in the availability of local natural resources (such as non-timber-forest resources).

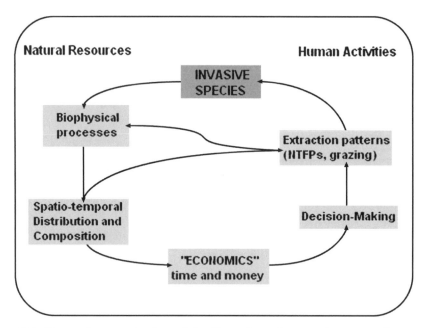

Figure 7.8 General conceptual model of how invasive species may affect
conservation of biodiversity and local people's livelihoods

Invasive species can affect the availability of local forest resources through both direct and indirect mechanisms. Poulsen (2001) has been modelled these relationships as given at Figure 7.8.

Protected areas, poverty and sustainable development

Many areas of great natural wealth that are protected as national parks, game reserves, strict nature reserves, or other types of protected areas, are found in the most remote parts of a country, farthest removed from the mainstream developments that may be bringing prosperity to other parts of the country. Not surprisingly, these remote, but nature-rich, areas also support some of the least economically prosperous segments of the country's human population, making the linkage between nature conservation and poverty alleviation especially challenging. The challenge has gone unaddressed for far too long and, indeed, the rural populations have sometimes been encouraged, or even forced, to abandon the areas designated to achieve conservation objectives. More recently, a very strong consensus has developed that protected areas need to make a solid contribution to poverty alleviation, going far beyond simply doing no harm (McNeely 2004). Many approaches to developing protected areas can also provide important economic benefits to rural populations. It is also important to recognise that poverty is not simply a lack of money, that human well-being (sometimes called 'sustainable livelihoods') also involves living in a healthy relationship with the environment, and that areas important for their natural values can also lead to significant benefits for local people, in terms of watershed protection, non-timber forest products and other such values. Many of the rural poor well recognise the value of conserving certain features or landscapes, and have established their own protected areas (sometimes called 'sacred sites') through their own cultural mechanisms. Thus the relationship between protected areas, poverty alleviation and SD has many complexities that we must begin to identify (McNeely 2004).

The CBD defines 'protected area' as 'a geographically defined area which is designated or regulated and managed to achieve specific conservation objectives', as given in Article 2. The modern approach to protected areas makes them essential parts of SD, again as given by McNeely (1999). The CBD has marked a significant shift in the perception of protected areas by governments. It has linked protected areas to larger issues of public concern, such as sustainable development, poverty alleviation, traditional knowledge, access to genetic resources, national sovereignty, equitable sharing of benefits and intellectual property rights. Protected area managers are now sharing a larger and more important political stage with development agencies, agricultural scientists, NGOs, anthropologists, ethnobiologists, lawyers, economists, pharmaceutical firms, farmers, foresters, tourism agencies, the oil industry, indigenous peoples, and many others. These competing groups claim resources, powers and privileges through a political decision-making process in which biologists, local communities, the private sector, and conservationists have become inextricably embroiled. The challenge is to find ways for the various stakeholders to work together most effectively to achieve the conservation and development objectives of modern society (McNeely 2004).

Ecosystem services from protected areas

Far more important than income from tourism or harvesting of renewable resources are the ecological services that protected areas can provide to local communities, the nation and the international community. Particularly important services at the community level include soil regeneration, nutrient cycling, pollination, recreation, provision of pure water, and maintenance of the functioning ecosystem which yields harvestable resources. Such benefits are often difficult to quantify, and even local people may take them for granted. Ecological services do not normally appear in corporate or national accounting systems, but they far outweigh direct values when they are computed. One of the most important ecosystem services, especially in view of the major investments in water resource management being made in much of the world, is the stabilising of hydrological functions. Experiences from various parts of the world demonstrate that protected areas are a cost-effective management option for maintaining healthy watersheds that produce a steady and reliable source of water (McNeely 2004).

Providing benefits to rural communities

Far more needs to be done to build support from local communities for protected areas. This will require a challenging combination of incentives and disincentives, economic benefits and law enforcement, education and awareness, employment in the protected area and employment opportunities outside, enhanced land tenure and control of new immigration (especially where the buffer zones around protected areas are targeted for special development assistance). The key is to find the balance among the competing demands, and this will usually require a site-specific solution. A key factor is the stability of rural communities, implying that governments need to be particularly cautious when contemplating major efforts at relocating people from one part of the countryside to another. Those people who have developed long-term relationships with particular settings, and have developed knowledge on how to manage the resources contained within those ecosystems, are likely to have very different relationships with the land and its resources from new immigrants who have no particular linkage to local resources and often receive considerable subsidies from outside; the new arrivals frequently are responsible for more destructive land-use practices than are the long-term residents, but of course new technologies and new markets can be expected to change behaviour of local villagers irrespective of their traditional conservation practices. It is possible that some local communities have a limit on their perceived needs, and once their basic needs are met, then they will reduce their impact on protected area resources. But this rosy assumption is far from a generality and most communities contain at least some individuals who happily will try to exploit more from a system than can be supported in a sustainable way, even if the social costs far outweigh the private benefits. This means that protected area management needs to be based on a clear understanding of rules and regulations, and must include effective means of enforcing them through various kinds of incentives (such as employment, clean water, various kinds of linked development, and so forth), and disincentives (such as public ostracism, fines and jail terms). Protected areas are created by people, so they are expressions of culture and serve as models of the relationship between people and the rest of nature. Thus the culture of each country is reflected in its system of protected areas, so each will tend to have different characteristics. The single over-riding issue for those interested in using protected areas to alleviate poverty is how to find the right balance between the generalised desire to live harmoniously with nature and the need to exploit resources to sustain life and develop economically. The problems facing protected areas are thus intimately related to socio-economic factors affecting communities in and around protected areas, including poverty, land tenure and equity; they also involve national-level concerns, such as land use, tourism, development, balance of payments, energy and resource management; and global concerns such as biodiversity, climate change and generation of new knowledge about life (McNeely 2004).

The SD programme for national protected area systems advocated here needs to include both firm governmental action and alliances with the other stakeholders at all levels. National governments cannot delegate their role as guarantors of the conservation of a country's cultural and natural heritage, so the appropriate authorities need to build the capacity to fulfil their regulatory and management duties and responsibilities. But civil society can share certain rights and responsibilities regarding the management of protected areas after careful preparations and an adequate definition of roles and responsibilities. Given the interests of NGOs, businesses, scientists, indigenous peoples and local communities who live within or close to protected areas, alliances can be created among stakeholders to enable each to play an appropriate role according to clear government policies and laws. Social and economic incentives can be used to reward land-holders that contribute effectively to protected area management. If governments and the general public recognise the many economic, social, cultural, ecological, developmental and political values of protected areas; if appropriate institutions are established to manage protected areas in close collaboration with other stakeholders; if sustainable economic benefits are enabled to flow to protected areas and their surrounding communities; and if information from both traditional knowledge and modern science can be mobilised to enable protected areas to adapt to changing conditions, then protected areas can be the engines for new forms of sustainable rural development that ensure a better life for all (McNeely 2004). Protected areas and their other importance will be discussed separately, because of the detailed effects.

A risk assessment framework for a formal resolution of the environmental risks

A risk assessment framework has been encouraged and recommended under a formal resolution of the environmental risks; this framework contains six steps, as shown in Figure 7.9 (van Dam et al. 2001):

1. Identification of the problem – identify the nature of the problem and develop a plan for the remainder of the assessment, including the objectives and scope.
2. Identification of adverse effects – evaluate the likely extent of adverse change.
3. Identification of the extent of the problem – estimate the likely extent of the problem.
4. Identification of the risk – integrate the results from the above steps.
5. Risk management and reduction – make decisions to minimise the risks without compromising other societal, community or environmental values.
6. Monitoring – verify the effectiveness of the risk management decisions.

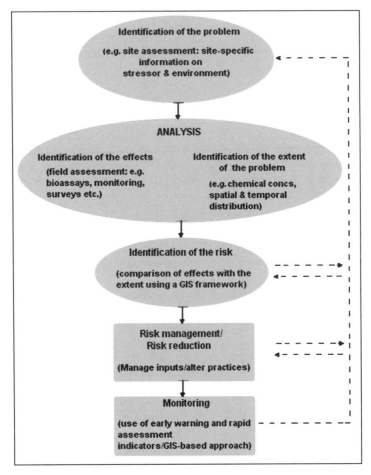

Figure 7.9 Model for environmental risk assessment

To identify the problem for risk assessment application it is necessary to determine the hazards first; trying to find the radical solutions for their reduction or removal are the main strategy for risk management system. The extent and consequences of such invasions can be assessed on the basis of existing information and recommendations made for control measures, including training and information gaps identified from the figure (van Dam et al. 2001).

As given by Rutledge et al. (2005), the aims of the New Zealand Biodiversity Strategy are to halt the decline in indigenous biodiversity by:

1. Maintaining and restoring a full range of remaining natural habitats and ecosystems to a healthy and functioning state, enhancing critically scarce

habitats, and maintaining modified ecosystems in production and urban environments.

2. Maintaining and restoring viable populations of all indigenous species and subspecies across their natural range and maintaining their genetic diversity.

The Strategy outlines the associated conservation challenges and reports recent progress to improve the measurement and monitoring of biodiversity to help its instigators to know *whether they are halting the decline for public good conservation purposes*. The Department is currently designing a Natural Heritage Management System (NHMS) that will help them monitor biodiversity trends and report the difference made by their conservation actions (Figure 7.10, Rutledge et al. 2005). 'The system consists of a decision-making process centred on government and community consultation, complimented by a toolbox that provides information to different stages in the process'. The system will allow the Department to:

1. specify monitoring techniques
2. collect, coordinate and curate data
3. report on and plan for conservation outcomes at a range of geographical and organisational scales
4. build agency accountability for knowing what progress has been made towards conservation goals.

Therefore, the outcome of discussions on biodiversity may produce serious impacts on the natural ecosystem in the future. Also, research and studies on the restoration and conservation of the present conditions can introduce a different perspective, for all the participants.

For this reason, it is essential to enlist the cooperation of government, local community institutions and, most importantly, of the people who, as consumers of the resources, can participate responsibly to avoid existing and future threats to local biodiversity. Strategic actions such as local management plans, restoration, control and eradication, research and the development of legal support for implementation are contributory factors in controlling and preventing the potential threats in environmental biodiversity. But environments fall within these five threat categories based on indigenous cover loss or poor legal protection.

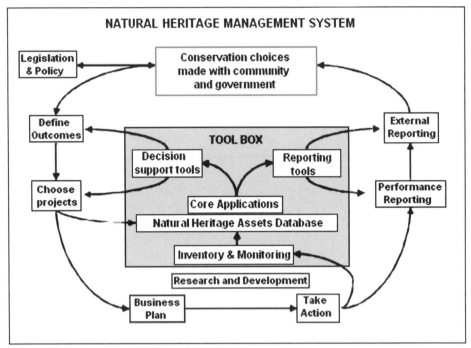

Figure 7.10 Design for a Natural Heritage Management System (NHMS)
for monitoring biodiversity trends, reporting differences and
identifying conservation actions

(*Source*: Rutledge et al. 2005)

Conclusions

Scientists are faced with the challenge of finding ways to apply the agreed goals
and targets to the national situation and to introduce them into policies, plans and
projects relevant to biodiversity management. This publication aims to provide
information on approaches taken in a variety of situations and environments
and to elucidate the scientific rationale of the methods applied. It presents – often
preliminary – results and thereby generates discussion and, hopefully, new initiatives
and research on ways in which science can support the monitoring of progress and
activities to achieve the 2010 target. All these targets will require implementing
a range of supporting activities, including for example the establishment of an
enabling policy environment, provision of financial and technical resources,
capacity building, monitoring and evaluation, and ensuring that protected areas
are established and effectively managed in an equitable and participatory manner.
Also, ecologically representative national and regional systems of a global network
contribute to achieving from all point of objectives of the Convention and the 2010
target to significantly reduce the current rate of biodiversity loss.

References

Altieri, M.A. (1999), 'The ecological role of biodiversity in agroecosystems', *Agriculture, Ecosystems and Environment*, 74, 19–31.

Altieri, M.A. (1994), *Biodiversity and Pest Management in Agroecosystems*, New York: Haworth Press.

Anon. (2006a), 'Environment. Corporate social responsibility. Corporate social responsibility – What does it mean? News and resources'. See <http://www.mallenbaker.net/csr/CSRfiles/Environment.html>.

Anon. (2006b), 'Social responsibility. What are we doing? Environment, health and safety', in 'Facing challenges – finding opportunities'. Gap Inc. 2004 Social Responsibility Report, pp 48–51, at <http://www.gapinc.com/public/SocialResponsibility/socialres.shtml>.

Anon. (2006c), 'Environmental management and accounting the relevance of environmental management systems', at <http://www.sustainability.org/international/index.htm> and <http://www.sustainability.org/international/Management-Development.htm>.

Anon. (2006d), 'Worldwide environmental policy', at <www.jnj.com/our_company/fast_facts/ social_and_environmental_responsibility.htm>.

Anon. (2005), 'Corporate Social Responsibility' (redirected from 'Corporate Social Responsibility'). Jump to: 'navigation', 'search'; see <http://en.wikipedia.org/wiki/Corporate_Social Responsibility>.

Büchs, W. (2003), 'Biodiversity and agri-environmental indicators – general scopes and skills with special reference to the habitat level', *Agriculture, Ecosystems and Environment*, 98, 35–78.

Büchs, W., Harenberg, A., Zimmermann, J. and Weiß, B. (2003), 'Biodiversity, the ultimate agri-environmental indicator? Potential and limits for the application of faunistic elements as gradual indicators in agroecosystems', *Agriculture, Ecosystems and Environment*, 98, 99–123.

Chiras, Daniel D. (1991), *Environmental Science: Action for a Sustainable Future*, 3rd edn, San Francisco: Benjamin/Cummings.

Convention on Biological Diversity (CBD), at <http://www.biodiv.org>.

van Dam, R., Walden, D., Begg, G. and Finlayson, M. (2001), 'Ecological risk assessment of cane toad, *Bufo marinus*, in Kakadu National Park, Australia', in *Assessment and Management of Alien Species that Threaten Ecosystems, Habitats and Species*, CBD Technical Series no.1, pp 21–4, Montreal: Secretariat of the Convention on Biological Diversity (CBD).

Dudley, N., Mulongoy, K.J., Cohen, S., Stolton, S., Barber, C.V. and Gidda, S.B. (2005), *Towards Effective Protected Area Systems: An Action Guide to Implement the Convention on Biological Diversity Programme of Work on Protected. Protected areas and the convention on biological diversity*, CBD Technical Series no. 18, Montreal: Secretariat of the CBD.

Food and Agriculture Organization (FAO) (2003), 'The role of biological diversity in feeding the world: the scope of agricultural biodiversity', at <http://www.fao.org/biodiversity/sci/foodsecu2.asp>.

Food and Agriculture Organization (FAO) (2001a), 'Food security: the role of biological diversity in feeding the world', at < http://www.fao.org./biodiversity for food & agriculture>, accessed 20 August 2001.

Food and Agriculture Organization (FAO) (2001b), 'The role of biological diversity in feeding the world: the scope of agricultural biodiversity', at <http://www.fao.org./biodiversity/sci/ foodsecu2.asp>.

Fresco, L. (2000), 'Scientific and ethical challenges in agriculture to meet human needs', *Food, Nutrition and Agriculture Alimentation*, 27, 4–13.

Gidda, S.B. and Mulongoy, K.J. (2004), 'Protected areas in the convention on biological diversity', in *Biodiversity Issues for Consideration in the Planning, Establishment and Management of Protected Area Sites and Networks*, CBD Technical Series no. 15, Montreal: Secretariat of the CBD, pp 9–13.

Hole, D.G., Perkins, A.J., Wilson, J.D., Alexander, I.H., Grice, P.V. and Evans, A.D. (2005), 'Does organic farming benefit biodiversity?', *Biological Conservation*, 122, 113–130.

Jones, C.G. and Lawton, J.H. (eds) (1995), *Linking Species and Ecosystems*, New York: Chapman & Hall.

Loew, T., Beucker, S. and Jürgens, G. (2002), *Vergleichende Analyse der Umweltcontrolling instrumente Umweltbilanz, Umweltkennzahlen und Flusskostenrechnung/Comparative Analysis on the Environmental Accounting Instruments Input-Output Balances, Environmental Performance Indicators and Flow Cost Accounting*, Berlin: INTUS-Project Diskussionspapier des IÖW DP 53/02. Gefördert durch das BMBF (Fkz: 01 RU 0009).

Lucas, N. (2003), 'Ecosystems and human well-being: a framework for assessment is the first product of the millennium', in *Facilitating Conservation and Sustainable Use of Biological Diversity*, CBD Technical Series no. 9, Montreal: Secretariat of the CBD, 27–9.

McNeely, J.A. (2004), 'Protected areas, poverty, and sustainable development', in *Biodiversity Issues for Consideration in the Planning, Establishment and Management of Protected Area Sites and Networks*, CBD Technical Series no. 15, Kuala Lumpur: Secretariat of the CBD, pp 14–22.

Mander, U., Mikk, M. and KuElvik, M. (1999), 'Ecological and low intensity agriculture as contributors to landscape and biological diversity', *Landscape and Urban Planning*, 46, 169–77.

Menne, B. and Bertollini, R. (2000), 'The health impacts of desertification and drought', WHO in United Nations Convention to Combat Desertification in Those Countries Experiencing Serious Drought and/or Desertification, Particularly in Africa (UNCCD), *Down to Earth: Newsletter of the UNCCD*, no. 14, December.

Pereira, H.M. and Cooper, H.D. (2006), 'Towards the global monitoring of biodiversity change', *Trends in Ecology and Evolution*, 21, 123–9. Also available at <http//ue.eu.int/ueDocs/cms_Data/docs/pressData/en/ec/00200-r1.en1.pdf>.

Poulsen, J.G. (2001), 'Impact of invasive species on biodiversity conservation and poor peoples's livelihoods', in *Assessment and Management of Alien Species that*

Threaten Ecosystems, Habitats and Species, CBD Technical Series no. 1, Montreal: Secretariat of the CBD, pp 21–4.

Rutledge, D., Lee, W., McGlone, M., Walker, S., Stephens T., Wright, E., Price, R. and Johnston, K. (2005), 'From outputs to outcomes: recent progress in measuring and monitoring biodiversity in New Zealand', in *Working Together for Biodiversity: Regional and International Initiatives Contributing to Achieving and Measuring Progress towards the 2010 Target*, Abstracts of poster presentations at the tenth meeting of the Subsidiary Body on Scientific, Technical and Technological Advice, CBD Technical Series No. 17, pp 65–7, Montreal: Secretariat of the CBD.

Saxena, K.G., Rao, K.S. and Ramakrishnan, P.S. (1999). 'Ecological context of biodiversity', in S. Shantharam and J.F. Montgomery (eds), *Biotechnology, Biosafety and Biodiversity: Scientific and Ethical Issues for Sustainable Developments*, Riverdale MD: US Department of Agriculture (Animal and Plant Health Inspection Series), pp 129–56.

Schauer, T. (2002), *Biological and Cultural Diversity in a Globalised Information Society. German Society for Rare Agricultural Plants*. Ulm: Universitatsverlag Ulm.

Social Inclusion (2000), at <http://www.socialinclusion2000.co.uk/csr.html>.

Topal R.Ş. (2005), 'Is it true that social responsibility studies can cause an assimilation problem, and why?', paper given at the 4th International Conference on Social Responsibility, 7–9 September 2005, Metropolitan University, London.

Topal R.Ş. (2004), 'Food unsafety problems in the world and Turkey: solution offer: from the site of social responsibility', paper given at the 2nd International Conference on Social Responsibility, 21–23 November 2004, Ansted University, Penang.

Topal R.Ş. (2003), *Sustainable Agriculture and Social Responsibility*. NATO Advanced Training Course on Ecological Agriculture, course book, pp 75–100. Invited NATO lecturer, Hamburg University (Germany), 30 October.

Topal, R.Ş. and Crowther, D. (2003). 'Bioengineering and corporate social responsibility', in D. Crowther and L. Raymen-Bacchus (eds), *Perspectives in Corporate Social Responsibility*, Aldershot: Ashgate, pp 157–72.

UNEP, UNICEF and WHO (2002), 'Children in the new millennium – environmental impact on health', *Global Environmental Problems*, Chapter 4, pp 87–98.

Van Overwalle, G. (2005), 'Protecting and sharing biodiversity and traditional knowledge: holder and user tools', *Ecological Economics*, 53, 585–607. Also at <www.sciencedirect.com>.

Waldhardt, R. and Otte, A. (2000), 'Zur Terminologie und wissenschaftlichen Anwendung des Begriffs Biodiversität' ['On the use of the concept of biodiversity'], *Wasser & Boden*, 52 (1/2), 10–13.

PART II

THE EMPLOYMENT RELATIONSHIP

Overview of Part II

The last couple of decades have seen considerable change in the structure of business organisations, caused largely by their desire to gain competitive advantage and by their desire to make use of the technological infrastructure available. Often this has been legitimated as a reaction to the increasingly deregulated free market environment brought into being as a consequence of globalisation. Equally often it has been legitimated as a reaction to the need to create value for shareholders. This has been manifest in activities of organisations, to cut costs primarily through reductions in employee costs and to flatten the hierarchical structures of organisation. As a consequence of these drivers of business management, organisations are now leaner and fitter, but inherent in these changes are certain dangers as organisations seek to capitalise on their restructuring and achieve continued competitive advantage and growth in this new environment.

More recently it has started to be discussed and recognised that this focus of organisations in cutting costs through labour force reductions, while providing short-term benefit, is not without its problems and that problems have been stored up for the future. Thus managers are starting to recognise that there is a need for them to manage their way out of the current short-term focus on business activity and build for the future. What is less certain, however, is that managers understand the implications of the actions of the last decades upon their existing, and potential, workforce, and the importance of the psychological contract between employer and employee and the way this has been changed by this new environment. Equally there is considerable uncertainty concerning what can be done to bring about changes to this contract and invest in the future of organisations.

The employment relationship is the concern of the contributors to this part of the *Ashgate Research Companion*. We have interpreted this in the broadest possible terms by considering that human rights – a fundamental aspect of CSR – are concerned with the employment relationship, among other things. In the first chapter Baptiste is concerned with the well-being of employees. She argues that there is a symbiotic relationship that exists between HRM practices and employee well-being in organisations when considered from a corporate social responsibility (CSR) perspective. She maintains that it is imperative that companies convince their key stakeholders (employees) that they are serious about CSR by demonstrating through HRM, good governance and ethical policies that the organisation aims to achieve the desired social, environmental and ethical outcomes. Therefore, it is the employees, rather than the board or a consultancy firm, who carry the main burden of responsibility for implementing ethical corporate behaviour in the daily working life of the company. In this chapter she reviews current knowledge in this area before arguing that there are considerable implications for the future of employee well-being and CSR in organisations.

The concern of Vandekerckhove is with whistleblowing, which he defines as 'the deliberate, non-obligatory act of disclosure, by individual with privileged access to data or information of an organization, about a non-trivial illegality or other wrongdoing under the control of that organization, to an entity who has the power to rectify the wrongdoing.' This chapter shows why whistleblowing policies are a CSR practice. It offers arguments for organisations to implement procedures that allow and protect internal and external disclosures. His argument is that this phenomenon is an essential part of corporate governance, and procedures are needed to protect the people who denounce this kind of wrongdoing. His survey of international practice shows that such protection exists in many countries and the value of the phenomenon is gradually being recognised internationally.

Vettori is concerned with an issue which is a major problem in Africa and a growing problem in other parts of the world – namely HIV and Aids. She takes a specifically South African perspective on the employer's duties towards employees infected with HIV/Aids. Her analytical lens is a legal one and she observes that the majority of legislation which exists is concerned – and phrased accordingly – with what an employer may not do. The purpose her chapter therefore is take an opposite view and to demonstrate that employers are in fact legally obliged to take positive steps to protect employees and even job applicants infected with the virus. Leaving aside any moral or ethical duty towards such employees her argument is that there is a financial imperative to take positive steps to address HIV/Aids issues at the workplace and the consequences of the current complacency are potentially very serious.

Although this section is concerned predominantly with the employment relationship and more generally with human rights, many of the main concepts introduced in the first section recur. Thus, issues concerning trust (or problems with a lack of trust), sustainability or stakeholder relations feature prominently. In this section, though, some of the language is different and some of the concepts are recast as issues of disclosure and accountability. Similarly, ethics – the subject matter of the next section – features prominently in this section.

The Symbiotic Relationship between HRM Practices and Employee Well-Being: A Corporate Social Responsibility Perspective

Nicole Renée Baptiste

Introduction

This chapter discusses the symbiotic relationship that exists between human resource management (HRM) practices and employee well-being in organisations from a corporate social responsibility (CSR) perspective. The chapter is primarily theoretically oriented and does not go into empirical studies. It gives an in-depth understanding of the relationship between HRM practices and employee well-being and what an organisation can do to promote the well-being of their employees, the key stakeholder. With this in mind, it is imperative that companies convince their key stakeholder (employees) that they are serious about CSR by demonstrating through HRM policies, effective line management leadership practices, good governance and ethical practices that the organisation mission, goals and objectives are to achieve the desired social, environmental and ethical outcomes. Therefore CSR will be demonstrated through the ethical behaviour of a company towards employees by management acting responsibly in their relationships with employees who have a legitimate interest in the business. Doukakis (2004) suggests that CSR is the continuing commitment by business to behave ethically and contribute to economic development while improving the quality of life of the workforce and their families as well as of the local community and society at large. Therefore, it is the employees, rather than the board or a consultancy firm, who carry the main burden of responsibility for implementing ethical corporate behaviour in the daily working life of the company (Collier and Esteban 2007). The achievement of those outcomes depends on employees' willingness to reciprocate and collaborate with positive attitudinal and behavioural characteristics. Gaining full support from employees and ensuring that they are motivated and committed to obtaining company objectives places challenges and complexity on line management leadership in the implementation of HRM policies within the organisation. The author argues that line managers' people-management strategies should involve, firstly, effective leadership through social exchanges with employees to generate support and develop trust; secondly, implementation of HRM practices; and, thirdly, promotion of a healthy organisational climate that is unique and conducive to employee motivation which in turn promotes well-being amongst workers to deliver on corporate performance. It is argued that the fundamental principles of CSR to promote employee commitment, job satisfaction and work/life balance satisfaction amongst employees is complex and multi-faceted and is based on the symbiotic relationship between corporate contextual factors (line managers' leadership practices; implementation of HRM policies; perceived organisational support and trust) and by employee reciprocation through positive attitudinal and behaviour characteristics that leads to enhanced key performance outcomes. The perspective discussed in this chapter is an individual employee perspective and not an organisational perspective. This places employees at the 'steering wheel' of organisations' policy formulation and strategic orientation.

The approach of this chapter adopts seven elements:

1. The first of these is the academic literature on the changing nature of work in the 21st century and the challenges and complexities placed on management of modern organisations.
2. The second is the human resource management literature from the context of CSR and ethical responsibility that discusses the commitment of organisations to contribute to working with employees to improve their quality of life.
3. The third source is represented by literature on line management implementation of HRM practices, which report on employee attitudes and behaviours relevant to trust and support that lead to ethics in the workplace through the promotion of employee well-being.
4. The fourth discusses the symbiotic relationship that exists between HRM practices and employee well-being and its effects on key performance outcomes.
5. Fifth, the discussion contributes to the literature on commitment, job satisfaction and work/life balance satisfaction that points to the importance of employee well-being as determinants of line management corporate responsibility involvement that promotes perception and support and trust amongst employees.
6. Sixth, it discusses increasing worker satisfaction and productivity, which is a goal for CSR.
7. The chapter concludes by examining the enhancing organisational corporate responsibility, knowledge and learning within organisations and its implications on employee well-being.

The changing nature of work in the 21st century and corporate responsibility

The changing context in which organisations operate in the 21st century continues to be a reality as ways in which companies and employees relate have changed substantially. Globalisation and advances in technological sophistication influence how companies are structured and where employees work. Demographic changes combined with government regulations will pressurise all companies to take account of the work health and well-being of their workforces. The economic drive in the workplace has resulted in increased work hours, jobs no longer for life, requirements for individuals to increase their working years and have shorter holidays, and an increasing amount of outsourcing. Alternatively, organisational change and restructuring are regular occurrences (Marchington and Wilkinson 2005); increasing multiculturalism within organisations is ordinary (Newell 2002); stress levels amongst employees appear to be increasing (HSE 2006); the introduction of new technology is hastening the pace of change (Currie 2001) and the demand for immediacy of response and dual-earning families is now commonplace and viewed as a normal family situation (Cox et al. 2005), creating problems of balance between work, family and life satisfaction (Cooper and Robertson 2001; Guest 2002). These changes have done little to enhance employee well-being, and have resulted in high levels of workplace stress, illness and employee dissatisfaction and the consequent rise in health-related costs to employers (Adams 2007). Therefore these changes challenge the management of corporate responsibility (CR) within organisations that encompasses social, environmental and financial issues as well as legal compliance. Moreover, Holme and Watts (2000) suggest that CR is the commitment of business to contribute to the sustainability of economic development, employees and their families, the local community and society at large to improve their quality of life.

Therefore, the challenges and complexities of management of modern organisations are likely to have an effect on employees' attitudes and behaviour towards the way they are treated within the organisation, which in turn can have a domino effect on key performance outcomes. Friedman (1993) holds the view that the only social responsibility of business is to maximise profits. However, this perspective has been challenged by the stakeholder model that regards business as not just about profit but also about the well-being of individuals and society (Marchington and Wilkinson 2005). In that, Doukakis (2004) argues that social responsibility towards stakeholders guides business activity. Therefore the stakeholder theory of the firm provides a foundation for the groups to whom the corporation is responsible. For the purpose of this chapter the focus will be on the employee stakeholder group. Hence, employees have an increased need to more fully understand and to critique the social and ethical performance of corporations in which they have an interest (Fombrum 1996). Therefore, in light of this view, cutting edge companies that have invested deeply in the well-being of their workforce are now reaping the benefits. Once organisations take CSR seriously, the context of human rights and ethical investment on the 'human capital' in organisations' internal workplaces will relate to fair-trading of staff. This fundamental issue involves the strategic purpose of businesses and the promotion of well-being amongst workers that is required for organisations to remain in operation.

Consistent with this chapter are the use of various terms and concepts. Before proceeding there are general points that should be noted. The first point is the notion of HRM as widely defined in the literature (Daniels 2006; Guest 1999; Huselid 1995) but for the purpose of this discussion HRM will be defined as a set of practices used to manage the workforce of an organisation; that is, recruitment and selection, training and development, worker involvement, pay and rewards, flexibility, involvement in decision-making, communications and employee welfare (Purcell 2004). The second general point is the notion of well-being, which has been researched within other disciplines to concern an overall sense of happiness (MacDonald 2005). Thus, from an HR perspective, well-being refers to the physical and mental health of the workforce (Currie 2001). In the context of this chapter, 'employee well-being' is discussed from an HRM perspective that looks after the quality of working life of employees through involvement by promoting attitudes and behaviours such as commitment, job satisfaction and work/life balance satisfaction. The phenomenon of employee well-being is specific to being at work. Peccei (2004) suggests that this type of well-being is an aspect of, and can certainly contribute to, people's overall sense of happiness, but is analytically distinct from general well-being. The three attitudinal and behavioural characteristics constitute employee well-being (commitment, job satisfaction and work/life balance satisfaction), which it is argued that when promoted can bring about continuous development and increased performance.

The third general point is the concept of corporate social responsibility. CSR definitions vary, however, from a broad perspective, Crowther and Rayman-Bacchus (2004) suggest that CSR is concerned with what is or should be the relationship between global corporations, governments of countries and individual citizens. In general, Lefkowitz (2006) points out that an organisation has an effective CSR policy when it manages its business in a manner that meets or exceed the ethical, legal, commercial and public expectations that society has for business. This requires a comprehensive set of policies, practices and programmes that are integrated into business operations, supply chains and decision-making processes throughout the company. Doukakis (2004) reinforces this view and suggests that the CSR concept refers to the corporate behaviour that is over and above legal requirements and is voluntarily adopted to achieve sustainable development. Thus, organisations need to integrate their economic, social and environmental impact in their operations and form corporate policy in light of their long-term interests of their corporate stakeholder (employees). Moreover, Crowther (2006) further defines CSR as the relationship between a corporation, its stakeholders and the local society in which it resides or operates. Similarly, promoting altruistic behaviour is regarded as morally right in pursuit of the greatest happiness for the greatest number (Crowther and Çalıyurt 2004). However, the central tenet of social responsibility is the social contract between all the stakeholders (employees) to society, which is an essential requirement of civil society. Crowther (2006) further maintains that social responsibility also requires a responsibility towards the future and towards future members of society. Therefore, Crowther (2006) suggests that CSR involves a concern with the various stakeholders to a business identifying socially responsible behaviour:

- It is primarily with those stakeholders who have power to influence the organisation. Thus organisations are most concerned with shareholders, less so with customers and employees and very little with society and the environment. CSR implies that they are all of equal importance.
- The definitions imply that CSR is a voluntary activity rather than enforced through regulation whereas in actual fact it is an approach to decision-making.
- Claiming a concern is very different to actually exhibiting that concern through actions taken (Crowther 2006).

Due to uncertainty surrounding the nature of CSR activity it is likely to be difficult to assess actions and activities. Therefore, Crowther (2002) and Schaltegger et al. (1996) suggest that it is imperative to identify such activity through three principles (sustainability, accountability and transparency), which together comprise all CSR activity.

Sustainability is concerned with the effect which actions taken in the present has upon the options available in the future. Therefore in practice, organisations should aim towards less unsustainability by increasing efficiency in the way in which resources are utilised. An example would be the promotion of well-being amongst employees that is likely to have a domino effect for enhanced organisational performance and sustainability. Crowther (2006) says that accountability is concerned with an organisation recognising that its actions affect both internal and external environments, and therefore assumes responsibility for the effects of its actions. In addition to the acceptance of responsibility, management must understand the power of stakeholders (employees) to affect the way in which those actions of the organisation are taken through employees' responses, which are reciprocated, based on the actions. Finally, the principle of transparency outlines the external impact of actions of the organisation through reporting significant facts openly. This can take the form of employees being advised of business issues and being involved in decision-making. Transparency can be seen to be part of the process recognition of responsibility (Crowther 2006) on the part of management for the external effects of its actions and equally part of the process of transferring power to stakeholders (employees). The growth of demand for knowledge-intensive workers places demands on employee expectations and what is good or bad for their well-being. Therefore, management need to focus its efforts on fulfilling its moral obligations to employees' higher expectations by developing an enabling organisational climate that promotes motivation, commitment and satisfaction amongst employees, ensuring work/life balance satisfaction, which holistically produces a happy workforce that moreover is likely to enhance corporate performance.

Therefore, if organisations' values are clearly set through normative frameworks and key actors (line managers) integrate ethical analysis into their decision-making schemes, this could foster the development of employee well-being. This view is supported by Kline (2005) who suggests that fostering development is easily modified to fostering socially responsible development. Managing stakeholders' interests is of paramount importance to organisations. According to de Wit and Meyer (2004), shareholders, employees, suppliers, customers, governments and communities all place demands on an organisation. These demands, which reflect each group's self-interest, are often conflicting. The managers of an organisation have to balance these sometimes competing expectations and attempt to secure broad stakeholder support for the firm's mission (Morand and Rayman-Bacchus 2006). However, the attainment of the company's mission cannot be materialised until the key stakeholder's (employees') well-being is promoted and maintained as a socially responsible behaviour by the organisation.

The importance of CSR in the new millennium

The CSR agenda refers to the idea that organisations should consider the interests of society and the environment when making decisions. Among the diverse changes undergone by organisations within the new millennium is the concept of transparency of information; therefore operational strategies are apparent to most consumers today. The activities in business are now extensive and widespread and changes to operations have been in response by business to social, political and ecological pressures that are largely instinctive and unplanned (Lucas et al. 2006). Therefore, the controversy surrounding the Bernard Matthews turkey brand in connection with the bird flu epidemic in recent times is a real sign that companies are obliged to taken into account social, political and ecological forces. Moreover, in the debate about obesity, fast food chain such as McDonald's have also succumbed to pressure by consumers.

Realising CSR initiatives within organisations is now high on organisational agendas in the setting of values, their integration with strategy as well as implementation and performance measurement and communication on the performance of CSR policy (Ligeringen and Zadek 2007). Ligeringen and Zadek (2007) suggest the need to 'fix values' which help establish 'what we do' and the management systems will determine how to integrate the policy with corporate strategy and the process guidelines in order to be able to measure and communicate what is done (Morand and Rayman-Bacchus 2006). However, both Hendry (2004) and Andrews (2003) suggest a similar process in that the principles associated with traditional morality and the maintenance of hierarchical order in society emphasise the duties and obligations to others to treat people honestly and with respect, to be fair and without prejudice, to help others when in need and to put the needs of others before one's own. Within organisations this poses a challenge for the leadership of senior managers to develop managers and employees as moral individuals. Another challenge can result if senior and middle managers may not feel that it is their duty to impart corporate values into day-to-day management and run the business organisation as a moral society (Hendry 2004: 27). Yet another challenge is learning through doing, affecting all managers and subordinate staff.

According to Morand and Rayman-Bacchus (2006) these challenges can be changed through organisations embracing value-setting, integration and implementation, and evaluation and communication. Corporate values stem from organisational culture, leadership and vision and should be embraced as encouraging a change in behaviour, which requires communication between the leadership and the workforce in order to shape company culture. Alternatively, the corporate vision can be transmitted throughout the organisation by management that reflects the universal standards, applicable across the organisations and functions in which the company is active. Moreover, Litgeringen and Zadek (2007) suggest that an organisation is likely to be challenged to integrate the concept of sustainable development into organisational and exterior relationships at both strategic and the operational levels. Kline (2005) observes that socially responsible behaviour begins with the individual, personal concern by consumers, managers and other stakeholders (employees) who connect communities and enable behavioural change. Therefore corporate values implemented by management have to inform company strategy and practices as well as becoming part of managing interpersonal relations with employees. In order for positive social exchanges to continue to thrive between management and employees there must be continual evaluation and communication of CSR policy initiatives, which is likely to provide the impulse for employee well-being, innovation and improvement.

Human resource management and corporate responsibility

Human resource management is a unitary system of management that attempts to elicit employees' commitment to (Guest 2001) and involvement in (Wood 1999) the purposes and goals of the organisation. Its principles and techniques influence how the whole organisation is managed (Marchington and Wilkinson 2005). Traditionally, HRM is believed to improve business performance in response to external threat of increasing competition (Guest 1999). However, Storey (1995) argues that the strategic orientation gives HRM a 'hard' utilitarian cast as it promotes the idea that workers are a resource that managers should exploit to their full potential, attaching little value to worker concerns. The 'hard' approach focuses on increasing efficiency and reducing labour costs through the application of rules and procedures that place emphasis on controlling workers. Contrary to this view is the developmental humanistic approach managing human resources that have been conflated with the 'soft' or 'high commitment' approach to HRM (Boxall 1996; Guest 1999; Pfeffer 2005). The humanistic or 'high commitment' approach suggests that effective HRM reflects attempts by management to create a work environment that emphasises practices such as participation, involvement in decision-making, teamwork, effective communication and training and development. Even further, organisations need to implement awareness of their corporate responsibility to encourage trust amongst their stakeholders, employees being the main stakeholders. Based on this view, it is important for employers to understand that ambitious agendas cannot be attained without the support of the business community (Marchington and Wilkinson 2005) and the workforce. CSR has been embraced by national corporate bodies like the EU Charter of Fundamental Rights and the Sustainability Strategy for Europe in addition to OECD guidelines and ILO labour standards, to name a few. Nevertheless, apart from national legislation, organisations face additional pressure from stakeholders to operate in the 'best practice' platform to create a competency framework and template to help managers integrate CSR into their organisations. The underlying idea is that the achievement of strategic objectives depends on taking into consideration stakeholders (employees) because they have the potential to either help or harm the corporation. Therefore the strategic management of stakeholders approach focuses on finding the best way to deal with employees as powerful stakeholders, whilst minimising damage to shareholder value.

Aside from legislation and policy initiatives, the motivation to adopt CR is diverse and overlapping (IRS 2002; Mullins 2004) although the business case and concern about loss of customers, investors and employees provides a major push. An organisation's repetition and image are important for profits and prospects of long-term survival. Lawrence (2002) argues that if suppliers comply with robust CR standards this can be a powerful incentive for the their own labour practices. By contrast, just as with the high commitment HRM, some organisations view CR as a means of providing competitive advantage through differentiation. Therefore, these practices invest in and develop innovative, flexible and committed employees who are valued and are high value-adding resources (Guest 1998). Hence, organisations adopting a 'soft' or 'high commitment' approach to HRM endeavour to enhance worker performance by empowering, developing and trusting workers to achieve organisational goals on the basis of mutuality of interests. In essence, the 'soft' approach focuses on HRM practices where employees are proactive rather than passive inputs into productive processes (Legge 1995), are capable of development, worthy of trust and collaboration, to be achieved through participation and informed choice (Whitener 2001). Therefore the emphasis from the 'soft' approach to HRM is on generating motivation (Collier and Esteban 2007) and commitment via communication and leadership (Legge 1995). Thus, 'high commitment' HRM practices are those that signal management's trust in employees.

High commitment HRM practices

Over the past decade, there has been much interest in the notion of 'best practice' human resource management, sometimes referred to as 'high performance work systems' (Appelbaum et al. 2000), 'high commitment' (Guest 2001) or 'high involvement' (Wood 1999). Many contemporary organisations use a range of high commitment HR practices and in many instances the practices themselves are not new but the rationale for using them has changed. For instances, managers are now endeavouring to develop a committed and qualified workforce in a climate of trust and comradeship (Gould-Williams 2004). Research on HRM focused on the impact of commitment seeking 'high performance' HR practices that are suggested to be able to improve employee and organisational performance (Wood 1999; Legge 1995). This approach contrasts with the orthodox view in which employees were used objectively and rationally as any other capital resource (Legge 1995). Even further, employee responses to HRM practices are at the heart of all HRM performance models (Purcell and Kinnie 2006) because it is the link between employee reactions and their subsequent behaviour that is critical. However, since CSR necessitates systematic change and involves expensive adjustments, organisations competing on cost are unlikely to make the investment. Similarly, it is argued that employer commitment to CR is superficial and used merely as a marketing ploy (Belal 2002). As in instances with problems with current reporting standards it is easy to use CR as 'window dressing' (Cerin 2002; Doukakis 2004). However, despite the perceived 'window dressing', organisations need to implement CR as their commitment to ethical practice for their employees to promote positive attitudes and behaviours.

Employee behaviour is usually subdivided into those concerning affective or attitudinal outcomes like job satisfaction and organisation commitment, referred to as organisational citizenship behaviour (OCB) (Purcell and Hutchinson 2007). All three variables together make up employee well-being. Furthermore, evidence suggests that when HR practices are used in conjunction with each other, the impact on performance will be greater than when used in isolation (Guest 1998). In other words, organisations attempting to introduce individual HR practices will observe minimal, if any, change in performance, whereas those organisations successfully introducing a range of practices (generally referred to as 'bundles') will experience a more dramatic change in performance (Gould-Williams 2004; Guest et al. 2003).

Similarly, Grant and Shields (2002) agree that the emphasis typically placed on the business case for HRM suggests a one-sided focus on organisational outcomes at the expense of employees. HR practices within a high commitment model are built around attempts to manage organisational culture and ensure that workers operate effectively within and for this culture (Guest 2002). Theoretical evidence on the relationship of HR practices with organisational effectiveness indicates that HR practices influence employee commitment and other performance measures which then lead to organisational effectiveness (Reichers 1985; Williams and Anderson 1991). Therefore, employees interpret organisational actions like human resource practices (Gallie et al. 2001) and the trustworthiness of management (Snape and Redman 2003) as indicative of the organisation's commitment to them (Wood and Albanese 1995).

The debate concerning HRM approach to employee well-being and relations has reached an interesting crossroad. Past research described a link between a particular style of HRM based around 'high performance' (Appelbaum et al. 2000) or 'high commitment' work systems (Wood 1999) and superior organisational performance (Guest 2002). Issues about organisational performance and about the link between HRM and performance are very important to organisations and their survival. Organisational performance is primarily based on the commitment of employees that is critically contingent on perceptions of justice, support and fairness in the perceived ethicality of the organisation itself. This is as a result of another important contextual factor that is based on the culture/climate of the organisation and the importance of line management, in the extent to which CSR is perceived to be championed by management, corporate leaders and by those with responsibility of embedding its principles and practice in hearts and minds, in decision-making structures and in the climate of the organisation's operation (Collier and Esteban 2007).

The effective delivery of corporate social and environmental responsibility initiatives is dependent on employee responsiveness (ibid. 2007). In order for employees to deliver on CSR requirements, they firstly have to be motivated to do so, and be committed to surmounting the challenges and attaining the goals of responsible corporate behaviour. Motivation comes first, commitment reinforces and embeds it. These attitudinal characteristics are promoted by organisations through the implementation of 'high commitment' HRM practices that forms the core (Pfeffer 2005), which signals managements' trust in employees. However, it is unlikely that any one organisation will utilise all these practices or even perform them equally well (Gould-Williams 2004). Therefore, the list should be regarded, in the first instance at least, as a standard by which mangers may monitor the level and extent of HR activity within the organisation.

The inter-related practices are: (1) employment security and internal promotion, (2) selective hiring and sophisticated selection, (3) extensive training, learning and development, (4) employee involvement, information sharing and worker voice, (5) self-managed teams, team working, (6) high compensation contingent on performance, and (7) reduction of status differentials/harmonisation. As highlighted earlier, it would be difficult to successfully implement one practice in isolation. For instance, the process of employment security and internal promotion should ensure employment security as much as possible by ensuring suitable candidates are chosen from within the organisation. This process can be more improved through personal training and development programmes that enhance the skills of workers. While the exact content and nature of these practices will vary between organisations, the underlying rationale for their adoption will be similar. Therefore, the following section will outline why and in what way these practices should be used.

1. Employment security and internal markets – contributes to employment security and makes an open and trusting employment relationship (Holman et al. 2003) and the notion of mutuality that is seen as a key component in partnership agreements relates to this. Internal promotion is generally seen as a critical corporate responsibility to retain key members of the workforce. Having recruited, developed and trained the 'right sort of people', it is unlikely that corporations and managers want to see these workers leave the organisation.

2. Selective hiring and sophisticated selection – is a critical element of HRM and when an organisation adopts a strategy of achieving superior performance

through the workforce, it will need the right people and will need innovative recruitment and selection strategies to obtain them.

3. Extensive training, learning and development – having recruited outstanding talent, employers need to ensure that these people remain at the forefront of their field in terms of professional expertise and product knowledge gained through training which facilitates learning so that people can become more effective in carrying out their work (Bramley 2003).

4. Employee involvement, information-sharing and worker voice – employee involvement is an essential component of the high commitment paradigm. Open communication about business matters ensures workers are informed about organisational issues and conveys a symbolic and substantive message that they are to be trusted in an open and positive manner (Marchington and Wilkinson 2005). Employee voice has been viewed as an aspect of 'high commitment' HRM, and is seen as essential so that workers should have the opportunity to express their grievances openly and independently, in addition to being able to contribute to management decision-making on task-related issues (Gould-Williams 2004).

5. Self-managed teams/teamworking – organisations that have tapped the power of teams have often experienced excellent results (Pfeffer 2005) through the pooling of ideas and improving work processes. It is suggested that, through teamworking, employees are encouraged to work together rather than on their own.

6. High compensation contingent on performance – there are a growing number of managers within the private sector who now reason that if employee performance results in enhanced organisational performance, then employees should share in the benefits received. In other words, they feel that workers should be appropriately and equitably rewarded for their effort.

7. Reduction of status differentials/harmonisation – this HRM practice conveys messages to manual workers and lower-grade office staff that they are valuable assets who deserve to be treated in a similar way to their more senior colleagues (Marchington and Wilkinson 2005).

The above review highlighting the seven 'high commitment' HR practices may not be appropriate in all settings, but core practices may be essential in gaining employee well-being and improved performance. Therefore managers need to consider each of these practices carefully to ascertain their relevance in relation to the context in which they are working. Consequently, it is suggested by Guzzo and Noonan (1994) that employees often interpret HRM practices in unintended and eccentric ways in that an HRM practice can have different consequences depending on the employees' predisposition. Thus, it is important to collect employees' views of HRM practices rather than relying on HRM policy directives.

HRM and employee well-being

Peccei (2004) argues that the heavy emphasis placed within the HR literature on the achievement of business-oriented performance outcomes has obscured the importance of employee well-being. Moreover, little research has investigated what HRM practices help to promote and underpin the well-being and happiness of employees within organisations. Similarly, Grant and Shields (2002) argue that the emphasis typically placed on the business case for HRM suggests a one-sided focus on organisational outcomes at the expense of employees. Winstanley and Woodall (2000) assert that employee well-being and the ethical dimension of HR policy and practice has been ignored, where the focus has shifted to 'strategic fit' and best practice' approaches. Marchington and Wilkinson (2005) argue that a high degree of alignment between HR employee champions and management can lead to extreme alienation of employees from both HRM and line management leadership practices, which has obvious implications for employee well-being. Marchington and Wilkinson (2005) further assert that this can be avoided if HR professionals effectively represent both employee needs and implement management agendas. Normative models of HRM tend to accept that employee well-being and organisation goals can always be aligned, through the creation of high commitment or high performance work practices (Purcell et al. 2003).

Conceptualising HRM in ways that acknowledge the complexities and tensions that line managers face in their attempt to develop the kind of 'high performance working' promoted by the CIPD (CIPD 2004) seems an essential goal which could be facilitated by a critically reflective framing of HR practice. This can provide a critical response to what Legge (1995) notes as a trend to represent employees in terms of a market-based discourse, facilitating HR practitioners to draw on strict economic criteria rather than social values to legitimise their practice, and regards as the gambling by HR practitioners with employee well-being in their efforts to gain strategic influence. These views are supported by Peccei's (2004) claims that it is vital to consider more explicitly the effects that HR policies and practices have on employees themselves and that this would help to realign HRM research with an important tradition of thinking in the social sciences. Particularly important in this respect are behavioural theories that suggest that the impact of HR practices on performance is mediated by employee attitudes and behaviour that include (for example) overall levels of worker satisfaction, employee commitment and well-being (Applelbaum et al. 2000; Guest 1999). Similarly, Peccei (2004) suggests that the adoption of progressive HR policies and practices (for example, selection, training, rewards, etc.) helps to maximise employee positive affective reactions at work, which in turn makes employees more willing to work hard and put in extra effort on behalf of the organisation, thus actively contributing to the overall productivity and effectiveness of the system. In essence, trying to gain a better understanding of the HRM line management leadership/well-being relationship in organisations is important not only in its own right, but also as a means of contributing to the CSR of organisations and to wider debates in the field of HRM about the impact of HR practices on organisational performance.

Line manager leadership: corporate responsibility in the promotion of social exchanges and trust

CSR standards, norms, principles and guidelines aim to provide generally accepted reference points for improving aspects of social and environmental performance (Ligteringen and Zadek 2007). Therefore CR can help drive and improve corporate performance through more responsible and accountable business practice. Moreover, business practice is likely to be implemented through the leadership behavioural practice of line managers. Thus, the array of codes, standards, guidelines and frameworks of CSR policies guide managers in integrating CR into their business strategies and management processes. Therefore, Glover et al. (2002) believe that management enhancement results from leadership amelioration through adaptive leadership. They argue that, in this model, leaders pay specific attention to their openness to change, to understanding a given context, to remaining flexible in the way in which they deal with problems, allowing them to be able not just to think 'outside the box' but also to 'change the box'. According to Glover et al. (2002), adaptive leaders take care to understand the culture of their organisation, whilst simultaneously seeking an adaptive relationship between the organisation and its external environment through creative problem-solving. Alternatively, the adaptive leader balances assimilative and accommodative thinking, acquiring and exhibiting cultural knowledge through information creativity and vision, creating synergy from diversity and anticipating sustainability (Adams 2007). It would appear, in light of the recent and highly publicised corporate scandals of Enron, WorldCom and Tyco (to name a few) that many corporate leaders are not particularly adaptive or highly imbued with vision or notions of sustainability, and if they are, not in a way that is ethically creditable.

Another current leadership theory/style used in the corporate world and receiving substantial research focus is that of transactional and transformational leadership (Bass et al. 1987). Transactional leadership involves a relationship in which the leader contracts or transacts with his/her subordinates to exchange a commodity that is of value to both parties. For instance, the line manager obtains the work efforts and skills of the employee, whilst the employee is given a salary and possible contingent rewards based on his/her performance. However, transactional leadership does not emphasise a relationship between the leader and the follower that address anything more than the pursuit of this transaction. Consequently, it is unlikely that a transactional leader would attempt to develop a mutual or ongoing relationship that lends itself to higher purposes, such as mutual attainment of a shared vision. Thus, according to Adams (2007), transactional leadership is more representative of management than actual leadership; managers are typically concerned with getting the most productivity out of their charges than in helping subordinates achieve their best. On the other hand, transformational leadership occurs when leaders interact with their followers in such a way that a personal transformation can occur which, according to Whittington (2001), involves an increase in both motivation and morality. Effectively transformational leadership involves a covenant relationship rather than a contractual one, which is characterised by reciprocity of interest and mutual vulnerability. Thus, this type of leader or manager would motivate individuals to do more than they initially expected they could do, raising their awareness of the significance of a given outcome. Transformational leaders also inspire a transcendence of self-interest for the good of the organisation by supplying employees with fundamental needs such as support, feeling of purpose, trust and perceived control (Whittington 2001).

According to Adams (2007), transformational leadership is commonly touted as an ethical leadership style. Kanungo (2001) claims that ethical leadership is that which is morally good and is considered morally right as opposed to what is considered legally or procedurally right, and believes that in order to behave ethically, leaders must pay attention to their motives, actions and character, the outcomes of which influence the moral development of both the leader and his/her followers. Moreover, Kanungo (2001) also suggests that, irrespective of the leadership style adopted, the legitimacy and credibility of managers is dependent on the moral standing and legitimacy of his/her views and actions. Thus, transactional leadership style is more likely to be rooted in self-interest, and ethical practices require that self-interest be put behind the interest of the organisation as a whole, so it is difficult to equate transactional leadership with ethical practice. In other words, transactional leaders use control strategies to induce compliance behaviour among their followers and seldom give rise for opportunities for greater autonomy, self-development or self-determination (Bass 1990). Similarly, transformational leaders are often seen as more ethical because they employ more empowering rather than controlling strategies (Kanungo 2001).

The role of line management

Research conducted by Purcell and Hutchinson (2007) on line management behaviour reflects the increasing recognition of the role that line managers play in the management of the employment relationship, in particular in terms of their potential to influence employee attitudes and behaviour. Daniels (2006) asserts that the role of managers and the relationship between employees and their managers can have a significant impact on the job satisfaction as expressed by the employee. Hutchinson and Purcell (2003) found that the behaviour of front-line management has a direct impact on the commitment, motivation and satisfaction reported by employees. They further stated that a poor relationship with a line manager could often be a key reason that employees leave the organisation, but this is not always demonstrated in data collected in exit interviews, because the interviews are often conducted by the line managers. The CIPD 2004 survey suggests that many managers are doing well, in that 63 per cent of employees felt that their immediate manager provided support when necessary 'most of the time'; 47 per cent felt that their manager motivated them to work effectively 'most of the time'; and 45 per cent receive regular feedback on how they are doing. Performance appraisals have a major impact on manager/employee relationships as employees may perceive that feedback and development support is poor, that appraisals can be subjected to management bias and can lack consistency, and that there might be a reluctance by managers to deal with poor performers (Purcell and Hutchinson 2007).

Other research conducted by the CIPD 2004 survey shows that the way front-line managers implement and enact HR policies (or 'bring policies to life') and demonstrate leadership plays a significant part in influencing employees' attitudes towards the organisation, their jobs and organisational performance. Therefore the role of line managers in people management, enacting HR practices and engaging in leadership behaviour means that they explain the relationship between HRM and organisational performance (Purcell and Hutchinson 2007). Employee responses to HRM practices are at the heart of all HRM performance models (Purcell and Kinnie 2006) and corporate responsibility because it is the link between employee reactions and their subsequent behaviour, which is critical.

Social exchanges

When viewed as an exchange, the employment relationship can be characterised as consisting of social and/or economic exchanges (Aryee et al. 2002). According to Blau (1964) social exchanges are 'voluntary actions' which may be initiated by an organisation's treatment of its employees, with the expectation that such treatment will eventually be reciprocated. The treatment can take the form of the implementation of 'soft' or 'high commitment' HRM practices that benefits the well-being of employees who in return display positive work characteristics that results in outcomes that benefits the organisation, such as reduction in sickness, absenteeism and turnover, or increased productivity and performance. Social exchanges describe the interpersonal relationships that exist between managers and subordinates. Research, they suggest, shows that more effectively developed relationships are beneficial for individual and work unit functioning and have many positive outcomes related to firm performance (Uhl-Bien et al. 2000: 138). In organisations, HRM practices are implemented by line managers who manage the workforce for organisational performance. Promoting social relationships by line managers is associated with employee beliefs and attitudes towards their employer, as seen in organisational commitment and job satisfaction (CIPD 2007). Eisenberger et al. (1990) suggest that the process of social exchanges (Blau 2006) is initiated by organisations when 'a general perception concerning the extent to which the organisation values employees' general contributions and cares for their well-being' is achieved. In social exchange, each partner in a relationship must somehow persuade the other of his/her trustworthiness (Haas and Deseran 1981). Trust is regarded as a critical factor underpinning social exchanges in that the act of initiating social exchange relationships requires the originator to trust that the recipient will respond in kind (Blau 2006; Haas and Deseran 1981; Aryee et al. 2002). Similarly, the accountability of corporate responsibility cannot always be measured but relies on the understanding that organisations would implement practices that will benefit their key stakeholders and the community and promote trust and a positive image of the organisation.

Trust in developing social exchange relationships

Trust is regarded as a critical factor underpinning social exchanges in that the act of initiating social exchange relationships requires the originator to trust that the recipient will respond in kind (Blau 1964; Haas and Deseran 1981; Aryee et al. 2002). Mayer et al. (1995) defines trust as the willingness of a party to be vulnerable to the actions of another party, based on the expectations that the recipient will perform a particular action important to the trustor, irrespective of the ability of the trustor to monitor or control the recipient. In the main, the general literature on trust is based on a consensus that trust between individuals and groups within an organisation are a highly important ingredient in the long-term stability and sustainability of the organisation and the well-being of its members (Whitener 2001). Similarly, interpersonal trust at work recognises that with regard to mutually dependent work groups within an organisation, trust may be categorised as: (1) faith in the trustworthy intentions of others, and (2) confidence in the ability of others, yielding ascriptions of capability and reliability.

According to Zeffane and Connell (2003) trust behaviours are those that build on individual confidence and eliminate fear as an operating principle. HRM and the psychological contract (Guest and Conway 1997; Rousseau 2003) suggest that the adoption of policies and practices associated with HRM is instrumental in formulating the psychological contract. Job satisfaction and employee commitment are attitudinal consequence of the psychological contract. Thus, a positive psychological contract assumes production of positive levels of job satisfaction and organisational commitment. The formation of trust within the workplace relationships is complex and elusive. Consequently, while workplace trust is increasingly referred to as necessary for the generation of competitive organisational advantage through support, cooperation and the improvement of coordination mechanisms (Zeffane and Connell 2003), research suggests that employees are becoming less trusting of their managers and employers (Kersley et al. 2006). The trend of declining trust within the workplace can be attributable to the stream of downsizing, restructuring and re-engineering programmes that have severely threatened employees' job security (Marchington and Wilkinson 2005). Consequently, Aryee et al. (2002) propose that managers should strive to develop trust where employees are required to share in cooperative working practices or deal directly with service users. Such views are consistent with those advocating that trust is the 'lubrication that makes it possible for organisations to work' and source of increased efficiency and effectiveness (Zeffane and Connell 2003).

Employees' trust in management

The levels of trust reflect employee loyalty and hence influence a myriad of organisational issues ranging from turnover to pilferage to successful organisational change. Research on trust remains somewhat ambiguous with conceptual challenges in receiving a clear answer to the issue of 'trust in whom?' (Gould-Williams 2002). Characteristics of the trustee/employee relationship highlighted in empirical studies include gender, ethnicity and tenure under a supervisor or manager.

Similarly, minority employees may feel as a function of historical discrimination less comfortable with extending trust to managers (Jackson and Alvarez 1992). According to McGee and Ford (1987), trust is a feature of relationships that forms over time wherein the person attributing trust observes and interacts with the object of trust to achieve a degree of predictability of behaviour. An employee's assessment of layoffs and management turnover are organisational features likely to affect trust. Therefore downsizing in an organisation raises questions amongst employees regarding the justice and administrative skill with which the layoffs are implemented, potentially leading to erosion of trust for managers (Gould-Williams 2004).

Consequently, the employee's subjective perception of the frequency of layoffs forms a conceptually useful indicator of trust. Alternatively, management turnover, whether in the context of downsizing or not, tends to create an atmosphere where it is more difficult to achieve higher levels of employee trust (Podsakoff et al. 1996). Therefore, if employees are treated differently and unfairly this tend to promote deep-seated resentments and alienation. Therefore, the concepts of emotional intelligence (Mayer et al. 1999) emphasised that leadership need to do more listening and responding to their employees and this is closely associated with transformational leadership (Bass 1990) that is considered to be essential for effective change management.

Symbiotic relationship model: HRM, line manager leadership and well-being

Using a mediated model approach, we can illustrate the contribution of the symbiotic relationship that exists in the link between HRM practices, line management leadership practices (social exchanges that promotes support and trust) and employee well-being. As institutional stakeholders, employees have become more pressing in their demands: at the same time companies are required to become more skilled in the use of social reporting through line managers.

Effective line management leadership is likely to result in organisational efficiency. Therefore, HRM practices that are actually implemented by line managers are as a result of their leadership behaviour as part of people management (Purcell and Hutchinson 2007). It is these practices and the way they are implemented in people management that employees perceive and react to. Employees' reactions to these practices are as a result of the interpersonal relationship that exists between the line managers and employees. The two moderating factors that result from this 'relationship' is that of perceived organisational support and trust in management. Therefore, once employees perceive that the organisation corporate approach to their welfare is ethical, fair and socially responsible in their dealings with stakeholders this indicates that the organisation cares about the treatment of its employees. In turn, it is likely that employees will be motivated and eventually reciprocate the organisation's treatment of them. Moreover, employee motivation has been researched by Adam (1997) whose equity theory suggests people will be better motivated if they perceive that they are being treated equitably (fairly) and will be demotivated if they perceive that they are being treated inequitably. Latham and Locke's (1991) goal theory suggests that motivation and performance are directly linked to the goals that have been set. Reviewing the theories of motivation makes clear the variety of factors that might result in the motivation of employees. Thus, understanding how to motivate different employees is a vital part of the process of developing the individual employment relationship, hence the importance of managers being able to understand and embrace this concept.

Once employees are motivated it is likely that they will display positive attitudinal and behavioural characteristics, such as commitment, job satisfaction and work/life balance satisfaction. These three job characteristics, once attained, are holistically known as 'employee well-being'. It is highly likely that at this point of 'well-being' the happiness of workers is promoted and can have a cascading effect on performance outcomes (such as reduction in absenteeism and sickness, and enhanced performance and productivity). Similarly, corporate social responsibility management is where businesses should recognise that their future profitability depends on their willingness to assume the responsibility for the social consequences of their employees and in turn their global footprint (Collier and Esteban 2007; Crowther and Rayman-Bacchus 2004). Thus the symbiotic framework in Figure 8.1 can be used to explore the HRM/line management leadership/employee well-being relationship.

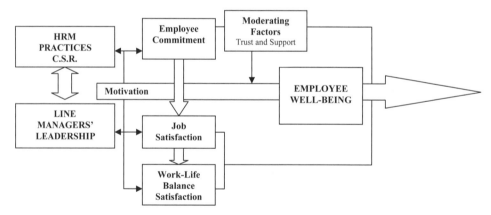

Figure 8.1 Symbiotic relationship model: HRM, line management leadership and employee well-being

Within the frame of reference of HRM, good employees – the 'human capital' – are considered to be the main asset of the organisation. This view is supported by Collier and Esteban (2007) who argue that companies will fail to convince stakeholders (employees) that they are serious about CSR unless they can demonstrate that their policies consistently achieve the desired social, environmental and ethical outcomes. From this point of view, it is only logical that organisations should seek to develop their 'human capital' by convincing employees that the organisation takes seriously threats to global society posed by business activity, and that the social impacts of exploitation and the results of hard choices will be minimised as far as possible. Therefore, it is evident that exposing a key stakeholder (employees) to needless stress and other threats to their well-being would be a foolish form of destruction of this human capital (Schabracq et al. 2003). Therefore, employees' well-being depends to an important extent on the degree to which line managers support workers and promote trust amongst employees. In addition, it also relates to managers behaving corporately responsible as leaders by displaying fairness, justice, honesty, respect and mindfulness as they relate with employees through the employment relationship as they work towards attaining the goals and objectives of the organisation.

It is not expected that all employees will have an understanding of the relational contract (Rousseau 2003) that exists between themselves and their line manager. However, they will be able to relate to the explicit relationship that exists with their line managers in terms of support, feedback, trust, perceived fairness and adequate explanations for job-related decisions (Blau 2006; Gould-Williams 2004). This relationship is what employees will view and perceive as an example of how they are seen by the organisation, which is based on the trust in management, perceived supervisory support and corporate social responsibility management over time. The symbiotic well-being model (Figure 9.1) theorises the importance of line management leadership practices and CSR in the implementation of HRM, which is moderated by support and trust to promote employee well-being. Once employees' expectations are met and 'happiness' results it is likely that employees will be more productive.

Employee well-being: a corporate social responsibility for organisations

The concept of employee well-being promotes the advantages to organisations of having a healthy workforce (Cooper and Robertson 2001). A healthy organisation is critical for survival in this competitive global environment in which we all live, work and operate. For new millennium organisations to be able to remain sustainable it is inevitable that promoting the health and well-being of its employees is a necessary need to enhance performance, and thereby survival and further development of the organisation (Currie 2001). This view is reinforced by Schuster (1998) who maintains that a significant relationship exists between attention to employees and superior organisational performance. Introducing the business case for employee well-being into business is likely to promote positive CSR strategy and an organisational climate that makes room for innovative practices that can produce positive organisational outcomes.[1] Social and economic history shows that it took centuries to develop the employment relationship where the well-being of employees is recognised as an organisational responsibility (Guest 2002; Cooper and Robertson 2001). Stemming from that, the Workplace Employment Relations Survey (WERS) 2004 survey suggests that employees' effective reaction to their work and environment have been a topic of perpetual interest to employers concerned with employment relations (Kersley et al. 2006). The next section discusses the three variables that constitute employee well-being, which are employee commitment, job satisfaction and work/life balance satisfaction.

Employee commitment

Organisational commitment is the heart of human resource management and the central feature that distinguishes HRM from traditional personnel management (Guest 1998). The concept of organisational commitment refers to a person's affective reactions to characteristics of his employing organisation (Cook and Wall 1980). It is concerned with feelings of attachment to the goals and values of the organisation, one's role in relation to this, and attachment to the organisation for its own sake rather than for its strictly instrumental value. The persistence of motivation is sustained by commitment – a force that binds an individual to a course of action that is of relevance to a particular target (Meyer and Herscovitch 2001). Commitment will encourage discretionary behaviours that will result in positive goal outcomes and hence reinforce employee commitment to the organisation. Work on commitment over the last decade has established that commitment can be directed towards various foci such as task, team, customer, career, etc. (Meyer et al. 2004). In the organisational context, commitment takes three forms: affective, normative and continuance. Affective commitment is viewed as an employee's positive attachment to the employing organisation and a willingness to contribute towards the attainment of organisational goals; normative commitment is grounded in the belief that there is an obligation to remain in the organisation; and continuance commitment is concerned with the perceived cost of leaving the organisation (Meyer and Allen 1991). Social exchange theory (Blau 1964) and the norms of reciprocity (Homans 1961) suggest that the commitment of employees to the organisation will be contingent on their perception of the value and benefit they receive from organisational membership (Wayne et al. 1997). This intuition is supported by evidence that high commitment HR practices and trust in management have a major impact on building employee commitment (Whitener 2001). Alternatively, the CSR initiatives and policies in an organisation can impact on

---

1   Historically, in the late nineteenth century employers paid little attention to employee well-being, though there are some exceptions in employers (the Quaker Cadbury family and the Lever Brothers) who generally cared about employees' well-being and introduced practices that assisted employees in the workplace and life outside work (Newell 2002). In contrast, most employers at that time held a different view and regarded employees as a necessary but burdensome financial evil: this was a far more frequent phenomenon (Currie 2001).

the organisation context, shape employee perceptions and thereby affect employee commitment and hence motivation.

Corporate culture flows from, and is the consequence of, corporate identity and is the fundamental style, quality, character and personality of an organisation, and it defines, motives and embodies the business mix, management styles, communication polices and practices, competences and competitive distinction (Downey 1986: 7). Therefore executives should assume responsibility and be proactive in ensuring ethical behaviour in their management practices. Therefore if top management is genuinely committed to ethical activity, they will seek to carry employees with them and to embed ethics policy in processes, practices and performance appraisal (Collier and Esteban 2007). People are an organisation's most important asset and their effective development and deployment offers a distinctive and non-imitable competitive advantage through employer and employee engagement. We now move on to job satisfaction.

Job satisfaction

Research conducted by the Economic and Social Research Council's (ESRC) Future at Work programme (Taylor 2002) found that a marked decline has taken place in levels of worker satisfaction and summed up that today's world of work is much less satisfying to employees than the one they were experiencing ten years ago. The Work Foundation warns that UK employees are becoming more critical of UK employers, producing a downward slide of satisfaction and effort. Alternatively, more recent research conducted by WERS 2004 suggested variable responses. Jernigan et al. (2002) assert that work satisfaction is one's sense of satisfaction not only with work but also with the larger organisational context within which work exists. Job satisfaction is more narrowly defined as a pleasurable or positive emotional state resulting from the appraisal of one's job or job experiences (Locke and Latham 1990). With this in mind, Fisher et al. (2004) claim that job satisfaction is the total of positive feelings associated with the rewarding aspects of a job that can intuitively lead to improved work performance. Currie (2001) suggests that satisfaction is related to the degree to which an individual is satisfied with the terms and conditions of employment and the factors that make up the physical work environment. For example, individuals may be satisfied with their salaries and how well they get on with their peers and work, or are satisfied with company policy. Therefore, job satisfaction and job involvement are attitudes which are determined by individual's perceptions of their total job situations, including the physical work environment, the terms and conditions of their employment and the degree to which they are given autonomy, responsibility, authority and empowerment in their jobs (Kersley et al. 2006). Alternatively, Tomer (2001) suggests that organisations wishing to implement high performance work systems (HPWS) pay attention to behaviour economics, which recognises that human input into any system is more complicated than the traditional motivational systems used by many organisations. Therefore for modern organisations to accurately access their human capital they need to invest time and resources into developing systems that actually help to enhance employee satisfaction, well-being and empowerment. We now move to the third factor which constitutes employee well-being.

Work/life balance satisfaction

The changing world of work has presented several challenges to the wide-ranging discourse of work/life balance. There are various social, political and economic changes that have served to raise the profile of work/life balance in workplaces (Daniels and French 2006). The changing demographic composition of the labour market, especially increasing female participation, has undoubtedly served to raise the tricky issue of balancing working lives outside household tasks (Houston 2005). According to Schmidt and Duenas (2002) the increasing numbers of dual-income families in which both partners work a greater number of hours per week than did their parents means that in excess of 66 per cent of people now have trouble balancing their work and home lives. Moreover, other researchers (Stevens et al. 2004) put this figure at closer to 80 per cent. Bratton and Gold (2003) define work/life balance as the need to 'balance work and leisure/family activities'. The leisure activities might include such things as the desire to travel, to be involved in community activities and the need to care for older relatives. This is further supported by Platt (1997) who suggests that a happy medium needs to be found between the demands of work and home and argues that there needs to be a 'balance' between work and life. According to the WERS 2004 survey an increasing number of employers have sought to address employment inequality since 1998 and this type of activity is still heavily concentrated in the public sector, larger workplaces and in workplaces with recognised unions (Kersley et al. 2006). However, unfortunately because of the predominant attitude that 'face-time' at work equals productivity, when people make efforts to redress this imbalance by taking more regular leave or refusing to work overtime, they are often punished indirectly for their perceived lack of dedication through the reduced likelihood of seniority, promotion or benefits (Schmidt and Duenas 2002).

The social and economic problems brought on by longer working hours, workplace stress, reduced health, the prevalence of work/life imbalance and its negative financial consequences has attracted the attention of both researchers and organisations. According to Wax (2004), workplaces need to be more sensitive to the needs of their employees as there is a greater need for highly skilled employees in the modern workplace and it is necessary for these people to interact effectively in order for the organisation to work successfully. Thus, it is likely that employee effectiveness can be generated through the promotion of employee well-being, which is the ethical and corporate responsibility of organisations. However, limitations such as hierarchical company structures and competition amongst workers for limited senior positions do not engender cooperation (Wax 2004). Therefore, when employees are forced to compete for advancement and when managers assume that company loyalty and employee productivity can be measured by the amount of time an employee spends at work, it is unlikely that the organisation will operate successfully, and there is a substantially increased likelihood of employee dissatisfaction (Adams 2007). Consequently, Wax (2004) believes that it is essential for managers to understand the consequences of this 'rat race' by realising that non-economic gains, such as workplace satisfaction and a consequent lower employee turnover, can in fact be profitable. Therefore, by decreasing reliance on escalating rewards, a hierarchical company structure, tournament-style promotion, and by increasing awareness of the work/life imbalance, senior management can embrace and implement their corporate responsibility towards enhancing employee well-being.

Conclusion

In conclusion, a question lingers: does it matter how managers treat their workers? Organisations and management make hundred of choices every day that have some influence on the lives and well-being of other people. Work in the UK may affect others in Europe, US and developing countries like India, China, Africa or the Caribbean, to name a few.

Bill Clinton, the former US president, speaking at the Dimbleby lecture (2001), highlighted some uncomfortable facts:

> In the twenty-first century, half the people on earth live on less than two dollars a day. ... A billion people live on less than a dollar a day ... while a billion people go to bed hungry every night and a billion and a half people – one quarter of the people on earth – never get a clean glass of water.

Corporate behaviour is more in the public domain in the twenty-first century than ever before. The mission statement of the code of practice will no longer be able to conceal corporate indifference to matters of social responsibility. Modern organisations are recognising that their actions and functions can move into the public domain faster than ever before. Therefore the subject of business ethics has been moving up the organisational agenda because bad publicity can adversely impact on sales and profits (Nieto 2006). Therefore the improvement in global communication has enabled consumers, employees and stakeholders to be more aware of how organisations behave. Furthermore, the increased knowledge of workers results in greater expectations and they are more likely to express a preference as to which organisation they can feel comfortable about. Based on this view, Nieto (2006) argues that in reality when there is more choice, matters of corporate behaviour rise further into the consumer's calculations.

Features of HR and organisational conduct is depicted by legislation where organisations have to comply with laws in areas such as discrimination, working conditions and minimum rates of pay. Similarly, practices like line management leadership behaviour can also be considered as ethical practices undertaken by an organisation. However, it would be unrealistic to suggest that because the law exists and modern organisations embrace 'best practice' that all organisational misbehaviour has disappeared. The application of business ethics accepts the minimum standards of caring for the interests of the organisation's stakeholders. This relationship between the organisation and stakeholders according to Crowther (2006) is referred to as corporate social responsibility, which embraces the concept that organisations have responsibilities regarding their behaviour to a range of stakeholders, internal and external, that are directly or indirectly affected by what they do and how they conduct their business (Crowther and Raymond-Bacchus 2004). Nieto (2006) suggests that this includes organisations in private, public, not-for-profit and non-governmental organisations.

In reality, there is no 'one size fits all'; instead each organisation has to reflect on what it believes to be the most appropriate action in each situation, taking care to promote organisational behaviour that will encourage the well-being of workers. Hence, it is important for managers to address the key issues of business ethics and corporate responsibility. Research by Trevino et al. (2003) indicated that ethical leadership requires more than personal integrity; it involves using the communication and the reward systems to guide ethical behaviour. Therefore, modern organisations cannot afford to ignore an increasingly informed public, which has become more proactive in vocalising displeasure regarding organisations that fail to perform in an ethical manner. Indeed, it is likely that consumer boycotts and political lobbying have played a part in making senior managers much more sensitive to their internal and external stakeholders. Thus, organisations, which might have regarded business ethics and employee well-being as a matter of second strategic importance have recognised the need to rethink their outlook.

References

Adams, J. (2007), *Managing People in Organisations: Contemporary Theory and Practice*, New York: Palgrave Macmillan.

Andrews, K.R. (2003), 'Ethics in practice', in B. Breeze, *Race to the Top: How Government, Business and Consumers can Drive Corporate Social Responsibility*, London: Social Market Foundation, pp 67–83.

Appelbaum, E., Bailey, T., Berg, P. and Kalleberg, A. (2000), *A Manufacturing Competitive Advantage: The Effects of High Performance Work Systems on Plant Performance and Company Outcomes*, New York: Cornell University Press.

Aryee, S., Budhwar, P.S. and Chen, Z.X. (2002), 'Trust as a mediator of the relationship between organisational justice and work outcomes: test of a social exchange model', *Journal of Organisational Behaviour*, 23 (3), 267–85.

Bass, B.M. (1990), 'From transactional to transformational leadership: learning to share the vision', *Organisational Dynamics*, 18 (3), 19–31.

Bass, B.M., Waldman, D.A., Avolio, B.J. and Bebb, M. (1987), 'Transformational leadership and the falling dominoes effect', *Group and Organisational Studies*, 12 (1), 73–87.

Belal, A. (2002), 'Stakeholder accountability or stakeholder management: a review of U.K. firms' social and ethical accounting, auditing and reporting (SEAAR) practices', *Corporate Social Responsibility and Environment Management*, 9, 8–25.

Blau, P.M. (2006), *Exchange and Power in Social Life*, with new introduction by the author, 10th edn, London: Transaction.

Blau, P.M. (1964), *Exchange and Power in Social Life*, New York: Wiley.

Boxall, P. (1996), 'The strategic HRM debate and the resource-based view of the firm', *Human Resource Management Journal*, 6 (3), 59–75.

Bramley, P. (2003), *Evaluating Training*, London: CIPD.

Bratton, J., and Gold, J. (2003), *Human Resource Management: Theory and Practice*, 3rd edn, Basingstoke: Palgrave.

Cerin, P. (2002), 'Communication in corporate environmental reports', *Corporate Social Responsibility and Environmental Management*, 9, 46–66.

Chartered Institute of Personnel Development (CIPD) (2007), *Rewarding Work – The Vital Role of Line Managers, Change Agenda*, London: CIPD.

Chartered Institute of Personnel Development (CIPD) (2004), *Flexible Working and Paternity Leave, Survey Report*, London: CIPD.

Clinton, B. (2001), *The Struggle for the Soul of the 21st Century*, The Dimbleby Lecture, 14 December, available at <http://www.bbc.co.uk/arts/news_comment/dimbleby/print_clinton.shtml>, accessed 20 April 2007.

Collier, J. and Esteban, R. (2007), 'Corporate Social Responsibility and Employee Commitment', *Business Ethics: A European Review*, 16 (1), 19–33.

Cook, J., and Wall, T. (1980), 'New work attitude measure of trust, organisational commitment and personal need non-fulfilment', *Journal of Occupational Psychology*, 53, 39–52.

Cooper, C. and Robertson, I. (2001), *Well-Being in Organisations: A Reader for Students and Practitioners*, Chichester: Wiley.

Cox, R.A.F., Edwards, F.C. and Palmer, K. (2005), *Fitness for Work: The Medical Aspects*, 3rd edn, Oxford: Oxford University Press.

Crowther, D. (2006), 'Standards of corporate social responsibility: convergence within the European Union', in D. Njavro and K. Krkac (eds), *Business Ethics and Corporate Social Responsibility*, Mate d.o.o. Publishes, Zagreb School of Economics and Management, Croatia, pp 17–34.

Crowther, D. (2002), *A Social Critique of Corporate Reporting*, Aldershot: Ashgate.

Crowther, D. and Çalıyurt, K.T. (2004), 'Corporate social responsibility improves profitability', in D. Crowther and K.T. Çalıyurt (eds), *Stakeholder and Social Responsibility*, Penang: Ansted University Press, pp 243–66.

Crowther, D. and Rayman-Bacchus, L. (2004), 'Introduction: Perspectives on Corporate Social Responsibility', in D. Crowther and L. Rayman-Bacchus, *Perspectives on Corporate Social Responsibility*, Aldershot: Ashgate, pp 1–19.

Currie, D. (2001), *Managing Employee Well-Being*, Oxford: Chandos.

Daniels, G. and French, S. (2006), *Regulating Work-Life Balance*, Keele: Centre for Industrial Relations, Keele University.

Daniels, K. (2006), *Employee Relations in an Organisational Context*, London: CIPD.

Davenport, T. (1999), *Human Capital*, San Francisco: Jossey-Bass.

De Wit, B. and Meyer, R. (2004), *Strategy: Process, Content, Context*, London: Thomson International Business Press.

Doukakis, I.P., (2004), 'The rhetoric and reality of corporate social responsibility from the perspective of the stakeholder model: balancing interests or window dressing?', in D. Crowther and K.T. Çalıyurt (eds), *Stakeholders and Social Responsibility*, Penang: Ansted Service Centre, pp 74–92.

Downey, S. (1986) 'The relationship between corporate culture and corporate identity', *Public Relations Quarterly*, 31 (4), 7–13.

Eisenberger, R., Fasolo, P. and Davis-Lamastro, V. (1990), 'Perceived organisational support and employee diligence, commitment and innovation', *Journal of Applied Psychology*, 75 (1), 51–9.

Fisher, C., Harris, L., Kirk, S., Leopold, J. and Leverment, Y. (2004), 'The dynamics of modernisation and job satisfaction in the British National Health Service', *Review of Public Personnel Administration*, 24 (4), 304–18.

Fombrum, C. (1996), *Reputation: Realizing Value for the Corporate Image*, Harvard MA: Harvard Business School Press.

Friedman, M. (1993), 'The social responsibility of business is to increase its profits', *The New York Times Magazine*, 13 September 1970. Reprinted in G. Chryssides and J. Kaler (eds), *An Introduction to Business Ethics*, London: Chapman and Hall.

Gallie, D., Felstead, A. and Green, F. (2001), 'Employer policies and organisational commitment in Britain 1992–1997', *Journal of Management Studies*, 38 (8), 1081–1101.

Glover, J., Friedman, H. and Jones, G. (2002), 'Adaptive leadership: when change is not enough (Part One)', *Organisational Development Journal*, 20 (2), 15–32.

Gould-Williams, J. (2004), 'The effects of high commitment HRM practices on employee attitude: the views of public sector workers', *Public Administration*, 82 (1), pp 63–81.

Gould-Williams, J. (2002), *The Extent to which HR Practices are Utilised within Local Government Departments: a Preliminary Study*, Cardiff: Local and Regional Government Research Unit, Cardiff University.

Grant, D. and Shields, J. (2002), 'In search of the subject: researching employee reactions to human resource management', *Journal of Industrial Relations*, 44 (3), 313–334.

Guest, D. (2002), 'Human resource management, corporate performance and employee well-being: building the worker into HRM', *The Journal of Industrial Relations*, 44 (3), 335–58.

Guest, D. (2001), 'Human resource management and performance: a review and research agenda', *International Journal of Human Resource Management*, 8 (3), 263–76.

Guest, D. (1999), 'Human resource management: the workers' verdict', *Human Resource Management Journal*, 9 (3), 5–25.

Guest, D. (1998), 'Is the psychological contract worth taking seriously?', *Journal of Organisational Behaviour*, 19, 649–64.

Guest, D. and Conway, N. (2001), *The Employer's Side of the Psychological Contract*, London: CIPD.

Guest, D. and Conway, N. (1997), *Employee Motivation and the Psychological Contract*, London: CIPD.

Guest, D., Jonathan, M., Conway, N. and Sheehan, M., (2003), 'Human resource management and corporate performance in the UK', *British Journal of Industrial Relations*, 41 (2), 291–314.

Guzzo, R.A. and Noonan, K.A. (1994), 'Human resource practices as communications and the psychological contract', *Human Resource Management*, 33 (3), 447–62.

Haas, D.F. and Deseran, F.A. (1981), 'Trust and symbolic exchange', *Social Psychology Quarterly*, 44 (1), 3–13.

Health and Safety Executive (2006), *Health and Safety Statistics Highlights, 2005/2006*, London: HSE.

Hendry, J. (2004), *Between Enterprise and Ethics, Business and Management in a Bimoral Society*, Oxford: Oxford University Press.

Holman, D., Wall, T., Clegg, C., Sparrow, P. and Howard, A. (2003), *The New Workplace: A Guide to the Human Impact of Modern Working Practices*, London: Wiley.

Holme, R. and Watts, P. (2000), *Corporate Social Responsibility: Making Good Business Sense*, Geneva: World Business Council for Sustainable Development.

Homans, G.C. (1961), *Social Behaviour*, New York: Harcourt, Brace and World.

Houston, D.M. (2005), *Work-Life Balance in the 21st Century*, New York: Palgrave Macmillan.

Huselid, M.A. (1995), 'The impact of human resource management practices on turnover, productivity and corporate financial performance', *Academy of Management Journal*, 38 (3), 635–72.

Hutchinson, S. and Purcell, L. (2003), *Bringing Policies to Life: the Vital Role of Line Managers in People Management*, London: CIPD.

IRS (2002), 'Corporate accountability', *IRS Employment Review*, no. 756, 22 July, 612.

Jackson, S. and Alvarez, E. (1992), 'Working through diversity as a strategic imperative', in S. Jackson (ed.), *Diversity in the Workplace: Human Resource Initiatives*, New York: Guilford Press, pp 13–29.

Jernigan, I.E., Beggs, J.M. and Kohut, G.F. (2002), 'Dimensions of work satisfaction as predictors of commitment type', *Journal of Managerial Psychology*, 17 (7), 564–79.

Kanungo, R.N. (2001), 'Ethical values of transactional and transformational leaders', *Canadian Journal of Administrative Sciences*, 18 (4), 257–65.

Kersley, B., Alpin, C., Forth, J., Bryson, A., Bewley, H., Dix, G. and Oxenbridge, S. (2006), *Inside the Workplace: Findings from the 2004 Workplace Employment Relations Survey*, London: Routledge, Taylor and Francis Group.

Kline, J.M. (2005), *Ethics for International Business: Decision-Making in a Global Political Economy*, London: Routledge.

Latham, G.P. and Locke, E.A. (1991), 'Self-regulation through goal setting', *Organisational Behaviour and Human Decision Processes*, 50, 212–247.

Lawrence, F. (2002), 'Sweatshop campaigners demand Gap boycott', *The Guardian*, 22 November.

Lefkowitz, J. (2006), 'The constancy of ethics amidst the changing world of work', *Human Resource Management Review*, 16, 245–68.

Legge, K. (1995), 'HRM: rhetoric, reality and hidden agendas', in J. Storey (ed.), *Human Resource Management: A Critical Text*, London: Routledge, pp 33–61.

Liff, S. (2003), 'The industrial relations of a diverse workforce', in P. Edwards (ed.), *Industrial Relations: Theory and Practice*, Oxford: Blackwell.

Ligteringen, E. and Zadek, S. (2007), 'The future of corporate responsibility codes, standards and frameworks, an executive briefing by the Global Reporting Initiatives and AccountAbility', available at <http://www.globalreporting.org/NR/rdonlyres/19BBA6F5-9337-42B0-B66D-A3B45F591938/0/LigteringenZadekFutureOfCR.pdf >, accessed 18 April 2007.

Lindsay, C. and Doyle, P. (2003), 'Experimental consistent time series of historical Labour Force Survey data', *Labour Market Trends*, 111 (9), 467–75.

Locke, E.A. and Latham, G.P. (1990), *A Theory of Goal-Setting and Task Performance*, Englewood Cliffs NJ: Prentice Hall.

Lucas, R., Lupton, B. and Mathieson, H. (2006), *Human Resource Management in an International Context*, London: CIPD.

MacDonald, L.A.C. (2005), *Wellness at Work: Protecting and Promoting Employee Well-Being*, London: CIPD.

McGee, G. and Ford, R. (1987), 'Two (or more?) dimensions of organisational commitment', *Journal of Applied Psychology*, 72, 638–41.

Marchington, M. and Wilkinson, A. (2005), *Human Resource Management at Work: People Management and Development*, London: CIPD.

Mayer, R.C., Davis, J.H. and Schoorman, F.D. (1995), 'An integrative model of organisational trust', *Academy of Management Review*, 20, 709–34.

Meyer, J.P. and Allen, N.J. (1997), *Commitment in the Workplace: Theory, Research, and Application*, London: Sage.

Meyer, J.P. and Allen, N.J. (1991), 'A three-component conceptualisation of organisational commitment', *Human Resource Management Journal*, 1 (1), 61–91.

Meyer, J.P. and Herscovitch, L. (2001), 'Commitment in the workplace: toward a general model', *Human Resource Management Review*, 11, 299–326.

Meyer, J.P., Becker, T.E. and Vandeberghe, C. (2004), 'Employee commitment and motivation: a conceptual analysis and integrative model', *Journal of Applied Psychology*, 89 (6), 991–1007.

Morand, M. and Rayman-Bacchus, L. (2006), 'Think global, act local: corporate social responsibility management in multinational companies', *Social Responsibility Journal*, 2 (3/4), 261–72.

Mullins, L. (2004), *Management and Organisational Behaviour*, 7th edn, London: FT/Pitman, London.

Newell, S. (2002), *Creating the Healthy Organisation: Well-being, Diversity and Ethics at Work*, London: Thomson Learning.

Nieto, M.L. (2006), *An Introduction to Human Resource Management: An Integrated Approach*, New York: Palgrave Macmillan.

Peccei, R. (2004), 'Human resource management and the search for the happy workplace', inaugural address, Erasmus Research Institute of Management, Erasmus University, Rotterdam.

Peccei, R. and Guest, D. (1998), 'The dimensionally and stability of organisational commitment', Discussion article no. 149, Centre for Economic Performance, London School of Economics, London.

Pfeffer, J. (2005), 'Producing sustainable competitive advantage through effective management of people', *Academy of Management Executive*, 19 (4), 95–108.

Platt, L. (1997), 'Employee work-life balance: the competitive advantage', in F. Hesselbein, M. Goldsmith and R. Beckhard, *The Drucker Foundation: The Organisation of the Future*, San Francisco: Jossey-Bass.

Podsakoff, P., MacKenzie, S. and Bommer, W. (1996), 'Transformational leader behaviours and substitutes for leadership as determinants of employee satisfaction, commitment, trust and organisational citizenship behaviours', *Journal of Management*, 2, 259–98.

Purcell, J. (2004), 'Business strategies and human resource management: uneasy bedfellows or strategy partners?', working paper presented at the international seminar on HRM, *What's Next?*, organised by Erasmus University Rotterdam, June 2004.

Purcell, J. and Hutchinson, S. (2007), 'Front-line managers as agents in the HRM-performance causal chain: theory, analysis and evidence', *Human Resource Management Journal*, 17 (1), 3–20.

Purcell, J. and Kinnie, N. (2006), 'HRM and business performance', in P. Boxall, J. Purcell and P. Wright (eds), *The Oxford Handbook of Human Resource Management*, Oxford: Oxford University Press.

Purcell, M., Kinnie, N., Hutchinson, S., Rayton, B. and Swart, J. (2003), *Understanding the People and Performance Link: Unlocking the Black Box*, Research Report, London: CIPD.

Reichers, A.E. (1985), 'A review and reconceptualisation of organisational commitment', *Academy of Management Review*, 10, 465–76.

Rousseau, D.M. (2003), 'Extending the psychology of the psychological contract: a reply to putting psychology back into psychological contracts', *Journal of Management Inquiry*, 12 (3), 229–38.

Schabracq, M.J., Winnubst, J.A.M. and Cooper, C.L. (2003) *The Handbook of Work and Health Psychology*, 2nd edn, Chichester: Wiley.

Schaltegger, S., Muller, K. and Hindrichsen, H. (1996), *Corporate Environmental Accounting*, Chichester: Wiley.

Schmidt, D.E. and Duenas, G. (2002), 'Incentives to encourage worker-friendly organisations', *Public Personnel Management*, 31 (3), 293–308.

Schuster, F.E. (1998) *A Strategy for High Commitment and Involvement: Employee Centred Management*, London: Quorum.

Snape, E. and Redman, T. (2003), 'An evaluation of a three-component model of occupational commitment: dimensionality and consequences among United Kingdom human resource management specialists', *Journal of Applied Psychology*, 88 (1), 152–9.

Stevens, J., Brown, J. and Lee, C. (2004), *The Second Work-Life Balance Study: Results from the Employees' Survey*, London: Department of Trade and Industry.

Storey, J. (1995), *Human Resource Management: A Critical Text*, London: Routledge.

Taylor, R. (2002), *Britain's World of Work – Myths and Realities*, Swindon: ESRC.

Tomer, J.F. (2001), 'Understanding high performance work systems: the joint contribution of economics and human resource management', *Journal of Socio-Economics*, 30 (1), 63–73.

Trevino, L.K., Brown, M. and Hartman, L.P.A. (2003), 'Qualitative investigation of perceived executive ethical leadership: perceptions from inside and outside the executive suite', *Human Relations*, 1 January.

Uhl-Bien, M., Graen, G. and Scandura, L. (2000). 'Indicators of leader-member exchange (LMX) for strategic human resource management systems', *Research in Personnel and Human Resources Management*, 18, 137–85.

Wax, A.L. (2004) 'Family-friendly workplace reform: prospects for change', *Annals of the American Academy of Political and Social Science*, 596 (1), 36–61.

Wayne, S.J., Shore, I.M. and Liden, R.C. (1997), 'Perceived organisation support and leader-member exchange: a social exchange perspective', *Academy of Management Journal*, 40 (1), 82–111.

Whitener, E.M. (2001), 'Do "high commitment" human resource practices affect employee commitment? A cross-level analysis using hierarchical linear modelling', *Journal of Management*, 27 (5), 515–535.

Whittington, J.L. (2001), 'Corporate executives as beleaguered rulers: the leader's motive matters', *Problems and Perspectives in Management*, 3, 163–9.

Williams, L.J. and Anderson, S.E. (1991) 'Job satisfaction and organisational commitment as predictors of organisational citizenship and in-role behaviours', *Journal of Management*, 17, 601–17.

Winstanley, D. and Woodall, J. (2000), 'The ethical dimension of human resource management', *Human Resource Management Journal*, 10 (2), 5–20.

Wood, S. (1999), 'Human resource management and performance', *International Journal of Management Reviews*, 1 (4), 367–413.

Wood, S. and Albanese, M.T. (1995), 'Can you speak of a high commitment management on the shop floor?', *Journal of Management Studies*, 32 (2), 215–247.

Wright, T. and Bonett, D. (1993), 'Role of employee coping and performance in voluntary employee withdrawal', *Journal of Management*, 14, 147–61.

Zeffane, R. and Connell, J. (2003), 'Trust and HRM in the new millennium', *International Journal of Human Resource Management*, 14 (1), 3–11.

Protect your Whistleblowers!

Wim Vandekerckhove

Introduction

Whistleblowing is the deliberate, non-obligatory act of disclosure, by an individual with privileged access to data or information of an organization, about a non-trivial illegality or other wrongdoing under the control of that organization, to an entity who has the power to rectify the wrongdoing. The growing number of whistleblowing policies implemented by organizations and enacted by governments have made the question whether or not that entity is internal or external to the organization less of an issue. Whistleblowing policies protect whistleblowers from retaliation under certain conditions. These conditions are stipulated in the whistleblowing policy. More precisely, whistleblowing policies specify who can make a protected disclosure (actor), about what disclosures can be made (subject), and to whom the disclosure should be made (recipient).

The protection of whistleblowers against organizational retaliation became an issue in the early 1970s, as a protest against the ethos of the 'organization man', which demanded absolute loyalty of the employee to the employer. Whistleblower activism denounced organizational closure and advocated that public interest should at all times take priority over an organization's interest in secrecy. A lot has changed since the early 1970s. Managers and auditors now start to recognize the value of procedures that allow concerns to be raised inside the organization rather than force responsible employees to go outside. And governments increasingly prescribe whistleblowing policies through legislation. Today, there are whistleblowing laws not only in the US, but also very important ones in Australia, the UK, South Africa, New Zealand, Japan and Belgium. Law proposals are being discussed in the Netherlands, Canada, Ireland and India. In many more countries, discussions towards legislation are under way.

This chapter shows why whistleblowing policies are a CSR practice. It offers arguments for organizations to implement procedures that allow and protect internal and external disclosures.

I also offer an overview of the research on whistleblowing. Change in research focus has had an impact on whistleblowing advocacy. It has certainly helped to clear out some misunderstandings about whistleblowers and has made the issue of protection and internal procedures accepted by management.

Nevertheless, some issues remain unsettled and this chapter closes with a discussion of some of those issues. For example, while most whistleblowing policies require disclosures to be made in good faith, it remains troublesome to defend this requirement. As whistleblowing policies are being implemented all over the world, the question to what extent cultural differences are restraining factors is an important but yet unresolved issue. Finally, whilst most internal procedures have been set up to receive anonymous disclosures, Europe seems to be heading in a different direction by preferring confidential disclosures to anonymous ones. The reasons for that are quite convincing; the responsibilities, however, are bigger as well.

Why are whistleblowing policies a form of CSR practice?

Although whistleblowing is always a matter of individual responsibility, having adequate whistleblowing procedures and policies is a matter of corporate social responsibility. This is so in at least two ways.

The first way that whistleblowing policies appear as a CSR practice is when we take a network perspective on the organization. To take such a perspective implies focusing on the interactions between organizational departments, between individuals within organizational departments, and between organizations. A central concern from the network perspective is how the pattern of interactions among these multiple actors affects the behaviour of members of the network. The overall pattern of interactions – the network pattern[1] – provides opportunities for and constraints on specific actions. If we would argue the ethicality of a particular organizational network, we would do so by pointing to the level of trust that exists between the different network participants. The participants are autonomous but interdependent actors. It is the level of trust between such actors that not only makes the network productive but also makes the participation worthwhile and fulfilling for the actors. Hence, a high level of trust in a network has both instrumental as well as intrinsic value and is therefore ethical.

Calton and Lad (1995) have argued that creating and maintaining trust within a network requires network governance, which amounts to institutional structures that are able to recognize and compensate the existence of power differentials. Corporate governance codes are an example of this. What corporate governance does is stipulate how management, board, shareholders and (to some extent) employees relate to one another within the organizational network. Corporate governance codes are important designers of the formal organization. They stipulate who gets and gives what information to whom, under what conditions a particular actor can question another actor's actions, and define the elbowroom for each actor. One of the concrete aims of corporate governance is to reduce

---

1   A network pattern can be determined in terms of densities (how many connections are there, how frequent, and how can they be characterized), trends (time-dimension) and processes (what interactions are presupposed in other interactions).

information asymmetries within organizational networks. The notion of 'imperfect information' is central to the theory of asymmetry of information (Sandmo 1999; Stiglitz 2000). Imperfect information reflects and results in an unequal power balance between actors in a network. The information can be imperfect in three ways – and hence give rise to three information asymmetries: (1) the information can be incomplete, (2) the receiver might be unable to interpret the information or there might be an information overload, (3) the information can be wrong. If we could have an institutional structure that can reduce the risk of information asymmetry, actors within the network could trust that the information they get is complete and accurate. Hence, to have such structure would amount to more ethical organizational networks. A whistleblowing procedure or policy is precisely such an institutional structure, able to create a power balance by identifying what asymmetries of information need to be balanced and how.

A second way in which whistleblowing procedures and policies appear as a CSR practice starts from the Aristotelian notion of *telos*, or 'purpose'. Robert Solomon (1993) argues that the social responsibilities of corporations are their very point of existence, because the purpose of business is to do what business has always been meant to do, which is to 'enrich society as well as the pockets of those who are responsible for the enriching' (Solomon 1993: 181). Solomon envisages responsibility and excellence as corporate virtues. Solomon states that excellence is to be measured by its *telos* or purpose and that the excellent corporation entails both cooperation and competition to the extent that they represent a contribution to the larger whole. But excellence is 'not skill for its own sake' (Solomon 1993: 159). Seen like that, market competition is secondary to external requirements and standards that point at the place of business as a practice in the larger whole – society. Solomon distinguishes goals from purposes. Business as a practice has a purpose, and goals are internal to the practice. The purpose of a practice is the reason for engaging in the practice. But the goals are defined and structured by the practice itself. Solomon explains this by giving the example of a football game. The purpose of the game is to kill time, but the goal of the game is to get the ball across a certain line more times than the other team. If in business goals would gain priority over purpose, then business is no longer regarded as a practice but rather as a game.[2] However: 'Business is not an isolated game, which the public may play if it will, and the point is not just to win, for the impact on the non-players is typically greater than the rewards for the participants' (Solomon 1993: 123). Hence, it is impact – and those who experience that impact are the stakeholders – that renders the practice of business a social responsibility. Its purpose refers to its place *in* society, and it is to produce and distribute goods and services that make life easier.

---

2   Solomon insists that game theory is not just a model for business, but an ideology because it is instructive. 'But however enticing the paradoxes of formalism (and they are indeed captivating), it is a mistake to think that by solving technical problems in a theory that is already off the mark we will thereby resolve the criticism that it is indeed off the mark' (Solomon 1993: 64).

Its social responsibility is to have a beneficial impact on society by meeting that purpose. The extent to which business is able to do so, is the level of its excellence.

So where does a whistleblowing policy fit in? Solomon notes that 'there is an unavoidable shift from ultimate purposes to internal goals, and the danger is that specific tasks and duties will eclipse the overall purposes of business altogether' (Solomon 1993: 262). Whistleblowing procedures and policies then, serve society by warning societal stakeholders when business goals are taking precedence over business purpose or, in other words, when the organization is off-track with regard to its *telos*, to bring about general prosperity. Hence, organizations that have whistleblowing procedures and policies in place guarantee society that there is a fall-back mechanism that will warn society should the organization fail to keep itself focused on its purpose. There lies the corporate social responsibility of whistleblowing procedures and policies.

The first way in which whistleblowing policies appear as a CSR practice concerns internal relations within an organization, and the second way concerns relations between the organization and society. True, perceiving organizations as networks blurs the organizational borders and hence makes the inside/outside distinction somewhat problematic. Still, a whistleblowing policy stipulates which network participants it recognizes as the whistleblower and as the recipient. In other words, it differentiates between stakeholders. Some are welcomed to raise concerns, some are appointed as receivers of 'bad news' whilst many others are not. In this sense, we can look at whistleblowing policies to find out who is to be considered 'inside' and who 'outside'.

A perspective that is driven by the inside/outside distinction is the systems perspective. An organization is a system and as a system it distinguishes itself from its environment. For Luhmann, the organization is an autopoietic system, which means that the organization reproduces itself as an organization through decisions (Luhmann 2000). Luhmann writes that organizations make self-descriptions, centralizing and bundling constantly occurring self-references, and having the function of making clear that it is always the same 'self', that it is always about a system which is identical to itself. And this self-description serves the system – the organization – as an official thought culture (*offizielle Gedenkkultur*), which can be communicated. More precisely, these communications are the organization's identity. Luhmann writes that organizations have no bodies, but they have text (Luhmann 2000: 422). Weick, too, has a similar view on the matter. He states that organizations are 'built, maintained, and activated through the medium of communication' (Weick 2001: 136). Communication can either strengthen the organization or make it more tenuous. But what shapes the interpretation process is shared language, authority relationships that assign rights of interpretation, norms of communication, and the communication itself. And this is the same for any organization, whether it is an NGO, government agency or corporation. This is why with regard to the issue of whistleblowing, it is perhaps more appropriate to speak of 'organizational social responsibility' rather than 'corporate social responsibility'.

The systems perspective, as described above, is very important to the issue of whistleblowing and the protection of whistleblowers through whistleblowing procedures and policies. Every act of whistleblowing involves a communication about the organization or about what is happening under the control of the organization. Very often, what whistleblowers communicate is that the organization is not identical to itself – in other words, it is doing one thing and saying another. The need for whistleblower protection shows that, indeed, organizations reproduce themselves through an official self-description that does not welcome dissent. The corporate and administrative scandals of the past and the present, however, show that the inside/outside differentiation can be very problematic for the outside, the society. This was precisely the issue when whistleblower activism first rose in the early 1970s. The call for protection of whistleblowers constituted a protest against organizational closure and thus against an absolute differentiation between organization and society, between inside and outside. Proponents of whistleblower protection, like Ralph Nader, argued that the interests of the public take priority over organizational interests and hence that society had a right to know what was going on inside organizations. This view was also argued in terms of corporate responsibilities. Those defending the primacy of organizational interest contested this view. James Roche, then chairman of General Motors, even compared whistleblowing to industrial espionage (Roche 1971, quoted in Walters 1975). Indeed, the early 1970s the discussion of whistleblowing and the protection of whistleblowing was in terms of a conflict between organization and society, or between system and environment, inside and outside.

We have certainly seen a change since then. The conceptual and argumentative shifts are documented in detail in Vandekerckhove (2006). The next section traces that shift in the academic literature on whistleblowing. What seems to have taken place is that the conflict is being contained by tiered whistleblowing procedures. As noted in the introduction to this chapter, whistleblowing procedures will stipulate who is allowed to receive whistleblowing information. These are the recipients. A 'tiered' whistleblowing procedure then prescribes a sequential order of recipients – for example, first the head of department, then the board of directors, then a specific government agency. There are many arguments in favour of tiered whistleblowing procedures. Besides having the advantage of recognizing both organizational and societal interests, the most important argument is that it is in the interest of society that organizational malpractices get corrected, but not necessarily that the public knows about it. Whistleblowing to the media can cause a scandal, but it is not a guarantee that things will go right from then on. A committed CEO or audit committee can do much more than a newspaper. Therefore, it makes sense to expect from whistleblowers that they raise their concern inside the organization first. Tiered whistleblowing procedures allow organizations to bring or keep their organizational practices in line with the public interest. Hence, it is not society that takes control over organizational practices. Only when organizations refuse or are unable to solve problems regarding their own practices can disclosures be made to a next-level recipient.

To sum up this section, whistleblowing procedures and policies constitute a CSR practice in the sense that they are a necessary mediation between the interests of the organization and those of society. In the framework of Wood (1991), they appear on the institutional level of CSR, meaning that the implementation of whistleblowing procedures and policies is an expectation that can be 'placed on all businesses because of their role as economic institutions' (Wood 1991: 695). To have such procedures and policies in place is part of what the principle of legitimacy requires.

Overview of research

All literature on whistleblowing traces the activity in an organizational context to 1971 (Walters 1975; Stewart 1980; Elliston 1982; Near and Jensen 1983; Dozier and Miceli 1985; Jensen 1987; Johnson and Kraft 1990; Near, Baucus and Miceli 1993; Perry 1998; Miceli et al. 1999) when, at a conference on professional responsibility, consumer advocate Ralph Nader raised the issue as a 'call for responsibility' and an 'encouragement to blow the whistle' defined whistleblowing as 'an act of a man or woman who, believing that the public interest overrides the interest of the organization he serves, blows the whistle that the organization is involved in corrupt, illegal, fraudulent or harmful activity' (Nader et al. 1972: vii). Sometimes there is consideration of a book by two editors of *Washington Monthly*, Peters and Branch, which is also from 1972, but Walters (1975) is clear that Nader et al. (1972) is 'the first published and still the best general treatment', though he also mentions a book by Fitzgerald (1972), which is an autobiographical case-report of whistleblowing on fraud on the part of the Pentagon and defence contractors.

Even though whistleblowing in an organizational context originated as an activist and hence politico-ethical concept, the momentum it gained in academic literature has also led to a de-activation of the concept.

The academic literature on whistleblowing kicks off in 1973, with a book review of Nader et al. (1972) in *Social Work*. The first article in a law journal dates from 1974 and is an overview of accountants' duties in relation to whistleblowing (Isbell 1974). From the same year is Vogel (1974) who argues that whistleblowing is an exponent of the politicization of the corporation. Publications on whistleblowing in law journals and in journals on politics and social issues remain constant but very scarce, with more book reviews than articles. Also, management journals join in pretty early, starting with Walters (1975) with an article in *Harvard Business Review*. The article files under the section 'Thinking Ahead' and warns companies to be on guard for the growing tendency of courts 'saying that matters traditionally considered an organization's own business may be the public's as well.' Court rulings at that time seem to take the US first amendment argument on free speech seriously, especially for government personnel. The tone of the article is that the future might very well bring laws protecting whistleblowers in private companies and installing whistleblowing as an exemption from the employment at will doctrine. An article from 1977 (Conway 1977) reviews that possibility. Overall, there seems to be a higher attention for whistleblowing from public management journals – starting with a special issue of *Bureaucrat* from 1977 that focuses on whistleblowing in terms of government accountability – than from management journals aimed at private sector organizations.

The issue of whistleblowing gains momentum in the academic literature from the 1980s on, but the growth in publications is mainly due to book reviews and editorials. The issue is particularly present in journals on engineering, information technology and scientific research. The 1980s also show whistleblowing studied from a sociological and psychological perspective. Sociological research on whistleblowing might have been triggered by the publication of a study by Anderson et al. (1980) of whistleblowing during the development of the Bay Area Rapid Transit system – BART – in California. The authors see the then available publications on whistleblowing consisting of 'brief descriptive accounts of specific incidents that are either journalistic or highly partisan in form' (Anderson et al. 1980: 16). Their book offers extensive descriptions of whistleblowing incidents at BART, but also sees the need to place the issue in the context of organization theory. They set out a set of research questions that seem to have been picked up by other scholars from the 1980s on. Anderson and his colleagues stated the need to 'identify the organizational conditions – authority structure, lines of communication, opportunities to participate in decision-making – that give rise to initial acts of disagreement with, or concern about, some organizational practice' (Anderson et al. 1980: 5). The most important authors in research on whistleblowing from a psychological perspective are Miceli and Near, who publish frequently on individual characteristics of whistleblowers from 1984 on. Glazer and Glazer (1989) are also to be situated in that field with their six-year study on employees blowing the whistle on their employers, researching the role of their belief system in their decision to blow the whistle and in coping with retaliation. Important to note is that, even though sociological and psychological research on whistleblowing keeps the politico-ethical undertone of power struggles within organizations and the public interest aspect of whistleblowing, the emphasis of the research is not on whistleblowing as a politico-ethical relevant practice, but rather on the whistleblower – personal characteristics of whistleblowers (their belief system, their organizational position) (Near, Baucus and Miceli 1993; Near, Dworkin and Miceli 1993; Glazer and Glazer 1986) – and on the act of whistleblowing – predicting whistleblowing and finding out what the determinants of organizations with a high risk of whistleblowing are (Rothschild and Miethe 1999; Barnett 1992). What they have found is that the perceived seriousness of the malpractice is an important factor on whether or not a person will blow the whistle – the more a practice is perceived as a serious malpractice, the more whistleblowing is likely to occur (Miceli and Near 1985; Near and Miceli 1987, 1995; Callahan and Dworkin 1994). However, Miceli and Near (1992) have shown that even for whistleblowers who disclose outside of the organization, it is very common to have tried internal channels prior to external whistleblowing. They also argued that organizational retaliation against whistleblowers encourages further whistleblowing. Other research argued that having internal whistleblowing procedures encourages internal disclosures but not external whistleblowing (Mathews 1987; Keenan 1990). Further, the research by Sims and Keenan (1998) shows that formal policies that support external whistleblowing are not a significant predictor of external whistleblowing.

Except for articles in law journals from the second half of the 1980s researching the effects of whistleblowing statutes and legislation (Rongine 1985; Dworkin and Near 1987; Parker 1988; Rosecrance 1988; Massengill and Petersen 1989), publications on whistleblowing protection are practically absent from the 1980s, but are more present in the first half of the 1990s and stem mainly from journals on nursing, medicine, engineering and auditing (Arnold and Ponemon 1991; Frader 1992; De Maria 1992; Doyal and Cannell 1993; Barnett et al. 1993; Ponemon 1994; Hooks et al. 1994; Hipel et al. 1995). It is only from 1998 onwards that the politico-ethical question with regard to whistleblowing is raised again in academic literature other than political journals.

Dworkin and Callahan (1998) argue that during the 1990s two conflicting trends have occurred. On the one hand, whistleblowers have gained more protection from retaliation through expanded legislation. But on the other hand, employers have increased the use of secrecy clauses to prevent information leaking out of the organization, which has resulted in more court cases in which judges were asked to enforce secrecy agreements against whistleblowers. Even though the motive for the disclosure, the identity of the information recipient, the seriousness of the wrongdoing and the strength of the evidence can safeguard a whistleblower from secrecy agreements being used to retaliate against them, Dworkin and Callahan (1998) claim employers have gained extra protection through such agreements, one important protection being that they can require that employees first report wrongdoing internally.

Perry (1998) charges the literature on whistleblowing with the unproblematic reproduction of the Enlightenment ideal; that is, combining individual autonomy and social rationality. Analyses of whistleblowing tell a story of moral man against immoral organization. The problem is that the empirical content of these studies contrasts with their narrative form. Whistleblowers are celebrated in these studies, but at the same time it is shown how bleak their fate is. Retaliation in terms of job loss and the disastrous consequences on the health and family life of whistleblowers is a constant. In effect, Perry argues, potential whistleblowers are cautioned against going public by the very same authors who commend the integrity of those who do. Perry calls for an alternative interpretation of whistleblowing practices as tracers of shifts and realignments within and between discursive and institutional structures, an approach which is more contextual and less axiomatically heroic. Such an approach sees whistleblowing as a signal of the state of social organization. Shifting relationships between business and state mean inter-institutional blurring and boundary-crossing. This is also associated with realignments in control and legitimation. Patterns of reward change and it is communication control which becomes functionally indispensable in uncoupling the production of conduct from the rhetoric of justification. In other words, there is a dualism between legitimating principles and operational practices of an organization. This is an uneasy coexistence which needs ritualized and ceremonial activity to keep it stable. Whistleblowing then, points at a failure of the attempt to stabilize that dualism. However, whistleblowers are truth-tellers (cognitive) who become whistleblowers (moral) because they need to speak in the narrative and dramatic conventions which the media produce. The text of the whistleblower becomes dissent through the process of media definition. In this sense too, whistleblowing is the product of inter-institutional realignments and discursive shifts.

Jubb (1999) comes to terms with the different ways in which whistleblowing has been defined over the years in academic literature. Without explicitly mentioning Nader, Jubb re-introduces the politico-ethical definition of whistleblowing emphasising dissent and the ethical dilemma of conflicting loyalties.

Vandekerckhove and Commers (2000) put whistleblowing in the context of loss of democratic control over society due to globalization and see whistleblowing laws and channels as candidates for a new guarantee for democracy and well-being of society.

O'Connor (2001) identifies whistleblowing as a form of resistance used by female scholars within the Irish academic community to raise awareness of gender inequality, but then argues that raising the awareness is not enough to resolve the problem.

Riesenberg (2001) reviews the Securities Exchange Act enacted by US Congress in 1995, which requires the reporting by independent auditors of illegal acts. He argues that the scope of those requirements is ambiguous, but concludes that an examination of the statutory language and legislative history of the act shows it is but a modest statute with limited significance.

Buchholz and Rosenthal (2002) elaborate on the moral dilemma arising from a market economy in which the corporation is the primary institution through which new technologies are introduced. Because corporations are primarily interested in economic goals, they cannot – or do not – ask adequate questions about the safety of a particular technology. Hence, concerns of engineers and technicians clash with managers' eagerness to favour organizational economic interests. Buchholz and Rosenthal argue that technology creates a moral situation which should provide the context for decision-making. Tensions within that context can be seen as a structural problem inherent in the capitalistic system, but they can also be seen as an organizational problem that requires facilitation of whistleblowing.

Grant (2002) puts whistleblowers on a pedestal, arguing that the moral sensitivity involved in whistleblowing approaches religious proportions in terms of courage, determination and sacrifice.

Vandekerckhove and Commers (2004) argue that the organizational discourse that carries flexibility as a key concept obliges organizations to rethink their demand for loyalty from their employees. Today absolute loyalty is untenable. What is consistent with the notion of flexibility is what Vandekerckhove and Commers (2004) call 'rational loyalty', which is a loyalty to the organization as defined in its mission statement. Organizations are hence obliged to protect those who are truth-tellers in the sense Perry (1998) had noted. If they demand loyalty from their employees, they have to reciprocate that by implementing whistleblowing procedures.

Finally, Vandekerckhove (2006) researches shifts in lobbying positions and argumentations for protecting whistleblowers. He studies law proposals, law texts and position papers from 1970 to 2005 in the US, Australia, the UK, New Zealand, South Africa, Japan, Belgium, the Netherlands, Ireland, Canada, India, Germany, Switzerland and at OECD and EU level. His findings are that the initial aspirations of the 1970s activism are at risk in the current argumentation. He stresses the importance of an open-ended final tier recipient (for example, the media or NGOs) in order to safeguard the individual from organizational enclosure.

These publications are examples of the re-emphasis on whistleblowing as a politico-ethical concept from the end of the 1990s onwards. It coincides with the rise of the anti-globalization activism and mass protests. But the politico-ethical question also reappeared in a different tone. Internal whistleblowing channels were 'in' again, and although the first half of the 1990s had seen some publications on internal disclosure policies (Dworkin and Callahan 1991; Barnett et al. 1993; Hooks et al. 1994; Ponemon 1994), the tone of the articles from the end of the 1990s onwards on internal whistleblowing channels is less politically protesting, less conflicting, but more morally laden in a legitimating sense.

The article of Benson and Ross (1998) is almost a corporate advertisement. The authors argue that the commitment of the management of Sundstrand is exemplary, and one of the reasons is that internal whistleblowing is encouraged and protected.

Gunsalus (1998) focuses on systemic elements for cultivating an ethical environment in organizations and argues that handling complaints and grievances at their earliest stages is important and that internal whistleblowing channels should be supported.

Gordon and Miyake (2001) review codes of conduct to get insight into corporate approaches to anti-bribery commitments and compliance management. Although the language and concepts used to describe bribery and corruption is very diverse, the authors regard the bribery codes as evidence of an emerging consensus on managerial approaches to combating bribery, and internal whistleblowing channels form one of those management tools.

Kaptein (2002) argues for an 'ethics helpdesk' characterized by low barriers, positive approach and simple procedures. Such a helpdesk can be seen as an internal whistleblowing channel, because it increases the chances of detecting unethical conduct which enable management to take adequate and timely measures.

Callahan et al. (2002) argue that establishing internal whistleblowing procedures form a way for corporations to improve efficiency and employee morale. The best way to do so, according to the authors, is through implementation of the BMI-model – Business as Mediating Institution – which offers beneficial aspects of both contractarian and communitarian forms of corporate governance. Their BMI-model with its internal whistleblowing channels is legitimized by linking it with the concepts of empowerment and shared values.

De Maria (1999) describes this promotion of new ethics regimes as an 'ethical meltdown', because those promoting them sound more like management consultants than like impartial critics of practice. It is interesting that De Maria regards whistleblowing as the 'test case' of how serious the ethics movement in management is. So, whereas in the early 1970s whistleblowing was a politico-ethical concept pointing at a conflict between organization and society, what we see in the last group of publications I described is that intra-organizational whistleblowing policies are presented as a politico-ethical concept able to eliminate conflict between organization and society, between the interests of private capital and the public interest. In *Whistleblowing and Organizational Social Responsibility* (Vandekerckhove 2006) I show the same shift occurs in public discussions about whether and how to protect whistleblowers.

It is also important to note that as whistleblowing legislation is being proposed and enacted around the world, we can expect more research covering employee reactions and attitudes towards whistleblowing. Existing examples of this are Thomas and Miller (2005) and Park et al. (2005). As the Sarbanes-Oxley Act (SOX) has implications for corporation around the world, we can also expect research covering compatibility of SOX requirements with local regulation (for example privacy regulation in Europe).

Current issues

Whether or not the whistleblower's motive is ought to be taken into consideration before offering protection remains an unresolved issue. Most policies explicitly mention 'good intention' or 'genuine whistleblower' as a precondition for protection against retaliation.

One reason might be that it is featured to counter the standard argument against protection, namely that disgruntled employees abuse whistleblowing procedures by telling lies about their colleagues or line manager, only motivated by personal gain. Another reason might be the portraying of whistleblowers in the media as moral heroes.

It is important to note here, however, that there is also a downside to mentioning motive as a condition for protection. Jubb (1999) left motive out of his definition of whistleblowing because motives may be mixed, misrepresented and very hard, if not impossible, to decipher. Whilst the quality of a whistleblowing procedure or regulation can be measured by the clarity and unambiguity of the conditions set on the protection, the introduction of a proper motive as a condition increases the arbitrariness of the protection. Who is to judge the whistleblower's motive? It makes raising concern much more risky for potential whistleblowers.

Moreover, the relevance of the whistleblower's motive is not that obvious, given the finality of whistleblower protection, namely to further the public interest. Indeed, as the report from the OECD work group on whistleblowing argued: 'as the purpose of a whistleblowing framework is to deter corruption rather than to encourage external disclosures, [labour representatives] were not persuaded that the motive or honesty of the whistleblower should be a critical factor in any new regime' (OECD 2000: 9).

The only whistleblowing policy that explicitly taps into whistleblowing motivated by personal gain is the False Claims Act in the US, which offers rewards for information. The Act establishes that anyone who sues in the name of the US government in relation to fraud also sues for herself. Basically, the idea is that the person or organization filing the lawsuit gets a percentage of the money the government is able to recover. Although the idea was raised during the parliamentary discussion in the Netherlands,[3] the False Claims Act provisions have not been taken over in any whistleblowing regulation so far. To reward whistleblowing which is motivated by personal gain seems to be a US idiosyncrasy.

This brings us to another issue regarding whistleblowing, namely whether or not cultural differences are of any explanatory relevance. Here, a distinction must be made between possible differences in attitudes towards whistleblowing on the one side and differences in whistleblowing schemes on the other. Current research (Thomas and Miller 2005; Park et al. 2005) seems to suggest that people from cultures where collectivism is more important than individualism are more likely to blow the whistle. However, whether they actually do so is not known and also depends on organizational and regulatory features.

When we look at whistleblowing schemes and legislation, the story is somewhat different. Intuitively, one would expect national culture to matter a great deal as to how whistleblower protection is advocated. Not only do whistleblowing policies affect an organization's autonomy with regard to the wider society, protecting whistleblowers is also a serious intervention in how people relate to one another within organizations. Therefore, one could argue that certain 'good reasons' might work in one region of the world, but not in another.

Contrary to that intuition, Vandekerckhove (2006) concludes that efficiency, accountability and corporate governance underpin whistleblowing schemes, regardless of national cultures. It is as if these arguments constitute a semantic 'fit' above national cultures. This is no surprise if we acknowledge that that describing and designing organizations and the relations between organizations and society through the concepts of flexibility, decentralization, governance, network and stakeholder, has become a global method. It appears as if this particular discourse on and from organizations has become more pervasive than national culture.

Of course, one could raise a point here and formulate things in a moderating way. More precisely, it might be more accurate to say that in those countries where organizations are increasingly described and problematized in terms of flexibility,

---

3   During that discussion, Marijnissen from the Socialist Party handed in a list of suggestions from his party towards a better and more effective fight against fraud. One of the suggestions was to offer whistleblowers, besides protection through labour law, a substantial reward. The same move was made by Halsema – from the Green Left – who called for a 'whistleblower fund' from which whistleblowers could be paid a financial reward if they come up with hard evidence on big fraud cases. (See *Handelingen Tweede Kamer* 56-3660-3710 and the notes on pages 3735–37.)

decentralization, governance, network and stakeholder, whistleblowing policies appear as a necessity and hence are being enacted into legislation.

This goes for Australia, where the antipathy towards 'dobbing' or betraying 'mateship' has withheld federal whistleblowing legislation covering the private sector, until HIH, Australia's second largest general insurer, collapsed in 2001. The HIH collapse could have been avoided, if only early warnings from an insider and several others to the Australian Prudential Regulatory Authority (APRA) asking to inspect HIH had been followed up. All of a sudden, the culture of 'mateship' was no longer convincing. Or rather, the restoring investor trust acquired an urgency that was able to convince beyond the importance of 'mates'. In September 2002, the federal government issued a policy proposal paper setting out ideas for protecting private sector whistleblowers. In October 2003, a draft bill was released and by June 2004, the CLERP Act (Corporate Law Economic Reform Program) was a fact. The point I am trying to illustrate is that certain situations are perceived as necessities and can as such wipe away cultural arguments. In the case of Australia, the 'cultural' argument that seemed to have blocked private sector whistleblower protection for ten years got washed away by one crisis. And all of a sudden, it is that same Australian private sector which is urging whistleblower protection to be legislated.

Another example is Japan where whistleblowing legislation was enacted in June 2004. For a country with one of the strongest corporatist cultures in the world, this sounds weird. Organizational loyalty in the old sense, the belief that illegality or malpractice should be overlooked or ignored for the sake of the corporation, is still very strong, but Japanese corporate culture is nevertheless showing cracks. Lifetime employment is fading, workforce reductions are taking place, and a lot of corporations have stopped offering low-price accommodation to their workers. Also the last ten years, notions such as 'accountability', 'freedom of information', 'governance' and 'business ethics' have been taken up in the language (Miki 2004). Thus, it is not national culture that seems most relevant, but rather the extent to which the conceptual hegemony of globalization is cracking up that national culture that is important.

A third issue is whether whistleblowers should be allowed to make anonymous disclosures. It is sometimes argued that anonymity is the best protection. It is also the easiest way to solicit information without having a duty to protect those disclosing the information. In this sense, it should be no surprise that nearly all commercially operated 'hotlines' are anonymous whistleblowing schemes. By definition, anonymous whistleblowers cannot be protected, for the simple fact that we do not know who it is that we should be protecting. Also, anonymous reports are harder to investigate because there is no way to obtain additional information from the whistleblower. Finally, anonymous reporting facilities might increase the risk of slanderous reporting. A good alternative to anonymous reporting is confidential reporting. In such a scheme, the recipient knows the identity of the whistleblower but keeps it confidential from management or other parties.

Just recently, policy-makers in Europe gave a clear signal that confidential schemes are to be preferred to anonymous ones. The provisions of the Sarbanes-

Oxley Act enacted in the US in 2002 had also implications for overseas corporations that were traded on the US stock market. More precisely, these corporations had to comply with Section 301 of the Act, which stipulates that 'Each audit committee shall establish procedures for ... the confidential, anonymous submission by employees ... of concern regarding questionable accounting or auditing matters.' In Germany and France, labour unions had argued that some whistleblowing schemes set up by corporations were unlawful. Court rulings confirmed this, by stating that whistleblowing schemes were not compatible with the European Directive on privacy (Directive 95/46/EC). Of course this caused a huge dilemma for some major European companies. Meanwhile, there is an advice paper from the Article 29 Working Party (approved in February 2006), which states that confidential reporting is to be preferred to anonymous reporting. Also, the French CNIL (Commission nationale de l'informatique en des libertés) issued a 'guideline document' in November 2005, in which it finds the encouragement of anonymous reporting unacceptable and suggests restrictive handling of anonymous reporting. If the guidelines from these authorities are followed up on, then it might very well be that the European whistleblowing scheme will differ from that elsewhere in the world.

References

Anderson, R.M., Perrucci, R., Schendel, D.E. and Trachtman, L.E. (1980), *Divided Loyalties: Whistleblowing at BART*, West Lafayette: Purdue University Press.

Arnold, D.F. and Ponemon, L.A. (1991), 'Internal auditors perceptions of whistle-blowing and the influence of moral reasoning. An experiment', *Auditing*, 10 (2), 1–15.

Barnett, T. (1992), 'A preliminary investigation of the relationship between selected organizational characteristics and external whistleblowing by employees', *Journal of Business Ethics*, 11 (12), 949–59.

Barnett, T., Cochran, D.S. and Taylor, G.S. (1993), 'The internal disclosure policies of private-sector employers. An initial look at their relationship to employee whistleblowing', *Journal of Business Ethics*, 12 (2), 127–36.

Benson, J.A. and Ross, D.L. (1998), 'Sundstrand: a case study in transformation of cultural ethics', *Journal of Business Ethics*, 17 (14), 1517–1527.

Buchholz, R.A. and Rosenthal, S.B. (2002), 'Technology and business: rethinking the moral dilemma', *Journal of Business Ethics*, 41 (1–2), 45–50.

Callahan, E.S. and Dworkin, T.M. (1994), 'Who blows the whistle to the media, and why: organizational characteristics of media whistleblowers', *American Business Law Journal*, 32 (2), 151–84.

Callahan, E.S., Dworkin, T.M., Fort, T.L. and Schipani, C.A. (2002), 'Integrating trends in whistleblowing and corporate governance: promoting organizational effectiveness, societal responsibility, and employee empowerment', *American Business Law Journal*, 40 (1), 177–215.

Calton, J.M. and Lad, L.J. (1995), 'Social contracting as a trust-building process of network governance', *Business Ethics Quarterly*, 5 (2), 275–96.

Conway, J.H. (1977), 'Protecting the private sector at will employee who "blows the whistle": a cause of action based upon determinants of public policy', *Wisconsin Law Review*, 77 (3), 777–812.

De Maria, W. (1999), *Deadly Disclosures: Whistleblowing and the Ethical Meltdown of Australia*, Kent Town (South Australia): Wakefield Press.

De Maria, W. (1992), 'Queensland whistleblowing. Sterilizing the lone crusader', *Australian Journal of Social Issues*, 27 (4), 248–61.

Doyal, L. and Cannell, H. (1993). 'Whistle blowing. The ethics of revealing professional incompetence within dentistry', *British Dental Journal*, 174 (3), 95–101.

Dozier, J.B. and Miceli, M.P. (1985), 'Potential predictors of whistle-blowing – A pro-social behavior perspective', *Academy of Management Review*, 10 (4), 823–36.

Dworkin, T.M. and Callahan, E.S. (1998), 'Buying silence', *American Business Law Journal*, 36 (1), 151–91.

Dworkin, T.M. and Callahan, E.S. (1991), 'Internal whistleblowing. Protecting the interests of the employee, the organization, and society', *American Business Law Journal*, 29 (2), 265–308.

Dworkin, T.M. and Near, J.P. (1987), 'Whistleblowing statutes. Are they working?', *American Business Law Journal*, 25 (2), 241–64.

Elliston, F.A. (1982), 'Civil-disobedience and whistleblowing – A comparative appraisal of two forms of dissent', *Journal of Business Ethics*, 1 (1), 23–8.

Fitzgerald, A.E. (1972), *The High Priests of Waste*, New York: Norton.

Frader, J.E. (1992), 'Political and interpersonal aspects of ethics consultation', *Theoretical Medicine*, 13 (1), 31–44.

Glazer, M.P. and Glazer, P.M. (1989), *The Whistleblowers: Exposing Corruption in Government and Industry*, New York: Basic Books.

Glazer, M.P. and Glazer, P.M. (1986), 'Whistleblowing', *Psychology Today*, 20 (8), 36.

Gordon, K. and Miyake, M. (2001), 'Business approaches to combat bribery: a study of codes of conduct', *Journal of Business Ethics*, 34 (3–4), 161–73.

Grant, C. (2002), 'Whistle blowers: saints of a secular culture', *Journal of Business Ethics*, 39 (4), 391–9.

Gunsalus, C.K. (1998), 'Preventing the need for whistleblowing: practical advice for university administrators', *Science and Engineering Ethics*, 4 (1), 75–94.

Hipel, K., Yin, X. and Kilgour, D.M. (1995), 'Can a costly reporting system make environmental enforcement more efficient?', *Stochastic Hydrology and Hydraulics*, 9 (2), 151–70.

Hooks, K.L., Kaplan, S.E. and Schultz, J.J. (1994), 'Enhancing communication to assist in fraud prevention and detection', *Auditing*, 13 (2), 86–117.

Isbell, D.B. (1974), 'Overview of accountants' duties and liabilities under federal securities laws and a closer look at whistle-blowing', *Ohio State Law Journal*, 35 (2), 261–79.

Jensen, J.V. (1987), 'Ethical tension points in whistleblowing', *Journal of Business Ethics*, 6 (4), 321–8.

Johnson, R.A. and Kraft, M.E. (1990), 'Bureaucratic whistleblowing and policy change', *Western Political Quarterly*, 43 (4), 849–74.

Jubb, P.B. (1999), 'Whistleblowing: a restrictive definition and interpretation', *Journal of Business Ethics*, 21 (1), 77–94.

Kaptein, M. (2002), 'Guidelines for the development of an ethics safety net', *Journal of Business Ethics*, 41 (3), 217–234.

Keenan, J.P. (1990), 'Upper-level managers and whistleblowing: determinants of perceptions of company encouragement and information about where to blow the whistle', *Journal of Business and Psychology*, 5 (2), 223–35.

Luhmann, N. (2000), *Organisation und Entscheidung*, Opladen (Wiesbaden): Westdeutscher Verlag.

Massengill, D. and Petersen, D.J. (1989), 'Whistleblowing: protected activity or not?', *Employee Relations Law Journal*, 15 (1), 49–56.

Mathews, M.C. (1987), 'Codes of ethics: organizational behavior and misbehavior', *Research in Corporate Social Performance and Policy*, 9, 107–30.

Miceli, M.P. and J.P. Near (1992), *Blowing the Whistle: The Organizational and Legal Implications for Companies and Employees*, New York: Lexington Books.

Miceli, M.P. and Near, J.P. (1985), 'Characteristics of organizational climate and perceived wrongdoing associated with whistle-blowing decisions', *Personnel Psychology*, 38 (3), 525–44.

Miceli, M.P., Rehg, M., Near, J.P and Ryan, K.C. (1999), 'Can laws protect whistle-blowers? Results of a naturally occurring field experiment', *Work and Occupations*, 26 (1), 129–51.

Miki, Y. (2004), 'The position in Japan', in R. Calland and G. Dehn (eds), *Whistleblowing around the world. Law, Culture and Practice*, Cape Town/London: ODAC/PCAW, 153–6.

Nader, R., Petkas, P.J. and Blackwell, K. (eds) (1972), *Whistle Blowing: The Report of the Conference on Professional Responsibility*, New York: Grossman.

Near, J.P. and Jensen, T.C. (1983), 'The whistleblowing process – retaliation and perceived effectiveness', *Work and Occupations*, 10 (1), 3–28.

Near, J.P. and Miceli, M.P. (1995), 'Effective whistle-blowing', *Academy of Management Review*, 20, 679–708.

Near, J.P. and Miceli, M.P. (1987), 'Whistle-blowers in organizations: dissidents or reformers?', *Research in Organizational Behavior*, 9, 321–68.

Near, J.P., Baucus, M.S. and Miceli, M.P. (1993), 'The relationship between values and practice. Organizational climates for wrongdoing', *Administration & Society*, 25 (2), 204–26.

Near, J.P., Dworkin, T.M. and Miceli, M.P. (1993b), 'Explaining the whistle-blowing process. Suggestions from power theory and justice theory', *Organization Science*, 4 (3), 392–411.

O'Connor, P. (2001), 'A bird's eye view. Resistance in Academia', *Irish Journal of Sociology*, 10 (2), 86–104.

Organization for Economic Cooperation and Development (OECD) (2000), *Whistleblowing to Combat Corruption – Report on a Meeting of Management and Trade Union Experts held under the OCED Labour/Management Programme*, PAC/AFF/LMP(2000)1, Paris: OECD.

Park, H., Rehg, M. and Lee, D. (2005), 'The influence of Confucian ethics and collectivism on whistleblowing intentions: a study of South Korean public employees', *Journal of Business Ethics*, 58, 387–403.

Parker, R.A. (1988), 'Whistleblowing legislation in the United States: a preliminary appraisal', *Parliamentary Affairs*, 41 (1), 149–58.

Perry, N. (1998), 'Indecent exposures: theorizing whistleblowing', *Organization Studies*, 19 (2), 235–57.

Ponemon, L.A. (1994), 'Whistle-blowing as an internal control mechanism. Individual and organizational considerations', *Auditing*, 13 (2), 118–130.

Riesenberg, T.L. (2001), 'Trying to hear the whistle blowing: the widely misunderstood "illegal act" reporting requirements of Exchange Act Section 10A', *Business Lawyer*, 56 (4), 1417–1460.

Roche, J. (1971), 'The competitive system, to work, to preserve, and to protect', *Vital Speeches of the Day*, 1 May 1971, 445.

Rongine, N.M. (1985), 'Toward a coherent legal response to the public-policy dilemma posed by whistleblowing', *American Business Law Journal*, 23 (2), 281–97.

Rosecrance, J. (1988), 'Whistleblowing in probation departments', *Journal of Criminal Justice*, 16 (2), 99–109.

Rothschild, J. and Miethe, T. (1999), 'Disclosing misconduct in work organizations: an empirical analysis of the situational factors that foster whistleblowing', in I. Harper and R.L. Simpson (eds), *Research in the Sociology of Work*, vol. 8, Ohio: JAI Press, pp 211–227.

Sandmo, A. (1999). 'Asymmetric information and public economics: the Mirrlees-Vickrey Nobel Prize', *Journal of Economic Perspectives*, 13 (1), 165–80.

Sims, R.L. and Keenan, J.P. (1998), 'Predictors of external whistleblowing: organizational and intrapersonal variables', *Journal of Business Ethics*, 17, 411–421.

Solomon, R.C. (1993), *Business and Excellence. Cooperation and Integrity in Business*, New York: Oxford University Press.

Stewart, L.P. (1980), 'Whistle blowing – implications for organizational communication', *Journal of Communication*, 30 (4), 90–101.

Stiglitz, J.E. (2000), 'The contributions of the economics of information to twentieth century economics', *Quarterly Journal of Economics*, 115 (4), 1441–78.

Thomas, J. Z. and Miller, D.L. (2005), 'Examining culture's effect on whistle-blowing and peer reporting', *Business & Society*, 44 (4), 462–86.

Vandekerckhove, W. (2006), *Whistleblowing and Organizational Social Responsibility*, Aldershot: Ashgate.

Vandekerckhove, W. and Commers, M.S.R. (2004), 'Whistle blowing and rational loyalty', *Journal of Business Ethics*, 53 (1–2), 225–33.

Vandekerckhove, W. and Commers, M.S.R. (2000), 'Het onderzoek inzake anti-corruptie. Een stand van zaken', *Ethiek & Maatschappij*, 3 (3), 39–61.

Vogel, D. (1974), 'The politicisation of the corporation', *Social Policy*, 5 (1), 57–62.

Walters, K.D. (1975), 'Your employees' right to blow the whistle', *Harvard Business Review*, 53 (4), 26–34 cont. 161–2.

Weick, K.E. (2001), *Making Sense of the Organization*, Oxford: Blackwell.

Wood, D.J. (1991), 'Corporate social performance revisited', *Academy of Management Review*, 16 (4), 691–718.

Legally Imposed Corporate Social Responsibility for the Protection of HIV-Positive Employees in South Africa

Stella Vettori

Introduction

There are various pieces of legislation that deal with employer duties regarding job applicants and employees infected with HIV/AIDS. Generally[1] these provisions are worded negatively. On the face of it, therefore, it may appear that these duties are confined to what employers may not do. Consequently, there seems to be no legislative imposition on employers to take positive steps to protect the interests and ameliorate the position of employees or job applicants infected with HIV/AIDS. Analysis of the legislation, read with the common law and 'soft law' will make it clear that employers bear a legally imposed social responsibility to employees infected with HIV/AIDS.

---

1   Positive duties imposed on employers concern the duty to provide a safe working environment and other minimum standards. In terms of section 8(1) of the Occupational Health and Safety Act 85 of 1993, an employer is obliged to provide, as far as is reasonably practicable, a safe workplace. This may include taking steps to minimise occupational exposure to HIV. The Basic Conditions of Employment Act 75 of 1997 provides certain basic minimum standards of employment, *inter alia*, in terms of section 22(2), a minimum amount of sick leave. Section 2(1) and section 5(1) of the Mine Health and Safety Act 29 of 1996 provides that an employer must provide, as far as is reasonable practicable, a safe work environment. Again, this may be interpreted to mean that the employer should take positive steps to minimise exposure to HIV. If an employee is infected with HIV as a result of occupational exposure to the virus, the employee is entitled to claim compensation in terms of section 22(1) of the Compensation for Occupational Injuries and Diseases Act 130 of 1993.

These duties have various sources: firstly there is 'soft law'[2] which, as opposed to legislation, is not enforceable in a court of law, but can in an indirect manner impose legal duties on the employers. This 'soft law' serves primarily as a guide to employers wishing to implement a policy on HIV/AIDS. In terms of the Employment Equity Act[3] (hereinafter the 'EEA'), the Code of Good Practice on HIV/AIDS must be used as an interpretive tool to give content to its provisions.[4] Consequently, employers may find that a legislative duty which on the face of it imposes only negative duties, such as the duty not to discriminate unfairly on the basis of a person's HIV status, in the light of the Code of Good Practice may ultimately entail a legal duty to take positive action.

The obligation in section 6(1) of the EEA not to discriminate unfairly on the basis of a person's HIV status, if read together with other provisions in the EEA, requires an employer to take positive steps to protect infected employees and job applicants from unfair discrimination on the basis of their HIV status.

The common law can also be interpreted to require employers to take positive steps to protect employees infected with HIV/Aids.

Finally, an employer's failure to take positive action to address discrimination of HIV-infected employees and to put policies in place by means of strategic action, in addition to attracting legal liability for the payment of compensation to the victim(s), is most likely to result in dire economic repercussions for the employer.

The Employment Equity Act (EEA)

Section 6(1) provides that no person may unfairly discriminate against an employee, or an applicant for employment, in any employment policy or practice, on the basis of his or her HIV status. An 'employment policy or practice' is defined as including but not being limited to the following:[5]

> (a) recruitment procedures, advertising and selection criteria;
> (b) appointments and appointment process;
> (c) job classification and grading;
> (d) remuneration, employment benefits and terms and conditions of employment;
> (e) job assignments;
> (f) the working environment and facilities;
> (g) training and development;
> (h) performance evaluation systems;

---

2   Code of Good Practice: Key Aspects of HIV/AIDS and Employment as promulgated in GN R1298 in GG 21815 of 1 December 2000. Another relevant source of 'soft law' in this regard is *The King Report on Corporate Governance for South Africa 2002*.
3   55 of 1998.
4   Section 3(c) of the Employment Equity Act 55 of 1998.
5   Section 1 of EEA.

(i) promotion;
(j) transfer;
(k) demotion;
(l) disciplinary measures other than dismissal;
(m) dismissal.

Although the term 'act or omission' is not used in section 6 with regard to an 'employment policy or practice', it is used in section 10(2) to describe the subject matter of a dispute about unfair discrimination. An omission or failure to do something, therefore, can amount to unfair discrimination. Consequently, section 6(1) read with section 10(2) can oblige an employer to take certain steps in order to avoid breaching the negatively worded terms of section 6(1).

Section 5 provides: 'Every employer must take steps to promote equal opportunity in the workplace by eliminating unfair discrimination in any policy or practice.' In *Harmse v City of Cape Town*[6] section 5 was found to provide a right to affirmative action. Affirmative action can loosely be defined as positive action by the employer in order to redress the imbalances of the past with regard to people who fall within the designated groups. Although persons living with HIV/AIDS are not a 'designated group',[7] it is commonly accepted that black women bear the highest risk of contracting the disease.[8] Therefore, a failure by an employer to take 'steps to promote equal opportunity in the workplace by eliminating unfair discrimination in any policy or practice' with regard to people infected with HIV/AIDS may constitute a breach of section 5.

Section 60 of the EEA provides *inter alia* that if an employer directly encourages or even by its inaction allows or condones conduct which is in breach of the EEA, it will be vicariously liable for damages flowing from such breach. It reads as follows:

(1) If it is alleged that an employee, while at work, contravened a provision of this Act, or engaged in any conduct that, if engaged in by that employee's employer, would constitute a contravention of a provision of this Act, the alleged conduct must immediately be brought to the attention of the employer.

(2) The employer must consult all relevant parties and must take the necessary steps to eliminate the alleged conduct and comply with the provisions of this Act.

---

6   [2003] 6 BLLR 557 (LC).
7   Section 1 of EEA defines 'designated groups' as 'black people, women and people with disabilities'.
8   South African statistics from the Department of Health National Antenatal Survey (1999) 21.

(3) If the employer fails to take the necessary steps referred to in subsection (2), and it is proved that the employee has contravened the relevant provision, the employer must be deemed also to have contravened that provision.

(4) Despite subsection (3), an employer is not liable for the conduct of an employee if that employer is able to prove that it did all that was reasonably practicable to ensure that the employee would not act in contravention of this Act.

In order to avoid liability on the basis of the above-quoted section an employer would be obliged to put in place policies and procedures in order to prevent the unfair discrimination of its employees infected with HIV/AIDS. Given the prevalent ignorance, intolerance, irrational fear, prejudice and social stigma surrounding the disease it is not difficult to imagine that a failure on the part of the employer to implement policies to prevent discrimination could easily result in HIV/AIDS-infected employees bearing the brunt of prejudices imposed on them by their fellow employees.

Secondly, in situations where employees were guilty of discriminating unfairly against fellow employees infected with the virus, the employer is obliged to 'to take the necessary steps to eliminate the alleged conduct'. Clearly section 60 obliges an employer to take positive steps in order to prevent unfair discrimination against *inter alia* its employees infected with HIV/AIDS.

The Labour Relations Act (LRA)

Section 187(1)(f) of the LRA[9] provides that if the reason for a dismissal is the employer's direct or indirect unfair discrimination on the basis of 'any arbitrary ground, including, but not limited to race, gender, sex, ethnic or social origin, colour, sexual orientation, age disability, religion, conscience, belief, political opinion, culture, language, marital status or family responsibility', such dismissal will constitute an automatically unfair dismissal.[10] In the case of other unfair dismissals the maximum compensation that can be awarded to an employee who has been unfairly dismissed is 12 months' salary.[11] In the case of an automatically unfair dismissal the maximum awardable compensation is 24 months' salary.[12]

Although the HIV status of an employee is not specifically named in section 187(1)(f) as a basis for dismissal which would result in an automatically unfair

---

9   Labour Relations Act 66 of 1995.
10   It is interesting to note that, despite the omission of HIV status as a prohibited ground for discrimination in this section, the Code of Good Practice: Key Aspects of HIV/AIDS and Employment at para 5.3.4 states: 'In accordance with section 187(1)(f) of the Labour Relations Act 66 of 1995, an employee with HIV/AIDS may not be dismissed simply because he or she is HI-positive.'
11   Section 194(1).
12   Section 194(3).

dismissal, it prohibits dismissal 'on any arbitrary ground'. An arbitrary ground is 'a ground which is capricious or proceeding merely from will and not based on reason or principle ... where the discrimination is for no reason or is purposeless ...' or 'even if there is a reason ... [where] the reason is not a commercial reason of sufficient magnitude that it outweighs the rights of the job seeker and is not morally offensive'.[13] On this basis, discrimination on the basis of a person's HIV status can constitute an automatically unfair dismissal in terms of section 187(1)(f) of the LRA.

However, where as a direct consequence of the disease the employee is unable to adequately perform his or her duties, provided fair procedures are followed the employer may dismiss the employee for reasons of incapacity.[14] Also, if an HIV-negative status is an inherent requirement of the job, a dismissal based on a person's HIV status will not be unfair provided the correct procedures are followed.[15] An inherent requirement of a job in the words of Waglay J in *Whitehead v Woolworths (Pty) Ltd*[16] is 'some indispensable attribute' which is 'so inherent that if not met an applicant would simply not qualify for the post'.[17] With regard to a person's HIV status constituting an inherent requirement of the job the Constitutional Court in *Hoffman v South African Airways*,[18] although conceding that there may be circumstances which render HIV-positive persons unsuitable for employment as cabin attendants, held that this did not justify 'a blanket exclusion' of all HIV-positive persons and that each case should be judged on its merits. The court found that refusal by South African Airways to employ the applicant on the grounds of his HIV status constituted unfair discrimination because the purpose of the discrimination on this basis on the medical evidence was not justified.[19] In similar vein, it was held in *IMATU & Another v City of Cape Town*[20] it was held that persons with insulin-dependent diabetes should not be automatically excluded as fire-fighters on the basis of inherent requirements of the job. The court held that each application should be assessed on its individual merits. In *PFG Building Glass (Pty) Ltd v CEPPAWU & Others*,[21] Pillay J, while conceding that there might be situations where a person's HIV status may qualify as an inherent requirement of a job, this would not easily be proved.

As seen, section 187(1)(f) prohibits both direct and indirect discrimination. Even though the HIV status of a person is not specifically mentioned in section 187(1)(f)

---

13   Per Landman J in *Kadiaka v Amalgamated Beverage Industries* (1999) 20 *ILJ* 373 (LC) at paras 42–43.

14   Section 188(1)(a)(i).

15   Section 181(2)(a).

16   [1999] 8 BLLR 862(LC) at paras 34–35.

17   See also *Association of Teachers & Another v Minister of Education & Others* [1995] 9 BLLR 29 (IC) at 60; *Woolworths (Pty) Ltd v Whitehead* [2000] 6 BLLR 640 (LAC) at paras 26 and 43.

18   [2000] 12 BLLR 1365 (CC) at para 35.

19   At para 29.

20   [2005] 11 BLLR 1084 (LC) at paras 107–112.

21   [2003] 5 BLLR 475 (LC) at para 59.

as a prohibited ground for unfair discrimination, given the fact that black females bear the highest risk of infection,[22] direct discrimination on the basis of HIV status will result in indirect discrimination on the basis of both the prohibited grounds of race and gender.

A dismissal need not necessarily take the form of positive action on the part of the employer. An employer's failure to act may constitute a dismissal. For example, if an employee has a legitimate expectation that his or her fixed-term contract will be renewed on the same or similar terms and the employer fails to renew the contract or renews the contract on less favourable terms, this constitutes an unfair dismissal.[23] A positive duty, therefore, rests on the employer to renew the contract of the employee where he or she has a legitimate expectation that it should be renewed. Failure to renew such a contract on the basis of the person's HIV status would in all probability constitute an automatically unfair dismissal in the absence of the employer being able to justify the discrimination on the basis of an inherent job requirement or possibly an operational requirement.[24]

Another example of dismissals occurring without there necessarily being any positive action on the part of the employer is in the case of constructive dismissals. A constructive dismissal occurs where the employer by its acts or omissions rendered continuation of employment by the employee intolerable.[25] This situation can be achieved by an employer's inaction. The lack of an HIV policy in the workplace or an employer's inaction with regard to the harassment of HIV-positive employees by fellow employees can render continued employment intolerable for the employee. Clearly then, in order to prevent liability for unfair dismissals including automatically unfair dismissals employers would be well advised to take measures to eliminate all forms of unfair discrimination against HIV-positive employees.

The common law

Employer's duty to take reasonable care of employee safety

The breach of the duty of care can also take the form of an omission.[26] Brassey states:

> *Since [employers] can be held liable for omissions, employers can be liable for failing to prevent people, such as suppliers, customers or employees, from causing their employees harm. They are likely to be held liable if they*

---

22 South African statistics from the Department of Health National Antenatal Survey (1999) 21.

23 Section 186(2).

24 See Vettori 'Operational requirements: a justification for discrimination?', (2000) 33 *De Jure* 336.

25 Section 186(1)(e).

26 See M. Brassey, *Employment and Labour Law*, Cape Town: Juta (2000), vol. 1, E4:29.

provided the opportunity or conditions for the injurious act or had the power to prevent it.[27]

Breach of this duty occurs if the employer fails to guard against injury or harm in circumstances where a reasonable person would have foreseen the likelihood of injury or harm.[28] Given the ignorance surrounding HIV/AIDS and the consequent stigma attached to the disease, possible (even probable) harassment by fellow employees is reasonably foreseeable. Therefore a common law duty on employers to take positive steps to prevent HIV-infected employees suffering harm or injury is most likely.

In *Media 24 Ltd & Another v Grobler*[29] the Supreme Court of Appeal held that it is 'well settled' that employers owe their employees a duty to take reasonable care of their safety.[30] The court opined that this duty is not confined to protecting employees from physical harm, but includes a duty to protect employees from psychological harm.[31] This case concerned an appeal by Media 24 to set aside the decision of the High Court in *Grobler v Naspers Bpk & 'n ander.*[32] The High Court had held Naspers vicariously liable for acts of sexual harassment committed by a fellow employee of Grobler against her. It ordered Naspers to pay Grobler an amount of R776,814 in compensation. On appeal the court found it unnecessary to deal with the question of the vicarious liability of the employer because the claim could succeed on the basis of Grobler's second cause of action, namely, the employer's common law duty to take reasonable care of the safety of its employees. The court found that the legal convictions of the community required an employer to take reasonable steps to protect its employees against acts of sexual harassment by other employees. Failure to do so would result employers having to pay compensation to the victim of such sexual harassment.

By analogy, it is not unreasonable to argue that the employer has a common law duty to take positive steps to protect HIV-positive employees from harassment, stigmatisation and discrimination at the hands of *inter alia* their fellow employees.

The following constitutional provisions further increase the likelihood of the existence of a common law duty on employers to take reasonable care of and to protect HIV-infected employees from physical and psychological harm arising from harassment, stigmatisation and discrimination at the workplace:

- Section 173 provides the High Courts, the Supreme Court of Appeal and the Constitutional Court with inherent jurisdiction to develop the common law, 'taking into account the interests of justice'.
- Section 39(1)(a) enjoins courts to promote the 'values that underlie an open and democratic society based on human dignity, equality and freedom'.

---

27   Ibid., E4: 30.
28   Ibid., E4: 30–31.
29   (2005) 26 *ILJ* 1007 (SCA).
30   See Brassey, E4:19–49.
31   *Media 24 Ltd & Another v Grobler* at para 65.
32   (2004) 25 *ILJ* 439 (C).

- Section 39(2) enjoins the courts to develop the common law in line with and giving effect to the spirit, purport and object of the Bill of Rights.
- Section 14 provides that all persons with HIV or AIDS have a right to privacy concerning their HIV status.
- Section 9(3) provides that no person may unfairly discriminate against anyone on one or more grounds including race, sex ethnic or social origin *et cetera*.
- Section 10 provides that 'everyone has the right to have their dignity respected and protected'.

Vicarious liability

Another possible common law basis for employer liability for failing to take steps to protect HIV-infected employees from harm is the vicarious liability of the employer. Unlike the direct liability based on the duty to protect its employees from harm, vicarious liability renders an employer liable for the wrongful acts of its employees. In *Grobler v Naspers Bpk & 'n ander* the court found the employer vicariously liable for the acts of sexual harassment of one of its employees. After considering the development of the doctrine of vicarious liability in other common law jurisdictions, the court concluded that of policy considerations justified its finding.[33] By analogy, an employer could be held liable on the basis of the common law doctrine of vicarious liability for the wrongful acts of its employees towards its HIV-positive employees. Nevertheless, given the statutory vicarious liability of the employer for unfair discrimination against employees infected with HIV,[34] it is not necessary to rely on the common law vicarious liability of the employer.[35]

Constructive dismissal (breach of contract)

If there is a 'sufficiently serious breach of a sufficiently important term' by one party to a contract, the other party will be entitled to cancel the contract.[36] Therefore if an employer renders performance of the employee's duties intolerable, this constitutes a material breach of contract entitling the employee to cancel the contract (resign) and claim compensation for breach of contract.[37] The breached term may be an express or an implied term. Implied in every contract of employment is a duty

---

33 A thorough discussion of the reasoning of the court is beyond the scope of this article.

34 Section 60 read with section 6(1) of the EEA.

35 As will be discussed under the heading 'Compensation' below, the EEA does not place a limit on the amount of compensation claimable in such a case and therefore there seems to be no advantage in claiming on the basis of the employer's common law liability in circumstances where the employer could be vicariously liable for the acts of its employees.

36 R. H. Christie, *The Law of Contract in South Africa*, Butterworth: Durban (2006), 5th edn, 514.

37 In *Stewart Wrightson (Pty) Ltd v Thorpe* 1977 2 SA 943 (A) 951–952 the court held that the employer had committed a material breach of contract by degrading the status of the employee. The employee was therefore held to be entitled to cancel the contract of employment and claim compensation for breach of contract.

of mutual trust and confidence.[38] This implied term[39] was derived from English law. This means that there is an implied term in every contract of employment 'that the employer will not, without reasonable and probable cause, conduct itself in a manner calculated or likely to destroy or seriously damage the relationship of confidence and trust between the parties.'[40] Since this is a material term, conduct inconsistent with it will entitle the 'innocent' party to cancel the contract of employment.[41] It is not necessary, however, for the party wishing to cancel the contract to prove that the other party intended to repudiate the contract.[42] What is of relevance is the effect that such breach has on the employee. If it has the effect, judged reasonably and objectively, that the employee cannot be expected to endure the situation, the employee will be entitled to resign.[43] Failure by an employer to implement policies and procedures in order to eliminate discrimination against HIV-positive employees can be construed as a material breach of the implied term of mutual trust and confidence rendering the employee's performance in terms of the contract intolerable.

Compensation

A refusal by an employer to take steps to ensure that its employees infected with HIV are not harassed and discriminated against can attract liability to pay compensation on more than one basis. For example, such inaction can result in the employer being liable to pay compensation for an unfair dismissal or unfair labour practice[44] as well as compensation for *contumelia*, pain and suffering, emotional trauma, loss of future earnings and the loss of amenities of life.[45]

---

38 See Craig Bosch, 'The implied term of trust and confidence in South African law' (2006) 27 *ILJ* 28.

39 This is a *naturalia contractus* of employment contracts.

40 *Council for Scientific & Industrial Research v Fijen* (1996) 17 *ILJ* 18 (A) at 26; *Pretoria Society for the Care of the Retarded v Loots* (1997) 18 *ILJ* 981 (LAC) at 985 para A.

41 Idem.

42 *Pretoria Society for the Care of the Retarded v Loots* (1997) 18 *ILJ* 981 (LAC) 984 para J; *Stewart Wrightson (Pty) Ltd v Thorpe* 1977 2 SA 943 (A) 951–952; Christie, 514.

43 *Pretoria Society for the Care of the Retarded v Loots* (1997) 18 *ILJ* 981 (LAC) at 985 para B.

44 An unfair labour practice is defined in terms 186(2) of the LRA as *inter alia* 'any unfair act or omission that arises between an employer and an employee involving' promotion, demotion, probation, training, the provision of benefits, suspension, disciplinary action short of dismissal and a failure to re-employ or reinstate an employee contrary to the terms of an agreement. In terms of section 194(4) of the LRA the maximum compensation for an unfair labour practice is 12 months' salary. This kind of conduct also constitutes a breach of the provisions of the section 6(1) of the EEA since the conduct would constitute an 'employment policy or practice' as defined in section 1 of the EEA.

45 See for example *Christian v Colliers Properties* 306c and 306d, where an order for compensation was awarded for sexual harassment in terms of section 50(1) of the EEA, in addition to an order for compensation for automatically unfair dismissal in terms of section 194 of the LRA.

This is what happened in *Ntsabo v Real Security CC*.[46] Ntsabo, a security guard, resigned after being sexually harassed by her supervisor. The employer, despite having been informed of the incidents of sexual harassment, consistently ignored the situation and in a complacent manner did nothing about it. The victim of the sexual harassment consequently resigned. The Labour Court found that the employer's inaction and complacency with regard to the situation had rendered it intolerable for Ntsabo to continue working and consequently Ntsabo was found to have been constructively dismissed.[47] The basis of the constructive dismissal was sexual harassment. Sexual harassment is not one of the prohibited grounds of discrimination listed in section 187(f) of the LRA, but it only qualifies as a ground for discrimination in terms of section 6(3) of the EEA. In consequence the court *per* Pillay J was unable to find that the dismissal was an automatically unfair dismissal in terms of section 187(f) of the LRA which attracts compensation of up to 24 months' salary. Nevertheless, the inaction of the employer was still found to constitute an unfair dismissal in terms of section 186(1)(e) of the LRA. The court made the maximum allowable award compensation for an unfair dismissal which is not an automatically unfair dismissal. This amounts to 12 months' salary,[48] which in this case amounted to R12,000.

The same inaction of the employer resulted in a further two awards for compensation. The employer was ordered in terms of the EEA to pay a further amount of R20,000 for future medical costs for psychiatric treatment, and an amount of R50,000 for general damages including *contumelia*. In addition, the employer was ordered to pay for the costs of the application.

Liability for future medical costs and general damages including *contumelia* was based on the statutory vicarious liability of the employer for the conduct of its employees created in terms of section 60 of the EEA.

Whether a claim is based on statute or the common law can have an effect on the amount of compensation awarded. Statute may place limits on the amount claimable with respect to statutory-based claims, as is the case with claims for unfair dismissals and unfair labour practices in terms of the Labour Relations Act.[49] These limits may, however, be of guidance for judges faced with the unenviable task of deciding how much compensation to award in the case of a common law breach.

A claim for a breach of the common law duty to take reasonable care of the safety of employees can either be based on delict or on contract.[50] For purposes of determining the amount of compensation claimable this distinction has no relevance because in both cases the amount would be the same. As Brassey explains:

---

46   [2004] 1 BLLR 58 (LC).
47   Section 186(1)(e) of the LRA.
48   Section 194(1) of the LRA.
49   Section 194 of the LRA.
50   Brassey, E4: 20.

In delict the employee is entitled to be put in the position he would have been in had the employer not committed the wrongful act or omission. In contract he is entitled to be put in the position he would have occupied had the employer fulfilled her duty to refrain from or prevent the wrongful act. In either case the remedy is aimed at a redress of the harm in so far as this is possible by the payment of money.[51]

Section 50(1)(d) and (e) of the EEA provide that the Labour Court may make any appropriate order including awarding compensation and damages 'in circumstances contemplated in this Act'. Section 50(2) of the EEA further provides that if the Labour Court finds that an employee has been unfairly discriminated against, it may make 'any order that is just and equitable in the circumstances, including (a) payment of compensation by the employer to the employee; (b) payment of damages by the employer to the employee.'[52]

Since the court can make an award that it deems to be just and equitable, there is no statutory limitation on the amount that can be awarded. Therefore, whether one's claim is for unfair discrimination is based on the common law (vicarious liability of the employer or on the duty to take reasonable care of the safety of employees) or on the statutory provisions contained in the EEA, the ultimate outcome concerning the amount of compensation will be determined by the judge's sense of what is right. It seems likely that a court will apply the same formula applicable to the award for damages for a common law of contract or for a delict: it will attempt to place the applicant in the same position he or she would have occupied had there been no breach of the EEA 'in so far as this is possible by the payment of money'.[53] Even though a judge will have the benefit of the opinions of expert witnesses concerning the extent of the injury, be it physical or psychological, as well as the results of calculations of actuaries, the fact remains that determining the amount of damages can never be an exact science. Inevitably there will always be an element of subjectivity in the final determination.

As discussed, the amount of claimable compensation for constructive dismissal and unfair labour practices is limited in terms of section 194 of the LRA. However, if instead of basing the claim on the LRA the applicant bases his or her claim on a breach of contract, there is no applicable statutory limit to the amount of compensation claimable. In *Pretoria Society for the Care of the Retarded v Loots*,[54] Nicholson JA, following English law, listed a number of guidelines that should be considered in determining the amount of an award for compensation.[55] This case concerned a constructive dismissal. It was decided in terms of the Labour Relations

---

51   Ibid., E4: 21.
52   In *Coetzer & Others v Minister of Safety & Security & Another* at 306, the primary remedy for unfair discrimination was held to be what the court deems just and equitable.
53   Brassey, E4: 21.
54   (1997) 18 *ILJ* 981 (LAC).
55   These were the factors mentioned by Combrinck J in *Ferodo (Pty) Ltd v De Ruite* (1993) 14 *ILJ* 974 (LAC) at 981 C–G.

Act 28 of 1956, which unlike the present LRA placed no limitations on the amount claimable for an 'unfair labour practice'.[56] These guidelines are as follows:[57]

> *(a) there must be evidence before the court of actual financial loss suffered by the person claiming compensation;*
> *(b) there must be proof that the loss was caused by the unfair labour practice;*
> *(c) the loss must be foreseeable, i.e. not too remote or speculative;*
> *(d) the award must endeavour to place the applicant in monetary terms in the position in which he would have been had the unfair labour practice not been committed;*
> *(e) in making the award the court must be guided by what is reasonable and fair in the circumstances. It should not be calculated to punish the party;*
> *(f) there is a duty on the employ (if he is seeking compensation) to mitigate his damages by taking all reasonable steps to acquire alternative employment;*
> *(g) the benefit which the applicant receives, e.g. by way of severance package, must be taken into account.*

In short, therefore, once again the judge is required to make a value judgment as to what is fair and reasonable in the circumstances.

Soft law

The Code of Good Practice: Key Aspects of HIV/AIDS and Employment

This Code was issued by the Minister of Labour in 2000. Its primary objective 'is to set out guidelines for employers and trade unions to implement so as to ensure individuals with HIV infection are not unfairly discriminated against in the workplace.'[58] Landman J in *Joy Mining Machinery (A division of Harnischfeger (SA) (Pty) Ltd) v NUMSA & Others*[59] stated with reference to this code that it 'is intended to provide guidance to a court and other persons applying the EEA. It may be assumed that a court would take a code into account in adjudicating a matter.' The guidelines in the Code provide for positive action on the part of the employer. This includes the prevention of unfair discrimination and stigmatisation by means of the following actions:

---

56 In terms of section 46(9) of the Labour Relations Act 28 of 1956, a constructive dismissal could constitute an unfair labour practice.
57 At 990 A–B.
58 Para 2 of the Code.
59 [2002] 4 BLLR 372 LC at para 9.

(i) the development of HIV/AIDS policies and programmes for the workplace;

(ii) awareness, education and training on the rights of all persons with regard to HIV and AIDS in the workplace;

(iii) mechanisms to promote acceptance and openness around HIV/AIDS in the workplace;

(iv) providing support for all employees infected or affected by HIV and AIDS; and

(v) grievance procedures and disciplinary measures to deal with HIV related complaints in the workplace.[60]

It is clear that the Code envisages positive action on the part of employers in the elimination of unfair discrimination against employees infected with HIV/AIDS. Given the fact that the in terms of section 3(c) of the EEA, its terms must be interpreted by taking into account 'any relevant code of good practice issued in terms of this Act ...', it is not difficult to imagine that an employer's failure to take these positive steps can be interpreted to be a breach of section 6(1) of the EEA. Secondly, such failure can contribute to the ease with which employees can contravene the provisions of the EEA, thus rendering the employer vicariously liable in terms of section 60 of the Act. This was the ultimate result in *Ntsabo v Real Security CC*.[61] Pillay in this case referred to the Code of Good Practice on the Handling of Sexual Harassment Cases which also provides for the setting out of procedures to deal with the issue of sexual harassment. He pointed out that the employer had not implemented 'a policy related to harassment in its operation let alone make plans in that regard'.[62] On this basis he concluded that this failure or omission could not serve as a veil behind which the employer could hide behind in order to avoid liability.[63] Similarly, a failure by an employer to develop policies plans, procedures, as provided for in terms of the Code of Good Practice: Key Aspects of HIV/AIDS and Employment, cannot serve as a basis to exclude liability on the part of the employer for its vicarious liability for the acts of discrimination committed by its employees against their HIV-infected fellow employees.

The King Report

The obligation on employers to take positive action to manage the effects of HIV/AIDS in an appropriate manner has two sources. As discussed above, a failure to ensure that HIV-infected employees are not unfairly discriminated against can result in the employer having to pay potentially huge amounts in compensation to the victim of the unfair discrimination. Secondly, such failure can have dire economic consequences for the organisation. Perhaps this second threat is even more

---

60   Para 6.2 of the Code.
61   [2004] 1 BLLR 58 (LC).
62   At 99.
63   Ibid.

compelling than the threat of civil litigation. Firstly, it is a more immediate threat. Secondly, such failure can result in the economic demise of the organisation.

In South Africa the King Commission drew up a code for good corporate governance[64] in the form of *The King Report on Corporate Governance for South Africa 2002* (The King Report). It provides guidelines for South African companies wishing to implement good corporate governance practices.[65] The King Commission subscribed to the view that in this global economy no corporation can afford to run its business without due consideration of the interests of all the stakeholders.[66] This view is commonly referred to as 'stakeholder theory'.[67] These stakeholders have been defined as 'those whose relations to the enterprise cannot be completely contracted for, but upon whose co-operation and creativity it depends for its survival and prosperity'.[68] This includes the community in which the company operates, its customers, employees and suppliers.[69] Since corporations are dependent on society for their survival, the necessity to conduct their affairs in an ethical and fair manner, taking the interests of society in general into account, is apparent.[70] For this reason, it makes no economic sense for employers to ignore the presence of HIV/AIDS in the workplace. Failure to take positive steps to address the issue and ameliorate the position of infected employees can only result in a tarnished company image and reputation which obviously is bad for business.

Even more pressing than the need for a favourable public image are the direct effects of the prevalence of HIV/Aids on the employer. The King Commission identified the following examples:

> ... *decreased productivity, e.g. through death, sick and compassion leave; increased overhead costs, e.g. health care and insurance; reduction in the available skills base (with attendant indirect recruitment and training costs);*

---

64   *The King Report on Corporate Governance for South Africa*, Institute of Directors: Johannesburg (2002).

65   Corporate governance is defined as 'the system by which companies are directed and controlled' by the Cadbury Report on Corporate Governance (UK). This is the meaning that is ascribed to the term in this article.

66   *King Report*, para 14, reads: 'In the global economy there are many jurisdictions to which a company can run to avoid regulation and taxes or to reduce labour costs. But, there are few places where a company can hide its activities from sceptical consumers, shareowners or protestors. In short, in the age of electronic information and activism, no company can escape the adverse consequences of poor governance.'

67   G. Vinten, 'Shareholder versus stakeholder – is there a governance dilemma?', *Corporate Governance*, 1 9, January 2001, 36, at 37.

68   *King Report* II page 98, para 1.4.

69   *King Report* II page 8, para 5.3.

70   See D. de Jongh, 'Know your stakeholders', *Finance Week*, 30 June 2004, 34, where he states: 'In today's CNN age everything we do as individuals and companies is exposed in seconds and therefore it's so important to understand exactly who all the stakeholders are that are affected by our business and how they again affect our business on a daily basis.'

a contracting consumer base[71] and changes in consumer spending patterns for some, predominantly retail, industry sectors; reduced profitability; and diminished investor confidence generally.[72]

Very significant and expensive internal risks for any employer include high rates of employee turnover with the attendant loss of client relationship, loss of workforce morale, reduction in productivity and increased absenteeism.

Therefore an employer should in its own interests

... ensure that it understands the social and economic impact that HIV/AIDS will have on business activities; adopt an appropriate strategy, plan and policies to address and manage the potential impact of HIV/AIDS on business activities; regularly monitor and measure performance using established indicators; and report on all the above to stakeholders on a regular basis.[73]

The strategy and plan would obviously have to include positive measures to protect employees from harassment from their fellow employees and from all forms of unfair discrimination.

Conclusion

As discussed, awards against employers as a result of a failure to take positive steps to address HIV/AIDS issues at the workplace are both potentially very high and impossible to predict with certainty. The financial repercussions of a poor public image as a result of such complacency are also impossible to calculate but nevertheless potentially very dangerous. Finally, the direct effects of HIV/AIDS mentioned by the King Report, such as decreased productivity, increased overhead costs, reduction in the available skills base (with attendant indirect recruitment and training costs), a contracting consumer base and diminished investor confidence, generally cannot be ignored if a corporation wishes to remain in business. Given the prevalence of HIV infection in South Africa, employers have no choice but to implement codes of corporate social responsibility for the benefit of HIV-infected employees.

---

71 According to *News 24* (E. Stoddard, 'Experts: Aids digging hole in SAB', Reuters, at <www.news24.co.za>, 12 April 2002), South African Breweries Limited is experiencing a diminishing domestic consumer base as a result of HIV/AIDS-related deaths. A study conducted by the company in 2002 predicted that the sale of beer would decline by 12.58 million litres in 2002 and that by 2006 it would decline by 41.68 million litres as a direct result of AIDS-related deaths reducing its consumer base.

72 *King Report*, para 4.4.

73 Ibid. at para 4.6.

PART III

Ethical Considerations

Overview of Part III

Thomas Hobbes is well known for discussing the concept of the social contract. In his construct, citizens would agree to vest absolute power in a sovereign power as the only way to avoid anarchy. In this way citizens give up their individual rights, including control of liberty and property, and possibly life. He argued that human self-interest is such that we would be willing to wage war on each other, the end result being a short and unpleasant life for all. This tradition accords with a utilitarian position (the pursuit of maximum welfare) and provides the test for whether corporate behaviour is morally right or wrong. Utilitarianism regards corporate activity as morally good if it maximises human welfare, and collective welfare may override individual welfare.

The concept of utilitarianism was developed as an extension of liberalism in order to account for the need to regulate society in terms of each individual pursuing, independently, his or her own ends. It was developed by people such as Bentham and John Stuart Mill, who defined the optimal position for society as being the greatest good of the greatest number. They argued that it was government's role to mediate between individuals to ensure this societal end. In utilitarianism it is not actions which are deemed to be good or bad but merely outcomes. Thus, any means of securing a desired outcome was deemed to be acceptable and if the same outcomes ensued then there was no difference, in value terms, between the different means of securing those outcomes. Thus, actions are value-neutral and only outcomes matter. This is, of course, problematical when the actions of firms are concerned because firms only consider outcomes from the point of view of the firm itself. Indeed, accounting, as we know, only captures the actions of a firm insofar as they affect the firm itself and ignores other consequences of the actions of a firm. Under utilitarianism, however, if the outcomes for the firm were considered to be desirable then any means of achieving these outcomes would be considered acceptable. In the nineteenth and early twentieth centuries this was the way in which firms were managed and it is only in more recent times that it has become accepted that all the outcomes from the actions of a firm are important and need to be taken into account. The development of utilitarianism led to the development of economic theory as a means of explaining the actions of firms. Indeed, the concept of perfect competition is predicated in the assumptions of classical liberal theory. From economic theory, of course, accounting was developed as a tool for analysis to aid the rational decision-making assumed in economic theory.

During the era of individualism in the 1980s, however, a theoretical alternative was developed in the US which became known as communitarianism, although the concept goes back to the earlier work of such people as Tonnies (1957) and Plant (1974). Communitarianism is based upon the argument that it is not the individual, or even the state, which should be the basis of our value system. Thus the social nature of life is emphasised alongside public goods and services. The argument is that all individuals, including corporations, have an obligation to contribute towards the public nature of life rather than pursuing their own self-interests. Underpinning the theories of communitarianism is the assumption that ethical behaviour must proceed from an understanding of a community's traditions and cultural understanding. Exponents (see Crowther and Davila-Gomez 2006) argue that the exclusive pursuit of private interest erodes the network of social environments on which we all depend, and is destructive to our shared experiment in democratic self-government. A communitarian perspective recognises both individual human dignity and the social dimension of human existence and that the preservation of individual liberty depends on the active maintenance of the institutions of civil society where citizens learn respect for others as well as self-respect. It is also where we acquire a lively sense of our personal and civic responsibilities, along with an appreciation of our own rights and the rights of others.

A perennial debate within the discourse of CSR has been the extent to which one's ethical ontology affects one's understanding of socially responsible behaviour. Similarly, the question of an ethical foundation, as opposed to a regulatory framework, being necessary for the operation of CSR is one which has caused considerable debate. There are of, course, no definitive answers to these questions and the contributors to this section do not attempt to provide any. Rather they focus upon a number of pertinent issues.

According to Davila-Gomez, social conscience may be assumed as a characteristic of a collective concerned for social well-being. However, the conscience of some individuals may not be aligned with what a group values as good, given that the existence of personality factors, life experiences and opportunities (or the lack of them) of gaining concern for others may influence the individual's behaviour towards their social moral duties. As such, apathy exists in our world and within some of our company directors. Thus, under the capitalist dynamics of a globalised economy, free market and human inequities, the need for managers to have greater concern for social responsibility is imperative. She explores the reality of these inequities, the ties with management theory and practice, as well as some psychological factors and environments that favour or disfavour the development of an individual's social conscience. She therefore proposes some academic orientations for conducting teaching and researching concerned for social sympathy and responsiveness, which include the occurrence of pedagogical and action-research environments that favour the student's awareness and the development of social conscience.

Debeljak and Krkač take a different starting point and wonder why people find change to be so stressful. Their chapter is an attempt to understand and analyse change. Thus, there is an analysis of the ontic structure of change. Since change is something that affects anything that comes in its way, the paper observes its relationship with business – namely the attempt at managing change in business, and the place of corporate social responsibility within the picture. They situate their analysis within the context of spiral dynamics and the ethics of care to show that change is inevitable not just in the world but in the firm as well. They argue that understanding change is manifest in leading change, and good leading means good understanding. They conclude that change should be governed in the light of the irreparable harm/damage principle and positively in the light of the care principle as a key tool for creating the future world in which people would prefer to work, live long and prosper.

The relationship between CSR and philanthropy on the part of corporations has received a great deal of attention within the CSR discourse. In the next chapter Phillips takes a different view of philanthropy by focusing on the behaviour of very rich individuals in their philanthropic giving. She contrasts the behaviour of these individuals with the giving patterns of the social elite, which is less ambitious in scope, and with corporate giving which is often seen to be for strategic purposes. Her suggestion for these people is that there is a significant element of personal aggrandisement in the public giving of very large sums to very high-profile charitable causes. In her analysis she uses a variety of theories of giving to help understand the phenomenon and concludes with a suggestion that this phenomenon has a role to play in helping to avert a global catastrophe.

Çalıyurt, by way of contrast, is more concerned with ethics and corporate governance. She focuses particularly upon Turkey, a developing country and candidate member for EU membership. The focus of this chapter is upon defining corporate governance in a Turkish context while explaining its relationship to both accounting and to Turkish law. As she states, the aim of her study is to give information about legislation changes that brought about closer integration of accounting studies after the banking scandals in the country. She echoes Aras when she states that sound corporate governance practices bring out advantages for companies and countries. With respect to companies, a high-quality status of corporate governance means low capital cost, increase in financial capabilities and liquidity, ability of overcoming crises more easily and prevention of the exclusion of soundly managed companies from the capital markets.

It is interesting to observe that the issue of stress in the workplace features prominently in this section, even though it is central to the concern of the previous sections with the employment relationship. Equally, as Çalıyurt shows, ethics and governance – one of our recurring concepts – are shown to be closely interrelated. Links to many of the other core concepts are also apparent in these chapters.

References

Crowther, D. and Davila-Gomez, A.M. (2006), 'I will if you will: risk, feelings and emotion in the workplace', in D. Crowther and K.T. Çalıyurt (eds), *Globalisation and Social Responsibility*, Cambridge: Cambridge Scholars Press, pp 166–84.

Plant, R. (1974), *Community and Ideology*, London: Routledge & Kegan Paul.

Tonnies, F. (1957), *Community and Society*, trans. C.P. Loomis, New York: Harper & Row.

Inquiring about Social Conscience

Ana-Maria Davila-Gomez

Corporations' excesses and individuals' choices

Without being the rule nor the traditional majority tendency in organizational theory and management discourses, there is nowadays an emerging literature in corporate social responsibility (CSR), mostly as a civil and moral response from some academics and a few practitioners who try to fix to a certain extent some of the damages that actual corporations continuously inflict on our entire world. This damage has been mostly documented in terms of detriment to the environment, impoverishment of social conditions with consequences in the quality of life, as well as in terms of taking advantage of the lack of legislation that protects human rights in developing countries. There is statistical evidence that reflects the former. There are various international organizations showing the situation (for example, United Nations 2006) in which, regardless of the fact that during the past 60 years we (as a collective) have begun to reflect about what we could call a 'global concern for sustainable development', it is well known that we are still far away from attaining a considerable global improvement.

At some point we identify that what is called a collective consciousness may represent a shared value or awareness; however, when what it is desired by this collective is not shared by a majority or, worse, when those who share it do not have enough power to produce a radical change, there is still a time frame of uncertain duration that must elapse in order to gain powerful adepts, or in order to produce a collective social movement in which the majority confronts the oppressive minority. For instance, history teaches us how the French Revolution took place, and how many of the actions carried out were inspired by the works of Rousseau (1712–78) (Rousseau 1999) or even Montaigne (1533–92), to name only two of the remarkable authors who contributed to enlighten the minds of many oppressed people at that time. Additionally, regardless of a shared intention as a collective, there are also individuals inside this collective who, despite sharing the same objectives, do not believe that the means used to attempt the goal are legitimate. We talk here about a legitimacy endorsed not only by laws, but also by common human sense, which leads us to the moral aspect, in the same sense that Socrates (see Plato 1997) and Rousseau (1964) referred to. Hereby, we make reference to those who question the legitimacy of governmental institutions that do not honour the promises made to the community or do not show advancement in their programmes.

In some way, we observe this kind of situation in the actual picture of our world, where, for instance, despite the implementation of many programmes seeking to improve the human situation worldwide (such as the World Bank investments and loans – see for instance World Bank 2007), the United Nations (2006) shows how the widening gap between rich and poor countries increases, as well as the gap between poor and rich people within each country. As such, we see that it is not necessarily true that in developing countries everybody is poor; on the contrary, reality shows that rich people, enclosed as an elite, hold the wealth of a nation and make a poor redistribution of it. In these terms, lack of protective legislation, which is by the way dictated by elitist governments regardless of their democratic composition, allows international companies to operate by means of offshore operation and outsourcing, which are represented to shareholders as a 'commodity' for decreasing production and distribution costs and also for targeting new markets.

With the previous example, we see how our behaviour is paradoxical given that, on the one hand, our governments participate actively in programmes of sustainable development and we participate actively in international organizational meetings (such as those of the UN or the OAS), but, on the other hand, seeking to improve our nation's indicators of economical performance we, as governments or social collectives, allow the neoliberalist dynamics of the free-market and increasing of shareholder value to dictate the rules of our nation's commerce and activities by means of organizational disregard towards social, human and environmental issues.

The collective conscience and the individual's will

These same kinds of events happen daily in the micro-level of organizational life. When pursuing productivity, managers offer, as a result of the process, a human development for employees and a social contribution through taxes and perhaps some CSR actions (such as parks, foundations, etc.). However, behind these promises of global development contribution of any organization's activity, we find marked disparities of the kind inside many organizations worldwide, as Epstein (1999) presents it:

> ... legitimacy questions – internal and external – underlie contemporary issues such as the high, some might even say exorbitant, levels of compensation received by some corporate leaders and the vast disparity between these amounts and what lower level employees earn; the substantial pressures form financial markets to focus business objectives on short-term rather than long-term goals; and the attenuated 'social contract' between the firm and the employees at all levels – CEO to baseline worker.

At one point, the two logics (macro and micro) need to be tied and reconciled, because in almost any country, some individuals are working on the macro-arenas at a macro-social level, and others, more as an individual's ethical choice (see Davila-Gomez 2005), are beginning to work in the humanistic details of organizational specificities. On top of that, some people work also in the aim to consolidate a global and collective consciousness for constructing a more sustainable and joyful place to live for future generations, and in that, non-governmental organizations and other entities place emphasis on benevolent efforts and not just on creating paid jobs.

The examples of incongruity and paradoxes presented before indicate that a high intellectual educational level does not necessarily grant moral behaviour to an individual. The classical case of this argument is the fact of corruption worldwide, where many of the corrupt practices are committed by some individuals in power who have attained these highly hierarchical jobs by means of university degrees and years of experience in government posts.

In this point, and regarding social responsible actions at the decision levels of organizations (whether public, governmental or private), we ask ourselves about what triggers in some individuals the desire and conviction to perform ethical actions with social concern, and what inhibits or invalidates this desire in others. With this questioning, we enter the field of purpose and, more than treating the organization as an entity, we question the motives and actions of powerful individuals who conduct the actions of organizations.

The question is therefore how, inside a collective conscience, some people question not only the aim pursued, but also the means used and the legitimacy and morality of the actions executed. Hence, we need to explore not only the organizational results as a collective of individuals, and their common shared values, but also the powerful individuals' conscience, their set of beliefs, and why some of them are truthfully concerned by social issues while others answer only to governmental regulation in order to continue operations.

As such, in our research, we arrive at the point of questioning the psychological motives of the individual; more precisely, those which prevent individuals from developing concern, compassion and empathy towards others. Mudrack (2007) suggests that believing in the rightness of social responsibility is tied to the individual's personality, where attitudes, values and thinking patterns have a great role to play in the way each one conduct and judges him or herself. We arrive at the point of questioning about sympathy or apathy towards social issues.

Apathy and the need for socialization

White (2004) elaborates on political apathy disorder (PAD) as a human behaviour:

> *Political Apathy Disorder (PAD) is proposed as a new Diagnostic and Statistical Manual of Mental Disorder (DSM) Axis II (Personality Disorder) category. … Who owns, manages, controls, distributes, and benefits from*

society's resources? ... a social conscience may have once existed but has since atrophied. Such individuals have moved past despair and demoralization into apathy where they no longer care about their lack of motivation to help others. ... The problem is that they lack sufficient empathy and compassion to compel action on behalf of those outside their inner circle. ... PAD reflects a failure in social functioning: failure to engage in activity designed to reduce the suffering of others. ... It is more likely that individuals with PAD are overmedicated. If anything is 'prescribed,' it should be more along the lines of participating in political action such as joining organizations, campaigns, and demonstration.

As such, apathy and disregard towards others may result from childhood experiences (see Winnicott 1965), nevertheless the hope for a cure exists. We see then how it is action and new social and political civil projects that may help individuals realize the need for concern, for helping others. Some individuals may only need to read about a particular situation, or just watch the news, in order to become aware. However, that is not the case for many individuals who need to experience the pain in the eyes of relatives or loved ones. In this sense, involvement with causes helps to create ties with individuals in need. In this way, socialization, interaction and communication help to generate concern for what may happen to the new people in the circle and, most probably, in which way it is possible to help in order to mitigate suffering to some extent. Socialization is a way of gaining deeper knowledge of issues, implications and consequences of others' needs.

Social awareness helps to develop the social conscience that awakens ethical behaviour and morals in our managerial decisions and actions. In this sense, Butterfield et al. (2000) define moral awareness as 'a person's recognition that his/her potential decision or action could affect the interest, welfare, or expectations of the self or the others in a fashion that may conflict with one or more ethical standards.' They develop a model in which the awareness is followed by judgement, intent and finally by action. For them, an action containing moral awareness also refers to what is conceived by the social group as good.

In these terms, for us, the individual's social conscience is related to the group's social conscience or, at least, taking advantage of our examples presented before, there is a relationship between the general ideal of the social project and the individual's will. However, the great directors do not always follow what the group would consider as good. As discussed before, our worldwide reality of inequities reveals that there is apathy in the world, and this, in powerful people, is particularly important, as they affect many individuals by their actions. We maintain, therefore, that when talking about social conscience, there is a need for the individual to pass from the conviction about something to the coherent action that represents its will. Moreover, as discussed by Singer and Smith (1997), in corporations, the individual's ethical action and moral behaviour will directly impact upon the organization image; therefore, deontology as a normative for the organization is not enough; it is imperative to count with the individual's will.

Equally, we identify that in a board of directors, in the case of public institutions, there is more openness to the participation of different stakeholders than in private firms. While taking decisions, there will be more awareness about the issues of different groups (stakeholders) if participation is allowed; therefore the possibility of developing a social conscience is greater. However, as we know, this participation is restricted in many private firms. Openness occurs mostly when governmental regulations of a particular country demands it, or when the free will of an overall majority of shareholders, who consider it a value, enables it to be so; otherwise, the board of directors will restrict outsiders to the limit of what laws demand. Clarkson (1995) shows how a social performance can be evaluated, not only in terms of the responses to the stakeholders, but also to the orientation and care towards society as a whole. The fact of not having representatives of every group of society in the board of directors, or in the stakeholders list, does not imply that the needs of those who are not present are negligible. Managers need to look for information outside their circle, they need to interact and socialize with other corporations, governments and international humanitarian organizations, among others. It is imperative to act right at the beginning – at the point at which individuals begin to form their sets of values and beliefs.

Academic moral involvement: research and teaching

Thinking about the continuous development of a manager's personality we maintain that along with technical education there is a need to develop the sense of judgement, the social sensibility and awareness to others' needs (that is, what Davila-Gomez and Crowther (2007) explain as the need to introduce a practical humanistic orientation in management education in both curricula and pedagogy). To complement this, and in order to nourish the humanistic concern for actual and future management students, we are interested in exploring some factors that put into context and favour the will for individuals to gain and develop social conscience. For this, as academics and former practitioners, we realize that a part of the answer is found in the discourse, experience and subjectivity of actual practitioners, whereas a deeper understanding of life experiences is granted by psychoanalysis and humanistic theories.

Therefore, while inquiring about social conscience, we suggest the conducting of research that follows a qualitative approach which emphasizes action research, discourse deconstruction (Chia 1996), critical analysis (Forester 2003) and subjectivity experience (that is, what Aktouf (1987) describes as participant observation, or what Torbert and Fisher (1992) present as autobiographical awareness).

For instance, as suggested by Reason (2006), the alternative of doing action research as a methodology enables not only to the gathering of knowledge from the practitioner's field, but also a contribution to improving the explored situation. As such, Reason (2006) includes with these practices the opportunity to building in democratic and participative events. In this way, we consider that there is more need to conduct academic studies in management concerning social responsibility by means of action research. On the one hand, we as professors will have information coming directly from the field, very certainly, and also we may participate as consultants in projects involving the improvement of social responsibility within organizations. We may become not only theoretical critics, but also direct change agents of the realities we study. On the other hand, academic projects of this magnitude should serve as the basis for students' thesis projects, allowing those students to achieve a thorough and factual understanding of the very real issues at stake in corporate social responsibility.

Additionally, these kinds of dynamics help to construct university–industry partnerships in social themes, and not only the traditional financial and technological ones. Our spectrum of influence is broader. Contrary to the market competition theory, this kind of action research projects enables inter-organization collaboration and cooperation, which are some of the behaviours valued as needed, by people (individuals) with social conscience. To become social actors of radical changes, organizations need to become collaborative, which implies in a way that they will act in some arenas in a different way than the traditional one of competition. There is a need to share, to be supportive towards those who are like us, and also towards those who are different; and this goes not only for individuals as separate beings, but also for organizations as collectives. Therefore, industry–public partnerships are more needed, and also cooperative social projects of various similar organizations grouped by consortiums, foundations, inter-organisational structures (see the 2005 interview conducted by *Revista de Empresa* with James Austin), among other ways of cooperation (see for instance Martínez et al. (2006) who present the case of the Carvajal Foundation in Colombia, where a private organization works united as a group with other public and non-governmental organizations for the educational, economic and social development of one of the most underprivileged sectors of society).

A critical pedagogy approach in management may help to unveil the owner's finalities of any case study (see Reynolds 1998). Balancing this, in order to favour social awareness in students, Selman and Dray (2003a; 2003b) discuss the need to pass from discourse and literature, to practice and the power of persuasion. Even though their texts are orientated towards school classes, their approach is congruent with our aim in the sense that they propose the need for socialization in students' school projects as we do and, mostly, the socialization and gaining of knowledge of other needs.

To us, in management, discussion, reflection and social comprehension are key components of the awakening the minds of the students. Additionally, we consider that socialization and listening to other individuals' interpretation of reality helps to explore their own issues, views and concerns. We claim the need for more intersubjectivity in pedagogy practices.

In this order of ideas, Epstein (1999) questions the influence that academic journals have on research and practice. The contents, epistemological orientation and themes treated in those journals lead our future and actual leaders who read those publications while studying for their MBAs, for instance. Not only do their contents affect those MBA students' reasoning and their continuous development of will, but also the methods they use in any learning process. Epstein (1999) proposes that professors use the available resources of information technology (IT) in a more constructive way to do their research and teaching, given that nowadays there is more data available about incongruence, paradoxes and worldwide needs than two decades ago, and also there is an increasing awareness among students of the aforementioned realities.

This indicates to us that academic and research activities should be pointed towards a questioning of legitimacy and validity and assessment of the power of individuals' roles in society and the collective. As such, an individual's conscience is influenced by what she or he reads; in a formal education, such as any administration programme, what is demanded by professors as mandatory reading also influences the modelling reasoning process of students. As the historical beings that we are, our behaviour answers to what we have learned throughout our lives, including practical experiences, reading, discussions, interactions with other people and, in all this, the values that each one of us extracts as valid. Therefore, while thinking about social conscience, the possibility of any manager becoming aware of social needs and the organizational responsibilities tied with those needs, and later acting on it, demands attitudes and behaviours based on concern for others, empathy towards others as well as a sense of compassion (see Kanov et al. 2004; Solomon 1998).

Conclusion

As apathy exists in our world, and very frequently is reinforced by globalization and free-market capitalism, the apathy about others' issues may increase and therefore, we academics, who are contributing to the education of tomorrow's managers, have the moral obligation to awaken a concern in our students for considering responsible practices, for helping them to increase their social awareness and, in consequence, their social conscience that will enable the occurrence of ethical action and moral decisions. In this sense, researching and teaching about CSR, and also management courses, should lean on research action techniques, critical reading and discussion, self and social reflexivity, and critical change propositions. Individuals continuously modulate their behaviours depending on the ongoing experiences in life. Academia has a moral responsibility to humanity and the planet in this arena.

References

Aktouf, O. (1987), *Methodologie des sciences sociales et approche qualitative des organisations: une introduction a la demarche classique et une critique*, Sillery: Presses de l'Université du Québec.

Butterfield, K.D., Trevino, L.K. and Weaver, G.R. (2000), 'Moral awareness in business organizations: influences of issue-related and social context factors', *Human Relations*, 53 (7), 981–1018.

Chia, R. (1996), 'The problem of reflexivity in organizational research: towards a postmodern science of organization', *Organization*, 3 (1), 31–59.

Clarkson, M.B.E. (1995), 'A stakeholder framework for analysing and evaluating corporate social performance', *Academy of Management Review*, 20 (1), 92–117.

Davila-Gomez, A.M. (2005), 'Beyond business ethics: managers' ethical challenges concerning community and employees', in D. Crowther and R. Jatana (eds), *Representations of Social Responsibility*, vol. 1, Hyderabad (India): ICFAI University Press, pp 74–104.

Davila-Gomez, A.M. and Crowther, D. (2007), 'Humanistic management education: richness, challenges and possibilities', in D. Bubna-Litic (ed.), *Spirituality and Corporate Social Responsibility*, Aldershot: Ashgate, forthcoming.

Epstein, E.M. (1999), 'The continuing quest for accountable, ethical, and humane corporate capitalism', *Business & Society*, 38 (3), 253–67.

Forester, J. (2003), 'On fieldwork in a Habermasian way: critical ethnography and the extra-ordinary character of ordinary', in M. Alvesson and H. Willmott (eds), *Studying Management Critically*, London: Sage, pp 46–65.

Kanov, J. et al. (2004), 'Compassion in organizational life', *The American Behavioral Scientist*, 47 (6), February, 808–27.

Martínez, J.L., Simón, C. and Agüero A. (2006), 'El reto de la sostenibilidad de la acción social: el caso de la Fundación Carvajal', *Revista de Empresa*, 15, 98–112.

Montaigne, M. de la (1967), *Oeuvres completes*, Paris: Gallimard.

Mudrack, P. (2007), 'Individual personality factors that affect normative beliefs about the rightness of corporate social responsibility', *Business & Society*, 46 (1), 33–62.

Plato (1997), 'Socrates' "Alcibiades", "Second Alcibiades", and "Menon" dialogues', in *Plato, Complete Works*, ed. J.M. Cooper and D.S. Hutchison, Indianapolis IN: Tacket, pp 557–608.

Reason, P. (2006), 'Choice and quality in action research practice', *Journal of Management Inquiry*, 15 (2), 187–203.

Revista de Empresa (2005), 'El verdadero líder tiene que saber más allá de los muros del negocio – Entrevista a James Austin', *Revista de Empresa*, 11, 120–124.

Reynolds, M. (1998), 'Reflection and critical reflection in management learning', *Management Learning*, 29 (2), 183–200.

Rousseau, J.J. (1999), *Du contrat social, livres I et II*, Paris: Hatier.

Rousseau, J.J. (1964), 'Discourse on the origin and foundations of inequality among men', in J.J. Rousseau, *The First and Second Discourses*, ed. R.D. Masters, trans. R. Masters and J. Masters, New York: St Martin's Press.

Selman, R.L. and Dray, A.J. (2003a), 'Bridging the gap: connecting social awareness to literacy practice', in R.L. Selman (ed.), *The Promotion of Social Awareness – Powerful Lessons from the Partnership of Developmental Theory and Classroom Practice*, New York: Russell Sage Foundation, pp 231–250.

Selman, R.L. and Dray, A.J. (2003b), 'The power of persuasion: who is the audience and where does it stand?', in R.L. Selman (ed.), *The Promotion of Social Awareness – Powerful Lessons from the Partnership of Developmental Theory and Classroom Practice*, New York: Russell Sage Foundation, pp 251–66.

Singer, D.D. and Smith, R. (1997), 'The ethical significance of corporate teleology', *Journal of Human Values*, 3 (1), 81–9.

Solomon, R. (1998), 'The moral psychology of business: care and compassion in the corporation', *Business Ethics Quarterly*, 8 (3), 515–533.

Torbert, W. and Fisher, D. (1992), 'Autobiographical awareness as catalyst for managerial and organizational development', *Management Education and Development*, 23 (3), 184–98.

United Nations (2006), *World Economic and Social Survey 2006*, see website at <http://www.un.org/esa/policy/wess/index.html>, accessed March 2007.

White, G.D. (2004), 'Political apathy disorder: proposal for a new DSM diagnostic category', *Journal of Humanistic Psychology*, 44 (1), 47–57.

Winnicott, D. (1965), *The Maturational Processes and the Facilitating Environment: Studies in the Theory of Emotional Developments*, New York: International University Press.

World Bank (2007), 'Project profiles' and 'Key development data and statistics – 2005', see website at <http://worldbank.org/>, accessed March 2007.

Change Management and CSR: An Essay in the Ontology and Business Ethics of Change/ Process Management

Jelena Debeljak and Kristijan Krkač

Introduction

Change management textbooks often reason change as an inevitable process, either occurring spontaneously, or as generated by people for the purpose of producing something better, or in order to accomplish certain progress. People tend to experience the first as either stressful, and therefore try to escape from it, or they ignore it, or use it as an opportunity to do something better. Taken in the latter positive sense, change as a stressful process usually leads to something better, and in the authors' opinion the level of stress is proportionate to the strength of one's opposition to it. The interesting part of the story is why, when it is a commonly recognized and constant factor of humans' lives, we have such a hard time accepting it, why we try so hard to keep the comfort of status quo and ignore or abolish change – it is another limitation of humankind. What does it mean to 'just to go with it' – to surrender to the course of change? The skill of managing change is possibly hidden somewhere within the answers to those questions. In that case, 'surrendering' to change and managing change are in a certain comparative relationship: the more one goes with it, the greater are the chances of managing it – in certain senses. This observation is applicable to our personal lives and to the lives of artificial objects whose lives we are governing every day, and in whose organisms we are situated – our organisations. When talking about the morality of the management of these processes, a combination of care and principles of pragmatic ethics is appropriate: the former because of the love and caring it represents in the choice of means/ motives of an activity – for love makes anything grow – and the latter because it is closest to everyday practical common moral thinking. Both can be easily improved in practice and can even be, let us say, *theorizing-free*, which appeals to people of the speedy media era, and to the never-satisfied element of human nature which is always striving towards more and better in every sense. This chapter is trying to understand change in this way. Thus, there is an analysis of the ontic structure of change. Since change is something that affects anything that comes in its way, the chapter observes its relationship with business – namely the attempt to managing change in business, and the place of corporate social responsibility within the picture.

The ontology and business ethics of change/process management

There are several significant reasons why our Western (especially European) economics, economies and businesses in general should be described and maybe even explained in terms of time-bound phenomena like change and process. The first reason is obvious. The ground idea of a market economy says that the market economy is essentially directed towards the future; that is, future profit.

'Capitalists, then, are people who make bets on the future. The essence of capitalism is a psychological orientation toward the pursuit of future wealth and property.'[1] So, businessmen are in constant expectation of future consequences of their present business actions. They are expecting certain changes to occur, and the whole phenomenon can be called a business process. The second reason seems to be obvious as well. Because of the rapid external changes in technology, society, environment and culture, as well as because of internal problems in business, change in business and especially in management is essential for understanding management practice and its results.

The one who recognizes and solves change-problems better or, in short, the one who adapts better, is the one who gets the job done better, contrary to the phrase 'people are resistant to change'. But what does it mean 'to solve change-problems' and to adjust 'better'? Change management is essentially management of change in business, and process management is the management of process in business. Understanding of 'what there is' seems to be essential for understanding of what there can be and cannot be and, what is more, what can be done and cannot be done; and change/process management unquestionably has some kind of underlying ontology and even certain ethics which partly arise from this ontology. If certain change, as part of a process, is partly governed by human agents and

---

1   See McCraw 2000. It is, however, historically interesting that the capitalism referrred to, which essentially means 'industrial capitalism' as affirmed by mainstream historians, is viewed as starting and developing not by the 'European miracle' (which is a part of the 'European myth' or 'Eurocentrism', especially by the 'Industrial Revolution'), but rather by colonialism (regarded as immoral at least, although nowadays viewed by differing moral standards or even from perspective of rigorous ethics such as Kantian ethics): this 'gave Europeans the power both to develop their own society and to prevent development from occurring elsewhere.' This is, of course, not the position of mainstream historians. See J.M. Blaut (1993), *The Colonizer's Model of the World* (New York, Guilford Press), 206.

affects other human agents and their environment as well, then according to the ontology of change and process it must be understood that change cannot be successfully completed if there is no underlying continuity, on the basis of which this very change can be performed, and more, so that it can be understandable and acceptable especially to those relevantly affected.[2] So, in order to understand change/process management we need to understand its underlying ontology and ethics, and to try to adjust CSR principles to these 'new circumstances'. Here we propose a certain process ontology and ethics, and implicitly also a change ontology and ethics that seem to explicate the central notions of change and process management. So, processes are the topic of this section, to be precise their ontology and ethics in terms of their content, structure, proceedings or dynamics, and dignity. Since we insist that change management is a part of a wider topic, namely process management and somehow interwoven with it, this must be elucidated. If change is a difference between succeeding stages and if continuation is succession between different stages, then we can see interdependence between change and continuity, moreover that a change is incomprehensible without continuity and vice versa.

The ABC of change/process ontology

Let us start with a few basics of process ontology.[3] Every process consists of stages which are mutually different or distinct stages of a certain process. At the same time all stages related within some kind of succession as continuity or continuation of a process. Every process consists also of at least one rule – that of succession and continuation of a process. A difference is the lack of absolute identity, or lack of relevant similarity. A succession is a stream, course, flow, series or sequence of stages one after another in time or space-time according to a rule. Change is difference between succeeding stages. Continuation is succession between different stages. The world consists of continuations and changes.[4] The world consists of processes, not of things, facts or events. Everything which is continuation in change and change in continuity is a process. What is given in every experience is no more than change

---

2   For example, the issue of the so-called 'most competitive knowledge-based capitalism in the world' as the goal of the EU. In other words, the achievement of 'sustainable business practices' (namely, being financially successful, environmentally friendly and socially responsible) is not to be conceived as one sole (legal, corporate, cultural or similar) action of a EU corporation, but rather as a long-term process of constant changes and adjustments to new circumstances in order to achieve these goals.

3   This subsection of the chapter is mostly based on a previous paper and lecture on process ontology which is nevertheless still unpublished. The topic of this section is process ontology and its application in the ontology of economic processes, namely management processes.

4   Regarding the context of such a claim, Rescher (2002b) formulates it quite precisely: 'The guiding idea of its [process philosophy's] approach is that natural existence consists in and is best understood in terms of *processes* rather than *things* – of modes of change rather than fixed stabilities. For processists, change of every sort – physical, organic, psychological – is the pervasive and predominant feature of the real.' See also Rescher (2002a). Here we conceptually presuppose solutions to the change problem.

and continuation. Let us examine change α. What is given in any experience is that in α, stage β, via the rule of becoming γ, is becoming and/or is replaced by stage δ (in terms of relative and absolute change). Change is difference or distinction between succeeding stages. Continuation is succession between different stages (harmony, accord in terms of proceeding between distinct stages).[5] Change is all there is; it includes becoming, duration and ceasing. Continuation (thick sense) is all there is; it includes initiation, continuation (thin sense) and cessation. Every kind of change/continuity is a process. Every kind of continuation (thin sense) is a process. Everything which has the starting point is a process. Everything which has continuation point/s is a process. Everything which has the ending point is a process. Everything which has distinct and succeeding stages is a process (at least temporal, if not spatio-temporal coherence or unity). All processes have three aspects: (1) stages/phases, (2) rule/s, and (3) energy/force manifested as proceeding/ movement (as a result of balance between the change aspect and the continuity aspect). Process force or energy seems to emerge from the simple coexistence of the starting phase or stage and a process rule. Every process is explicit and *sui generis*. There are no hidden processes. They are transparent via daily experience.[6] Every process consists of its rule/s, its stages and emergent energy. Every process consists of at least three stages. These three stages are initiation, continuation and cessation. Every process has at least one rule. Rules and stages cannot exist outside of their process. Process stages and process rules are in relationship resembling that of stuff/pile and its shape. Every process is self-governed.[7] Every process is governed by its rule. Every rule of a process is *sui generis*. The rule of a process is implicit in the process. The rule of a process manifests itself in the process. A particular rule of a particular process is its trope as rhythm (of succession). Every process is composed out of fabric. Stages are fabric or bits and pieces of a process. Every stage is connected to at least two other stages. Stages are mutually connected, compacted (path-compacted), and integrated as a whole. Every stage is explicit and *sui generis*. There are no hidden stages. Every stage is an element of a process as sequence. Every stage can be a stage of more than one process. All processes can be divided according to the kind of movement they display.[8] There are at least four kinds of process. A process is either one turning into another, or one replaced by the other. The first can be called continuous and the second a discrete process. Processes can

---

5   Regarding the problem of change, especially substantial change, see Lowe (forthcoming, 2007).

6   The problem of 'hidden' was mentioned to me by N. Rescher.

7   Non-natural processes are also self-governed since they just seem to be governed from outside. The point is that, for example, a person who is taking care of the process of an engine running regularly, or of the process of a corporation performing properly as a legal person running regularly, is a part of this process; in other words, the actions of caring for an engine or for a corporation are stages in the process of the engine running regularly and performing properly.

8   From the Latin *processus* means *movement*. Process is a naturally occurring or designed sequence of changes of properties/attributes of a system/object.

be divided into physical, biological, technical and logical.[9] Every process has its dynamics; that is a rhythm according to which it proceeds. The rhythm of a process is a rule according to which the process proceeds from stage to stage. There are at least two kinds of dynamics of processes: one stage becoming another according to a rule, and one stage being replaced by another according to a rule. This explicates distinction between continuous and discrete processes. Processes are connected in a web of different connections. The basic types of connections are: linear, circular, sequenced, parallel, crossed/overlapped, convergent and divergent. They can be classified by different criteria; for example, sharing a stage or not, convergent or divergent, etc. Pairs of opposite processes which can be mutually connected are: linear–circular, parallel–crossed, detached–overlapping, convergent–divergent, etc.[10] This much concerning the ontology of processes seems to be enough as an introduction to the ethics and CSR of processes and changes in business and management.

Process ontology for business and management

Processes are given in daily experience as compact, integral, complete and indivisible wholes, like self-governed moving-wholes (echoing the nature of Leibniz's monads). However, processes can be known only as conceptual constructions from such experiences; that is, processes as wholes composed out of their parts. In that sense every process is knowable as being composed from stages/phases which proceed according to a rule, every process can be known (via experience) as a whole composed from its parts (mereology[11]), every stage is a construction in terms of an event, and finally every rule is a construction in terms of some formal law, or law-like relationship. Finally, things, facts and events are generalizations of stages and rules; that is, out of changes and continuations.

Processes also seem to have certain morality in terms of dignity. For example, natural processes have dignity in terms of not being interrupted or in being free to proceed

---

9   The flowing of a river is an inorganic or physical process. The growing of a child, eating, sleeping, moving, playing, feeling (in terms of sentiments), willing, thinking and perceiving are all kinds of organic or biological processes. The movement of a steam engine is an artificial or technical process. Movements of a computer program (in terms of states and events like kinds of stages) are formal processes. Most processes are blended from these basic kinds. For example, forms of life are in fact forms of culture, and the underlying ontology of forms of culture seems to be process ontology; namely, culture as process. Nevertheless, processes are mostly mutually webbed. Another example might be the performance of a corporation as a legal person. The corporation is a process composed of stages that are its actions.

10 I wish to thank Professors J. Lowe and N. Rescher for valuable comments regarding some issues regarding process ontology explicated in this section of the chapter (K. Krkač).

11 Mereology is that part of ontology (metaphysics) which is concerned with understanding 'being' as composed of parts, so comprehending the relationships between the parts is the most important way of grasping the structure of the whole. The first text concerning mereology is a small note in Aristotle's *Metaphysics*.

from stage to stage according to their rules. Also non-natural processes or humanly governed processes should be governed in the same way.[12]

Processes which we bump into on a daily basis, and of which we are a part, are mostly blended or mixed out of basic kinds of processes (mentioned previously). Forms of life, for example, as one of Wittgenstein's crucial categories from his later period, are in fact forms of culture and (as it seems) cultural processes, and business is just one form of life among others (producing, marketing, selling, bargaining, buying, etc.).

Business is a process; that is, change in continuity and continuity in change. As such, it includes at least realization of long-term values (and profit seems to be just one among many values, at least according to the stakeholder theory of corporation), and as such it requires long-term planning and management. Business process is a complicated web of basic processes: organic, artificial, physical, formal.[13]

But let us turn to another subject matter, namely management. Management is surely culturally bounded – not just international management, but management in principle.[14]

Change is a dynamic process, a necessary and natural condition affecting both individuals and organization.[15] It can be classified as:

- transactional (affecting behaviour),
- transitional (affecting behaviour and beliefs), and
- transformational (affecting behaviour, beliefs and mindset).

The moral applications of these change-types are: minimal, moderate, and significant.[16]

---

12 Just to give a few examples, human actions and practices as processes obviously have dignity to be performed *lege artis*, or according to the rules of a profession. Also the processes of the working of machines and engines should be governed with sufficient care or without actions that produce any kind of irreparable damage or harm to the machine, or in fact to the process of running itself.

13 Regarding business in general and especially capitalism as a time/future-bound phenomenon see Kagin et al. 2005.

14 For relations between business, culture and CSR, see Debeljak and Krkač 2006.

15 See Horniman 1997: 104.

16 Contrary to what seems obvious, transformational change is not by itself morally right or wrong. For example, transformational change from a communist to a market economy seems to be morally right, at least in the light of private property and its value. On the other hand, bossing as a type of transformational change is surely morally wrong. But, the question is in principle – is it morally right to change the mindset of another person for the purpose of maximization of profit even if the person agrees with such a change; and if it is, then on which grounds? (We wish to thank A. Mušura for explaining some psychological effects of mindset change on personality.) Ethically speaking and from a Kantian perspective it would be wrong to change a person's mindset without that person's knowledge, acceptance and approval (however, Jelena disagrees on the 'approval' addition).

Change management is essentially theory and practice (like a list of recommendations which can govern our practices) *of managing change* (mostly including groups). So, if business and management are essentially processes, then the ontology and, above all, ethics (and CSR) of business and management should be the ontology and ethics (CSR) of processes.

The formal definition of a process (that is, change in continuity and continuity in change) affects management and we must realize that change in business takes place only against the background of the certain continuity of business. A change is in fact the change from one stage to another, but this change, no matter how radical (maybe even discrete as pure replacement) is possible and intelligible only against the background of certain business process as a whole. On the other hand, a process as the continuity is merely a continuity of changes and nothing more.[17]

So *management of business is in fact the management of constant change*, and the only continuity in such constant change can be the very rule of a process. Managing business changes comes down to governing business processes as wholes, not as particular stages, particular manifestations of process energy or of process rules.

Business undergoes changes because of objective circumstances, and also because of subjective reasons like decisions made by CEOs and/or owners. Change in business is often called 'development'; in other words, changes as being planned as something essentially positive and good (but this seems to be a question of the simple rhetoric of business correctness, or of 'selling' change).[18] Nevertheless, change as development process can be objectively needed regarding the following spheres of business:

- sales development
- new product development
- new market development
- business organization, shape, structure and processes development
- tools, equipment, plant, logistics and supply-chain development
- people, management and communications (capabilities and training) development
- strategic partnerships and distribution routes development
- international development
- acquisitions and disposals

So the task for business is to transform quickly as a reaction to new business circumstances, since the only stability is that of a change. Regarding the rules for governing business process and change we must mention 'Ten principles of change management' by John Jones, DeAnne Aguirre and Matthew Calderone (see

---

17 This seems to be quite important in a time when change is introduced in business; in other words, that all affected should remember that the very same business also changed before and also that it started probably because of an original idea of how to adapt to new circumstances in business.

18 See Aune 2001; Crowther and Jatana 2005.

References) since they emphasize 10 crucial elements. Change management can be defined in the following way:

> *The concept of change management describes a structured approach to transitions in individuals, teams, organizations and societies that moves the target from a current state to a desired state. Stated simply, change management is a process for managing the people-side of change. The most recent research points to a combination of organizational change management tools and individual change management models for effective change to take place.*[19]

However, the most important part of any change and process in business, especially in management, is change *among* people and change *of* people which is comprehensible only against the background of organizational change (see comments above on transformational change). One of the best-known and recognized models for such change is the following. Research conducted by Prosci with more than 1,000 organizations from 59 countries shows that people must achieve five building blocks in order for change to be realized successfully. These building blocks are described as the 'ADKAR model':

- Awareness – of why the change is needed
- Desire – to support and participate in the change
- Knowledge – of how to change
- Ability – to implement new skills and behaviours
- Reinforcement – to sustain the change

In particular, regarding change in human resources, a change must be *realistic, achievable* and *measurable*.

These aspects are particularly relevant in managing personal change. But there is surely an application of the caring principle or at least of the harm principle in change/process management. *Change needs to be understood and managed in such a way that people can cope effectively with it.* In other words, change needs to be understood and managed in such a way that people who engage in it at least do not perform irreparable damage or harm to stakeholders and, if possible, it should be performed with sufficient care for involved relevant stakeholders, no matter how 'sufficient' or 'reasonable' is defined since it is often defined as negligence or malpractice regarding certain business professions.[20]

This understanding of change can be applied then to the *principles of managing change*:

---

19 See 'Change management' entry in Wikipedia. Here we must emphasize that change is defined as part of a discrete rather than a continuous process: we must disagree with this since business processes are blended also out of organic processes which are fundamentally continuous.

20 For the harm principle, ethics of care and CSR, see Debeljak et al. (2007).

- At all times involve, and agree support from, people within the system (the system being: environment, processes, culture, relationships, behaviours, etc., whether personal or organizational).
- Understand where you are/the organization is at the moment.
- Understand where you want to be, when, why, and what the measures will be for getting there.
- Plan development in appropriate achievable measurable stages.
- Communicate, involve, enable and facilitate involvement from people, as early and openly and as fully as possible.

There are, however, at least *four basic important steps for change management*:

- recognizing the need for change based on the corporation's internal and/or external changes
- deciding on the change to make
- implementing the change
- evaluating the change.[21]

However, all of these principles (including the ADKAR model for personal change of attitudes as well as the organizational change mentioned previously) include certain ethics and eventually certain CSR.

CSR regarding change and process in any kind of business includes relevant and necessary care for at least internal stakeholders according to relevant legal norms, codes of ethics, organizational culture and goals of the business organization.

However, we must differ between:

- ethics of change in business or process business ethics (which in fact should be the code of ethics for business change)
- the influence of the ethics of constantly changing business on external stakeholders (the balance between the profitability and the morality of business that relevantly affects society)[22] and
- the influence of social ethical norms on business (and vice versa).

Nevertheless it seems that the same rule can be applied to internal as well as to external social and non-social stakeholders; in other words, the harm principle or the rule of relevant care.[23] But this is not so obvious. In order to make it obvious we must apply some ideas from the ontology of process and change to business. Suppose we have a process of the work of a certain machine, for example a steam-

---

21 Jones et al. (2000), 572–609.
22 We must notice, contrary to many CSR defenders, that in principle the misbalance between profitability and morality in favour of morality sometimes can harm stakeholders more than would be predicted.
23 See Barry (2000) and McCann (2000) for the discussion between these two authors, especially with regard to explication of positive and negative CSR as defined by Solomon and discussed by McCann.

powered engine. Given that processes are wholes, a man who keeps the engine running properly is a part of the process of an engine running properly. Suppose also that the steam engine is a part of a locomotive which is a part of a train. So the rule of the process of the engine running smoothly is closely connected to the labour of a stoker and others in the locomotive. The simple process of the running of a steam-powered engine in a locomotive influences the whole bundle of processes and is comprehensible only against the background of the whole process of the railroad business. Taking care of the steam engine in a proper manner directly influences taking care of a railroad company for their customers. So the whole context of business, including internal and external stakeholders as well, seems to be just one process.

The 'postmodern corporation' is essentially a process of constant realization of corporate goals of sustainable business through series of changes as adjustments (sustainable meaning being: financially successful, environmental friendly and socially responsible; that is, according to EU directions). The stages of a corporate process include all relevant internal and external stakeholders.

Stakeholders are not simply parts of a corporation, but rather perspectives on the corporation itself (for example, a corporation from the perspective of the relevant environment).

The dignity of a corporate process is the dignity of all the stakeholders in a way that their interests must be taken into account as much as it is (technically, organizationally, financially, and humanly) possible against the background of the goals/end points of a corporate process.

- The governing of any business/corporate process *lege artis* (*lege artis* procedure being something that basically includes constant adjustments to new circumstances in view of the goal of financial success), with necessary and sufficient care for the process itself.
- It is the indispensable and basic task of a management to seek to accomplish this without producing irreparable harm/damage to any of its stakeholders (in view of the goals of being environmentally friendly and socially responsible).

Change/process management and CSR

This leads us to at least two lessons from process and change ontology for process and change management in terms of financial performance as well as in terms of CSR.

- The first lesson from process philosophy/ontology is that changes will occur and processes will proceed with or without us, since many processes are basically beyond our control, even some corporate processes (for example, far future harm or the benefit of corporate process on environmental processes, or on future generations of employers and employees).

- The second lesson is that corporate changes are occurring all the time, not just when they are induced and/or governed by managers as a response (for example) to recognized problems or challenges in performance. There are some changes and processes that we can provoke and govern, and there are some that we cannot. The corporate process is a mixture of processes that can be controlled and governed and those which cannot. It is a mistake to assume that a process which cannot be governed by the corporation is chaotic, because if it is not governed by a government or by some other legal person, surely it is self-governed. This leads us to the problem of change in business.

Every change is a part of a certain process, and so are business changes. As well as processes, changes also can be organizationally governed and self-governed. A change from good to bad performance in terms of profit as well as in terms of CSR can be a result of changes happening outside of the corporation (for example, the emergence of low-cost foreign competitors) while the corporation itself performs in the same way. There can be an opposite case also. The same corporation can be just such a foreign competitor regarding some other corporation and because of its internal processes and changes in performance it cannot recognize an opportunity for entering a new market. Of course, there can be also a mixture of these examples. Since a corporation is in fact a corporate process, the question is how it is possible that such a corporate process achieves CSR goals in principle, through the irreparable harm principle and the necessary and sufficient care principle, and through particular rules while still remaining financially successful. These principles are expressed in the organization's code of ethics which derives from (1) societal values, (2) professional ethics, and (3) individual ethics, as manifested in actions of a corporation. This is also called 'proactive approach' to CSR.

The proactive approach to CSR is a strong commitment to CSR or eagerness to do more than the law requires and to use organizational resources to promote the interests of all organizational stakeholders.[24] Of course, we must notice that the law requires much more in the EU due to its legal systems than in the US, but it seems to be important that such a definition of a proactive approach in view of the ethics of care as covering values of CSR affirms not just *due* care for stakeholders but even actions of *extraordinary* care. The question is why a corporation ought to act in this way. A corporation should perform in this way because it is a person, although legal, and as such it is a member of society, and not vice versa.

> *The guiding idea of its [process philosophy] approach is that natural existence consists in and is best understood in terms of processes rather than things – of*

---

24   Such companies as Hewlett-Packard, The Body Shop, and Johnson & Johnson, for example, are at the forefront of campaigns for causes such as a pollution-free environment, recycling and conservation of resources, minimizing or avoiding the use of animals in drug and cosmetic testing, and reducing crime, illiteracy and poverty (see Jones et al., 2000: 162). For problems with The Body Shop, see Barry (2000).

*modes of change rather than fixed stabilities. For processists, change of every
sort – physical, organic, psychological – is the pervasive and predominant
feature of the real (Rescher 2002b).*

And we can add that this seems to be correct not just of natural process, but also
of social, organizational and business processes. Business process improvement
works by: (1) defining what the organization's strategic goals and purposes
are (*Who are we, what do we do, and why do we do it?*); (2) determining who the
organization's customers (or stakeholders) are (*Who do we serve?*); and (3) aligning
the business processes to meet the customer's requirements (*How do we do it
better?*)[25] The underlying idea is to make changes now! The change process should
be done repeatedly, not merely once. Waiting for a perfect solution would mean no
solution. Understanding business and management in terms of process rather than
change from time to time assures that everyone relevantly included can cope with
the process itself.

It must be realized that the corporation as a corporate process is a certain
continuity composed entirely and solely of changes that occur from stage to stage
by its very procedural nature. Some of these changes can be governed by the actions
of members of the corporation since corporate process is a process blended of many
different basic processes – organizational, organic, inorganic, mechanical, formal,
etc. This is so because the corporate process or processes are mostly overlapped
with many different corporate processes (including other corporations) and also
with non-corporate processes in its social, cultural, and natural environment.

The actions of a corporation or of a corporate process are in fact stages of
corporate process. The goals of a corporation are long-term values and goals as
ending points of a corporate process. CSR is just a perspective on the stages of
the corporate process, just as financial performance, management performance
and others are too. There are no special processes such as 'CSR process' or special
stages in corporate process such as 'reasonable caring for employees, society, and
environment'.

The very essence of a business process 'going on smoothly' implies 'goods
producing process' and 'process producing good'; in other words, financial-moral
success. Just as it is nonsense to say business 'and' financial success, so it is nonsense
and insensitive in a certain way to say business 'and' moral correctness. There is no
'and' here. Either financial and moral successes are both side-effects of our neutral
human actions, or they are both essential to our economic actions.

The business actions of a corporation, being stages of a corporate process as
such, are entirely neutral and only interpreted as economic (being financial-moral),
but nevertheless they can, they ought to be, and should be interpreted as financially
successful or not, ethically responsible or irresponsible, etc., by all the stakeholders
according to their relevance (as a perspective) to the process. Such a narrative,
while being a narrative and nothing more, is essential for economic, business, and

---

25   See 'BPI' entry in Wikipedia, at <http://en.wikipedia.org/wiki/Business_Process_
     Improvement>.

management process as well as to any other process and itself is a basic part of a corporate process.

Change management, CSR and ethics of care

Christians believe that the world is created for spiritual ends. Are we coming closer to those ends with change management and its background philosophy reflected in a fairly newly created term, sonorously called 'evolutionary leadership?' Is stakeholder theory (realized in corporate social responsibility) an evolutionary/developmental step forward from the pure shareholder way of thinking business on the timescale of human reasoning? Is it possible, after realizing and accepting this new concept in doing business, to talk about a certain spiritual development of humanity? And could maybe a concrete implication of Hegel's theory of the development of absolute spirit in the history of mankind or Whitehead's process ontology be recognized here as well? If CSR is a kind of proof of some moral evolution of the way of doing business, or evolution of corporations, where corporate intuitions are being purified, their morality is reflected in the simplicity, easiness or even purity, if you like, of their numerous (business) relationships. Or, as in the opinion of some, humankind as such does not evolve through history at all. A modern/new way of thinking and observing conceptual models of the world, namely the idea of 'spiral dynamics', would not quite agree, as its proponents argue that human nature cannot to be fixed. Spiral dynamics (SD) is defined as:

- 'a way of thinking about complexities of human existence and understanding the order and chaos in human affairs. It explains deep forces in human nature which shape our values, and lays out both a pattern and trajectory for change'.
- Further on, it is a multidisciplinary approach that 'describes differences in how people think, but not the worth of how they think ... it reflects a variety of worldviews and conceptions on what life is about'.
- 'It describes variability in thinking, behaviour, and conceptualization, not the worth or decency of a person ... [it] is about moral and ethical standards; it addresses where those decisions come from and how they are made. Its focus is on why people adopt the values they do – not what those values are' (<http://www.evolutionleader.com/topics/paradigms.htm>).

The purpose is to facilitate the functioning of organisations, to help people to learn and live better. The SP model takes an integral approach, trying to synergize the efforts of all stakeholders, and is applying this approach in dealing with any one of the world's problems. Judging by values placed at the top of the list, CSR is basically a new way of thinking or a 'paradigm' or even a worldview, the discourse the world needs at this point, rather than forming new organisations. Being on this track it seems that the theories of Hegel and Whitehead and spiral dynamics integral theory are comparable. But I am not going into this analysis here, just mentioning it as a possibility.

CSR has outgrown its first stage of development – its emergence (see above); it has surfaced again in the 1990s after a period of silence, and now is in the stage when we are trying to understand it and to find programmes/models of implementing this new way of thinking in existing organizations.

Change management helps at this point because it is about managing change within an organisation, and 'change can only be effected by working with and through people' (Crowther 2006). There are theories suggesting the right way of managing change during an organization's transition. Change management training show that change starts with an individual (change). So, depending on the direction one chooses to go (better consciously than not), we are talking about positive and/or negative change. Change management is trying to *manage* change towards a positive outcome/change – something people are pursuing by nature, and is also psychologically more desirable. Since change begins with an individual self (commonly we would say 'it's all in one's head', and there is where everything starts), and is influentially spreading on to others/environment, we are originators of the kind of the world we live in. So, can we speak together with Hegel, Whitehead and Beck about the history of the development of the (human) spirit? If the individual has consciously understood that they shape their world by bringing their own thought out – starting therefore with their own way of thinking, through speaking/words coming from their mouth, all ending up in their outward deeds – then it becomes clear that they can *manage* change.

Therefore, we could agree here with Beck that 'we simply need to awaken to new ways of thinking' and that 'it's not that we need to form new organisations'.

How can change management, presented by the SD thinking approach, come together with care ethics and corporate social responsibility? Most of us would agree that change is difficult and none of the ever-appearing new change management programmes are of much use.

That is why we would like to consider the way-people-think approach (that is, SD) since '… it is only through change that a person can grow, and management is all about people – the people managing and the people being managed, and we all both manage and are managed in our organisational lives' (Crowther 2006). As spiral dynamics, consequentially to its starting point, emphasizes importance of 'powerful conversations', which could be also called quality conversations, for the development of human relations with the purpose of creating the future together, their *idea* fits well within the ethics of care way of thinking. The ethics of care derives from the so called *women's way of knowing*; that is, the feminine approach to morality, which is implanted in receptivity, relatedness and responsiveness, and thus views morality through the glasses of typically womanly traits – intimacy, caring and personal relationships – all related to so-called *soft skills* that the modern way of doing business requires.[26]

---

26   Debeljak et al. (2007).

So, SD and the ethics of care, each in their own way, realize the importance of relationships in the creation of modern sustainable businesses by contributing the quality of informal structures or social networks in the organization, and what about CSR?

Working on CSR projects, organizational team works on positive change creation – for the organisation's well-being, and also the broader environment, that of other stakeholders.

We have mentioned above that SD researchers look at some new integral paradigms[27] in dealing with social problems, and engage business as a dominant institution nowadays, especially their leaders, in taking responsibility for the impact of their decisions; this is because through those decisions our organizations and broader stakeholders – organic and inorganic – are being affected, our world's layout designed and the atmosphere we live in created. Through some of those newly forged paradigms (the 'language and conversations paradigm', the 'learning organization and living systems paradigm', the 'ecological and sustainable paradigm', the 'conscious evolution paradigm'), such ways of thinking that bring about sustainable enterprises, institutions, communities, societies and environment (all of those ideas presented in stakeholder theory, that is, CSR) are being presented. They also include conservation, cooperation, collaboration, quality, love, trust and partnership. These values relate to care ethics. Now, by becoming aware of responsibility and choice about the kind of future they want to emerge, it becomes possible for humans to generate positive change, or in terms of SD thinkers, engage in a conscious evolution in order to create a sustainable future.

A possibility of positive creativity is what makes spiral dynamics integral an attractive theory:

- It offers leeway for total positive change at an organizational level (smaller 'living system') that consequentially stretches out onto bigger living systems – the broader community.
- It offers an option between destructive ways of thinking (which unfortunately shape a great share of our world – through their way of dealing with interpersonal conflicts, starting with family quarrels, and stretching out as far as global and interstate tensions) and constructive – an option that can be found in some of SD paradigms.

If positive changes are what we want for our organizations and broader organizational systems/living systems, then the constructive way of thinking is what we are going to choose and follow all the way. Our thoughts shape/go over to our sentences/conversations that shape our world, organisation, community, etc.

---

27   A paradigm can be defined as a group of assumptions, beliefs, values and social practices shared by a community of people; an invisible cultural structure through we perceive, filter, and make meaning of the world; influences that we perceive as reality, our possibilities and what we believe is beyond question. See <http://www.evolutionleader.com/topics/paradigms.htm>, accessed 27 February 2007.

This makes future our choice, and this makes us managers of the change we want to see and maintain – starting with our organizations' layout.

Concluding remarks

Change as such is the only constant value of the speedy post-modern media era. That is why it is worth getting acquainted with it, especially in business. In this text we have tried to elucidate some connections between the ontology of change, change management, spiral dynamics and the ethics of care. The basic idea was to show that changes are inevitable, not just in the world but in the firm as well. Understanding change is manifest in leading change, and good leading means good understanding; for example, what is within one's control and what is not, what can and ought to be done individually, and what must be done socially or as a group, etc. Most changes that can and should be governed in groups and by the groups, especially organizations (business as well) should be governed in the light of the irreparable harm/damage principle and positively in the light of the care principle as a key tool for creating the future world in which we prefer to work, live long and prosper.

References

Ontology, process ontology and the philosophy of economics
Anderson, E. (1995), *Value in Ethics and Economics*, Cambridge MA: Harvard University Press.
Aune, J.A. (2001), *Selling the Free Market, The Rhetoric of Economic Correctness*, New York: Guilford Press.
Beabout, G.R. (2001), 'The primacy of culture', *Markets & Morality*, 4 (2), Fall, 344–50.
Crowther, D. (2006), *Change Management*, manuscript.
Hausman, D.M. (2003) 'Philosophy of economics', in the Stanford Encyclopedia of Philosophy, at <http://plato.stanford.edu/entries/economics/>.
Lowe, E.J. (2007), 'How real is substantial change?', forthcoming in *Monist*, 2007.
Lowe, E.J. (2002), *A Survey of Metaphysics*, Oxford: Clarendon Press.
Lowe, E.J. (1998), *The Possibility of Metaphysics: Substance, Identity, and Time*, Oxford: Clarendon Press.
Rescher, N. (2002a), 'On situating process philosophy', at <http://www.religion-online.org/showarticle>.
Rescher, N. (2002b), 'Process philosophy', at <http://plato.stanford.edu/entries/process-philosophy/>.
Rescher, N. (1996), 'Idealism', in J. Dancy and E. Sosa (eds), *A Companion to Epistemology*, Oxford: Blackwell.
Rescher, N. (1973), *Conceptual Idealism*, Oxford: Blackwell.

Tunehag, M. (2006), *Transformational Business*, manuscript.

Zaratiegui, J.M. (1999), 'The imperialism of economics over ethics', *Markets & Morality*, 2 (2), Fall.

Zúñiga, G.L. (1999), 'An ontology of economic objects: an application of Carl Menger's ideas', *American Journal of Economics and Sociology*, 58 (2), April.

Change management and CSR

Barry, N.P. (2000), 'Do corporations have any responsibility beyond making profit?', *Markets & Morality*, 3 (1), Spring, at <http://www.acton.org.publicat/m_and_m/2000_spring>.

Barry, N.P. (2000), 'Do corporations have any responsibility beyond making profit? A response to Dennis P. McCann', *Markets & Morality*, 3 (1), Spring, at <http://www.acton.org.publicat /m_and_m/2000_spring>.

Conner, D.R. (1993), *Managing At the Speed of Change*, New York: Random House.

Crowther, D. and Jatana, R. (2005), 'Modern ethics and corporate well-being', in D. Crowther and R. Jatana (eds), *Representations of Social Responsibility*, vol. II, Hyderabad: ICFAI University Press.

Debeljak, J., Koričan, M., Krkač, K. and Mušura, A. (2007), 'Caring principle and practices in CSR', in A.M. Davila-Gomez and D Crowther, *Ethics, Psyche and Social Responsibility*, Aldershot: Ashgate.

Debeljak, J. and Krkač, K. (2006), 'Influence of culture on European business, ethics, and business ethics', in K. Krkač and D. Njavro (eds), *Business Ethics and Corporate Social Responsibility*, International Conference Papers, MATE, ZSEM, Zagreb, 2006, pp 110–125.

Hiatt, J. (2006), *ADKAR: a Model for Change in Business, Government and our Community*, Loveland CO: Prosci Research.

Horniman, A. (1997), 'Change', in P.H. Werhane and R. E. Freeman (eds), *The Blackwell Encyclopedic Dictionary of Business Ethics*, Oxford: Blackwell, pp 104–7.

Jones, G.R., George, J.M. and Hill, C.W.L. (2000), *Contemporary Management*, Boston MA: Irwin McGraw-Hill.

Jones, J., Aguirre, D. and Calderone, M. (n.d.), 'Ten principles of change management', at <www.strategybusiness.com/resilience/rr00006?pg+all>.

Kagin, J., Krkač, K. and Mušura, A. (2005), 'Time, credit and debt. An essay in philosophy of economics', in F. Stadler and M. Stölzner (eds), *Proceedings of 28th International Wittgenstein Symposium*, Kirchberg am Wechsel, 2005, pp 127–31.

Kotter, J.P. (1996), *Leading Change*, Boston MA: Harvard Business School Press.

Krkač, K. (ed.) (2007), *Introduction to Business Ethics and CSR* (in Croatian), ZSEM, MATE d.o.o. Zagreb.

Krkač, K. and Njavro, D. (eds) (2006), *Business Ethics and Corporate Social Responsibility*, International CSR Conference Papers, ZSEM, MATE, Zagreb.

LaMarsh, J. (1995), *Changing the Way We Change: Gaining Control of Major Operational Change*, New York: Prentice Hall.

McCann, D.P. (2000), 'Do corporations have any responsibility beyond making profit? A response to Norman P. Barry', *Markets & Morality*, 3 (1), Spring, at <http://www.acton.org.publicat /m_and_m/2000_spring> (two responses).

McCraw, T.K. (2000), *Creating Modern Capitalism*, Cambridge MA: Harvard University Press.

O'Donovan, G. (2006), *The Corporate Culture Handbook*, Dublin: Liffey Press.

Spiral dynamics integral theory, see website at <http://www.evolutionleader.com/topics/paradigms.htm>.

Tycoon Philanthropy: Prestige and the Annihilation of Excess

Mary Phillips

Introduction

Bill Gates, founder of Microsoft, one of the world's most successful corporations, is the world's richest man. He also appears to be among the world's most generous men, having endowed one of the richest foundations in the world (the Bill and Melinda Gates Foundation) and largely with his personal fortune.[1] He is not alone among wealthy American business tycoons, where large-scale personal philanthropy is almost commonplace. Other examples include Warren Buffett, the second wealthiest man in the world and the world's most generous philanthropist according to *Business Week* (2006). Buffett, Chief Executive of Berkshire Hathaway, plans to give away most of his personal wealth, a figure that exceeds $40 billion. Gordon and Betty Moore (third on the list), co-founders of Intel, have given over $7 billion to environmental and scientific causes. George Soros, founder of Soros Fund Management, founded the Open Society Institute which 'aims to shape public policy to promote democratic governance, human rights, and economic, legal, and social reform' (Open Society Initiative 2007) and has given away nearly $6 billion of his personal fortune. Ted Turner was the founder of CNN and went on to be Vice Chair of Time Warner AOL, amongst other media ventures. He is the largest private landowner in the US and, in keeping with his environmental concerns, owns the largest bison herd in the world. In 1998, he pledged $1 billion over ten years to the UN, as well as making philanthropic grants in the areas of the environment and population control through the Turner Foundation. Although lagging behind

---

1   The list of '50 most generous philanthropists' produced by *Business Week* is dominated by men. Of the seven women who appear solo on the list, one is an heiress and five are widows of successful businessmen. Only Oprah Winfrey (number 32 on the 2006 list) appears in her own right. A further 14 women are named in partnership with their businessmen husbands.

their US counterparts, UK business magnates have also been generous with their personal fortunes. Tom Hunter, who sold his footwear retailing business to JJB Sports for a personal gain of £250 million, has pledged £55 million to Bill Clinton's Global Initiative and has established the Hunter Foundation with an initial pledge of £100 million (Moss 2005). Lord Sainsbury, whose Gatsby Charitable Foundation has already donated over £400 million in 35 years, hopes to be the first Briton to give away £1 billion in his lifetime (Moss 2005). This is giving on a massive, even gargantuan, scale as these enormously rich and powerful men seem almost driven to dispose of their personal fortunes. There is something exuberant about it, something excessive and beyond the rules of logical, rational economic behaviour.

The personal philanthropic ventures of these high-profile business leaders seem to differ from the giving behaviour of the social elites and from corporate philanthropy. Ostrower (1995) found that most of the wealthy donors in her study emphasised the personal and familial meanings associated with their giving and rarely mentioned it as a way of attaining broader social or political goals. Most gave large amounts of money to 'precisely the kinds of educational and cultural organisations that are used by, and have prestige among, the elite' (Ostrower 1995: 39). These might include Ivy League universities, art galleries and museums. Schervish and Havens' (2001) large-scale survey of US households enjoying a net worth at or above $5 million found that giving was focused on influencing the improvement of education, promotion of arts and culture and strengthening family stability, causes that created and supported the elite's own success, although the reduction of poverty and hunger also featured. While some of the top givers identified by *Business Week* and *The Chronicle of Philanthropy* (Di Mento and Lewis 2006) also supported such causes, ambitious goals such as finding vaccines for malaria and HIV/AIDS, preventing nuclear proliferation or global warming and tackling poverty are foremost among the causes receiving support. Thus there would seem to be greater support for broader social impact than among the mass of wealthy individuals.

In terms of establishing a common culture and identity among top business givers, it could be that tycoon philanthropists share some of the characteristics of the social elite. Ostrower (1995) found that while individual donors regarded their own giving as personally motivated, it was, in fact, highly institutionalised. Philanthropy was a way into the higher echelons of society and support of the 'right cause' a symbol of having arrived. Benefits, charity balls and golf tournaments were, and still are, boundary-setting mechanisms that contribute to the production of a particular class based on wealth. The nature of tycoon giving, both in terms of size and causes supported, may also be becoming institutionalised along similar lines.

There would also seem to be some points of similarity with corporate philanthropic gestures. This, scholars and practitioners have noted, is becoming increasingly strategic. Although the existence of this trend is most often represented by anecdotal evidence, a growing body of research shows that firms are seeking clear business benefits from their support. Corporate philanthropy is designed to improve the firm's strategic position in a competitive marketplace, either in terms of reputation enhancement, legitimation or marketing (Saiia et al. 2004; Griffin, 2004; Harrow et al. 2006; Moir and Taffler 2004; Porter and Kramer 2002; Werbel and Wortman 1998; Wulfson 2001). It has also been noted that corporate giving in response to high-profile disasters such as the December 2004 South Asia tsunami seems to share some characteristics of the celebrity and rock star support for events such as Band Aid. This includes the one-off nature of donation and a herding approach in 'a quasi-competitive form of compassion' (Harrow et al. 2006: 319) that may be linked to legitimacy. While a desire to legitimise their wealth and influence and even competitive compassion may well be behind some tycoon philanthropy, it differs from much corporate giving in that gifts are generally made on a regular rather than a once-only basis.

However, neither setting the boundaries for an elite class nor a focus on legitimation nor their espoused motivations for giving seem to be an adequate explanation for the lavish philanthropic ventures of Bill Gates, Warren Buffett or George Soros. I have therefore turned to gift theory, drawing on lines of thought developed by Mauss, Bataille and Baudrillard, to examine whether the disposal of excessive wealth has broader, structural, economic, political or social functions. In the following section, therefore, I outline these theories in some detail before showing how it can be applied to the philanthropic gestures of business tycoons.

Theories of giving – potlatch, excess and annihilation

Mauss's theory of the gift, and in particular the ways in which it is manifest through the ceremony of potlatch, forms the basis both for Bataille's principle of loss and Baudrillard's notion of symbolic exchange value. Mauss (1967) focused on consumption as an alternative explanation for the circulation of goods as opposed to the utilitarian calculations of production and exchange of rationalist economics. He wanted to explore the ways in which a gift might be socially significant, and what the practices of giving might reveal about those doing the giving and the receiving. He studied what he referred to as 'archaic societies' – for example, Maori and Samoan societies, and the native societies of Northwest America. According to Mauss, gift-giving is bound up with obligation, receiving and repaying. A gift is given because of an obligation to give, while the recipient is, in turn, obliged to receive the gift and to return the gift with interest. Gift exchange is thus distinguished from the commodity exchange of buying and selling in which a buyer's obligation and relationship to the seller ends when payment is made. Mauss emphasises that the threefold sequence of obligation (giving, receiving and reciprocating) forms a cycle of exchange. Groups or individuals are obligated to receive while the groups or individuals with whom an exchange relationship is established are obligated to give. Failure to fulfil obligations can have serious consequences:

> To refuse to give, to fail to invite, is – like refusing to accept – the equivalent of a declaration of war; it is a refusal of friendship and intercourse. Again, one gives because one is forced to do so, because the recipient has a sort of proprietary right over everything which belongs to the donor (Mauss 1967: 10).

Thus the receipt of a gift means that the recipient is under pressure to give a gift back so continuing the cycle of exchange.

The Maussian notion that giving creates an interdependent relation between donor and receiver has been criticised for overstating the obligation created by the transaction (Testart 1998; Laidlaw 2000). It has been pointed out that there are 'free gifts', such as giving money to a beggar, when nothing is expected in return except perhaps a salved conscience or the warm glow of altruistic endeavour. However, the competitive aspect of gift-giving notable in the phenomenon of the potlatch does appear to be relevant to the activities of tycoon philanthropists. This form of gift-exchange is described by Olsen (2002) as 'an orgy of generosity', where the emphasis is on an agonistic display of luxury and excess. The prestige and honour of an individual is closely tied to expenditure and to the duty to return gifts with interest. Mauss relates that: 'Consumption and destruction are virtually unlimited. In some potlatch systems one is constrained to expend everything one possesses and to keep nothing. The rich man who shows his wealth by spending recklessly is the man who wins prestige' (1967: 35). Goods are destroyed rather than given in this war of wealth, to give the appearance that reciprocation is not necessary, and to 'level and crush a rival' (ibid.: 35). However, the rival has an obligation to destroy an even greater value of goods, because refusal to participate is proof of inferiority and an inability to meet the challenge offered. Precious copper goods are shattered and thrown in the sea, slaves have their throats cut, and entire villages burnt to the ground. But through the destruction of wealth, the individual gains status and prestige and their superiority is recognised by their contemporaries.

It was the excessive nature of giving and of destruction inherent in potlatch that provided Bataille with a point of departure for his overall conception of the general economy (Bataille 1988). Bataille conceived the general economy as a meta-category linked to the movement of energy through the universe, of which classical economics, with its focus on isolatable systems of operation and on scarcity, is a sub-category. Bataille argues that all living organisms receive more energy (and he traces this back as far as the energy emitted by the sun) than is necessary for the maintenance of life. Excess energy (or wealth) can be used for growth, either of the individual organism, or through reproduction of the species. If the excess cannot be absorbed by growth, 'it must necessarily be lost without profit, it must be spent, willingly or not, gloriously or catastrophically' (1988: 21). For living matter in general, as opposed to particular or limited populations of living beings, energy is always in excess. Because of his position at the 'summit' of the living world, man is destined to useless consumption. The ways in which a society chooses to annihilate the store of excess energy it produces defines that society:

> On the whole, a society always produces more than is necessary for its survival; it has a surplus at its disposal. It is precisely the use of this surplus that determines it: The surplus is the cause of the agitation, of the structural changes and of the entire history of society. But the surplus has more than one outlet, the most common of which is growth. And growth itself has many forms, each one of which eventually comes up against some limit. Thwarted,

demographic growth becomes military; it is forced to engage in conquest. Once the military limit is reached, the surplus has the sumptuary forms of religion as an outlet, along with the games and spectacles that derive therefrom, or personal luxury (Bataille 1988: 106).

Current examples of outlets for surplus might include the staging of the Olympic Games or the space race. Which brings us back to Mauss's essay. Bataille shows how the custom of potlatch challenges capitalist economics based on the acquisition of wealth, by revealing not a desire to gain, but a need to give away, lose or destroy excess. However, he goes on to say that:

The gift would be senseless (and so we would never decide to give) if it did not take on the meaning of an acquisition. Hence giving must become acquiring a power. Gift giving has the virtue of a surpassing of the subject who gives, but in exchange for the object given, the subject appropriates the surpassing. He regards his virtue, that which he had the capacity for, as an asset, as a power that he now possesses (Bataille 1988: 69).

The act of giving or destroying cannot be done privately or there would be no compensation, no power would result, but if the object is destroyed or given away in front of another person, the giver acquires the power of destroying or of giving. Bataille notes the absurdity of gift-giving – 'to give is obviously to lose, but the loss apparently brings a profit to the one who sustains it' (ibid.: 70). What the giver gains through potlatch is not the return of more lavish gifts, but prestige, glory and rank. Thus surplus must be squandered, but paradoxically, squandering becomes a means of acquisition: 'he must waste the excess, but he remains eager to acquire even when he does the opposite, and so he makes waste itself an object of acquisition' (ibid.: 72). The more ostentatious the squander, the greater the superiority attributed to the squanderer.

Bataille suggests that surplus must be annihilated and that failure to do so will result in war, death and destruction. In this, there is considerable resonance between his view of the consuming nature of wealth, and that of Baudrillard (Wyschogrod et al. 2002). Baudrillard believes that current society is in a state of hypertrophied growth, excessive growth and development, in which materiality is reduced to hyperreality and simulation, to the randomness of simulacra, images without originals. Objects and commodities are no longer characterised by economic exchange value (the object as commodity, marked by the logic of equivalence) or by symbolic exchange value (the object as symbol or gift, marked by the logic of ambivalence) but rather by sign exchange value (the object as sign, marked by the logic of differentiation). Drawing on Saussurean linguistics, Baudrillard argues that just as words take on meaning according to their position in a differential system of language, so sign values take on meaning according to their place in a differential system of prestige and status. Commodities are therefore purchased and displayed primarily for their sign value in terms of what they express about luxury, power and prestige, to such an extent that sign value now constitutes the commodity and consumption. Society has become so infected by sign value that it is organised around the consumption and display of commodities through which prestige, identity and standing are signified (Baudrillard 1998).

Thus, for Baudrillard, as for Bataille, consumption rather than production has become the chief basis of the social order: 'There is all around us today a kind of fantastic conspicuousness of consumption and abundance, constituted by the multiplication of objects, services and material goods' (Baudrillard 1998: 29). This is an exuberance, a profusion of luxuriant abundance and, through the conspicuousness of surplus, 'our markets, major shopping thoroughfares and superstores also mimic a new-found nature of prodigious fecundity' (ibid.: 26). We are living in the fantasy world of the plenitudinous Land of Cockaigne. Moreover, Baudrillard goes on to say:

> *And this metonymic, repetitive discourse of consumable matter, of the commodity, becomes once again, through a great collective metaphor – by virtue of its very excess – the image of the gift, and of that inexhaustible and spectacular prodigality which characterizes the feast (ibid.: 26).*

There are echoes here of both Mauss and Bataille. Consumer goods have the appearance of being offered as gifts which place the consumer in a position of being obligated to receive, while the orgy of consumption mimics the feast. Note that Baudrillard also argues here that the *discourse* of consumables is a product of its own surplus – so it is not just the 'real' production of objects that creates an excess that must be destroyed as in Bataille, but now the presentation of objects, the ways in which objects signify, produces an excess. Following Bataille, the focus of Baudrillard's analysis is not the typical production of objects in consumer society, but of the need of that society to destroy objects through fundamental and systematic wastage as its foundational principle (Baudrillard 1998). While conferring rank and prestige on those who can consume the most, at same time symbolic exchange is reduced to sign exchange. Although Baudrillard argues that the spectacular squandering of the potlatch has lost much of its symbolic and collective signification, becoming individualised and 'mass-mediafied' (ibid.: 46), destruction 'is fated to become one of the preponderant functions of post-industrial society' (ibid.: 47). Baudrillard also believes that elements of potlatch can still be detected in relationships between individuals and in objects which function as 'displays of antagonism' (1981: 41).

Against this backdrop, Baudrillard sees the gift as having a liberating potential that, rather than confirming value, wealth and rank, annihilates it. The gift was presented by Baudrillard as an escape from the problems of commodity exchange, calculation and political economy. His argument is that in a society where everything is a commodity that can be bought and sold, alienation is total.[2] In contrast, gift or

---

2   The idea that all social life is becoming commodified is by no means universally accepted (for example, Williams 2002), particularly Baudrillard's version of it which has stirred up much controversy and antagonism.

symbolic exchange establishes personal qualitative relations between the people transacting. While money cancels obligations between people and things, gifts establish obligations between people through things. Thus, Baudrillard champions symbolic exchange which resists capitalist values of utility and monetary profit. The gift is held out as the nearest representation of symbolic exchange because the object given is both arbitrary and particular, and thus ambiguous, and is invested with the power to signify 'the concrete relation in which it is exchanged, the transferential pact that it seals between two persons' (1981: 64). The gift has no use value or economic exchange value because it cannot be independent of the giver and recipient. To give means to both invest a part of the self in the gift, while at the same time giving something away. This is what makes gift exchange ambivalent – it is always 'a medium of relation *and* distance: it is always love and aggression' (1981: 65). However, Baudrillard also claims that symbolic exchange in a consumer society is parodic, a simulacrum of the rivalry of the potlatch that is industrially produced and mass-mediafied 'no longer arising in the personal reciprocity of challenge and exchange' (1981: 119). This is crucial because symbolic exchange relies on the *counter-gift*. It is the challenge posed by the necessity of the counter-gift rather than the unilateral gift that will initiate symbolic exchange. The undermining of sign value is predicated on 'the reversibility of the gift in the counter-gift, the reversibility of exchange in the sacrifice ... the reversibility of life in death' (1993: 2).

Thus for Bataille, there is an inevitable surplus of energy which has to be spent unproductively in order to maintain a balance between expenditure and accumulation and this constitutes a general economy. For Baudrillard, the surplus of accumulation is ever increasing and cannot possibly be entirely spent either productively or unproductively. This is increasingly leading to catastrophe to which the only possible response is to practise potlatch individually, challenging oneself and others 'to receive, to give, to return, to destroy – if possible, all at once' (1981: 207).

Tycoon gift-giving

When we take a closer look at tycoon philanthropy, we find strong resonances with the work of Mauss, Bataille and Baudrillard as we can see elements of the competitive aspects of potlatch, the drive to annihilate excess and, just possibly, spending as a means of fending off impending catastrophe. We will also ask whether this lavish gift-giving constitutes a site of resistance to sign value and the logic of commodification (Urry 2000), a 'space of hope' (Harvey 2000), or whether it is yet another simulacrum.

As there is scant academic work on this subject, my method has been to excavate and explore data gleaned from the websites of foundations established by top business givers, the news media and comment from organisations such as the Capital Research Centre and *The Chronicle of Philanthropy*. Much of this is inherently biased, either pro or anti individuals and their causes. However, it could be argued that many philanthropists and those who disapprove of their charitable ventures use print, broadcast and electronic media to publicise their activities and thus play a powerful role in shaping public perceptions of philanthropists and the issues they espouse (Rindova et al. 2006; McCombs and Shaw 1972). Baudrillard would argue that such media contribute to the constitution of the sign value of charitable giving.

It should also be noted that an exploration or critique of the motives or political affiliations of the donors is beyond the scope of this essay. I am not presenting any normative view about the philanthropic ventures supported or suggesting that the resources expended have no impact, or that philanthropists should not give.

The potlatch revisited – as sign value

The gift-giving of some of the 'super-rich' seems to have a competitive edge that fits with the agonistic aspects of potlatch, to 'defy rivals through the spectacular destruction of wealth' (Bataille 1985: 121). In the UK, an organisation called the Fortune Forum was recently set up to appeal to 'individuals of extreme wealth' to give as lavishly as possible, and it was launched at a gala dinner. There is, of course, a long history of this kind of charity event in the US, where tickets cost a small fortune in themselves and where it is important that socialites and celebrities are seen (Ostrower 1995). Tickets to the Fortune Forum dinner cost £1,000 or more, where 500 guests heard Bill Clinton, Michael Douglas and Zac Goldsmith (a politician, a movie-star celebrity and a member of the Goldsmith dynasty turned eco-warrior) exhort them to take 'personal and individual action against global poverty and environmental degradation' (Cohen 2006; Temko 2006; Willman 2006). The highlight of the evening was a project auction during which 'golden goddesses', attractive women in golden costumes, collected pledges from the audience. The desire to be seen giving, to outdo the others' gifts by outbidding them in an auction for 'treats' such as a weekend on a luxury yacht off the French Riviera or a music session with a rock star – all examples of useless luxuries – are exactly the agonistic elements of potlatch described by Mauss and Bataille, designed to confer rank and status on the giver, in a society which, Bataille claims, has reduced giving by the wealthy to a form of commodification. Drawing on Baudrillard's observations of commodities and consumption as sign values, giving in this context does not establish contact between people as there can be no counter-gift, but is yet another form of consumption that signifies status and prestige.

It also conforms to the boundary-setting behaviours reported by Ostrower (1995) and described above. Bataille argues that, in current society, luxurious consumption and excessive giving retain something of the original function of potlatch in that the rich man proves his superior nobility, honour and rank to other rich men. However, its ultimate goal is to demonstrate his separation from those who are destitute. The exuberance of giving in the archaic forms of potlatch has been reduced to handouts and the wealthy who give away their possessions are lying to themselves, because they are reducing giving to 'a commodity of exploitation, a shameless source of profits' (Bataille 1998: 75).

The organiser, fashion designer Renu Mehta, is reported as saying that 'very fortunate individuals like me – captains of industry, celebrities, activists – [have found] that we were all feeling the same way. We were looking for the missing ingredient in our lives, an ingredient that could offer personal fulfilment. I've since discovered this only comes with the serenity of giving something back' (Cohen 2006). However, this is a serenity that is purchased. This resonates with Baudrillard's idea that pecuniary human relationships are substituting for social relationships based on obligation and reciprocity. Experiences, such as the feeling of serenity, have to be paid for and have become part of Baudrillard's sign value, as other people's time, affections, regard and attention become paid-for experiences that signify social worth. Serenity has a sign value.

Warren Buffett's justification for giving to the Bill and Melinda Gates Foundation rather than increasing the size of existing Buffett foundations is that 'the feedback on philanthropy is very slow and that would bother me. I'd have to be too involved with a lot of people I wouldn't want to be involved with and have to listen to more opinions than I would enjoy' (Loomis 2006a). For Buffett, the instant gratification of giving seems to be as important as the outcome of the gift, while he positively turns away from establishing relationships with other stakeholders. Tom Hunter also seeks the 'fun' of giving and explains his plans to give away his wealth now rather than let others do it after his death as 'Why give someone else all the fun? Why do it once you're dead? I want to do it now' (Moss 2005). Although Hunter insists on the impact of his gifts being evaluated through audits and performance indicators, this is because 'I like to control things' (Moss 2005). The experiences of fun and of feeling in control, something that Hunter now finds lacking in his business dealings, have been bought with the gift.

The Fortune Forum dinner also highlights the celebritisation of the business magnate. Guests and prospective members of the Forum are 'heads of the world's largest foundations, global leaders, captains of industry and finance, academics and celebrities' (Fortune Forum n.d.). Note how celebrities and business magnates are described as being in attendance at the dinner, and how Fortune Forum groups them together as prospective participants. The cult of the celebrity CEO is something that has been noted particularly in the practitioner business journals (for example, *Strategic Direction* 2003). The celebrity chief executive is constructed largely through the media, usually achieving iconic status for their perceived business acumen, distinctiveness of action and idiosyncratic personalities (Hayward et al. 2004). They publish best-selling autobiographies and 'how to' books. They are given soubriquets; Warren Buffett is dubbed 'the Sage of Omaha' for his homilies to shareholders, while Ted Turner is known as 'the Mouth of the South' for his outspoken views. Marshall sees celebrity as incorporating two faces of contemporary capitalism: 'defaced value and prized commodity value' (1997: 4). Even though the value of celebrity lacks any material basis – celebrities often conform to the axiom of being famous for being famous – achieving the visibility of celebrity status is the *sine qua non* of prestige today, the primary signifier of success. Celebrity exists in the realm of signs. Rein et al. argue that professionals who have attained celebrity status, or who aspire to, recognise that their visibility confers significant power, opportunities and rewards. They are willing to work with the invisible industry that generates and markets celebrities to achieve such visibility. Spectacular giving adds to this celebrity status, not only through the glitz surrounding occasions such as the Fortune Forum dinner, but through the publicity that the gifts generate. Warren Buffett's gift was widely reported at the time in newspapers and TV, and he has published his letters to Bill and Melinda Gates and to his children on the Internet. The letters themselves are formulaic and very nearly identical, but through their publication and other publicity, Buffett acquires the power of giving noted by Bataille. Ted Turner's 1998 billion dollar pledge to the UN was the cover story in *Newsweek* even though the gift itself is problematic and concerns have been raised regarding its legality. By 2003, he had run into financial problems and still owed $600 million of the pledge (Hudson 2003). The billion-dollar pledge, the publicity and controversy it generated, and Turner's insistence that 'that's not my money' (*New York Times* 2003, cited in Torbert 2004), despite his financial problems, is an example of gift-giving as spectacle. There was even talk of Turner being awarded a Nobel Prize (Kincaid n.d.).

Annihilating excess

Although the individual may dispose of his wealth to gain prestige, Bataille argued that the destruction of excess inherent in potlatch served a more general economic function, and we will now therefore turn to this element of tycoon philanthropy.

Warren Buffett claims that it was always his intention to give back his wealth to society:

> *In that we agreed with Andrew Carnegie, who said that huge fortunes that flow in large part from society should in large part be returned to society. In my case, the ability to allocate capital would have had little utility unless I lived in a rich populous country in which enormous quantities of marketable securities were traded and were sometimes ridiculously mispriced. And fortunately, for me, that describes the US in the second half of the last century (Loomis 2006a: n.p.).*

What Buffett seems to be implying is that individuals with his skills and drive will inevitably amass an enormous surplus through the operation and manipulation of exchange. Bataille would say that he can either use the surplus to produce an even greater accumulation, and thus build up an even greater pressure to dispose of it, or he has to dispose of it in a way that is unproductive.

Buffett's means of disposal is to gradually give away $40 billion of his personal fortune made up with shares from his company Berkshire Hathaway. Some will go to the four family trusts (three foundations each headed by one of his three children, and the Susan Thompson Buffett Foundation named in honour of his late wife) but the largest share (five-sixths) will go to the world's largest philanthropic organisation – ironically the $30 billion Bill and Melinda Gates Foundation. The gifts are phased so that each year a set of shares, starting with 602,500 in 2006, and then decreasing by 5 per cent per year will go to the five foundations (Loomis 2006b). The excess represented by Buffett's fortune will be annihilated as it will be largely destroyed. The Buffett family foundations will have to sell the shares given to them in order to generate money to give away.

It is reported that Bill and Melinda Gates have also said that 'almost all their fortune will go to charity' (Loomis 2006c). Moreover, the Gates Foundation funds research into finding solutions to some of the world's most intractable problems; for example, to discover a vaccine against HIV/AIDS and to deliver antiretrovirals to those already infected with the disease. Bill Gates has calculated that the annual cost of treatment to everyone in world who is HIV-positive would be more than $13 billion (Gates 2006) so the project could, potentially, consume expenditure on a massive scale. Indeed, it could almost be argued that such projects would suck resources into a black hole, something of which Gates seems to be aware. He acknowledges that he has been criticised for emphasising research into big health breakthroughs (Gates 2005) and for trying to find big, costly and technological solutions to big, costly problems. He has said: 'We can afford to have a lot of failures. We're going to have a lot of failures. I will not stop working on malaria, TB or AIDS because of failures' (Boseley 2006). Although finding an AIDS vaccine could cost billions, he will not give up. The philanthropic aims of other tycoons are equally ambitious and large-scale. Ted Turner's Foundation attempts to halt nuclear proliferation and prevent environmental disaster; George Soros wishes to promote worldwide democracy and one of the initiatives promoted by the Gordon and Betty Moore Foundation is to 'preserve the Amazon Basin, protect North Pacific salmon ecosystems and improve marine management resources to revolutionise the management of coastal oceans' (Moore Foundation 2006). Just one of the ambitions espoused by John Sperling is to extend the human lifespan indefinitely. He also spent seven years and $19 million in vain trying to clone a dog (*Wired* 2004). The scale of these projects dwarfs the most generous giving and will annihilate much of the excess fortune generated and amassed by these individuals.

Fear of impending catastrophe

The espoused motivation behind much of the lavish giving could almost be inspired by Baudrillard's exhortation to individually spend, destroy, to stave off catastrophe.

This is partly to prevent annihilation on an individual basis. Of the philanthropists identified in the list of 'The 50 most generous philanthropists' (*Business Week* 2006), 41 have endowed foundations that carry their names, and several of these, and some without a foundation, have art collections, libraries, university research centres or chairs, law centres and programmes named after them. Philanthropy can achieve a form of immortality; literally in the case of John Sperling whose giving, as noted above, supports human longevity research (*Wired* 2004).

The threat of annihilation which lavish expenditure seems to try to forestall is, however, on a greater scale than the annihilation of the individual. Bataille believed that societies attempt to expend excess through religious festivals or monuments, artistic endeavour or through a proliferation of the services that increase leisure time today, but that expenditure has always been inadequate. This has doomed human beings and their goods to the destruction of wars. Industrialisation, which brought a focus on production as its principal goal, had a double effect. At first, it used up a portion of the surplus energy in order to drive growth, but eventually it produced a larger and larger surplus that had to be expended. So now the imperative is not to further develop the forces of production, but to spend, or squander, their products. Bataille sees the two world wars as the greatest orgies of the squandering of wealth in history.

At the time that Bataille wrote *The Accursed Share* (1988), the major threat to world peace came from a possible (Bataille thought almost inevitable) conflict between the US and the USSR. The American economy, driven inexorably by growth, is 'the greatest explosive mass the world has ever known' (ibid.: 171) so that the only thing that prevented the inevitability of war was the idea that 'the economy ... might continue it by other means' (ibid.: 171). Bataille therefore believed that the US would conduct a war by non-military means:

> One can envisage a vast economic competition, which, for the competitor with the initiative, would cost sacrifices comparable to those of war, and which, from a budget of the same scale as war budgets, would involve expenditures that would not be compensated by any hope of capitalist profit (ibid.:172).

This non-military means was the Marshall Plan – a way of competing economically with the USSR. By 'sacrificing' $5 billion for non-military ends, the Americans were engaging in an enormous potlatch. Now, of course, the USSR is no longer a superpower and, with the loss of the 'salutory fear of the Soviets (or some analogous threat)' (ibid.: 183) there is no equivalent of the Marshall Plan. Indeed, George Soros has pointed out that:

> The Cold War was an extremely stable arrangement. Two power blocs, representing opposing concepts of social organization, were struggling for supremacy, but they had to respect each other's interests, because each side was capable of destroying the other in an all-out war. This put a firm limit on the extent of the conflict; all local conflicts were, in turn, contained by the larger conflict. This extremely stable world order has come to an end as the result of the internal disintegration of one superpower. No new world order has taken its place. We have entered a period of disorder (Soros 1997).

The stability of the Cold War threat has been replaced with the disorder of the 'War on Terror'. Bataille believed that the US had to continue using up its excess to raise the global standard of living so that global conflict could be avoided. In fact, US aid has declined from around 0.6 per cent of gross national income in the 1960s to just over 0.1 per cent in 2001, rising to 0.2 per cent in 2006. Most of the increase can be accounted for by reconstruction and other aid to Iraq and reconstruction and anti-narcotics programmes in Afghanistan, and what is given is tied to a greater extent to US interests. Reconstruction in Iraq, for example, is largely in the hands of US organisations (OECD 2006; Sachs 2001).

A fear of apocalyptic global catastrophe, in the form of either nuclear war or global environmental disaster, is relatively common among top givers. For example, one of the aims of the Susan Buffett Foundation is to prevent the spread of nuclear weapons. Ted Turner has established the Nuclear Threat Initiative whose stated aim is 'to reduce the global threats from nuclear, biological and chemical weapons', including keeping 'weapons of mass destruction out of terrorist hands' (Nuclear Threat Initiative, n.d.). The Turner Foundation is committed to preventing damage to ecosystems and, among other activities, supports radical environmental groups such as Greenpeace and the Ruckus Society. In a Reuter's interview, Turner warned:

> *Global warming, nuclear weapons, nuclear proliferation, population explosion, environmental degradation that's occurring in virtually every ecosystem all over the world … We've already got a catastrophe on our hands. Without precedent in the history of the world. And if we don't get it straight, just on global warming alone, God forbid a nuclear war springing up (Turner 2006).*

It is interesting to speculate whether these wealthy US businessmen are performing the economic and political function of filling the gap left by the relative paucity of US state-sponsored spending on social and environmental initiatives. Indeed, Turner's avowed purpose behind his $1 billion pledge to the UN was to compensate for the $1 billion arrears owed by the US government; he gave because the 'United States just wasn't paying its dues'. It is therefore the tycoon philanthropists who are fulfilling Bataille's vision of defusing the potentially explosive surplus produced by the US in order to avert catastrophe.

Conclusion

Whatever the espoused motivations behind tycoon philanthropy – to give back, to achieve serenity, to have fun, to save the planet – there are strong indications of the aggrandising and agonistic aspects of potlatch noted by Mauss and Bataille. The spectacle of the second-richest man in the world giving the bulk of his fortune to the charitable foundation of the richest man in the world particularly resonates with the concept of potlatch. However, at the same time, it also seems to be parodic of potlatch having become a means of personalisation and differentiation, a shared sign which makes the members of the group of super-rich businessmen different from any other particular group. Moreover, what is given is not material goods or even the material signifiers of exchange such as notes and coins, but intangible and invisible flows of capital such as stocks or pledges. Spectacular giving is no longer a spectacle, we cannot see it except through its manifestation on the pages, screens and websites of the mass media. There is little sense that this giving has the liberating potential of establishing personal, qualitative relations between the giver and receiver, or of establishing reciprocal obligations championed by Baudrillard. On the contrary, it is impersonal and carried on at arm's length through family foundations. Buffett has expressly stated that he does not want to be involved, while the awkwardness of Bill Gates and his reluctance to engage with the recipients of his charity was noted on a recent visit to Africa (Boseley 2006). It is a simulacrum of potlatch, rooted in sign value. As such, its potential to act as a space of hope against the onward march of commodification seems limited.

And yet, the actions of the tycoon philanthropists also seem to fulfil the wider economic imperative of annihilating excess noted by Bataille. Their hugely ambitious programmes, gargantuan in terms of scope, could consume far more than even the most generous donor could give, while Gates, Buffett and others say they intend to dispose of the bulk of their fortunes. Annihilation can never be complete as much of the expenditure leads to yet more production (new drugs or new technologies) and the creation of wealth in Western economies to pay for, for example, research and development activities by pharmaceutical or engineering firms. But finding an AIDS vaccine, tackling pollution or global warming, or promoting Soros's particular vision of open governance around the world will absorb resources on a massive scale. It will also result in some transfer of resources away from the US, making a contribution to fulfilling what seems to be an ethical imperative set by Bataille to defuse the explosive mass that is the US to avert global catastrophe.

References

Bataille, G. (1988), *The Accursed Share: An Essay in General Economy*, vol. 1, trans. R. Hurley, New York: Zone.

Bataille, G. (1985), 'The notion of expenditure', in A. Stoekl (ed. and trans.), *Visions of Excess: Selected Writings 1927–1939*, Manchester: Manchester University Press, 116–129.

Baudrillard, J. (1998), *The Consumer Society: Myths and Structures*, trans. C. Turner, London: Sage.

Baudrillard, J. (1993), *Symbolic Exchange and Death*, trans. I. Grant, London: Sage.

Baudrillard, J. (1981), *For a Critique of the Political Economy of the Sign*, trans. C. Levin, St Louis: Telos.

Boseley, S. (2006), 'Wealth and experience', *The Guardian*, 20 July.

Business Week (2006), 'The 50 most generous philanthropists', at <http://bwnt. businessweek.com/philanthropy/06/index.asp>, November, accessed December 2006.

Cohen, N. (2006), 'Save me from the super-rich and their competitive compassion', *The Observer*, 24 September.

Di Mento, M. and Lewis, N. (2006), 'How the wealthy give', *The Chronicle of Philanthropy*, 23 February.

Fortune Forum (n.d.), at <http://www.fortuneforum.org/the-club.htm>, accessed November 2006.

Gates, W. (2006), 'XVI International AIDS Conference Keynote Speech', at <http://www.gatesfoundation.org/MediaCenter/Speeches/Co-ChairSpeeches/BillgSpeeches/BGSpeech2006AIDS-060813.htm>, accessed November, 2006.

Gates, W. (2005), 'Speech to the 2005 World Health Assembly', at <http://www.gatesfoundation.org/MediaCenter/Speeches/Co-ChairSpeeches/BillgSpeeches/BGSpeechWHA-050516.htm>, accessed November 2006.

Griffin, J. (2004), 'Corporate restructurings: ripple effects on corporate philanthropy', *Journal of Public Affairs*, 4 (1), 27–43.

Harrow, J., Palmer, P. and Bogdanova, M. (2006), 'Business giving, the tsunami and corporates as rock stars: some implications for arts funding?', *Cultural Trends*, 15 (4), 299–323.

Harvey, D. (2000), *Spaces of Hope*, Edinburgh: Edinburgh University Press.

Hayward, M.L.A., Rindova, V.P. and Pollock, T.G. (2004), 'Believing one's own press: the causes and consequences of CEO celebrity', *Strategic Management Journal*, 25, 637–53.

Hudson, A. (2003), 'Tough times shut down Turner philanthropy', *The Washington Times*, 18 June.

Kincaid, C. (n.d.), 'Ted Turner's United Nations Foundation: making the UN a pawn for tax-exempt special interests', at <http://www.apfn.org/apfn/turner.htm>, accessed November 2006.

Laidlaw, J. (2000), 'A free gift makes no friends', *Journal of the Royal Anthropological Institute*, 6, 617–634.

Loomis, C. (2006a), 'A conversation with Warren Buffet', at <http://money.cnn.com/2006/06/25/magazines/fortune/charity2.fortune/index.htm>, accessed October 2006.

Loomis, C. (2006b), 'Warren Buffet gives away his fortune', at <http://money.cnn.com/2006/06/25/magazines/fortune/charity1.fortune/index.htm>, accessed October 2006.

Loomis, C. (2006c), 'The global force called the Gates Foundation', at <http://money.cnn.com/2006/06/25/magazines/fortune/charity4.fortune/index.htm>, accessed October 2006.

McCombs, M.E. and Shaw, D.L. (1972), 'The agenda setting function of the mass media', *Public Opinion Quarterly*, 36, 176–87.

Marshall, P.D. (1997), *Celebrity and Power: Fame in Contemporary Culture*, London/Minneapolis: University of Minnesota Press.

Mauss, M. (1967), *The Gift: Forms and Functions of Exchange in Archaic Society*, New York: Norton.

Moir, L. and Taffler, R.J. (2004), 'Does corporate philanthropy exist? Business giving to the arts in the U.K.', *Journal of Business Ethics*, 54, 149–61.

Moore Foundation, Gordon and Betty (2006), 'Foundation Five Year Report', at <http://www.moore.org/docs/GBMF_5YearReport.pdf>, accessed January 2007.

Moss, S. (2005), 'The tycoon who wants to save the world', *The Guardian*, 23 September.

Nuclear Threat Initiative (n.d.), at <http://www.nti.org/>, accessed December 2006.

Olsen, C. (2002), 'Excess, time and the pure gift: postmodern transformations of Marcel Mauss' theory', *Method & Theory in the Study of Religion*, 14, 350–374.

Open Society Institute (2007), 'About us', at <http://www.soros.org/about>, accessed January 2007.

Organization for Economic Cooperation and Development (OECD) (2006), 'Briefing document', at <http://www.oecd.org/document/54/0,2340,en_2649_201185_37799158_1_1_1_1,00.html>, accessed January 2007.

Ostrower, F. (1995), *Why the Wealthy Give: The Culture of Elite Philanthropy*, Princeton NJ: Princeton University Press.

Porter, M.E. and Kramer, M.R. (2002), 'The competitive advantage of corporate philanthropy', *Harvard Business Review*, 80 (12), 56–68.

Rein, I., Kotler, P. and Stoller, M. (1997), *High Visibility: The Making and Marketing of Professionals into Celebrities*, Lincolnwood IL: NTC Business Books.

Rindova, V.P., Pollock, T.G. and Hayward, M.L.A. (2006), 'Celebrity firms: the social construction of market popularity', *Academy of Management Review*, 31 (1), 50–71.

Sachs, J. (2001), 'What's good for the poor is good for America', *The Economist*, 12 July.

Saiia, D.H., Carroll, A.B. and Buchholtz, A.K. (2004), 'Philanthropy as strategy: when corporate charity "begins at home"', *Business & Society*, 42 (2), 169–201.

Schervish, P.G. and Havens, J.J. (2001), 'The mind of the millionaire: findings from a national survey on wealth with responsibility', *New Directions for Philanthropic Fundraising*, 32, 75–107.

Soros, G. (1997), 'The capitalist threat', *Atlantic Monthly*, 279 (2), 45–58.

Strategic Direction (2003), 'Welch, Dunlap and Nasser have now left the building: is it time we got rid of the celebrity CEO?', 19 (3), 5–8.

Temko, N. (2006), 'Stars queue to join Clinton at ball', *The Observer*, 24 September.

Testart, A. (1998), 'Uncertainties of the "obligation to reciprocate": a critique of Mauss' in W. James and N.J. Allen (eds), *Marcel Mauss: A Centenary Tribute*, New York: Berghahn Books.

Torbert, S. (2004), 'Ted Turner: down but not out', *Foundation Watch*, November.

Turner, T. (2006), 'Ted Turner: telling it like it is', at UN Dispatch, September, <http://www.undispatch.com/archives/2006/09/telling_it_like.html>, accessed October 2006.

Urry, J. (2000), *Sociology Beyond Societies: Mobilities for the Twenty-First Century*, London: Routledge.

Werbel, J.D. and Wortman, M.S. (1998), 'Strategic philanthropy: responding to negative portrayals of corporate social responsibility', *Corporate Reputation Review*, 3 (2), 124–36.

Williams, C.C. (2002), 'A critical evaluation of the commodification thesis', *Sociological Review*, 50 (4), 526–42.

Willman, J. (2006), 'Celebrities show gift for charity', *Financial Times*, 30 September.

Wired (2004), 'John Sperling wants you to live forever', February.

Wulfson, M. (2001) 'The ethics of corporate social responsibility and philanthropic ventures', *Journal of Business Ethics*, 29, 135–45.

Wyschogrod, E., Goux, J.-J. and Boynton, E. (2002), *The Enigma of Gift and Sacrifice*, New York: Fordham University Press.

Corporate Governance Studies on the Accounting Environment in Turkey

Kiymet Tunca Çalıyurt

Introduction

There is a direct relationship between corporate governance and the accounting world. Recent accounting scandals have placed an increasing importance on corporate governance. In actual fact, firstly, corporate governance is created to protect shareholders' rights. Parkinson's study published in 1994 declared that institutional investors strongly agree that corporate governance is '… the process of supervision and control intended to ensure that the company's management acts in accordance with the interests of shareholders' (Solomon 2007: 13). The scandals of the last few years came as a shock not just because of the enormity of failures like Enron and WorldCom, but because of the discovery that questionable accounting practice was far more insidious and widespread than previously envisioned. A definite link between these accounting failures and poor corporate governance is beginning to emerge. Adelphia, for example, was given a very low 24 per cent rating by Institutional Shareholder Services on its corporate governance score. In Europe, Parmalat and Royal Ahold ranked in the bottom quartile of companies in the index provided by Governance Metrics International. The Corporate Library had issued early failure warnings on WorldCom and Enron. An increasing number of researchers are finding that poor corporate governance is a leading factor in causing poor performance, manipulated financial reports and unhappy stakeholders. Corporations and regulatory bodies are now trying to analyse and correct any existing defects in their reporting system (Ramaswamy n.d). The Corporate Governance Reporting Institution has published reports to warn the public about potential scandals before them happening. Accordingly Farber's study shows that results indicate that analyst following and institutional holdings do not increase in fraud-related firms, suggesting that credibility is still a problem for these firms. However, the results also indicate that firms that take actions to improve governance have superior stock price performance, even after controlling for earnings performance. This suggests that governance improvements appear to be valued by investors (Farber 2004).

Turkey is a candidate member for the EU. As such, in every area there is legislation, and this extends to the areas of accounting and corporate governance. Corporate governance studies are necessary for a better accounting world in Turkey. The experience of banking scandals has been defined as 'Turkey's Enron' by managers of publicly held companies (Demircan 2007: 113). After the banking scandals, corporate governance and relevant (related) legislation has shown important changes and improvements in Turkey too.

In this study, it is necessary to define corporate governance because it is one of the most topical subjects of recent years. The amount of corporate governance research has increased dramatically during the last decade. A search of Social Sciences Research Network abstracts containing the term 'corporate governance' results in more than 3500 hits (Gillian 2006).

There are different definitions of corporate governance which are dissimilar from that applied in Turkey. Because it is a familiar and usually undefined term, it is unsurprising that corporate governance appears to have as many meanings as it has users. In an everyday sense, the verb 'to govern' is typically defined as 'ruling by authority'. It is commonly associated with the activities of the state. In the corporate sense, however, corporate governance seems to be a term used almost universally in a less stringent sense of directing, regulating or controlling. With this mind, it is therefore relevant to ask:

- What corporate activities are directed, regulated or controlled?
- Why is directing, regulating or controlling corporate activities necessary?
- How is directing, regulating, or controlling corporate activities conducted? (Lee 2006: 21)

The Turkish Industrialists' and Businessmen's Association has defined corporate governance as 'any corporation's management regulation that people have composed for reaching to an aim in modern life'(Sanayici and Dernegi 2002).

So the question must be asked as to why has corporate governance been more important during the last 20 years and not before. This can be answered by prioritizing in a different way: firstly, the privatization phenomenon in the world; secondly, retirement pensions reforms and growing personal savings; thirdly, the integration and regulation of capital markets; fourthly, the Asian crisis that happened in 1998; and lastly, the company collapses and financial scandals in the 1990s (Becht et al. 2002).

The advantages of a corporate governance approach are as follows:

- The corporate governance concept and regulations about this promotes (and encourages) discussions on subjects relevant to corporate governance.
- It stimulates the application of several standards by companies, firstly by application of generally accepted accounting principles and auditing standards, then of accepted standards in the managerial area.

- It helps to explain to investors more easily both the legal obligations of management and common corporate governance applications.
- It simplifies the performance evaluation of top-level executives and the board of directors.
- It facilitates preparation of the necessary changes in capital market legislation and company law (Demirbaş and Uyar 2006: 19).

The aim of this study is to give information about legislation changes that have caused accounting studies to align themselves more closely after the banking scandals in Turkey. The Banking Regulation and Supervision Agency, the Capital Markets Board, the Ministry of Finance and the Accounting Standards Board all took important decisions that will affect the accounting and corporate governance worlds.

The legislation studies on accounting in Turkey in corporate terms

The Turkish Capital Market Board's corporate governance workings on audit

The following paragraphs have been added to Article 11 of Communiqué Serial X, No. 16 Regarding Independent Auditing in Capital Markets, published in the *Official Gazette* dated 4 March 1996, no. 22570:

Independent auditing firms, their auditors and other staff shall not provide any issuer or intermediary, contemporaneously with the audit, any non-audit service, with or without fee, including;

a) book-keeping and other related services,
b) financial information systems design and implementation services on management, accounting and finance,
c) appraisal or valuation services and actuarial services,
d) internal audit outsourcing services,
e) legal services and expert services,
f) any other consultation services.

However, within the framework of the Law No. 3568 on Independent Accountancy, Independent Accountancy Financial Advisory and Sworn-in Financial Advisory, it is not prohibited to examine financial statements and tax returns and verify their conformity and to give opinion and prepare reports in accordance with tax legislation. Any consulting firm that is related with any independent auditing firm by way of capital or management shall not provide any consulting service to any issuer to which the related independent auditing firm provides audit service for the same period. This prohibition includes consulting services rendered by shareholders or directors of the independent auditing firm.

In special and/or annual audit, independent auditing firms are selected by the board of directors of the company for no more than 5 years. The audit engagement signed with selected independent auditing firm comes into effect after the approval of the board of directors of the issuer. In an annual audit, selection of independent auditing firm made by board of directors is presented to approval of stockholders' meeting. After 2 accounting periods, independent auditing firm could provide audit service to the same issuer.

Listed companies have to establish an audit committee that has at least two members who shall be selected by and among the board of directors. If the committee has two members, then neither of them (or if the committee has more than two members, the majority of them) cannot occupy an executive post such as that of general manager or executive committee member in the board of directors. Non-listed companies can voluntarily establish an audit committee according to principles regulated in this article and disclose its membership to the public.

The audit committee oversees implementation and effectiveness of accounting systems, disclosure of financial information to the public, independent auditing and internal control systems. Also, the following operations are realized under the oversight of the audit committee: the selection of the independent auditing firm, the beginning of the auditing process by signing an audit engagement with an independent auditing firm, and every phase of services rendered by the independent auditing firm. Selection of an independent auditing firm and audit services rendered by independent auditing firms shall be presented to the board of directors of the issuer after pre-approval by the audit committee. The independent auditing firm shall produce a timely report bringing the following issues to the notice of the audit committee of the issuer:

- all critical accounting policies and practices to be used
- all alternative treatments and disclosure options of financial information within generally accepted accounting principles that have been discussed with management officials of the issuer
- possible results of the use of such alternative disclosures and the treatment preferred by the auditing firm
- other material and written communications between the auditor and client management.

The audit committee shall establish procedures for:

- the receipt, retention and treatment of complaints received by the issuer regarding accounting, internal controls and auditing matters, and

- the confidential, anonymous submission by employees of the issuer of concerns regarding questionable accounting and auditing matters.

The audit committee shall present annual and interim financial statements with its evaluations to the board of directors after taking the opinion of responsible directors of issuers and auditors regarding a true and fair view and conformity to accounting principles of the issuer.

The audit committee shall have the authority to engage independent counsel and other advisers, as it determines necessary to carry out its three duties. Funding for payment of compensation to any advisers employed by the audit committee shall be provided by the issuer. The audit committee shall meet at least once every three months, at least four times in a year, and the results of these meetings shall be presented to the board of directors in a written form. The audit committee shall present immediately problems and suggestions which are related to the committee's task and responsibility area to the board of directors of the issuer in a written form. The task and responsibility of audit committee cannot abolish the task and responsibility of the board of director defined in Turkish commercial law (Gokalp 2005).

The Turkish Capital Market Board's corporate governance principles

The Turkish Capital Market Board (CMB) has announced corporate governance principles in 2003 and has revised them in 2005. The President of the Board made a speech about their reasons for applying such principles for publicly held companies:

> Today's global financial marketplace sets the scene for outstanding and swift developments. In light of such developments and latest novelties, the competitive power of the markets is more important than ever. The global trends need to be clearly identified to ensure efficient functioning of capital markets for the purpose of the country's development. Although national borders maintain their physical existence, they are becoming less significant in today's world which is becoming a smaller place to live in. Recent trends in globalisation and improvements in information technology have enabled funds to move from one market to another in just a few seconds. On the other hand, as governments across the world and international finance institutions have realised the need for closer cooperation, international standard setting is becoming a must in many areas.

Companies and even governments no longer feel restricted to limit their financial capacities with their own domestic markets, but rather seek to utilize their opportunities in the international financial arena. International competition is becoming a lot more essential in order to best utilize the flow of capital movements across the world. As new funds and new innovations enter the world financial markets, investor preferences are getting enhanced with each day. In parallel with these developments, regulation of the problems and standard issues being faced in today's financial markets is becoming more complex.

Due to the increase in competitive conditions within financial markets, countries are being required to harmonize their legislation with the international level and realize a set of regulations in order to attain and sustain development. Within this context, restructuring the Turkish capital markets is becoming highly significant, especially for public companies, in terms of providing global liquidity and expanding the fund provision capabilities of international financial markets. It is widely accepted that bad management practices have triggered the financial crises and company scandals that have broken out in recent years. This has clarified the importance of the concept of sound corporate management practices. The importance of the issue has been growing at an international level and the quality of corporate governance practices, which is deemed to be as important as financial performance in investment decisions, has become a subject of more serious consideration. Empirical studies indicate that international investors now better realize the significance of corporate governance practices on the financial performance of companies than ever before and, while adopting investment decisions, international investors believe that this issue bears more importance for countries that are in need of reforms, and that they are more ready to pay higher premiums for companies having sound corporate governance practices.

Sound corporate governance practices bring out advantages for companies and for countries also. With respect to companies, the high-quality status of corporate governance means a lower cost of capital, an increase in financial capabilities and liquidity, ability to overcome crises more easily and prevention of the exclusion of soundly managed companies from the capital markets. On the other hand, with respect to the country, sound corporate governance means improvement of a country's image, prevention of outflow of domestic funds, increase in foreign capital investments, increase in the competitive power of the economy and capital markets, overcoming crises with less damage, more efficient allocation of resources attainment and maintenance of a higher level of prosperity.

There are several factors to define the corporate governance atmosphere of a country including, for instance, the general conditions of a particular country, the capital market's level of development and individual company practices. The factors of a country in general are: economic status, financial conditions, level of competition, banking system, level of development of property rights and similar factors. Factors concerning the capital markets are: market regulations and infrastructure, market liquidity, existence of a sophisticated investment community and the level of implementation of international standards, primarily accounting standards. Mainly, issues bearing substantial importance in company practices are public disclosure of financial and non-financial information, equal treatment of shareholders, practices and independence of the board of directors and financial benefits provided thereto, capital structure, level of free float, liquidity of stocks, level of participation of stakeholders in the decision-making process, sensitivity of the company to the environment and level of social responsibility.

Several studies have been made and others are still being realized in the area of corporate governance. These studies emphasize the fact that no single corporate governance model is valid for every country. Accordingly, the model to be established should be compatible with the conditions peculiar to each country. However, the concepts of equality, transparency, accountability and responsibility appear to be the main (*sine qua non*) concepts in all international corporate governance approaches that are widely accepted. *Equality* means the equal treatment of shareholders and stakeholders by the management in all activities of the company and it thus aims to prevent all possible conflicts of interest. *Transparency*, on the other hand, aims to disclose company-related financial and non-financial information to the public in a timely, accurate, complete, clear, understandable manner, easily reachable at low cost, excluding trade secrets and undisclosed information. *Accountability* means the obligation of the board of directors to account to the company as a corporate body and to the shareholders. Finally, *responsibility* defines the conformity of all operations carried out on behalf of the company with the legislation, articles of association and in-house regulations together with the audit thereof.

Efforts to establish a framework for corporate governance around the globe continue rapidly. The World Bank, the Organization of Economic Cooperation and Development (OECD) and the Global Corporate Governance Forum (GCGF), which has been established in cooperation with the representatives of these two organizations and the private sector, lead the way in handling the issue. Many countries, including those with developed economies, have reviewed their own legislation or are in the process of reviewing current legislation. For example, the US has passed a new law (Sarbanes-Oxley) after the company scandals of the previous year. Similarly, Germany has adopted its corporate governance principles as law and the principles became a legal obligation; similarly Japan has also re-examined and improved its company law; and Russia has announced its new corporate governance regulations. Many countries have been restructuring and publishing their current legislation within the framework of the best corporate governance principles.

In parallel with the current practices worldwide, the CMB of Turkey has established its corporate governance principles (the Principles). Distinguished experts and representatives from the CMB, the Istanbul Securities Exchange and the Turkish Corporate Governance Forum have participated in the committee that was established by the CMB for this purpose; additionally many qualified academicians, private-sector representatives, as well as various professional organizations and NGOs have stated their views and opinions, which were added to the Principles after the required evaluations. Accordingly, these Principles have been established as a product of contributions of all high-level bodies. Regulations of many countries have been examined, and generally accepted and recommended Principles – primarily the 'OECD Corporate Governance Principles' of 1999 – together with the particular conditions of our country have been taken into consideration during the preparation of these Principles. The Principles mainly address publicly held joint stock companies. However, it is considered that other joint stock companies and institutions, active in the private and public sectors, may also implement these Principles. The implementation of the Principles is optional. However, the explanation concerning the implementation status of the Principles, if not detailed reasoning thereof, conflicts arising from inadequate implementation of these Principles, and explanation on whether there is a plan for change in the company's governance practices in the future should all be included in the annual report and disclosed to public. Within the framework of the regulations to be enforced by the CMB, the rating institutions conducting rating of corporate governance will determine the implementation status of the Principles.

Within the Principles, the 'comply or explain' approach is valid. However, the (R) letters attached to some of the Principles indicating that those are recommendations only. With respect to non-conformity with these Principles, which are only recommendations, no disclosure is required. Additionally, the Principles marked as recommendations may be subject to the 'comply or explain' approach in the medium and long term.

The Turkish Capital Market Board's Corporate Governance Principles were published in 2003 and revised in 2005. Principles titles are as follows:

Part I – Shareholders
1. Facilitating the Exercise of Shareholders' Statutory Rights
2. Shareholders' Right to Obtain and Evaluate Information
3. The Right to Participate in the General Shareholders' Meeting
4. Voting Rights
5. Minority Rights
6. Dividend Rights
7. Transfer of Shares
8. Equal Treatment of Shareholders

Part II – Public Disclosure and Transparency
1. Principles and Means for Public Disclosure
2. Public Disclosure of Relations between the Company and its Shareholders, The Board of Directors and Executives
3. Periodical Financial Statement and Reports in Public Disclosure
4. Functions of External Audit
5. The Concept of Trade Secret and Insider Trading
6. Significant Events and Developments That Must Be Disclosed to the Public

Part III – Stakeholders
1. Company Policy Regarding Stakeholders
2. Stakeholders' Participation in the Company Management
3. Protection of Company Assets
4. Company Policy on Human Resources
5. Relations with Customers and Suppliers
6. Ethical Rules
7. Social Responsibility

Part IV – Board of Directors
1. Fundamental Functions of the Board of Directors

2. Principles of Activity and Duties and Responsibilities of the Board of Directors
3. Formation and Election of the Board of Directors
4. Remuneration of the Board of Directors
5. Number, Structure and Independence of the Committees Established by the Board of Directors
6. Executives.

(These can be explored on the website <http://www.spk.gov.tr/ofd/KurumsalYonetim/index.html?tur+ilkeler>.)

Corporate governance workings of the Banking Regulation and Supervision Agency

The regulation about banks' corporate governance principles was published in the Official Gazette dated 1 November 2006, No. 26333. In the regulation, there are several arrangements about banks' different agencies, managers and policies that will implement in terms of gaining trust of investors and public are determined.

Corporate values and strategic objectives must be formed in banks. A bank's board of directors must determine its mission and vision and disclose them to the public. The board of directors should firstly define the strategies that direct the bank's continuity of proposed activities and it must be the initiator of composing corporate values and ethical rules for itself, top management and other personnel. The corporate values and ethical rules that will be developed must reflect the importance of evaluating problems in time, particularly the prevention of illegal and unethical attitudes such as bribery and corruption, both inside and beyond the bank's operations. Appropriate communication channels must be formed along which personnel can confidently transmit information to the relevant authorities about activities and operations that do not correspond with corporate values and moral principles. The board of directors should satisfactorily determine any possible conflicts that may occur because of top management's role in the bank's activities and then execute the necessary policies for preventing or administering these.

The authorities and responsibilities in banks should be determined clearly (openly) and implemented. The board of directors should define the authorities and responsibilities of top management and board members, monitor top management's activities and check whether they conform or not to the policies determined by the board of directors. Top management should clearly identify the authorities and responsibilities of personnel for conformity with policies, implementation procedures, moral principles and professional applications, and for the monitoring of how the defined authorities and responsibilities are performed or not performed. All personnel should be aware that they are finally responsible to the board of directors.

Board members must have the ability to assume their duties in a efficient way and be aware of their role in corporate governance: an independent audit should evaluate the bank's activities. Members of the board of directors must:

- execute their duties to bank and shareholders honestly
- understand the mission under the direction of the bank
- spare enough time for the bank's actions and participate in board meetings
- assume their duties in a cautious (provident) way and within the framework of the goodwill rules
- have a thorough knowledge of the legislation (regulations) to which banks are subjected and satisfy the efficient relationship (correlation) with the bank's regulatory and auditor authorities
- not create any adverse impression of the bank and to this end they should not accept material benefit from other sources
- not give deficient or biased information with the aim of misleading other members (see <www.bddk.gov.tr>).

The improvements (reforms) in corporate governance in the new Turkish Commercial Law (Code)

Turkey made changes in the Turkish Commercial Law No. 6762 that was in force until 1 October 1957 in the adaptation process to EU standards. The new bill brings in several changes, especially about auditing. This law highlights accounting and consultancy business from the first section to last. Independent auditing firms will do the auditing of corporations. At least two Chartered Accountants or two Certified Public Accountants will audit small corporations. It is specified in the new Turkish Commercial Law bill that:

- The financial accounts and annual reports of corporations and multinational enterprises are controlled by the auditor.
- The financial accounts and annual reports that are not controlled by the auditor are regarded as unmanaged.
- If the financial accounts and annual reports of such bodies are changed after submitting the audit report and such changes affect the auditing report, then the accounts and annual report must be re-audited. Re-audit and its report are explained specially. The auditor's acceptance in writing must identify the extensions (additions) that reflect re-auditing (Ficici n.d.).

Reforms of corporate governance in the Corporate Tax Law

In Turkey's conformity process to the EU, an first important step was taken in tax and corporate governance applications by getting 'transfer pricing' into Corporate Tax Law (CTK). The new CTK, which has been a long time in preparation and has now become law, includes very important changes and improvements. There are changes about 'camouflage of earning' in section (entry) 17. Actually, the subject entry has not changed in essence but 'Camouflage of Earning's Distribution by Transfer Pricing' has defined more expansive and apparent expressions. The new section's text is on the whole compatible with general transfer pricing principles which were published as a report study for multinational companies and tax administrations by the OECD in 1995. In this context, new definitions are clearly made in the text and this time some concepts which are also expressed in the current law section are announced as technical terms (Demircan 2007: 20).

The workings of the Turkish Accounting Standards Board

Turkey's most important workings on corporate governance about accounting is its Financial Reporting Standards, which have been promulgated very similarly to International Reporting Standards. The list on page 278 shows the Turkish Financial Reporting Standards and the dates they were announced.

Discussion

After the banking scandals in Turkey, important legislation changes and revisions have been made. The reasons for the changes and revisions are to strengthen confidence in public companies with corporate governance. When the regulation changes that are classified in this study are examined it is maintained that banks and public companies (in particular) in Turkey have started implementing international accounting standards. In this regard, Turkey is a reliable country for foreign investors. A fact that known by everybody is the importance of executing laws rather than enforcing them.

In addition to the serious legislation changes that affect the corporate governance and accounting world in Turkey, the Turkish Commercial Code draft is also important. After acceptance of the Code (which was prepared by contributors from different areas such as academics and accountancy experts from 1999 onwards), there will be improvements, especially in the auditing world. Companies must have websites and issue fiscal reports in their websites as mandatory. All capital stock companies must have independent auditing. With this bill, corporate governance of companies will become stronger and confidence in the accounting world will be provided.

By renewing the Turkish Commercial Law, important parts of corporate governance studies of companies in Turkey's tax, accounting and auditing areas will be completed.

Standard	Official newspaper date & number
Conceptional Framework	16.01.2005 - 25702
TAS 1: First-time Adoption of International Financial Reporting Standards	16.01.2005 - 25702
TAS 2: Inventories	15.01.2005 - 25701
TAS 7: Cash Flow Statements	18.01.2005 - 25704
TAS 8: Accounting Policies, Changes on Accounting Estimates and Errors	20.10.2005 - 25972
TAS 10: Events After the Balance Sheet Date	20.10.2005 - 25972
TAS 11: Construction Contracts	26.10.2005 - 25978
TAS 12: Income Taxes	28.03.2006 - 26122
TAS 14: Segment Reporting	03.03.2006 - 26097
TAS 16: Tangible Fixed Assets	31.12.2005 - 26040
TAS 17: Leases	24.02.2006 - 26090
TAS 18: Revenue	09.12.2005 - 26018
TAS 19: Benefits for Workers	30.03.2006 - 26124
TAS 20: Accounting for Government Grants and Disclosure of Government Assistance	01.11.2005 - 25983
TAS 21: The Effects of Changes in Foreign Exchange Rates	31.12.2005 - 26040
TAS 23: Borrowing Costs	09.11.2005 - 25988
TAS 24: Related Party Disclosures	31.12.2005 - 26040
TAS 26: Accounting and Reporting by Retirement Benefit Plans	01.03.2006 - 26095
TAS 27: Consolidated and Individual Financial Statements	17.12.2005 - 26026
TAS 28: Investments in Associates	27.12.2005 - 26036
TAS 29: Financial Reporting in Hyperinflationary Economies	31.12.2005 - 26040
TAS 30: Disclosures in the Financial Statements of Banks and Similar Financial Institutions	25.03.2006 - 26119
TAS 31: Shares in Joint Ventures	31.12.2005 - 26040
TAS 32: Financial Instruments: Disclosure and Presentation	28.10.2006 - 26330
TAS 33: Earnings Per Share	28.03.2006 - 26122
TAS 34: Interim Financial Reporting	02.02.2006 - 26068
TAS 36: Impairment of Assets	18.03.2006 - 26112
TAS 37: Provisions, Contingent Liabilities and Contingent Assets	15.02.2006 - 26081
TAS 38: Intangible Fixed Assets	17.03.2006 - 26111
TAS 39: Financial Instruments: Recognition and Measurement	03.11.2006 - 26335
TAS 40: Investment Property	17.03.2006 - 26111
TAS 41: Agriculture	24.02.2006 - 26090
TFRS 1: First Application of Turkish Financial Reporting Standards	31.03.2006 - 26125
TFRS 2: Share-based Payments	31.03.2006 - 26125
TFRS 3: Business Combinations	31.03.2006 - 26125
TFRS 4: Insurance Contracts	25.03.2006 - 26119
TFRS 5: Non-current Assets Held for Sale and Discontinued Operations	16.03.2006 - 26110
TFRS 6: Exploration for and Evaluation of Mineral Resources	31.01.2006 - 26066
TFRS 7: Financial Instruments: Disclosures	30.01.2007 - 26419

References

Becht, M., Bolton, P. and Roell, A. (2002), 'Corporate governance and control', *Finance Working Paper*, 02/2002, October, 5–168.

Demirbaş, M. and Uyar, S. (2006), *Kurumsal Yonetim Ilkeleri ve Denetim Kurulu*, Istanbul: Guncel Yayincilik, 1.Baski [1st edn], s. [p] 19.

Demircan, S. (2007), 'Sarbanes Oxley Yasası ve Bağımsız Denetime Etkileri'['The Sarbanes Oxley Act and its effects on independent auditing'], Yayınlanmamış Yüksek Lisans Tezi [unpublished MBA thesis], Trakya Universitesi Sosyal Bilimler Enstitüsü, Mart 2007, s. [p] 113.

Farber, D. (2004), 'Restoring trust after fraud: does corporate governance matter?', Social Science Research Network, 4 October, at <http://papers.ssrn.com/sol3/papers.cfm?abstract_id=485403>.

Ficici, B. (n.d.), 'Turk Ticaret Kanunu Tasarisi, Turkiye nin Muhasebe Sitesi', at <http://www.muhasebtr.com/yazarlarimiz/bulent/002/>.

Gillian, S. (2006), 'Recent developments in corporate governance: an overview', *Journal of Corporate Finance*, 12 (3), June, 381.

Gokalp, F. (2005), 'Genel Hatlari ile Sarbanes Oxley Kanunu ve Turkiyedeki Sirketlere Etkisi', *Analiz*, Cilt [vol.] 5, Yil [year] 14, Sayi [issue] 14, Ekim 2005, s. [p] 107–115.

Hits, G.L. (2006), *Journal of Corporate Finance*, 12 (3), June, 381.

Lee, Thomas A. (2006), *Financial Reporting, Corporate Governance*, Chichester: Wiley.

Ramaswamy, V. (n.d.), *Corporate Governance and Forensic Accountant*, The CPA Journal Online, at <http://www.nysscpa.org/cpajournal/2005/305/essentials/p68.htm>.

Sanayici, T. and Dernegi, I. (2002), *Kurumsal Yonetim En Iyi Uygulama Kodu: Yonetim Kurulunun Isleyisi ve Yapisi*, Istanbul: Aralik, Yayin [publication] no: TUSIAD – T/2002-12/336.

Solomon, J. (2007), *Corporate Governance and Accountability*, 2nd edn, Chichester: Wiley.

PART IV

IMPLEMENTING CORPORATE SOCIAL RESPONSIBILITY (CSR)

Overview of Part IV

Recently the selfish indulgence of the 1980s and 1990s has been replaced by a concern for social responsibility – and CSR is again back on the agenda of corporations, governments and individual citizens throughout the world. Previously this concern has been known by such terms as environmental responsibility, stakeholder involvement or some similar term. It is only in its current manifestation that it has become generally known as corporate social responsibility or CSR. Thus the term 'corporate social responsibility' is in vogue at the moment but as a concept it is vague and means different things to different people.[1] There is no agreed definition of CSR so this raises the question as to what exactly can be considered to be corporate social responsibility.

Most people initially think that they know what CSR is and how to behave responsibly – and everyone claims to be able to recognise socially responsible or irresponsible behaviour without necessarily being able to define it. So there is general agreement that CSR is about a company's concern for such things as community involvement, socially responsible products and processes, concern for the environment and socially responsible employee relations (Ortiz-Martinez and Crowther 2006). Issues of socially responsible behaviour are not, of course, new and examples can be found from throughout the world and at least from the earliest days of the Industrial Revolution and the concomitant founding of large business entities (Crowther 2002) and the divorce between ownership and management – or the divorcing of risk from rewards (Crowther 2004).

According to the European Commission, CSR is about undertaking voluntary activity which demonstrates a concern for stakeholders. But it is here that a firm runs into problems – how to balance up the conflicting needs and expectations of various stakeholder groups while still being concerned with shareholders; how to practise sustainability; how to report this activity to those interested; how to decide if one activity is more socially responsible than another. The situation is complex and conflicting. In this final section, therefore, the contributors are concerned with the arguably most immediate problem for business of how to actually implement CSR in practice.

In the first chapter Sharma and Kwatra investigate social advertising in India. They show that the applicability of marketing principles used to sell products

---

1   See Crowther and Rayman Bacchus (2004) or Crowther and Çalıyurt (2004), and the contributions in each, for a wide variety of definitions and concerns.

to the consumers into the marketing of ideas, attitudes and behaviour has long been appreciated, almost as soon as the early 1970s. This realisation paved the way for the evolution of the discipline of social marketing, whose roots lie in social advertising. They explain that social advertising does not result in financial profit but is undertaken to about bring awareness of the quality of life or a social issue. In India, where awareness and scientific temper among the masses are at an evolutionary stage, the government as well as other social organisations have started campaigns to educate people in different areas of social interest. From this they investigate the purpose and effectiveness of a variety of campaigns.

Yumuk is concerned with the tax system in Turkey and the problem of avoidance which is prevalent there. As she states, law comprises those measures that provide the order in society and indicates the organising power of the government, whereas ethics is an important component that provides continuity in business and includes various kinds of attitudes, work and relations with the rights and privileges of groups and persons. However, in our society the legislation that shows the sanction power of government can sometimes be in contradiction with the moral values of business life. One of the areas in which we often see this dilemma is that of tax amnesty. In order to cover the expenses of society, according to the financial positions of citizens, within the rules of legislation, the government raises taxes, by force when it is necessary and without any repayment. Sometimes a tax amnesty is applied and it affects these in a negative manner so this shows that although many applications are legal from the point of business life, they are not necessarily ethical. The is especially true when the taxpayers do not pay the taxes because of a tax amnesty. Those who do pay regularly are affected in a negative way. In the long term it reduces the habit of tax payment. In this work, results have been evaluated statistically by asking 135 accounting students to evaluate a sample case on tax amnesty.

Often it is argued that CSR has no place in the behaviour of either small and medium enterprises (SMEs) or in developing countries. This issue is tackled by Stevens, Kim, Mukhamedova, Mukimova and Wagner through their research in their country of domicile, Uzbekistan. Their research shows that the behaviour attributable as CSR had been in existence long before the term itself became recognised, a situation which is the case in many countries. Nevertheless, they identify some important issues and behaviours which are identifiable and pertinent to the debate. They also consider the cultural context which is particular to their country – given its history and recent origin – while also discussing some features which are absent from the repertoire of CSR behaviour in Uzbekistan. Such a case study gives many pointers to the development of CSR in many other countries.

Meza-Cuadra focuses on the opposite side of the world when she considers the mining industry in Peru. Her concern is with the integration process of sustainable development by the Peruvian mining industry because, as she states, most of the international mining companies have been adopting sustainable development as the CSR strategy for the sector. Her analysis leads to the conclusion that although the mining industry has always been one of the most dynamic sectors of the Peruvian economy, which has been promoted through privatisation and favourable tax rules, combined with high prices in the early 19902, this did not translate into a reduction of poverty. She argues therefore that there has been some improvement but more is needed.

David and Abreu, like Yumuk, are also concerned with taxation and its avoidance, with their focus being upon Portugal. Their view is that in a society in which firms and citizens want to promote the morality of the tax system, it is essential that the system must be balanced, without overpayment or underpayment of taxes for specific firms and citizens and by equal treatment for all. This provides a basis for the investigation of tax evasion and fraud, not just in Portugal but elsewhere too. Thus, this chapter discusses the concept of evasion and fraud and subsequently presents the understanding of the role of ethics and discusses the importance and effects of the code of ethics. The European and the Portuguese fight against fiscal evasion and fraud is presented and argued, before the chapter concludes that the research was undertaken to assess the level of taxation and fiscal evasion, as well as measures or precautions against evasion and fraud in the European and the Portuguese situations.

According to Papasolomou, in the final chapter, many business are seeking to align their social responsibility agendas with their business strategy. This leads to a consideration of the phenomenon of cause-related marketing. For this contributor, cause-related marketing (CRM) is a prime example of the partnership formed between corporations and charities to raise both money and brand awareness while also demonstrating the corporation's socially responsible behaviour. A corporation's reputation is, of course, shaped to a considerable degree by the signals it gives about its nature. Such signals are subsequently received by different target audiences and are used to form perceptions and feelings about the organisation. She concludes therefore that CRM can undoubtedly be one of these signals or cues, which an organisation can offer as a form of expression and as a tool for enhancing its corporate reputation.

Inevitably, in a section about the actual implementation of CSR by a variety of businesses, most of the key concepts discussed in the previous sections recur. Thus issues such as ethics, the employment relationship, sustainability and the environment feature prominently. So, too, do concepts such as governance, accountability and disclosure. More significantly, this final section shows that the examples from around the world exhibit both the ubiquity of the concepts of corporate social responsibility and the difficulties of in putting these into practice. In doing so, it highlights both commonalities and differences in the approach taken, which are replicated throughout the world and no approach is specific to any particular region or industry. Diversity of approach – one of the main aspects of this book – is shown to abound. For us, this is good, as we do not believe in a 'one-size-fits-all' approach to corporate social responsibility and do not believe that this is possible.

References

Crowther, D. (2004), 'Limited liability or limited responsibility?', in D. Crowther and L. Rayman-Bacchus (eds), *Perspectives on Corporate Social Responsibility*, Aldershot: Ashgate, pp 42–58.

Crowther, D. (2002), *A Social Critique of Corporate Reporting*, Aldershot: Ashgate.

Crowther, D. and Çalıyurt, K.T. (eds) (2004), *Stakeholders and Social Responsibility*, Penang: Ansted University Press.

Crowther, D. and Rayman-Bacchus, L. (eds) (2004), *Perspectives on Corporate Social Responsibility*, Aldershot: Ashgate.

Ortiz-Martinez, E. and Crowther, D. (2006), '¿Son compatibles la responsabilidad económica y la responsabilidad social corporativa?', *Harvard Deusto Finanzas y Contabilidad*, 71, 2–12.

The Effectiveness of
Social Advertising:
A Study of Selected Campaigns

Tejinder Sharma and Geetanjali Kwatra

Introduction

Marketing has a large role to play in a rapidly transforming and diversified society like India. While economic prosperity is improving the living standards of the citizens, the transformation of attitudes, beliefs and values is a much slower process. The inherent inertia in the transformation of attitudes, beliefs and values can seriously jeopardise the process of social transformation, particularly when large sections of the society suffer from poverty, illiteracy, superstition, poor health standards, etc. In order to sustain economic and technological development in society, it is essential that a planned effort be made to achieve a commensurate social development as well. It is at this juncture that the power of marketing tools and techniques can be extrapolated to achieve changes in social behaviour.

The transferability of marketing principles used to sell products to the consumers into the marketing of ideas, attitudes and behaviour has long been appreciated, from the early 1970s onwards. This realisation paved the way for the evolution of the discipline of social marketing, whose roots lie in social advertising. In India, and also in several other developing countries, social advertising has been used frequently to spread social awareness on a variety of issues, ranging through health, communal harmony, reduction of superstition, etc. Interestingly, even for marketing the commercial products, firms are beginning to rely upon social advertising, which indicates its potential to achieve the desired outcome. Figure 15.1 plots the organisational purpose against organisational ownership to show the types of organisations relying upon social advertising.

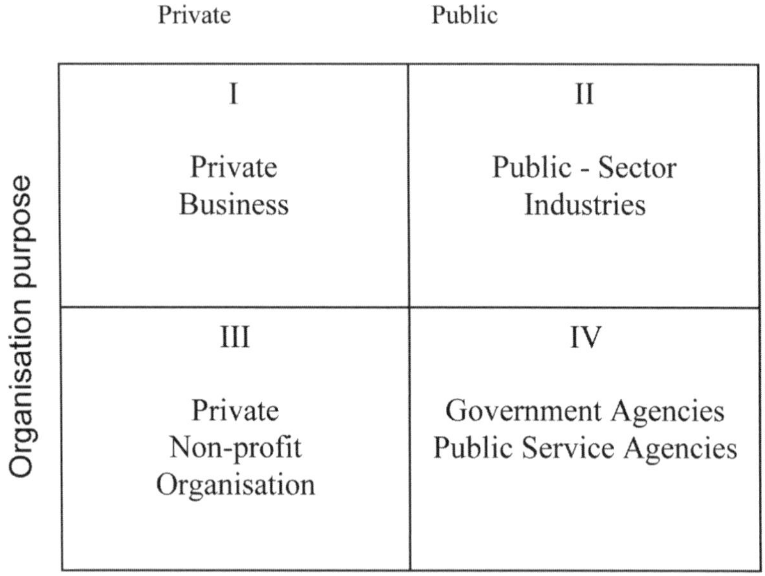

	Private	Public
Organisation purpose	I Private Business	II Public - Sector Industries
	III Private Non-profit Organisation	IV Government Agencies Public Service Agencies

Figure 15.1 Organisations relying on social advertising

Social marketing to social advertising

The roots of social marketing lie in social advertising. Social advertising does not result in rupee profit but is undertaken to raise awareness about a quality of life or a social issue. In India, where awareness and scientific temper among the masses are at an evolutionary stage, the government and other social organisations have started campaigns to educate people in different areas of social interest.

Social advertising has followed the success of commercial advertising and uses the same principles. For social advertising, a social problem is identified and then a campaign is designed to solve this problem. The problem may be related to some kind of behaviour in which individuals are indulging. Although it may be risky (such as smoking or taking drugs), the consumer may be unaware of some service or product which can improve their lives (family planning, health care, etc.), or a group may be unresponsive to the needs of others by ignoring issues like environmental pollution. Social advertising is an effort to control the process of change so that the change is in a desirable direction and leading to favourable results. The efforts encompassing various aspects of social marketing go beyond simple advertising. For instance, in order to strengthen the campaign against smoking, in addition to social advertising, firms can make use of seminars, distributing special products to alleviate desire to smoke, and initiating publicity aimed at the general public. Social advertising remains central to any such actions addressing important social issues.

Social advertising: the concept

The use of advertising to plead a cause rather than sell a product is not new. Yet we are currently witnessing a surging growth in the area of what is loosely termed 'issue' or 'causes' advertising. Social advertising covers a wide variety of objectives, audiences and communication tools.

No one term satisfactorily conveys the meaning of this type of advertising. At various times, it is referred to as 'public service', 'institutional', 'idea', 'non-product', 'social', 'advocacy' or 'public relations' advertising. Sometimes it is derogatorily termed 'propaganda'. Researchers have pointed out that there is a lack of agreement on terminology in this regard. However, a few commonly used terms in this context are: public-interest advertising, public affairs advertising, viewpoint advertising, strategic advertising, opinion advertising, advocacy advertising, cause and issue advertising, etc.

'Public service advertising' is that kind of advertising, either government- or association-sponsored, which promotes causes and activities generally accepted as desirable. By its nature, public service advertising is usually controversial. It may be paid or presented by the media without charge. Such advertising may be undertaken by public bodies such as municipal corporations but may also be undertaken by business concerns in the public interest. As the name of the company will normally appear in the advertisement, some pay-off from such advertising to the company's benefit may result. However, when the primary purpose of such advertising is to promote a social cause, it may be considered non-commercial and there can be no categorical classification of advertisements.

Some of the characteristics of social advertising can be stated as follows:

- Its main focus is on some matter of social importance.
- It is a type of public relations advertising.
- It deals with social, economic or cultural issues.
- It promotes those causes and activities which are generally accepted as desirable.
- It may be sponsored by the government, voluntary organisations or sometimes by a business house.

Social advertisements in India

One of the crucial areas of the development of a nation is its progress on the social front. Committed efforts towards social causes can contribute a great deal to the overall development of a nation. The existing social scenario of India is a matter of great concern for policy-makers, voluntary organisations, business houses, etc. There already are a lot of problems on the social scene, such as health, family welfare, drugs, safety, national integration, welfare of girl children, etc., and the cultural changes add more problems on top. In a developing country like India, such problems can be effectively tackled by social advertisements. Repeated exposure of the public to such campaigns can bring about attitudinal and behavioural changes among the mass of people. As compared to the West, social advertisements are of recent origin in India. Government-sponsored social advertisements on family planning appeared for the first time in 1964.

In late 1960s, with the increase in socio-economic problems and popularisation of TV, social advertising gained increasing attention. Since then, it has become part and parcel of life and the government sanctions the expenditure of millions of rupees for the televising of various social advertisements. Various government department/ministries, national and international agencies, voluntary organisations and autonomous bodies also address various social issues from time to time.

In the context of social problems, advertising can play an important role and can help in social upliftment and transformation. If today Indians are aware of family planning, iodised salt, drinking water and pulse polio, it is due to effective social advertising. Social advertising has helped in generating awareness about environment protection and a change in the attitude of the people towards environment. For example, it has created awareness of the need to wear a helmet while driving a motor bike. It has increased the awareness of the social evils of female infanticide. In recent years, some of the areas covered under social advertising are health care (pulse polio), pollution, safety, drug abuse, literacy, women education, girls' welfare, untouchability, population, etc.

Review of the literature

The importance of social marketing has been realised long ago and many researchers have contributed to increasing the awareness of social advertising and the social responsibility of business (Bloom and Novelli 1981; Robin and Reidenbach 1987, Laczniak et al. 1979; and so on). During these formative years, it was observed that the marketing principles used for commercial products could be used for the marketing of the ideas on social issues as well. Non-product advertising soon began to appear in the media, taking a variety of forms. In India, studies examined how social advertising could influence social behaviour (Rao and Gupta 2004; Sivalogonathan 2001; Mann 2001; etc.). A marketing paradigm was observed, where well-designed social advertising and an efficient logistics system was observed to be necessary for meeting social objectives. Shankaraiah et al. (2001) correlated social marketing with welfare marketing for society, wherein social advertising increased the acceptability of social ideas so that they could make a major positive impact on the social problems. Drumwright (1996) found how economic and non-economic objectives could be harmoniously blended in an individual campaign, through a portfolio approach to communication programmes. Lichtenstein et al. (2004) have reported research evidence suggesting that a corporation's socially responsible behaviour can positively affect consumers' attitudes towards the corporation. The effect occurs, both directly and indirectly, through the behaviour's effect in customer-corporation identification.

Research problems

As suggested by the literature, in tackling social problems, advertising can play an important role, particularly in a diverse society like India. However, there is a need to study the effectiveness of social advertisement in terms of its recall and its influence on the behaviour. Specifically the objectives of research are stated as:

- to study the recall of social advertising campaigns
- to study the perception on social advertising
- to find out the effect of social advertising on the behavioural intentions of the target audience.

Methodology

The required data for the study was collected from both primary and secondary sources. Primary data was collected personally by means of a self-administered structured questionnaire, a copy of which is enclosed as Annexe 1. Secondary data was collected from various magazines, articles, newspapers and journals, etc.

A sample of 140 respondents, comprising an equal proportion of both male and female groups, was chosen to represent an upcoming town (in District Kurukshetra, Haryana) of North India. The sample was fairly evenly distributed to represent various age groups of the population. The data generated by the survey was tabulated and analysed. The descriptive analysis was done by computing mean scores and standard deviation, while the data on perceptions of social advertising was studied with the help of factor analysis. The impact of social advertising on behavioural intentions was studied by means of regression analysis. The Cronbach alpha value computed to study the reliability of measurement (0.6490) was fairly acceptable for an exploratory survey of this nature.

Findings

Recall rate of social advertising

In the recent past (years 2005–06), three campaigns of social advertising on the issues of vaccination against pulse polio, AIDS awareness and water conservation have appeared in the Indian media. The respondents were asked to recall the advertisements aired on these subjects and the percentage of advertisements recalled on the subjects was taken as the unaided recall rate of these campaigns. After administering this question, the respondents were given cues on the advertisements on these subjects and then asked to recall them. The cues comprised of the punchline of these advertisements, or the celebrity model projected in the advertisements. Table 15.1 shows the aggregate aided and unaided recall rates of the social advertisement campaigns.

As expected, the unaided recall rate of the social advertisements is far below the aided recall rate. It is noteworthy that the aided recall rate is very high, indicating a high degree of awareness of the respondents on these subjects.

Table 15.1 Recall rates of social advertising, by age group

Age group	No. of respondents	Aided recall rate – %	Unaided recall rate – %
> 18 years	30	100	20.00
18–25 years	40	96.67	25.00
25–40 years	40	83.33	37.50
> 40 years	30	80.00	30.00

Table 15.2 Recall rates of social advertising, by gender

	All three recall – %	Only 3 recall – %	One recall – %	No recall – %
Male	5.00	19.29	12.86	12.14
Female	12.14	22.14	11.43	5.00
	17.14	41.43	24.29	17.14

Table 15.2 shows that the female respondents had higher recall rates than their male counterparts, possibly indicating their greater sensitivity and responsiveness to social advertisements.

Priorities for product purchase

While preparing to make a decision to purchase, several factors influence a consumer (Table 15.3). On the basis of the mean score of the various priorities for product purchase, it may be concluded that price is the most important consideration while purchasing the product. The next set of almost equally important considerations are its functional utility, durability and safety. However, the social cause, as a consideration for purchase, does not receive a high importance score from the respondents. This seems to indicate that the 'rational' set of variables seems to dominate consumers' purchase behaviour.

Table 15.3 Priorities in product purchase

Sr. no.	Variables	Mean	S.D.
1	Price	4.29	1.014
2	Quality	4.19	1.125
3	Safety	4.17	1.031
4	Durability	4.14	1.088
5	Brand image	3.83	1.073
6	Easy availability	3.83	1.268
7	Functional utility	3.81	1.131
8	Size	3.76	.910
9	Colour	3.65	1.163
10	Social cause	3.54	1.034

Perception of social advertisements

The respondents' perception of social advertisements was studied with the help of 18 statements, which solicited their responses on various aspects of social advertisements. The responses were taken on a five-point scale. The mean scores and the standard deviations of the responses to these statements are shown in Table 15.4. Further, the perception of social advertising was analysed with the help of factor analysis by using principal component method. The tables showing Eigen values, with cumulative percentages of variance of the statements, and the rotated component matrix of opinion on different statements are shown as Tables A and B in Annexe II. Table 15.5 shows the summary of the factors extracted from various opinion statements, which are explained in the subsequent discussion.

Table 15.4 Opinions on social advertisements

Sr. no.	Variables	Mean	S.D.
1	Ready to buy product because of social cause	3.47	1.083
2	Handloom products because they are cheap	3.66	1.149
3	Social advertising is boring and useless concept	3.61	1.091
4	Carpet industry employs child labour, so I don't like it	3.98	.893
5	Maruti Euro-III is preferred because it reduces pollution	3.69	1.087
6	Social advertising helps in identifying and highlighting problems of society	3.28	1.258
7	Handloom products help cottage industries	3.64	1.005
8	Social advertising is cost-effective way to disseminate social message	3.22	1.336
9	Social advertising is wastage of money	3.65	1.092
10	Social advertising helps in mobilising public participation	3.72	1.093
11	Pollution is not my concern; Euro-III is better car because it give more mileage	3.72	1.093
12	Ready to pay extra for a product with a social cause	3.80	.946
13	Quality gives me more satisfaction rather than social issues	3.92	.898
14	People don't act after seeing social advertisements	3.96	1.014
15	It is satisfying to buy eco-friendly products	3.45	1.375
16	Social advertisements increase faith in products	3.61	1.233
17	Consumer is affected by the personalities featured in advertisements	3.73	1.285
18	People ignore social advertisements	3.73	1.285

Table 15.5 Summary of factors

Sr. no.	Factor name	Constituent variable	Factor loading
Factor 1	Cognitive reinforcement	Personality	.925
		Ignore	.925
		Faith	.823
Factor 2	Involvement	Boring	.740
		Cost-effective	.708
Factor 3	Environmental consciousness	Reduce pollution	.774
		Help public participation	.561
		Satisfaction	.511
Factor 4	Rational dimension	More satisfaction	.809
		Don't act	.689
		Ready to buy	.484
Factor 5	Social concerns	Child labour	.803
		Help society	.438
		More average	.428
Factor 6	Socio-economic advantage	Help cottage industry	.810
		Handloom cheapness	.655
Factor 7	Monetary aspects	Wastage of money	.719
		Pay extra	.475

Factor 1 (Cognitive reinforcement) The constituent variables of the first factor have a high positive loading and indicate that social advertisements increase the faith of the consumers about the product. The personalities featured in the advertisements have an influence on the consumers and the people recall the social advertisements because of them, although they may ignore the social message contained therein. The social advertisements emerge as the overt influencers on the consumers, who seem to be banking upon them for a *cognitive reinforcement* of their purchase, otherwise ignoring them for all other purposes.

Factor 2 (Involvement) The variables constituting the second factor show a high positive loading, and relate to the same dimension of the 'consumer involvement' in the social advertisements. However, both the variables are almost opposite in the content, which shows that the respondents demonstrated two extreme dimensions of involvement with the social advertisements. There seems to be a piecemeal approach in the minds of the respondents while assimilating the social advertisements, whereas the content and the consequences are analysed separately. While the respondents are favourably disposed towards the consequences, the content seems to be perceived as being monotonous. Possible reasons could be the presentation of social advertisements and the absence of direct personal benefits from them. People appreciate the significance of social advertisements to society as a whole, but are lackadaisical in approach when placing themselves at the locus of control. This factor relates to the issue of *involvement*, and is accordingly named.

Factor 3 (Environmental consciousness) High positive loadings are observed on these variables, all of which relate to environmental aspects. Safeguarding the environment and conserving it from pollution is an important issue projected in social advertising. So the statements related to such issues have shown higher covariance among themselves, indicating a high degree of environmental consciousness and a drive to purchase products that do not harm the environment. This factor has been described as *environmental consciousness*.

Factor 4 (Rational dimension) This factor comprises three variables, of which two are positively loaded while one is negatively loaded. One of the positively loaded variables shows that quality is the major consideration while purchasing the product. The other two variables indicate that the respondents do not act upon the social advertisements and rely on tangible and rational factors, such as quality, for purchasing the products. The social issues benefit the society at large and do not give benefits to an individual. So they are secondary while purchasing and the product characteristics seem to be dominant in these situations. In line with the findings, this factor is designated as *rational dimension*.

Factor 5 (Social concern) The variables comprising this factor have high positive loadings, indicating that they share high covariance among themselves. These variables relate to the social concerns often portrayed in social advertisements. The respondents shared their concern on the social issues such as child labour and showed their commitment towards helping their society. The social advertisements have contributed towards increasing the social awareness and motivated the people to work towards the betterment of society. Since society and the social issues are the prime concerns reflected in this factor, this has been the given the name *social concern*.

Factor 6 (Socio-economic advantage) High positive loading are observed in the variables handloom cheapness and helping cottage industries. It indicates that the lower price creates the customer quest to purchase that product. People buy handloom products because they are cheap and it helps the cottage industries. They prefer those products which are cheap and give advantage to society. Hence, this factor is named as *socio-economic advantage*.

Factor 7 (Monetary aspects) The last factor consists of two variables – that social advertisements are a waste of money, and that consumers are ready to pay extra for the social cause concerned. It shows that respondents link their decisions with money and they are price-conscious. While preparing to buy the product they may think that social advertisements are a waste of money because they do not influence the buying decisions of consumers. However, at the same time they are ready to pay extra for a social cause. While taking the final decision, the respondents take financial convenience into consideration. Hence, this factor named as *financial convenience*.

Discussion

The above findings show that respondents have awareness of social advertisements, but that there is little commitment towards them. The responses reflect a sense of doubt towards the social advertisements. The assertion that social benefits influence buying intention is not supported empirically. Therefore, it may be inferred that when purchasing a product, the product characteristics and the functional advantages that accrue to the consumer emerge as the prime factors. Social benefits do not accrue to an individual directly; therefore there seems to be little interest in taking buying decisions on their basis. Respondents seem to be relying on rational decisions, over the social decisions, while purchasing a product. They are not very overt in their opinions as to whether social advertisements are desirable or undesirable.

Behavioural intention and purchase variables

The relationship between various factors influencing the purchase and purchase intention was studied by applying regression analysis, and the results are shown in Tables 15.6 and 15.7.

Table 15.6 Results of regression analysis of purchasing factors

Sr. no.	Variable entered	Un-standardized coefficients B (beta)	R-square	Significance
1	Brand-image	.375	.055	.001
2	Colour	.307	.101	.005
3	Durability	.274	.136	.021

Table 15.7 Variables excluded from regression analysis

Sr. no.	Variables	Value	Significance
1	Price	.788	.432
2	Size	1.001	.319
3	Social cause	.815	.417
4	Functional utility	1.260	.210
5	Qty	.914	.362
6	Safety	.065	.948
7	Easy availability	.830	.408

The emerging model has relatively low coefficient of determinance (0.137), but does indicate a broad relationship between the factors assumed to be influencing the purchase behaviour and buying intentions. The brand image, colour and durability are the major variables that have been found to be statistically significant influencers of behavioural intentions, while the rest of the variables have been excluded from the model. The role of social benefits associating the social cause with buying intention is found to be insignificant. It may be inferred that the buying intentions are a function of the product characteristics and functional advantages that accrue to the consumer directly, while the social issues do not give any direct individual benefit and are weak influencers of buying intentions. The rational approach seems to be influencing the purchase behaviour over the social concerns. The respondents seem to have valued the direct tangible benefits accruing to them personally over the social issues that have an overt benefit to them.

Conclusions

Social advertising is being viewed with interest and is contributing to the social development of the developing countries. The use of celebrity endorsement, branding of social products and punch line, jingles, etc., contribute to improving the recall rate for social advertising. The people rely upon social advertisements for cognitive reinforcement of their purchase decisions and show a fair degree of involvement in the issues addressed in the social advertisements. Specific issues in social advertising, such as environmental consciousness, social concerns, etc., attract greater involvement. However, at the time of purchasing, the consumers give more weight to direct functional benefits over the social issues. The marketers can supplement their marketing efforts by addressing social issues, but exclusively banking upon social issues for marketing may not yield the desired results.

Further research

The model linking behavioural intentions and purchase variables, particularly those related to social issues, needs to be further developed and tested in diverse market segments.

References

Bloom, P.N. and Novelli, W.D. (1981), 'Problems and challenges in social marketing', *Journal of Marketing*, 45, 79–88.

Drumwright, M.E. (1996), 'Company advertising with a social dimension: the role of non-economic criteria', *Journal of Marketing*, 60 (1–4), 84–7.

Fox, K.F.A. and Kotler, P. (1980), 'The marketing of social causes: the first 10 years', *Journal of Marketing*, 44, 24–33.

Gupta, N.S. (1975), 'Social responsibility of business houses', *Indian Journal of Commerce*, 28 (1), 19–22.

Lacznaik, G.R., Lusch, R.F. and Murphy, P.E. (1979), 'Social marketing: its ethical dimension', 43 (Spring), 29–36.

Laturkar, V.N. (2001), 'Social marketing', *Indian Journal of Marketing*, 31 (1–2), Jan.–Dec., 13–16.

Leiss, W., Kline, S. and Jhally, S.U.T. (1990), *Social Communication in Advertising*, 2nd edn, New York: Routledge.

Lichtenstein, D.R., Drumwright, M.E. and Braig, B.M. (2004), 'The effects of corporate social responsibility on customer donations to corporate-sponsored non-profits', *Indian Journal of Marketing*, 68 (October), 16–32.

Mann, B.S. (2001), 'Effectiveness of social advertising', *Indian Journal of Commerce*, 54 (4), 142–6.

Rao, N. and Gupta, D. (2004), 'Social responsibility by public sector', *Indian Journal of Commerce*, 57, Jan.–March, 45–9.

Rao, P.S. (1975), 'Social responsibility of business houses', *Indian Journal of Commerce*, 28 (1–4), 23–26.

Robin, D.P. and Reidenbach, R.E. (1987), 'Social responsibility, ethics and marketing strategy: closing the gap between concept and application', *Journal of Marketing*, 51 (1–4).

Shankaraiah, A., Saibaba, R. and Pervaram, S. (2001), 'Social marketing: an approach to rural development through Janam Bhasmi Programme', *Indian Journal of Marketing*, 54 (4), 138–41.

Wilkie, W.L. and Moore, E.S. (1999), ''Marketing's contribution to society', *Journal of Marketing*, 63 (1–4), Jan–Oct., 198.

ANNEXE I
QUESTIONNAIRE

1.   NAME ....

2.   AGE ....

3.   SEX   Male .... Female.........

4.   Occupation:
Business/Salaried/Self-employed/Retired/Housewife/Student/Any other

5.   Income:
       *   Less than 10,000   ( )
       *   10,000–20,000   ( )
       *   20,000–30,000   ( )
       *   More than 30,000   ( )

6.   Age group:
       *   Below 18   ( )
       *   18–25   ( )
       *   25–40   ( )
       *   Above 40   ( )

7.   Education:
       *   Matric   ( )
       *   Higher secondary   ( )
       *   Graduate   ( )
       *   Post-graduate   ( )

8.   Can you recall any of three social advertisements?
                i)   ....
                ii)   ....
                iii)   ....

9.   Which product is projected in the advertisement 'DO BOOND ZINDAGI KI'*
       *   Milk   ( )
       *   Ariel   ( )
       *   Pulse polio   ( )
       *   Water   ( )

10.   The AIDS advertisement is anchored by which famous cricket player?*
       *   Rahul Dravid   ( )
       *   Sachin Tendulkar   ( )
       *   Virender Sehwag   ( )
       *   Can't say   ( )

11.   The slogan 'SAVE TWO BUCKETS OF WATER DAILY' is related to which product?*

* Surf Excel   ( )
* Ariel   ( )
* Wheel   ( )
* Can't say   ( )

12.   What is the punchline of the Blood Donation Campaign?

13.   What will be your priority while going to purchase the product?

	Very important	Important	Neutral	Unimportant	Very unimportant
1. Price	( )	( )	( )	( )	( )
2. Size	( )	( )	( )	( )	( )
3. Brand image	( )	( )	( )	( )	( )
4. Social cause	( )	( )	( )	( )	( )
5. Function or utility	( )	( )	( )	( )	( )
6. Quality	( )	( )	( )	( )	( )
7. Durability	( )	( )	( )	( )	( )
8. Safety	( )	( )	( )	( )	( )
9. Colour	( )	( )	( )	( )	( )
10. Easy availability	( )	( )	( )	( )	( )

14.   Please state your opinion on the following statements?

	Strongly agree	Agree	Neutral	Disagree	Strongly disagree
1. I am ready to buy a product because of a social cause.	( )	( )	( )	( )	( )
2. I buy handloom products because they are cheap.	( )	( )	( )	( )	( )
3. Social advertising is a boring and useless concept.	( )	( )	( )	( )	( )
4. Carpet industry employs child labour so I don't like it.	( )	( )	( )	( )	( )
5. Maruti Euro-III is preferred because it reduces pollution.*	( )	( )	( )	( )	( )
6. Social advertising helps in identifying and highlighting problems of society.	( )	( )	( )	( )	( )
7. I buy handloom products because it helps cottage industries.	( )	( )	( )	( )	( )
8. Social advertising is cost-effective way to disseminate social message.	( )	( )	( )	( )	( )
9. Social advertising is wastage of money.	( )	( )	( )	( )	( )

10. Social advertising helps in mobilising public participation.	( )		( )		( )		( )		( )
11. Pollution is not my concern; Euro-III is better because it give more mileage.	( )		( )		( )		( )		( )
12. I am ready to pay extra for a product with a social cause.	( )		( )		( )		( )		( )
13. Quality gives me more satisfaction rather than social issues.	( )		( )		( )		( )		( )
14. People don't act after seeing social advertisements.	( )		( )		( )		( )		( )
15. I feel satisfied by buying eco-friendly products.	( )		( )		( )		( )		( )
16. Social advertisements increase faith in products.	( )		( )		( )		( )		( )
17. Consumer is affected by personalities featured in advertisements.	( )		( )		( )		( )		( )
18. People ignore social advertisements.	( )		( )		( )		( )		( )

Explanatory notes: The above questionnaire contains some of the punchlines in Hindi. The models/brands being portrayed in the advertisements have also been mentioned in the questionnaire.

ANNEXE II

Table A Eigen values and cumulative percentages of customers' variance of opinion on different statements

Component	Eigen value	% of variance	Cumulative % of variance
1	2.754	15.302	15.302
2	2.629	14.607	29.909
3	1.766	9.811	39.720
4	1.330	7.388	47.108
5	1.160	6.446	53.554
6	1.049	5.826	59.380
7	1.016	5.643	65.022

Table B Rotated component matrix of opinions on different statements

Variables	F_1	F_2	F_3	F_4	F_5	F_6	F_7	H_2
Ready to buy product because of social cause	-.115	.484	.384	-.439	.329	.056	-.067	.703
Handloom products because they are cheap	.030	.267	-.259	.165	-.123	.655	.193	.647
Social advertising is boring and useless concept	-.048	.740	.019	.197	-.138	-.039	.095	.618
Carpet industry employs child labour so I don't like it	.009	-.016	-.016	.055	.803	-.113	.050	.664
Maruti Euro-III is preferred because it reduces pollution	-.004	-.75	.774	.026	-.054	-.101	.274	.694
Social advertising helps in identifying and highlighting problems of society	-.012	.335	.401	-.135	.438	-.118	.120	.512
Handloom products because it helps cottage industries	.014	-.258	.138	.008	.032	.810	.020	.743
Social advertising is cost-effective way to disseminate social message	-.075	.708	.156	-.008	.241	-.007	-.004	.589
Social advertising is wastage of money	.166	.170	.217	.080	-.049	.026	.719	.630
Social advertising helps in mobilising public participation	.009	.182	.561	-.037	.101	.108	-.043	.372
Pollution is not my concern; Euro-III is better because it give more mileage	.111	.141	.144	.042	.428	.286	-.118	.333
Ready to pay extra for a product with a social cause	.082	-.022	.009	.165	.338	.319	.475	.476
Quality gives me more satisfaction rather than social issues	-.066	.049	.041	.809	.308	-.049	.028	.761
People don't act after seeing social advertisements	.115	.108	-.029	.689	-.171	.244	.080	.596
Satisfying to buy eco-friendly products	.202	.241	.511	.351	.116	-.057	-.501	.752
Social advertisements increase faith in products	.823	.047	.104	-.057	-.080	.015	-.237	.757
Consumer is affected by personalities featured in advertisements	.925	-.108	-.036	.077	.087	.037	.215	.724
People ignore social advertisements	.925	-.108	-.036	.077	.087	.037	.215	.929

Is Everything that is Legal Ethical? Research on the Turkish Tax System

Gülsevim Yumuk

Introduction

The Turkish tax system runs within the principles that are specified and established by the tax laws. The organization of the rights, responsibilities and authority of both taxpayers and the state is a requirement of both the principle of Law of State and the 73rd item of the Constitution. The government has to have a legal support for the money that is transferred from the private sector to the public sector freely and definitely in order to meet the public demands. The collection system has to be based on the feeling of justice, the right time and the right circumstances. In this adaptation, some circumstances which are legal but can be discussed ethically might emerge from time to time as a result of the political pressures and economical profits. The most obvious one of these implementations is the tax amnesties which are widely seen in the Turkish tax system and defined as the elimination of the sanctions that are applied to the people who break the laws of tax.

Tax amnesties cannot be against the Constitution since there is a hierarchy between the rules of law. No law and governmental decision can be against the Constitution. The suitability of every law made in this respect for the constitution is inspected by the Court of Constitution. However, equality in tax amnesties is out of the question since people do not have a right to take advantage of an amnesty as part of their basic rights and freedoms (Baykara 2003). First of all, frequent amnesty laws are against the policy of crime and punishment. A person who is determined to commit a crime and thinks that he/she will evade the punishment partly or totally as a result of an amnesty law will certainly commit that crime. This situation eliminates the threat and discouragement of the punishment.

Over time, there has been a continuous decline in the respect of the public and the taxpayers for the government and the ethics of tax payment (Yayman 1999). This situation damages the present stability among those taxpayers who pay their taxes by declaration, whose tax is paid before they get their payment demand and who pay their taxes indirectly.

In this study, tax amnesties whose legality is unquestionable but whose ethical side causes controversies will be discussed and we will also evaluate the thoughts about business and tax ethics of a sample of university students who are studying accountancy.

Tax law and the Turkish tax system

Tax is the economic value that is taken from people's incomes and possessions unilaterally by authority of the state in order to meet public expenditure (Erginay 1990). In earlier times the duty of the state was only to provide the internal and outer security of the citizens, whereas today the state has to meet the other demands of the citizens (such as education, health and social services) in accordance with the principles of a social state. Thus, the state needs financial power in order to perform these new duties it has undertaken. Consequently, the state needs to get money from its citizens.

Although taxation has the quality of interference with people's rights and freedoms and possessions, it is also an important and effective tool that finances the democratic regime for the state and provides the ruling political party with the realization of their economic and social policies (Çağan 1982a). There are important items about tax in almost all contemporary constitutions. And, as is stated in the 73rd item of the Turkish Constitution, paying tax is a duty not only for taxpayers but also for all citizens (<www.tdb.org.tr>).

Law constitutes the method and rules that organize the relationships among the people who live in a society. While the rules that organize the relationship between the people and the state constitute the public law, tax law is one of its subdivisions. In this respect, the collection types of the financial values that will be taken from the citizens, their rates and the solutions to the contradictions related to these processes are stated in order to compensate for the expenditures that the state will make to serve its people (Battal 2003).

A country's tax system constitutes all public revenue laws that are in force in that country at a given time. The tax system structure of countries, however, depends on the legal, political, economic and social conditions of that country (Aksoy 1989). Over time the changes in the legal, political, economic and social conditions of countries also modify their tax systems. The tax collection of the country under different names almost emerged together with its social organization. Taxation, which appears to be restricted in primitive communities, has spread, become more varied and become better organized over time.

It is understood that the first taxation practices were developed in Mesopotamia, ancient Egypt, Palestine and the Hittite Empire by looking at ancient documents. It can be said that the authority of taxation in these ancient important civilizations depended on the state's or ruler's actual power rather than a legal basis. In history therefore, the first state structure that legalized taxation was seen in the Roman Empire (Uluatam and Methibay 2001).

The settled tax structure changed greatly after the collapse of the Roman Empire and it became differentiated as a result of the arbitrary practices of kings and feudal lords after the establishment of feudal structures in Europe during the Middle Ages. The historical development of taxation authority changed when democratic regimes were adopted after the autocratic ones. As a reaction to the limitless power of the absolute state power and the ruler's arbitrary taxation, the sovereignty of the later state was made somewhat limited and some basic principles of public law were adopted.

As for the Turkish tax system, it was seen that state revenue was constituted by various taxes which were partly religious and partly traditional. That unique state structure which was thought to be able to meet the demands during a few centuries of the Ottoman Empire's expansion became inadequate when the state stagnated. With this aim, the Sened-i İttifak (Charter of Alliance) was signed in 1809, restricting the sultan's exercise of power and delegating some powers to the senate of the empire. This measure required the collection of revenues to be undertaken fastidiously and the same held true for expenditures; it also required prevention of excessive taxation of the poor and the public.

Islahat Fermanı was declared on 28 February 1856: this was a reform programme prepared by the UK, France and Austria at the end of the Crimean War – Istanbul was compelled to accept it as a condition of peace. This measure tried to abolish taxation imposed according to people's religion and denomination. The constitutional government declared in 1876 brought an further important change in taxation, requiring it to be based on law by dividing the authority of taxation between the sultan and the council. However, those decisions could not be carried out and the loss of the economic power of the Ottoman Empire in time, its failure in paying its external debts and the protection of creditors' rights made it necessary to establish Düyun-u Umumiye for the collection of tax and other revenues. Düyun-u Umumiye, or the General Administration of Debts, was an institution formed by some of the European states to audit the external debts of the Ottoman Empire between the years of 1881 and 1928. The establishment of Düyun-u Umumiye and the Ottoman Empire's loss of the right of taxation, which was the most important element of being an independent state, also put an end to the independence of the empire.

With the start of the War of Independence, the authority of Düyun-u Umumiye was disregarded and the rates and amounts of tax were changed by protecting the qualities of available income laws in order to cover the war expenditures. The tax authority that belonged to the Ottoman sultans was given to the Council on 23 April 1920.

The Ankara government issued a notification in October 1922 and claimed that the authority of taxation belonged to the National Assembly and as a result of this, it declared that the treaties signed between the İstanbul government and Düyun-u Umumiye concerning taxes were invalid (Çağan 1982b).

After the treaties were signed between the Turkish Republic and Düyun-u Umumiye in 1928 and 1933, the authority of the organization was given to the Ministry of Finance (Uluatam and Methibay 2001). Afterwards, some other regulations were added in the 1961 and 1982 Constitutions.

As in almost all countries, tax revenues which constitute the most important income source of the state in Turkey firstly depend on the perfect implementation of the tax system. However, the applicability of the system does not only depend on the tax authority. Taxpayers have to be reminded about their public responsibilities on this topic and be made conscious of the need and purpose. The taxpayer has to be convinced that the tax is used on behalf of the country, to raise the welfare of the public, to guarantee the current and future needs, also that the tax is fair and that non-payers will be punished (Yılmaz 2003).

Tax amnesty and the practice in Turkey

All countries have carried out some studies so that they can deal with the lack of harmony in tax, which has several negative effects such as reducing the revenues of the state and the destruction of people's feeling of fairness and to increase the tax harmony (Tunçer 2001). The tax amnesty is one of the most important of these tools in order to temporarily suspend the administrative legal sanctions applied to people who do not obey the tax laws. The benefactors of these amnesties are the people and organizations that have to be taxpayers or taxpayers that have not paid all the tax they were responsible for (Güner 1988).

Taxes have increasingly become the most important source of revenue for the government as it seeks to ensure fiscal sustainability and reduce its dependency on foreign loans (Purnomo 2004). As a result of this, the state changes the tax laws from time to time and frequently declares amnesties in order to discourage people who do not want to pay their taxes (Esen 2003a).

The main reason for the state to declare amnesties is to meet the demand for the increasing revenue that emerges as a result of the lack of voluntary participation in the costs of the increasing public necessities. The second most important reason is to have more taxpayers in the tax system through amnesties due to the radical changes that will be made in it (<www.eso-es.net>).

The criminal aspect of tax amnesty is of importance, as it would involve the moral hazards problem and people's sense of fairness. The moral hazards problem arises when people expect to be offered another amnesty, and this would lower their willingness to pay tax in anticipation of the future tax exemption. Those honest taxpayers would also react negatively to the fact that evaders were being given concessions and they might choose not to comply in the future (WorldSources Online 2004). Experts have cautioned that frequent tax amnesties would be an incentive for unscrupulous taxpayers to defer tax payments until the next amnesty is declared (Felipe 2004). Especially frequent tax amnesties have several negative effects on tax harmony and causes evaders to distort the tax system (Andreoni 1991). Every amnesty creates an expectation in the public mind for a new amnesty that is much more comprehensive than before and this probably has some potential problems apart from its advantages (Başaran 2003).

So far no tax amnesty law has included a statement to compensate honest taxpayers. And the same taxpayers have taken advantage of each tax amnesty and, as a result, the amnesty laws have become 'adherent laws'. So, while it has created some advantages for those out of the list, it has treated unjustly the taxpayers who supported the state in economic crisis (Esen 2003b).

Tax punishments have been made invalid as a result of the amnesty laws that have been made since 1961 (Kırbaş 2002). While political reasons are effective in the fiscal amnesties that were declared formerly, in the amnesties of the 1980s, technical and economic reasons were more effective (Keleş 2002). About 40 amnesty laws were made in Turkey. It is estimated that in Turkey the informal economy is about 50 per cent of the formal economy. If 1 per cent of people could be registered with every tax amnesty, the informal economy in Turkey would be reduced to 10 per cent. However, it can be still seen that the dimensions of the informal economy go beyond 50 per cent of the formal economy (Doğrusöz 2003). As a result, the government must provide tax amnesty as part of its efforts to lure back billions of dollars parked overseas by the country's conglomerates, and to encourage them to pay the real amount of their tax obligations in the future (Purnomo 2004).

Research

The superiority of the law is of utmost importance for countries. People have to live according to some norms as a requirement of being a part of society. However, it should be kept in mind that society does not have to depend on formal obligations because some responsibilities that are not found in the laws are taken from time to time and some ethical behaviour is expected. The services that accountants carry out in society and the responsibilities they take make it necessary to regulate their occupation according to ethical rules (Fatt 1995). Thus, in this part of the study, students who studying at the Faculty of Business Administration and Economics in Turkey, considered as accountants of the future, were asked questions about the ethical aspect of the tax amnesties that play an important role in the Turkish tax system and the following results were obtained.

Demographic characteristics of the students participating in the survey

The study was of students studying at Faculty of Business Administration and Economics; it can be seen from Figure 16.1 that 52 per cent of the students who answered the questionnaire were male and 48 per cent were female.

Gender

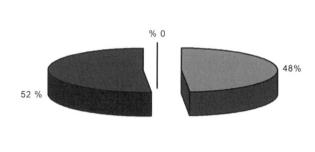

Figure 16.1 Students participating in the survey, by gender

When the distribution of the students according to their age is examined, it can be clearly seen from Figure 16.2 that most of the students that participated in the survey are about the ages of 21 or 22.

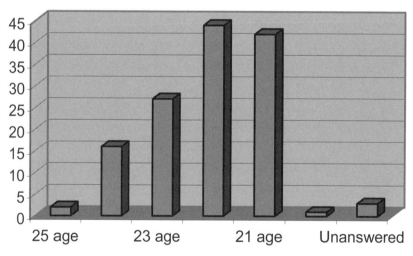

Figure 16.2 Students participating in the survey, by age

Education about job ethics at universities, and the students' definition of ethics

We define job ethics as the integrity that individual and public ethical norms constituted as a result of experiences in the business world and organizational cultures (<www.insanbilim.com>).

The system of values determines the fundamental principles of ethics. The values people have are, however, the preference of one single behaviour, event or situation over others. When we asked the participants whether they studied job ethics at university, we observed that 132 out of 134 (98.5 per cent) of them did not take such a class. When we look at the students' definitions of ethics we can easily recognize their lack of education about this subject (Tables 16.1 and 16.2).

Table 16.1 Survey participants who took a job ethics class at university

	Job ethics class		Total
	Yes	No	
Trakya University		74	74
Marmara University	2	58	60
Total	2	132	134
%	1.5	98.5	100

Table 16.2 Definitions of ethics by the survey participants

	%
Morals	34.4
Being moral in business life	23.7
Obeying social rules and laws	19.4
Being honest to yourself	3.2
Being honest	3.2
Behaving according to the situation	3.2
Respecting personal rights and freedoms	3.2
Respecting universal rights	2.2
Being neutral	1.1
Others	7.5

Most of the students (34.4 per cent) stated that they perceive the concepts of ethics and morals as being the same. The participants who define it as being moral in business life are around 23.7 per cent. Apart from this, those who define ethics as 'obeying social rules and laws' are 19.4 per cent, as 'being honest to yourself' are 3.2 per cent, as only 'being honest' are 3.2 per cent and as 'behaving according to the situation' are 3.2 per cent. People defining it as 'respecting personal rights and freedoms' are 2.2 per cent, as respecting universal rights are 2.2% and as being neutral are 1.1%.

The answers to the question 'Do you think everything legal is ethical?'

In the study, it was found (Table 16.3) that 87 per cent of the students who participated in the research do not consider every legal practice as ethical. The concept of law includes the systems and norms that organize the relationships among people who live in the society. However, the principles that are employed to provide justice in societies are exploited as a result of some legal practices of the state. One of the best examples of this is the differences in points of view about the tax amnesties that can be frequently seen in tax systems.

According to item 73/3 of the Constitution, the principle 'The tax situation, expenditure and similar financial obligations are declared, changed and abolished by law' has been put forward as a requirement of being a legal state. This principle makes it necessary to organize the practices about taxation and also to change or abolish the available regulations by law.

Therefore, it can be said that tax amnesties are not always positive and equal in practice; they affect the ethics of tax negatively even though each of them has a legal base because they cause honest taxpayers to seem irrational whereas the tax evaders seem rational (User 1992). In this respect, tax amnesties are thought to be unethical since they punish honest taxpayers, encourage tax evasion and non-payment of taxes and raise future amnesty expectations.

Table 16.3 Participants' answers to the question 'Do you think everything legal is ethical?'

	Number	%	Explanation
Yes	9	7.8	(F= 3, M=6)
No	100	87	(F=50, M=50)
Unanswered	6	5.2	
Total	115	100	

The students participating in the research were given a case study describing the behaviour of a taxpayer expecting a tax amnesty in the future is. Their thoughts about the ethical standards of the behaviour are discussed below.

Case study

Mr Osman has been the financial counsellor of Akın A.Ş. for 12 years. The owner of Akın A.Ş., Mr Ali, is a person who pays his taxes regularly. However, since there is an expectation of a tax amnesty at the end of the year, he calls Mr Osman to tell him to delay the tax payments. Mr Ali tells him that the other businesses pay less tax than his does, so he has to be more careful about his financial counsellor in the crisis time and adds that he may look for another financial counsellor to work in these conditions. After that talk, Mr Osman does not pay the taxes.

The gender classification of the students supporting the behaviour of Mr Osman Of the 135 students who answered the questionnaire, 48 thought that the financial counsellor was right. When we look at the reasons why they thought he was right (Table 16.4), we understand that the problem of employment (20 people: 8 females, 12 males), competition (8 people: 3 females, 5 males), the future of the employment and business (5 people: 3 females, 2 males) and profitability (5 people: 2 females and 3 males) were the reasons for their support.

Table 16.4 Participants who thought the financial adviser was right, and their reasons

	Female	Male	Total
Problem of employment	8	12	20
In order to be able to compete (because of competition)	3	5	8
Employment and for the future of the business	3	2	5
Profitability	2	3	5

Also, the relationship was studied between the reasons why Mr Osman's behaviour was thought to be right and the student's gender: since the result of the Pearson chi-squared test was found to be bigger than 5 per cent (0.915), it was understood that there was no relationship between them and that the reasons found were not affected by gender but rather resembled each other.

The gender classification of the students who thought Mr Osman was wrong, and their reasons Those who thought the incident mentioned was wrong consisted of 60 students and constituted 55 per cent of the respondents (Table 16.5). The most important reason for finding it wrong was its unethical nature: of the 40 students who supported this opinion, 22 were female and 18 of them were male. The second most important reason was that they thought the financial counsellor should pay the tax on time without considering the possibility of a future tax amnesty. Of the 15 students that supported this opinion, 7 were female and 8 of them were male.

Table 16.5 Participants who thought the financial adviser was wrong, and their reasons

	Female	Male	Total
Because of not being ethical	22	18	40
Because of not paying the tax on time (other reasons)	7	8	15
Other reasons	3	2	5

How could Mr Osman solve the problem by behaving ethically? Ethics in the occupation of accounting is the presentation of credible information to society clearly by giving importance to the laws, the occupation laws and the standards of judgement accepted by the society (Sözbilir and Yenigün 2002) Those employed as accountants have to adopt the ethical rules and take them into consideration in the period of decision (Çoban and Daştan 2003) In this respect, 44.4 per cent (48 out of 108) of the respondents thought the financial counsellor, Mr Osman, was right and 55.6 per cent (60 out of 108) of them thought the opposite (Table 16.6).

Table 16.6 How Mr Osman could solve the problem by behaving ethically

	%	Number
By paying the tax on time	48.3	29
By convincing the boss	28.3	17
By quitting the job	6.7	10

The students' opinions about an ethical solution to the problem were asked. However, 44 per cent of the participants did not answer that question. Of those who did, 48.3 per cent thought the best solution was to pay the tax on time and 28.3 per cent thought the boss should have been persuaded out of waiting for the amnesty. Also, 6.7 per cent of them thought the counsellor should not make a concession if the boss forced him to and that he could leave his job as a solution.

The students were asked about the sanctions that could be experienced by the financial counsellor as a result of this case study (Table 16.7). It was understood that the students did not have enough information about the sanctions that the counsellor could experience since they were not informed about the ethics of accounting during their education.

Table 16.7 Sanctions that the financial adviser might encounter

In the view of:	Likely sanctions	%
– the law	He will be punished	74.4
	No sanctions	16.3
– business in general	His reputation will be damaged	23.3
	No sanctions	11.6
– society as a whole	He will lose his respectability	48.9
	No sanctions	17.8
– his professional association	His membership of the association will be cancelled	45.2
	He will be criticized	19.4

Regarding possible legal sanction, 135 students, 43 (32 per cent) answered that question: of these, 74.4 per cent said that he could be punished by law and 16.3 per cent stated that there were no sanctions.

Again 32 per cent of the students answered the question about sanctions from the business community: 23.3 per cent of them stated that his reputation would be ruined, 23.3 per cent thought he would be prevented from doing his job, and 11.6 per cent thought there were no sanctions.

Of the participant students, 33 per cent answered the question about society's view of his actions: 48.9 per cent of the 45 students said that the financial counsellor would lose his reputation but 17.8 per cent said there were no sanctions. Some students even stated that, apart from the lack of sanctions, the person might gain reputation in society and this in turn would be a good promotion for him and provide him with more job opportunities in the future. The worrying thing here is that some unethical practices are approved by some parts of the society.

On the question about his treatment by his professional association, 23 per cent of the participant students (31 out of 135) did not answer this question and 45.2 per cent of the respondents stated that his membership of the association would be cancelled.

When all these answers are studied, it can be understood that they are unrealistic, since the students did not take any courses about job ethics at university and they need serious education about it. The study included senior students, so it shows that they may have serious problems in the future since they will soon become members of the business world. In this connection, the professional associations are responsible for this in the first place but more importantly this gap has to be filled during university education.

Conclusion

The revenues that the state obtains from different sources within the constitutional borders in order to realize the functions it has undertaken are known as the public revenues. The most important characteristic of tax that makes it different from other revenues is its being compulsory. However, the obligation imposed by tax is not the only important thing for the state to be successful in collecting tax. What it has to do to be successful is to make the citizens believe that the tax they pay is a requirement of their responsibilities for society. However, sometimes it may be necessary to create an opportunity to open a clear page for the people who have not declared their income or declared less than the real amount they earned (perhaps because they could not fulfil their tax responsibilities due to financial problems) and this may provide them with the opportunity to align with the future tax system. With this aim, tax amnesties, which we perceive as the opportunity for the taxpayers to pay (with little interest) the taxes they hitherto could not or did not pay, may be declared.

While frequent tax amnesties and their anticipation encourage tax crimes economically, they also create an inequality for the people who honestly pay their taxes on time. This situation shows that the tax ethic in our society is at a lower level than general ethics.

It is a constitutional duty of a state to provide taxpayers with regulations and practices about taxation and documentation which will not resist tax, break tax laws or require a new tax amnesty and also which will be suitable for their jobs and procedures. So, while the state is making some regulations, it has to establish legal bases for them.

However, we can claim that not all legal practices are fair and equal and also that the ethic of tax amnesties, which are widely accepted in the Turkish tax system, can be discussed. In our study aiming at this, the students who will be financial counsellors or may be taxpayers in the future were asked about their thoughts about the legal and ethical sides of tax amnesties.

But it was found that the students had difficulty even in defining ethics because they did not have such a class at university. If we define the concept of ethics as the evaluation system of the behaviour of people who do any kind of job, this has the same meaning as morals for many students. When we study the concepts of law and ethics, we have found out that the students do not consider all legal practices as ethical. It is also surprising that 35.5 per cent (48 out of 135) of the participants think taxpayers are right when they do not carry out their responsibilities and cause their accountants to behave immorally as a result of amnesty expectations. In this connection, it has been understood that the students who will soon become financial counsellors have insufficient information about ethics and they will seek their own advantage while performing their jobs in the future.

Illegal behaviour certainly has a sanction. However, the practices that are against job ethics do not have legal punishments and they emerge because society encourages them whereas they have considered as more important than the public ones.

When individuals make some decisions, they must not only think about their businesses and themselves, but also about society, because profit is not the only measure of performance. As a result of this, they must protect both themselves and the people around them from the negative effects of the highly competitive business world. Social, economic and political structures that are changing rapidly, individuals who have become more conscious and the nature of the environment in which the business operates all force individuals and businesses to obey certain rules. The importance the managers give to the morals that are applied around them are a dimension of the culture in its social structure: those involved should urge businesses to make some moral rules and obey them.

References

Aksoy, Şerafettin (1989), *Vergi Hukuku ve Türk Vergi Sistemi*, Filiz Kitabevi: İstanbul.

Andreoni, James (1991), 'The desirability of a permanent tax amnesty', *Journal of Public Economics*, 45 (2).

Başaran, Murat (2003), 'Vergi Barışı Kanunu Üzerinden Mali Af Arayışları', *Vergi Sorunları Dergisi*, Sayı 173, Şubat.

Battal, Ahmet (2003), *Hukukun Temel Kavramları*, Gazi Kitabevi: Ankara.

Baykara, Bekir (2003), 'Vergi Barışı Kanunu 14. Maddesinin Anayasal Durumu', *Vergi Dünyası*, Sayı 261.

Çağan, Nami (1982a), 'Anayasa Tasarısında Vergi ve Benzeri Yükümlülükler', *Vergi Dünyası*.

Çağan, Nami (1982b), *Vergilendirme Yetkisi*, Kazancı Yayınları: İstanbul.

Çoban, Metin, and Daştan, Abdulkerim (2003), 'Muhasebe Mesleğinde Meslek Etiği: Trabzon İline Yönelik Anket Çalışması', *Vergi Dünyası*, Sayı 261.

Doğrusöz, Bumin (2003), 'Kayıt Dışı ile Mücadele Konusunda Bazı Düşünceler', at <www.turmob.org.tr>.

Erginay, Akif (1990), *Vergi Hukuku, İlkeler- Vergi tekniği, Türk Vergi Sistemi*, Savaş Yayınları: Ankara.

Esen, Ahmet (2003a), 'Vergi barışı ve /veya vergi affı', *Maliye Postası*, Sayı 539, Özel sayı.

Esen, Ahmet (2003b), 'Rica ile Vergi Toplamak', *Maliye Postası*, Sayı 542, Özel sayı.

Fatt, James P.T. (1995), 'Ethics and the accountant', *Journal of Business Ethics*, Sayı 14.

Felipe, F. Salvosa (2004), 'Business group bucks tax amnesty, says it will encourage delinquency', *Business World*, Manila, 1 November.

Güner, Ayşe (1988), *Vergi Afları-Vergiye Uyum İlişkisi Üzerine*, MÜ Maliye Araştırma ve Uygulama Merkezi Yayın no.10, İstanbul.

Keleş, Y. (2002), 'Yine Mi Af? Mükellefler ne Zaman Vergi Öderler?', *Vergi Dünyası*, Sayı 249, Mayıs.

Kirbaş, Sadık (2002), *Vergi Hukuku, Temek kavramlar, İlkeler ve Kurumlar*, Siyasal Kitabevi: Ankara.

Purnomo, Hadi (2004), 'Tax chief fears misuse of planned amnesty facility', *Jakarta Post*.

Sözbilir, Naciye, and Yenigün, Tekin (2002), 'Muhasebe Meslek Gruplarının Bağımsızlık ve Tarafsızlıklarının Korunmasında Risk Alanları ve Bir Anket Çalışması', *Muhasebe ve Finansman Dergisi*, Sayı 13.

Tunçer, Mehmet (2001), 'Vergi Aflarının Vergi Uyumuna Etkisi', Cumhuriyet Üniversitesi, İ.İ.B.F., İktisat Bölümü, Araştırma Görevlisi.

Uluatam, Özhan, and Methibay, Yaşar (2001), *Vergi Hukuku, Genel Esaslar, Türk Vergi Sistemi*, İmaj Yayınevi: Ankara.

User, İnci (1992), 'Vergilemenin Sosyal Psikolojik Sınırı', Yayınlanmamış doktora tezi, MÜ Sosyal Bilimler Enstitüsü, İstanbul.

WorldSources Online (2004), 'Caveats within Susilo's tax amnesty plan', *Jakarta Post*, at <www. proquest.umi.com>.

Yayman, Derya (1999), 'Vergi Denetiminde Etkinliğin Sağlanması', Yayınlanmamış doktora tezi, Dokuz Eylül Üniversitesi Sosyal Bilimler Enstitüsü Maliye Anabilim Dalı, İzmir.

Yilmaz, Kazım (2003), 'Tutarlılık ve Vergi Toplayabilme', *Sabah Gazetesi*, 6 March.

<www.eso-es.net>
<www.insanbilim.com.tr>
<www.tdb.org.tr>

How Far Can CSR Travel? Reflections on the Applicability of the Concept to SMEs in Uzbekistan

Daniel Stevens, Alexey Kim, Lobar Mukhamedova, Malika Mukimova and Rowan Wagner

The question of the relevance of CSR for small and medium enterprises (SMEs) in Uzbekistan represents an interesting case study of how far the concept can travel from its origins in the debate over the role of large corporations in the West. On the one hand it could be argued that the issues raised in the CSR debate are particular to the Western context and that the problems of small businesses struggling to survive in the context of a gradual transition to the market economy, as is the case in Uzbekistan, are quite different. On the other hand one could argue that the idea that businesses have a responsibility before their communities is a universal one, and equally relevant everywhere, even amongst small entrepreneurs in a relatively remote region of the world.

In this chapter we seek to address this question by drawing on the findings of a research project undertaken by Westminster International University in Tashkent (Uzbekistan) in collaboration with the Chamber of Commerce and Industry of Uzbekistan[1] which examined the extent to which the concept of CSR is relevant for SMEs in the country. This is the first research of its type in the region. What research has been carried out focuses mainly on larger, mainly international companies (Mirkhanova 2006), and is more often journalistic in style and related to other countries in Central Asia.[2] In particular we examine the question from a number of disciplinary perspectives – those of economics, law, management studies

---

1   We very much appreciate the assistance of the Chamber in conducting the research, and also the British Embassy in Tashkent, Uzbekistan, who funded the project.

2   For example see the debate about the actions of a mining company in Turdueva (2006).

and sociology – seeking to show what role the concept can play in these different frameworks of analysis.

Introduction – how far can CSR travel?

When introducing the research project on 'CSR amongst SMEs in Uzbekistan' we invariably met with a moment of incomprehension. Either our conversant was unfamiliar with Uzbekistan as a country, given that it has only been an independent country for 15 years following the break-up of the Soviet Union, or if they were familiar with (and often from) Uzbekistan it was the term 'CSR' that gave rise to some puzzlement. Even if the respondent was familiar with CSR *and* Uzbekistan, the focus on SMEs was somewhat novel. In short, the combination of CSR, SMEs and Uzbekistan is quite unusual, reflecting the fact that the emergence of CSR as a modern concept was very much rooted in the West and large corporations.

It is difficult to pinpoint the exact time when the term 'corporate social responsibility' became popular, but already by the 1970s the CSR debate was being referred to and analysed (Walters 1977). What is clearer than the date is the location of the centre of the debate – namely the US. This is not because the US is more attuned to social questions than other societies, but because of its nature as a 'business civilization'[3] where limited government involvement and greater reliance on the market means it has greater influence over, and thereby responsibility for, society. The result is that the issue has become an integral part of business practice and management education in the US (Alsop 2006). It has also been widely discussed in Europe where it fits with a tradition of state–business partnership in dealing with social issues.

However, as any review on the literature on CSR will testify, the concept has gone global as a result of the way in which globalisation has given rise to powerful multinationals, often with greater economic power than individual countries. If 'corporations rule the world' (Korten 1996), then there is a need for them to take responsibility commensurate with their power. Globalisation has also, by promoting competition between national economies, undermined the welfare state, with the consequence that the state's ability to shape society is shrinking at the same time as the role of business is expanding. And thirdly, the globalisation of scholarship has propelled the concept around the world – to take just one example, in 2007 the 6th International Conference on Corporate Social Responsibility will be held in Malaysia, the previous year having been in Turkey.

Just as the concept got its impetus in the US, but is now expanding internationally, so the concept was originally linked primarily to big business, but is now being applied to SMEs. Initially those corporations with the visibility and economic weight to attract the attention of campaigners were the focus of the debate, and

---

3   This term, used by the liberal American economist Robert Heilbroner, expresses the idea that the central institution of society is the corporation (as opposed to the government, civil society or household).

by the same token they were the most motivated and best able to try and seize the initiative by developing corporate social responsibility departments. However, while the behaviour of large multinationals may dominate the headlines, it is the practice of SMEs which have at least as much, if not more, impact on society.

The result is that some now see the concept as of universal relevance for all types of business in all countries, based on the observation that the concerns underpinning the CSR concept date back right back to the origins of the modern corporation. Ideas of charity, fairness and stewardship were a feature of earlier eras (van Marrewijk 2003: 96) and, to a greater or lesser extent, are an issue for all civilizations both ancient and modern. For example, one Chinese writer argues that, 'regardless of whether a country is Eastern or Western, developed or developing, everyone expresses their understanding of CSR similarly – that is, in their pursuit of profit, enterprises must also take responsibility for the needs of the environment, society and stakeholders' (Chen 2006: 8).

That the concept of CSR has gone global is clear, but even if one accepts that the concerns about business being sensitive to society are universal, does this mean that the assertion that 'in their pursuit of profit, enterprises must also take responsibility for the needs of the environment, society and stakeholders' is equally valid, and appropriate for all societies at all stages of development? Just as there are cultural backlashes against such 'universal' concepts of democracy, so maybe there is a need to subject this global advance to scrutiny. Even on its home turf the concept remains controversial; witness the recent 2005 survey in *The Economist* which argued that it was a 'pity' that 'the movement for corporate social responsibility has won the battle of ideas' (Crook 2005: 3). There remains a healthy debate about the proper role of business in society, particularly outside of the US (Avtonomov 2006).

To help address this question of how far the concept can usefully travel we draw on a survey of over 200 small and medium enterprises in Uzbekistan, together with more in-depth interviews with 28 managers, as well as 15 community leaders, representing seven regions of the country. We also draw on the experience of conducting this research project, and running workshops and developing a multimedia resource for SMEs to help them reflect on the questions posed by the CSR concept. Using this common data set, we also set out to answer the question from a variety of disciplinary perspectives, starting with that of the economist.

The economics perspective

While the activities of powerful multinational companies (MNCs) often capture the public imagination, economists are often more concerned with the activities of small firms and private entrepreneurs since they represent the cornerstone of many economies. They are especially important in economies in transition from a command economy to a market economy, as is the case in Uzbekistan. While it is usually argued that CSR is mainly an activity of MNCs, there are numerous reports and findings which prove that SMEs are also heavily engaged in the implementation of CSR. Certainly an SME has a different perspective on CSR from that of an MNC. As the World Bank series on CSR indicates (World Bank Institute 2004), SMEs are more proactive in incorporating elements of CSR into their core activities and they usually provide help in kind, rather than financial support, compared to MNCs. SMEs perceive CSR as a complementary tool in gaining competitive advantage over their rivals, unlike MNCs.

Most of the economics literature on the subject is concentrated on testing the underlying motivations for implementing CSR, such as profit maximization or manager's utility maximization. Unfortunately, studies in this area often lack firm level-specific analysis of underlying motives, besides they are more focused on big enterprises. Aggregated data irons out motivational differences and has intrinsic biases that are reflected in the controversial conclusions of such studies. There are only a few event studies that explore the relationship between CSR and profitability, but they do not test the underlying motives.

Using a unique data set we were able to explore the main motives for pursuing CSR in Uzbekistan. We used the World Bank classification of 'small enterprises', such that:

1. micro enterprise: less than 10 employees; total assets less than US$100,000 and total annual sales less than US$100,000
2. small enterprise: between 10 and 50 employees; total assets between US$100,000 and US$3 million and total sales between US$100,000 and US$3 million.

The combination of in-depth interviews and aggregated data allow us to test the following hypotheses:

Hypothesis 1: profit maximization is a primary motive to pursue CSR

It is usually assumed that in contexts of transition small developing businesses are focused upon survival. Therefore entrepreneurs pursue some elements of CSR purely for profit-maximizing purposes. And indeed both our survey and in-depth interviews showed that SME managers are doing CSR to maximize their profits in the long run. Around 62 per cent of respondents indicated that they pursue CSR for purely profit-maximizing purposes, since entrepreneurs believe that elements of CSR help them to boost their sales figures. Taking into account local cultural aspects, it has a tremendous impact on the sustainability of the business.

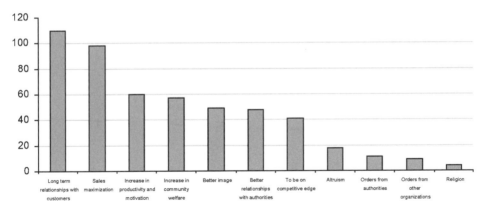

Figure 17.1 Motivational factors to pursue CSR among SMEs in Uzbekistan (March 2007)

Hypothesis 2: companies are more likely to engage in sponsoring certain social events, rather than simply giving to charities

Since sponsoring is usually associated with free advertising and the promotion of the business in the community, while charitable donations are often more anonymous, we hypothesize that SMEs will prefer the sponsorship option. In fact the survey showed that entrepreneurs spend three times more on charitable donations than on sponsoring social events (see Figure 17.1). In-depth interviews revealed that religious factors and altruistic behaviour play a significant role in the decision to donate. Moreover, altruism and simply the desire to help people was the main driving force for charitable donations. Rather than donating money, entrepreneurs give free lunches, or their own goods, to poor people and for special associations.

Hypothesis 3: the bigger the company, the more it is engaged in CSR

Since bigger companies have larger financial resources, it is easier for them to engage in CSR, compared to smaller businesses that are struggling to survive (Figure 18.2). Companies are twice more likely to engage in CSR if the number of workers increases by 20. Since any company's financial results include sensitive information, we therefore used the number of workers engaged in a firm as a proxy for the size of the business. Companies with 30 and more workers also have more diversified CSR activities. These activities vary from charitable donations and environmental protection to providing financial assistance to staff members in the event of marriage, and free staff education and retraining programmes.

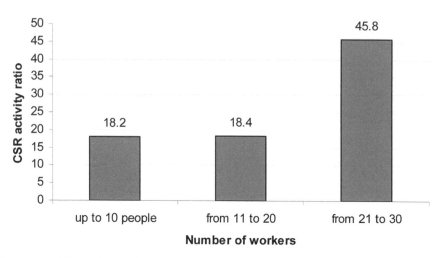

Figure 17.2 **Firm size and engagement in CSR in Uzbekistan (March 2007)**

Hypothesis 4: the more intense the competition in the market, the more likely SMEs are to engage in CSR

CSR in this sense would create a competitive advantage in the eyes of the community. The closer the business is to the community the more likely it is to be successful in that region. Our survey results confirmed the hypothesis. Competitive companies are twice more likely to engage in CSR than companies that operate as monopolies. It is interesting to note that firms in the city are more likely to engage in CSR than firms in rural areas. This can be partially explained by a higher concentration of people in the community in the city, and hence much larger exposure of business activities to the community. In the rural areas, neighbours are sometimes located a few kilometres away from each other.

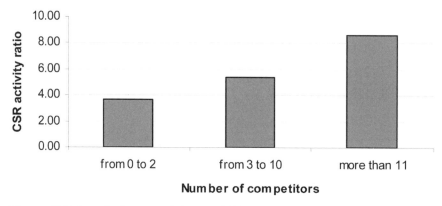

Figure 17.3 **Level of competition and CSR**

Hypothesis 5: improved relationships with local authorities play a significant role for SMEs to engage in CSR

SME engagement in CSR has a certain effect on better relationships with government authorities, but not to a great extent. This 'stick' motive takes only fifth place after the 'carrots' of profit maximization and building better relationships with customers and the community (see Figure 17.1).

Hypothesis 6: firms in the capital give less than firms in the regions

This hypothesis was derived from the cultural aspects of people living in Uzbekistan and an assumption that people in the regions are more likely to support each other than people living in the capital. In fact the survey results showed that business in the capital is more likely to engage in CSR than in the regions (Figure 17.4). This phenomenon could be partially explained by the level of competition in the capital and regions. It is evident that competition amongst SMEs in the capital is much more intense than in the regions. Therefore we can observe a much higher CSR activity in the capital, which is reconfirmed by hypothesis 4.

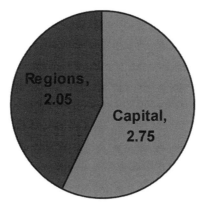

Figure 17.4 CSR activity ratio in the capital and regions of Uzbekistan (March 2007)

Generally our survey shows that the bigger the company and the more competitors it has, the more likely it is that it will be engaged in CSR. Firms engage in CSR not only as a result of profit maximization motive but also as a consideration of managerial utility, where managers satisfy their altruistic desires and also play the role of 'champion'. Companies will be engaged in CSR only when managers – champions – pursue CSR themselves. 'Stick' policies from local authorities seem to play an insignificant role in CSR development.

This analysis illustrates that the concept of CSR does seem relevant for SMEs in a transition economy. The main conclusion is that, far from concerns for survival crowding out an interest in CSR, SMEs in competitive industries see activities such as sponsorship of community events, and donations to the needy (particularly using in-kind products or services), as important to their sustainability as well as immediate survival. This, of course, is not the only reason, since the study also indicated that religious mores and cultural notions of altruism, along with the 'stick' of government pressure', also motivate SMEs to engage in such activities, but what is clear is that amongst a significant number of SME managers there is an understanding that building good relations with the community is good business.

The management perspective

To examine this further, we take the case of one of the authors (who is a small-business owner and international academic working in Uzbekistan) who has come to appreciate how sensitive his business and other small businesses like his are to the influences of local culture and social norms, as they operate on thinner margins and often are dependent on the communities they serve on a day-to-day basis for their own survival (Salmones et al. 2005). Other non-financial aspects such as image and reputation in the communities where SMEs operate are extremely important as they can directly impact the profitability of the business (Luken and Stares 2005). What is hard to figure out in this unique and interesting environment is what to actually execute that will reap both the rewards of helping society and the company's bottom line.

Uzbekistan is unique and challenging in many aspects. First, as has been mentioned, it is a country in transition from a Soviet socialist state based upon a centralized command and control economy to something not quite determined but more orientated towards the global free market. Additionally, however, Uzbekistan is a doubly land-locked country and is limited in access by its surrounding neighbours who at times have less than cordial relationships when it comes to trade and economic interplay, based upon leadership quirks and differing senses of history. This particular history has shaped the understanding of CSR as based on a communal sense of supporting local needs in times of instability and promoting local support of local sports, education and social activities, normally through local *mahallas* (neighbourhood organizations) or other semi- and fully government-supported offices. Also globalization and the access to other goods and service options that better match the wants and desires of local community members is also shaping the business environment.

So, using this foundation and the actual need to make profit for long-term sustainability of a business, this author has been using some select CSR concepts that, so far, in the relative short term of six months, have paid off in the form of a significant pool of repeat customers, made some profit, and reduced the hassle of unwarranted inspections and undue bureaucracy from local authorities and administrative bodies.

The specific activities that have been carried out are ensuring the safety of the products sold as well as keeping the prices down, donating sport equipment and books to the local elementary school, and periodic donations to the local community (*mahalla*) social support fund. These have links to what is commonly understood as corporate social responsibility (for example, not selling harmful products), also to transparency and community actions in support of community needs, which relates to what many SMEs are doing in other parts of the world (Enderle 2004).

Our survey results indicate that some activities are more widespread than others. Particularly there is still a lack of appreciation of product safety, though recently there has been some strengthening of consumer protection laws, mostly in response to large reported cases of abuse. This leads us on to considering the development of the legal framework for CSR.

Legal perspective

From a legal perspective, the principle of the social responsibility of organizations and individuals is not entirely new for the post-Soviet states. The social protection of the citizens, education and environmental protection were considered to be very important issues and were well developed during the period of the Soviet Union. After the break-up of the Soviet Union the newly independent states realized the need to develop the market economy based on private entrepreneurship as well as the need to create a new national idea of a sovereign state. In Uzbekistan, social policy was considered to be one of the most important principles to bear in mind when transitioning to a market economy based 'state with a great future'.

Several factors have made it increasingly important for companies to demonstrate social responsibility; in other words, to 'operate a business in a manner that meets or exceeds the ethical, legal, commercial and public expectations that society has of business' (Business for Social Responsibility 2006). In the case of Uzbekistan, it is clear that legal expectations have a large role to place – our research findings indicated that regulatory supervision by the government was a major factor as many CSR issues are grounded in binding legal obligations, often derived from international law. While, as noted above, this is not the overwhelming motive, still 15 per cent of all respondents (owners or employees of small businesses) in our survey specified that the main motive for them to conduct socially responsible activities stems from their legal obligations.

The legislative base for the social support is vast and profound. The year 2007 was proclaimed by the government to be a 'year of social protection': a State Programme of Social Protection has been developed and includes provisions for developing and updating the existing legislation on social protection, improving the effectiveness and fairness of social aid distribution in the areas of support of population with special needs, national health (especially women's protection), and financial and spiritual support of youth and young families.

These legislative provisions create certain legal responsibilities for small businesses to operate in socially responsible ways. Such areas as taxation, environment, labour law and health and safety are the most heavily influenced by these requirements. In addition there are a number of tax incentives provided by the government to encourage entrepreneurs to conduct activities which benefit society on the whole or special needs populations in particular.

On the one hand, overregulation does not let voluntary CSR practices develop fully: on the other hand, regulatory intervention is important to redress the balance in cases of, for example, negative externalities such as pollution, public nuisance or harm to others.

Thus the balance should be achieved between the national rules and legislative framework on one side and the broader, supranational framework of shared values on the other. The experts point out that we are globally witnessing the emergence of 'increasingly hybrid governance structures in which social needs are no longer the exclusive realm of the state' (Luetkenhorst 2004).

In Uzbekistan, another unique source of addressing social needs is the activities of *mahallas*, the self-governing neighbourhood bodies. These are, in effect, semi-governmental bodies that exercise governmental supervision over many fundamental aspects of Uzbek life. They are required to assist various state bodies in carrying out their functions and in most cases monitor the social contribution of small businesses situated or registered on their territory. So the research showed, all respondents in one way or another are involved in the provision of financial and other support for the *mahalla* activities which include, for example, support for low-income families, disabled people and pensioners, landscape development, medical care, training and education, and creating employment opportunities.

The sociological perspective

From the perspective of sociology one of the issues of interest is how the concept of CSR is understood locally. In Uzbekistan is it clear that there are a variety of understandings of this concept. Those who grew up during the period of socialism assume that corporations and enterprises should address all social problems, since historically they were extensively used by the state in the provision of social services. Now, since the withdrawal of the Soviet state, the fact that these enterprises cannot continue this role leads to a sense of disappointment in the mass consciousness, a break in the social contract between state and citizen.

A new understanding held by some new entrepreneurs is that each business has a responsibility solely to its own employees – providing them with good salaries – and the wider responsibility to the community is fulfilled simply by paying taxes. However, located in the culture there is still a sense that 'there is a need to share' and so there is a strong pressure for SMEs to be involved in charity work.

What is distinct in the understanding in Uzbekistan, as compared to Europe for example, is that there is less emphasis on issues such as product safety, workplace discrimination, and restriction of competition through the use of cartels and exploiting a monopoly position in the market. Some of these omissions are particular to the Central Asian context where a broader discussion of what CSR entails has yet to appear in the media, unlike for example in Russia.[4]

This understanding of CSR, which emphasizes charity, is (as in other cases) seemingly rooted in existing moral norms (Blagov 2004). As Islam is the main religion in Uzbekistan, Islamic ethics in particular have a significant influence on the basic norms and ethics of business dealings. Analysing the influence of religious Islamic ethics on economics, Muslim theorists investigated the interrelation between the moral instructions of Islam, its spiritual-moral values and the concept of the person and his/her economic behaviour. The research discovered that these values promote basically strong-willed and enterprising character traits and virtues that form a person capable of self-development and being guided by common sense. There were also changes in the attitudes to work and labour activity. The ability to work effectively for the benefit of oneself, family and society are promoted by Islam to the rank of a moral duty. In the system of values of the business world, honesty and responsibility are prominent, and it is noted that the process of manufacturing should be directed to the achievement of the prosperity of society. However, much of the study of the influence of Islamic ideology on entrepreneurship and business culture nowadays is not as systematic as it could be (Nurlina 2004: 5). We were able to draw from our empirical data, and in particular our interviews with the heads of businesses, an understanding of the way in which entrepreneurs are guided by the canons of Islam, in particular the principle of general equality of Moslems before each other, before the law and before God.

Two basic postulates are the concepts of *riba* (prohibition of loan interest) and *zakyat* (a duty and an obligation to pay part of one's income to the needy). Islam encourages the individual to increase their wealth, but then to use it for the good of society. Representatives of small businesses, in particular, identified this as a motive for philanthropy. Thus, while they may not be familiar with the term 'CSR', their traditions, education and religion have ingrained an understanding that business is not just about profit, but is also for the good of society.

It is, however, not just religious traditions that shape the understanding of CSR in Uzbekistan. For, as mentioned already, central to the system of local governance in Uzbekistan is the *mahalla*. The *mahalla* (an Arabic term referring to a part of the city) has roots far back in the Middle East in general[5] and also in Uzbekistan and, what is more, it continued its influence during the period of the Soviet Union as a focal point for the association life of its residents. It remained central to people's lives in organizing the community rituals, particularly the rites of passage – ceremonies of circumcision, marriage and burial. Given its historical legitimacy,

---

4   For example, a round-table discussion on 'Social responsibility business' (held on 29 October 2003 and reported by the TASS-URAL press center, Interregional mass media club, Moscow), included on the agenda the need for a fuller, more European understanding of the concept.

5   When Nosir Khisrav, a poet and writer of the 11th century, had been travelling in the countries of the Middle East and visiting Mecca on a pilgrimage, he wrote of 'the city of Cairo comprised of 10 *mahallas*'. This fact testifies that *mahallas* have existed for several centuries in the countries of the East.

and the need for new mechanisms of control in the absence of the Communist party, since independence in 1991 the institution has also been incorporated into the government as a unit of administration (providing welfare payments as playing a supporting role to the security services in ensuring social control). Thus in its current form it is a fusion of local solidarity expressed in the activities of organizing ceremonies and public events, and an important element and executor of social policy in Uzbekistan. It is promoted as the fundamental institution of 'civil society'.

In the course of our research we interviewed representatives of the organizing committees of 13 *mahallas* across seven different regions. It was found that, for the most part, the activities of a *mahalla* centre around securing social support for and providing assistance to the poor, handicapped and old. It also has an impact on the activities of businesses, regardless of their size. Based on the results of the survey, it was found that the *mahalla* assists in carrying out such events as cleaning up various areas within the community, conducting festivals, providing facilities for business, and assigning young people to educational facilities and to work duties. Amongst the surveyed entrepreneurs, only 14 per cent of the respondents do not work in close relationship with the *mahalla* committee.

The elders (leaders) of *mahallas* conduct talks with the representatives of small businesses and write letters and ask entrepreneurs to participate in the activities of *mahallas*. From the opinion of the *mahalla* committees it is evident that there is a need to make a clear case for representatives of small and medium businesses to actively participate in the life of *mahallas*. In addition there is an expectation that the existence of a wider information interchange between *mahallas* and enterprises, and the increase of knowledge about such concepts as social responsibility, will help entrepreneurs and the representatives of *mahalla* committees to work in closer cooperation.

Conclusion

This overview of some of the findings of our research, from a variety of different perspectives, allows us to make a number of conclusions in answer to the question posed – of how far the concept can travel and to what extent it is applicable to the struggles of SMEs in an emerging market economy such as Uzbekistan.

Firstly, it is clear that, just as the 'New World' existed long before it was 'discovered' by European colonial explorers, so 'CSR' amongst small businesses in Uzbekistan existed long before the modern-day concept arrived on its shores (metaphorically speaking – with no shores to speak of, communication between Uzbekistan and the outside world is now largely mediated by modern communication technologies). Our survey and interviews uncovered significant patterns of CSR-related activities driven by a variety of factors. The assumption that economic man, when running a business, seeks to maximize profits seems to hold true amongst SMEs in Uzbekistan, and that many managers have made the connection between good community relations and the bottom line of profit. Crucially, one factor which influences this is the level of competition in the market (possibly one reason why CSR is practised more heavily in urban rather than rural areas, where more companies are in more direct competition, given the greater population density).

This conclusion is confirmed when looking at the regulatory regime in Uzbekistan, reflecting the Soviet structure which, in its own way, paid great emphasis to the broader role of economic enterprises in society, using them to deliver social services, and giving rise to whole communities structured around one particular, normally large-scale, industrial enterprise. Regulation of business is a particularly pertinent issue, and the findings of our report hint at the difficulty of getting it right – providing streamlined regulation that is effective in channelling economic activity towards the public good, without stifling entrepreneurial activity in the process. The way forward seems to be identified from a sociological perspective, in looking at the institutions which already exist. Our research has identified the significant extent to which Islamic norms and the institution of the *mahalla* have spurred and shaped the development of charity and philanthropic activity within local communities.

So if CSR already has a past amongst SMEs in Uzbekistan, what about the future? Our research also provides some pointers for ways in which SMEs can be further encouraged to think long term, to invest in positive community relations and to develop sustainable business practices that will benefit society at large.

Firstly, the economic perspective, focusing on structural causes, suggests that as competition is strengthened so will CSR practices become more widespread. Managers will be spurred to find new ways of finding new customers for their products or services, and will value their existing customers more, given the threat that they might leave for a competitor. From a legal perspective, there is a need to have more targeted regulation that focuses on externalities and provides greater freedom for social initiatives of SMEs which should facilitate a gradual move away from the dominance of governmental control. As the discipline of market competition begins to take the place of government directives, so CSR practices would become more diverse, innovative and sensitive to the changing needs of the community. It would also, of course, directly address one of the underdeveloped elements of CSR in Uzbekistan – an appreciation of the ethics of fair competition and an equal playing field created by the government. The discipline of competition would also promote a greater focus on another underdeveloped aspect, that of product safety. For while government legislation has a role, the ultimate drive for product quality has to be the business logic of retaining customers with safe products, and avoiding media scares that would drive them to competitors.

Another lesser developed area of CSR relates to issues of workplace discrimination and ensuring fair opportunities for all in employment. These relate to more cultural issues and the sociological perspective highlights how the emphasis on charity relates to the religious norms as well as the institutions into which individuals have been socialized. And yet by the same token, the emphasis in Islam on the equality of man discussed above and the solidarity of the *mahalla* do contain within them the start of a focus on equal opportunities for all, regardless of family or ethnicity. This is reinforced by the pronouncements of the government of Uzbekistan about the need for equality of access to social services, and the importance of developing the SME sector in order to enhance the development of the country. Though barriers do exist, there are signs that the country is keen to build on its past and embrace best practices in the area of CSR. This suggests that while CSR arrived a long time ago, there is a continuous need to engage in discussion with the international community in order to learn from best practice, and also to share the country's own insights internationally.

References

Alsop, Ronald (2006), 'The top business schools: something old, something new', *The Wall Street Journal Online*, 20 September, at <http://www.careerjournal.com/reports/bschool06/20060920-alsop-mblede.html>, accessed 22 September 2006.

Avtonomov, Vladimir (2006), 'Balancing state, market and social justice: Russian experiences and lessons to learn', *Journal of Business Ethics*, 66, 3–9.

Blagov, Y.E. (2004), 'The conception of corporative social responsibility and strategic management', *Russian Journal of Management*, 3, 17–34.

Business for Social Responsibility (BSR) (2006), 'Online introduction to CSR', at <www.bsr.org/BSRLibrary/TOdetail.cfm?DocumentID=138>, accessed October 2006.

Chen, Ying (2006), *Will CSR Work in China? Leading Perspectives*, in the Trends and Solutions Series, Business for Social Responsibility, Summer 2006, pp 8–10.

Crook, Clive (2005), 'The good company: a survey of corporate social responsibility', *The Economist*, 22 January.

Enderle, G. (2004), 'Global competition and corporate social responsibilities of some small and medium-sized enterprises', *Business Ethics: European Review*, 13(1), 51–63.

Korten, David (1996), *When Corporations Rule the World*, West Hartford CT: Kumarian Press.

Luetkenhorst, Wilfried (2004), 'Corporate social responsibility (CSR) and the development agenda: should SMEs care?, SME Technical Working Papers Series, UNIDO, September, at <www.unido.org/file-storage/download/?file%5fid=29500>, accessed October 2006.

Luken, R. and Stares, R. (2005), 'Small business responsibility in developing countries: a threat or an opportunity?', *Business Strategy and the Environment*, 14, 38–53.

Marrewijk, Marcel van (2003), 'Concepts and definitions of CSR and corporate sustainability: between agency and communion', *Journal of Business Ethics*, 44, 95–105.

Mirkhanova, Umida (2006), 'The development of CSR in Uzbekistan', paper presented at the conference: *Problems and Success Factors in Business: Perspectives from Emerging Markets and Transition Economies III*, Bishkek, September 2006.

Nurlina, G. (2004), *Islamic Ethic of Business*, Moscow: Umma.

Salmones, G., Crespo, C. and Bosques, I. (2005), 'Influence of corporate social responsibility on loyalty and valuation of services', *Journal of Business Ethics*, 61, 369–85.

Turdueva, Aziza (2006), 'Kyrgyzstan: rural communities seek share in prosperity', *IWPRS Reporting Central Asia*, 463, 12 September, available at <IWPR.net>.

Walters, Kenneth D. (1977), 'Corporate social responsibility and ideology', *California Management Review*, XIX (3), 40–51.

World Bank Institute (2004), *Can Small be Responsible? The Possibilities and Challenges of Corporate Social Responsibility among Small and Medium Enterprises*, ed. M. Jarvis, report of e-conference organized by World Bank Institute, 19 January–8 February 2004, available at <http://infor.worldbank.org/etools/docs/library/126862/small_responsible.pdf>.

Corporate Social Responsibility in the Peruvian Mining Industry

Sonia Meza-Cuadra

Most of the international mining companies have been adopting sustainable development as their corporate social responsibility (CSR) strategy for the sector since the middle of the 1990s. As Peru is the number one worldwide producer of silver, second of zinc and bismuth, third of copper, tin and tellurium, fourth of lead and molybdenum, and fifth of gold, the Peruvian mining industry is an important case for analysing how this process has occurred in the context of a developing country.

This chapter aims to examine the integration process of sustainable development by the Peruvian mining industry since the 1990s which coincided with the opening of the Peruvian economy to foreign investment. To this end, the first two sections give the necessary background on the economic, political and social evolution of mining in Peru. The third section analyses the mining industry and the roles of its main stakeholders. In the next section, we move on to review the evolution of mining legislation as a effort made by the government to integrate a sustainable development approach for the first time in Peru. Finally, we include an evaluation of the progress of CSR programmes, based on secondary sources of information, in the last two sections.

Economic, political and social background information on Peru

The Inca Empire was the ancient Peruvian civilization which was captured by the Spanish conquistadors in 1533. The Spanish ruled the country until 1821 when independence was declared. During its republican period, Peru had unstable democratic and military governments. The last military government stayed in power 12 years (1968–80) and took several radical measures, such as the nationalization of foreign companies and an agrarian reform. In 1980, Peru returned to democracy but, during that decade, experienced economic problems and the growth of a violent terrorist group.[1] From 1985 to 1990 a populist regime led by President Alan Garcia resulted in a collapse of the Peruvian economy that reached a hyperinflation with an annual rate of 7,000 per cent by the end of his term.

During the 1990s the Peruvian government embarked on economic reforms following the 'Washington consensus'. The main measures aimed to improve competitiveness through reductions in import tariffs, privatizations, and financial reforms including liberalizations of interest rates and free movement of capitals, and the allowing of flexibility in the labour market.

In 2001, Peru elected its first president of indigenous origin, who continued this economic policy, resulting in remarkable macroeconomic results and the outperformance by Peru of the neighbouring countries. One of the most impressive results was a doubling of exports from US$7,000 million in 2000 to US$17,000 million in 2005. This increase was driven mainly by the boom in commodity prices, particularly mineral exports, but also by the growth in production of new mining and hydrocarbon[2] projects, as well as agricultural products, fisheries and textiles. As we can see in Table 18.1, fiscal and monetary policy has achieved steady decline in public sector deficits and low, stable inflation rates. The public sector deficit has come down every year since 2001, mainly due to the increase in revenue from mining taxes.

Table 18.1 Key indicators for the Peruvian economy

	2000	2001	2002	2003	2004	2005	2006e
Annual GDP growth rate	3.0	0.2	5.2	3.9	5.2	6.4	6.6
Inflation rate	3.7	-0.1	1.5	2.5	3.5	1.5	1.5
Overall Public Sector Balance/GDP	-3.3	-2.5	-2.2	-1.7	-1.0	-0.3	0.6
Public Sector Debt	45.7	46.1	46.9	47.5	45.1	37.8	32.8
Exports (FOB); % change p.a.	14	1	10	18	41	35	31
Imports (CIF); % change p.a.	9	-2	3	11	19	23	26
External Current Account/GDP	-2.9	-2.3	-2.0	-1.6	0.0	1.4	1.1

Note: Figures for 2006 involve some estimations
(*Source*: Peruvian Central Bank)

---

1   During the mid-1980s and 1990s a terrorist group called Shining Path (Sendero Luminoso) spread violence. According to the 2003 report of the Truth and Reconciliation Commission, an estimated 69,000 Peruvians died from political violence (<http://www.cverdad.org.pe/ingles/ifinal/index.php>).

2   The largest boost comes from the Camisea gas project that will cost about US$1.6 billion and will enable Peru not only to become self-sufficient in energy but also a net exporter.

Notwithstanding, there are some economic indicators that have not improved. For instance, unemployment and underemployment rates remain very high (approximately 10 per cent and 50 per cent respectively). Also, inequality and poverty remain the greatest problems. Despite the steady improvement in three key social indicators (infant mortality, life expectancy and literacy rates[3]), the national poverty rate dropped only two percentage points between 2002 and 2004, and half the population (51.6 per cent) still lives in conditions of poverty. Income inequality also remains relatively high, with the Gini coefficient having improved slightly from 0.52 to 0.50 during the same period (see World Bank website).

Another challenge in Peru is its centralized political administrative system which has only begun a slow decentralization process since 2000. The economic centralism has been an important limitation for regional development since 54 per cent of GDP is generated by Lima (the capital) and all of the other 23 regions added together produce the remaining 46 per cent. This decentralization process has proved to be very difficult because regional and local governments lack administrative and financial management capacity. Moreover, 'this process has been left somewhat incomplete, halfway between central government agencies, in particular sector ministries, and regional government. Where responsibilities have been transferred, they often lack adequate and predictable funding' (ICMM 2006: 57).

There are two characteristics of Peru that are important for understanding the limited state presence in large portions of the country: its rough geography and its migration patterns. The Andes Cordillera divides the country into three very different geographic and cultural regions: the coast, the Andean highland and the Amazonian jungle. More than half of the extremely poor population resides in the rural highland, though it has less than a quarter of the national population. Indigenous peoples comprise an estimated 15 per cent of the population, but have a poverty rate of 70 per cent. Social services, especially in isolated, conflict-prone regions of Peru's highlands and jungles, are inadequate. Regarding migration patterns, 30 per cent of the total population live in Lima, a result of high rural Andean to urban coastal migration.[4] The urban population has increased from 35.4 per cent of the total in 1940 to 75 per cent in 2004.

A final challenge for Peru is its poor performance in governance indicators, as the country has a legacy of eroded public institutions. The Inter-American Development Bank considers that the Peruvian public administration suffers from poor accountability and inadequate policy coordination. As a result, organizational confusion, duplication of programs, and excessive centralization has restrained its performance (<www.iadb.org>). Governance has only relatively recently been acknowledged to be a key area for the achievement of development. The following

---

3   Infant mortality dropped from 54 to 32 deaths per 1,000 live births between 1990 and 2000, while maternal mortality decreased from 265 to 185 deaths per 100,000 between 1993 and 2000. From 1997 to 2001, there was an important expansion in the access to secondary education. Attendance increased to 74 per cent in urban areas (up 3.5 per cent) and 44 per cent in rural areas (up 7 per cent) (ICMM 2006).

4   Migration from the countryside to big cities, especially Lima, was increased during the decade of terrorism.

table compares Peru's governance performance with two other mining developing countries: Chile and Ghana in 1996 and 2004. We can see that Peru has mixed results comparing both years. Overall, Peruvian governance has better indicators than Ghana but worse than Chile.

Table 18.2 Governance indicators compared, 1996 and 2004

Indicator	Peru		Chile		Ghana	
	1996	2004	1996	2004	1996	2004
Voice and accountability	-0.73	-0.04	0.93	1.09	-0.35	0.39
Political stability	-0.90	-0.68	0.75	0.89	-0.10	-0.06
Government Effectiveness	-0.18	-0.58	1.20	1.27	-0.07	0.17
Regulatory quality	0.65	0.17	1.52	1.62	-0.14	-0.28
Rule of law	-0.35	-0.63	1.26	1.16	-0.12	-0.16
Control of corruption	-0.10	-0.35	1.28	1.44	-0.47	-0.17

Note: A score of -2.5 is the worst, with a score of +2.5 being the best
(*Source*: ICMM 2006)

Consequently, although Peru's economy is growing, there are strong social and political pressures throughout the country which present major challenges for the new government. Peru saw the return of Alan Garcia as president in July 2006, who this time promises to follow the same economic policy as his two predecessors, based on the promotion of private investment,[5] as well as the improvement of social conditions.

The impact of mining on the Peruvian economy

Mining has been a major economic activity since the time of the Inca Empire, especially for gold and silver. Nowadays, as mentioned in the introductory paragraph to this chapter, Peru is an important worldwide provider of minerals and metals. It was considered the most attractive country for mining investment based on its pure mineral potential in the 2005–06 Attractiveness Survey carried

---

5   Peru is expected to sign a free trade agreement with the US in 2007.

out by the Fraser Institute (see the Fraser Institute website, <www.fraserinstitute. org/commerce.web/product_files/Mining20052006.pdf>).

Recent history has seen three distinct periods in terms of economic policy governing the mining sector. After the Second World War, following the world's trend, mining was re-launched when Peru modified its mining law to attract foreign investment. Two big American mining companies arrived in Peru: the Southern Peru Copper Corporation and the Marcona Mining Company. All mining companies were privately owned in the 1950s and 1960s. By the end of the 1960s, a military regime expropriated most of the foreign-owned extractive companies except the Southern Peru Copper Corporation. Mining production increased, particularly of copper, in the 1970s, but in the 1980s state-owned mining companies stagnated because of their limited investment. Stated-owned companies were, during that period, the state's reference for their surrounding communities. For instance, people around a project in the central highland of Peru, La Oroya, received a monthly payment in compensation for the company's contamination (Damonte et al. 2003). Additionally, this privatization led to a reduction in state provision (via these companies) of 'social wages' (for example, subsidized food, health services and education), with consequent negative socio-economic impacts (Warhust 2000).

In the early 1990s, the government, again following the worldwide trend, encouraged private investment and foreign investment in particular, through new laws that we will review later on. Investment in exploration worldwide increased by 90 per cent and quadrupled in Latin America between 1990 and 1997, but the exploration growth in Peru had the impressive rate of 2,000 per cent. Furthermore, when mineral prices fell in 1997, worldwide exploration was significantly reduced yet Peru managed to maintain its share of the total. This explains why Peru has doubled its production now that the prices are high again. Another way of seeing the effect of this mining boom is the fourfold territorial extension of mining activities going from 8 billion hectares in 1992 to 33 million hectares in 2004 (Glave and Kuramoto 2001).

Mining exports, production and taxes have also been steadily growing since 1992. Traditionally, mining exports were 40 per cent of Peruvian exports but since 2003 they are now over half of them. Thus, in 2003, they were 51.1 per cent and in 2004, 54 per cent of the total of Peruvian exports, which amounted $16.5 billion. The contribution of mining to the GDP increased from an average of 5.2 per cent during 1970–2000 to 7 per cent of the GDP in 2004, and one third of the income tax paid to central government came from the mining companies in the same year.

Mining employment indicators also show an improvement. In 2004 there were 81,447 mining workers compared with 42,915 in 1994 (CARE 2005). Moreover, given the Ministry of Energy and Mining's (MEM) estimations that each direct employee generates five indirect jobs, more than 400,000 indirect jobs should have been created. However, 75 per cent of mine workers lived in surrounding communities in 1989 (Long and Roberts 2001), whereas only 16.8 per cent of the direct employees of Antamina[6] presently live near the mine (ICMM 2006).

---

6   Antamina is one of the most important worldwide combined copper/zinc mines, based in Peru and owned by BHP Billiton, Xstrata, Teck-Cominco and Marubeni companies.

Most of the mines in Peru are located in remote and economically depressed areas with low employment rates and poor-quality educational programmes, and the inhabitants are usually of indigenous origin. Consequently, direct and indirect employment opportunities are heavily linked with the level of poverty indicators. It has been suggested that the industry is an important powerhouse sector in Peru, but has this translated into trickle-down economic success?

At odds with the mining sector's positive outcomes, the impact of mining on poverty is disappointing. There has not been an improvement in poor rural areas where mining projects have been located. Further, the correlation between the GDP of mining regions with the UN Human Development Index (HDI) is negative. De Echave and Torres's research on this subject shows that mining regions with mining GDPs higher than 4 per cent of total GDP have a strong inverse correlation coefficient of 0.90 (De Echave and Torres 2005).

Moreover, another study compares the rise in mining production with the increase in the HDI between 1999 and 2003 showing that in Cajamarca and Ancash (where 45 per cent of national mining production is concentrated as the biggest new mines are located here), the HDI grew by around the same as the average of other regions, yet both remain among the poorest areas in the country. Furthermore, that study shows that the best improvement in HDI came from a region where mining output fell by 20 per cent (ICMM 2006).

These figures demonstrate that while companies and the country in general are benefiting from the positive performance of the sector, the areas where the mines are located not only have to face the negative environmental impact, but they do not take advantage of the mining investment. This situation generates frustration which encourages social instability and polarization against the mining industry (Glave and Kuramoto 2001).

As a result, in the last three years, there have been 62 conflicts related to mining operations (Oxfam America 2005). One defining trait of mining stakeholders is the lack of trust among them, which has contributed greatly to conflicts currently present in several mining areas. It is the latest in a historical set of cumulative effects since the start of colonial times, when Andean people were forced to work in mines for the Spanish conquistadors, and the existence of several environmental liabilities in more recent times explains the stakeholders' mistrust.

The Peruvian mining industry

The Peruvian mining industry consists of around 1,000 large,[7] medium and small/artisanal mining companies and three smelting and refinery companies. Large mining companies are mainly owned by foreign multinational mining companies, while most of the medium and small companies have Peruvian owners. Table 18.3 summarizes the main mining projects run by these companies at different levels of development.

---

7   Large companies are classified as producing more than 5,001 metric tonnes per day, medium ones 351–5,000 metric tonnes, and small ones less than 351 metric tonnes or having no more than 2,000 hectares of production area.

Table 18.3 Stages of industrial development in the Peruvian mining industry

1. Mining companies at exploration stage

During the 1990s, exploration was an activity principally carried out by 'junior' companies (currently there are around 60 of these, mainly Canadian[1]). However, today large companies (previously focused on mining production), medium-sized (Peruvian) companies and small mining operators are all engaged in exploration. There are three big exploratory projects by large companies: Toromocho, La Granja and Las Bambas. The last two have been recently given in option to worldwide leader companies such as Rio Tinto and Xstrata, respectively. These two projects, as well as Alto Chicama, owned by the Canadian Barrick Gold Company, have just started production and have included a significant community participation process since the start of the exploration stage. This is regarded as the new standard for community engagement and development. Another important project at exploration level is Rio Blanco, owned by the junior British company Monterrico Metals. This project has been facing opposition from its surrounding communities during the last two years. There is also an important gold project under construction, Cerro Corona owned by South African company Gold Fields, which is the world's fourth largest producer of gold.

2. Mining companies at production stage

Large-scale mining operations are generally run by foreign companies and one of them, Yanacocha, is a partnership between an American company (Newmont) and the most important Peruvian mining group: Buenaventura. Companies that have currently operations in production[2] are Barrick Gold, Phelps Dodge, BHP-Billiton, Noranda, Teck-Cominco, Marubeni, Glencore, Goldsfield, Xstrata, Grupo Mexico, Doe Run and Shougang. Large-scale Peruvian-owned companies are Cia. Minas Buenaventura, Minsur, Volcan Mining, Atacocha, Hochschild group and Milpo Mining Co. Most of the large mines in Peru have become worldwide leader producers[3] of gold and copper. Peruvian-owned companies have also opened mines in other countries. For instance, Milpo owns a mine in Chile, Hochschild has investments in Chile, Mexico and Argentina; and Benavides has been exploring in Ecuador.

Medium-scale mines are owned mainly by Peruvian companies and their production primarily comes from underground mines. These companies have fewer resources and capacity to operate in a manner compatible with environmental standards, and therefore their activities can be very damaging and polluting. However, they are less conflict-prone than large companies.

Small and mining artisans is a heterogeneous group of around 50,000 informal miners who mainly exploit gold with a very rudimentary technology, polluting the environment and putting their health at risk. Many of these small miners exploit minerals in the territories of medium or large mines, becoming stakeholders of the larger mining companies.

3. Smelting and refinery companies

There are currently three smelters and refineries in the country: The smelter and refinery at La Oroya (which processes copper, lead, zinc, silver, gold and other minerals). It is now owned by Doe Run. The zinc refinery in Cajamarquilla, located near Lima, privatized in 1995 in a sale to Teck-Cominco and Marubeni; and the copper smelter at Ilo (in southern Peru) belongs to the Southern Peru Copper Corporation. The smelters at La Oroya and Ilo are known to have had serious past and ongoing environmental problems.

Notes to Table 18.3

[1] <http://www.cooperaccion.org.pe/modulo/boletin>
[2] Most of these companies start investing in Peru after 1992, with the exception of Southern which has been working there since 1958. Southern was previously owned by the American Asarco and sold to Grupo México in 1999.
[3] Antamina is the third biggest mine in the world and the biggest combined mine for copper and zinc. Yanacocha is the biggest gold mine in Latin America and the second biggest in the world.

During the last three years, mining companies' profits have been steadily growing. Estimation of profits shows that among the most profitable companies, two are Peruvian-owned. Volcan had a profit growth rate of 1,200 per cent, Atacocha 150 per cent and Cerro Verde – owned by Phelps Dodge – 130 per cent in 2005. In absolute values, Southern Peru was the company with most profits, US$2,050 million, followed by Cerro Verde with US$536 million, Buenaventura with US$453 million, and MINSUR with US$153 millions. In 2007, there is a prediction that there will be a slight fall in mineral prices, yet mining companies will continue to be the most profitable industry in Peru (CooperAcción 2006).

The main stakeholders in mining

Peruvian mining companies, as their worldwide peers, have established a special relationship with a varied group of stakeholders.[8] However, the big impact on the environment and on the communities where mines are located makes both elements into prominent stakeholders. Government, at national, regional and local levels, has also had similar importance for the industry, not only because of their regulating control but also because they could facilitate or obstruct the relationship between companies and the other stakeholders. Additionally, Peruvian and international NGOs have also played an active role in compensating for the asymmetry of power between the communities and companies.

Amongst the different governmental institutions with mining responsibilities, the Ministry of Mining and Energy (MEM) is the most important. Since the 1990s, MEM received the responsibilities for promoting private investment and regulating and controlling the mining policy, including its environmental impact. It was converted in a 'one stop window' which has been dealing with all mining procedures. We move on now to analyse the extensive mining regulation put in

---

8   Mineral and metals end-clients have little influence on mining management decisions about sustainable development because the final individual customers 'are eight steps removed from the ... mining companies' (Diamond 2005: 467), making it impossible to penalize or boycott non-responsible companies. However, a good example of customer power was when Tiffany & Co., the jewellery company, decided to choose Rio Tinto, a responsible company, as its gold company providers when they faced protesters about cyanide release (Diamond 2005).

place by the national governmental institutions in order to comply with both responsibilities.

The legal framework of the mining industry

The integration of sustainability into the legal framework has been a challenging process for Peru because it has had to reconcile this process with fierce competition from other countries for attracting funds for mining (Bastida 2002; World Bank 2005). Policy-makers in Peru started the process by attracting important amounts of investment but, as we have seen, by the end of the decade it was clear that promoting investment was not enough to guarantee positive social and economic development. Consequently, new command and control environmental and social regulations have been passed throughout the last 15 years. Peruvian legislation is thus considered to be leading the process of integrating a sustainable development approach in Latin America (Bastida 2005).

Before turning to the mining legislation, it is also important to mention that the management of the transfer of resources from central government to regional and local authorities, among them the taxes paid by mining companies, has been heavily affected by decentralization regulations. The Ministry of Finance (law 28056) requires the approval of concerted development plans and participative budgets by regional and local levels before any transfer is done. In addition, a system (SNIP) was set up to ensure the sustainability of projects and this has established a strict set of rules for projects before their authorization.

Promoting mining investment

The current mining legislation is part of the policies to promote private investment established in 1991. This legislation – Legislative Decree 708 and 674 – created a regime of legal stability for foreign investment that eliminated earlier restrictions on foreign ownership and control of assets. In 1992, the General Mineral Law created an administrative system offering attractive tax terms, a convertible current regime and the freedom to repatriate earnings. Net earnings became the basis of central government taxation and many of the contracts contained stability clauses for periods of 10 to 15 years.[9]

Three new instruments for environmental control were introduced: the Environmental Impact Assessment (EIA) for the new operations, the programme for Environmental Management Adaptation Plans (PAMA) and the Environmental Auditing. Before these laws were passed, mining companies, whether private or state owned, and even foreign mining companies that had rigorous environmental and social performance in their countries of origin, failed to be proactive in taking measures to ensure good environmental management (World Bank 2005). This is

---

9   Legal stability was deemed very important to attract investment since developing countries tend to have very unstable governments and rules.

the reason for the existence of around 800 mining liabilities which fuel the negative perception about mining.

Environmental and social regulations

Sustainable development regulations affecting the whole mining life cycle are analysed in this section.

Mining concession Since 2003, before any company starts exploration, it is required to make a stated commitment (compromiso previo) under Decree 42-2003 that includes the following pledge:

1. To aim for environmental excellence.
2. To respect local institutions' cultures.
3. To keep continuous and appropriate communication with the local and regional authorities by providing information about their mining operations.
4. To work together with the area residents affected by the mining operations in the creation of an office for local development if the mining project is implemented. For this purpose, studies should be performed to contribute to the creation of local development opportunities which should continue even after the completion of the mining operations.
5. To prefer and encourage local employment providing the required training opportunities.
6. To prefer local services and goods.

This decree is very important because it aims to tackle some of the reasons for mining conflicts. The commitment to preferentially hire local people and buy local goods and services is probably the most important mechanism by which wealth 'trickles down'. The case of Chile's success in reducing poverty in mining areas is explained by consumption linkages at local level[10] (ICMM 2006).

Another regulation relevant to the mining concession stage is Law 26570, passed in 1996, that approved a Servidumbre Minera (Mining Easement/Covenant) which, in the case that an agreement is not reached between company and land owner, entitles the government to pay an amount of compensation and give the company the right to use the land for a determined number of years under certain conditions. According to Peruvian legal framework the landowners only own superficial lands but the state is the owner of the ground.

The exploration stage This has been specifically regulated by D.S.38 since 1998, including the requirement of a limited environmental impact assessment before the start of exploration. This regulation also defines that before beginning exploration

---

10   Chile does not have any mechanism to transfer taxes to mining areas equivalent to the Peruvian Canon Minero.

a previous agreement with the superficial land owner or the Servidumbre Minera process had to be finished.

This limited EIA regulation does not require an analysis of the potential impact on the affected stakeholders. However, while exploration could present a small environmental risk, the social impact is very significant. Some companies at exploration level, since they are not sure if the investment is going to be profitable, are not very keen to make important investment in building a good relationship with those living in the vicinity.

In Peru, bad experiences of exploratory operations have made big impacts on conflicts. Tambogrande's concession to the junior Canadian Manhattan Mineral is an emblematic case because it illustrates how mismanagement of community relationships at exploration level can hold up further development of the project. Tambogrande is an agricultural town located in Piura, a region which is not a traditional mining area. In 1989, a concession without prior consultation with Tambogrande's inhabitants was granted. However, the project would require the relocation of about one fourth of the town residents, around 8,000 people. A feasibility study and an environmental impact statement (EIS) which led to a referendum were in the process. However, the referendum showed that 93 per cent of the community rejected the mine development. This opposition was based upon fears by local inhabitants of water pollution and damage to their crops and to the tropical dry forest ecosystem, and that this would result in a loss of agricultural jobs leading to widespread poverty within the region. In December 2003, the MEM rejected the Manhattan Company's Tambogrande mine development proposal. Several NGOs and the Church were involved in supporting community claims.

The development stage This can start after a complete EIA is approved, the superficial lands are acquired, right to road access, source of energy, mineral process plant, and tailing impoundments are obtained.

The Environment Impact Assessment (EIA)'s current regulation aiming to improve participation of the affected community was passed in 2002. Establishment of workshops in the mining area, previous information with the community, an EIA public hearing and inclusion of comments in the EIA are among the changes introduced in this regulation.

Regarding the assessment of the social impact, which has to be part of the EIA, there is no specific regulation for its management. However, there is a non-binding *Guideline* for the evaluation of the social impact of the mining, hydrocarbon and energy projects. The guide recommends:

* establishing a code of conduct for employees, contractors and subcontractors;
* a local employment policy;
* a transparent and informed relationship with the identified groups of interest;
* a Community Relation Plan containing a CSR committed vision and mission;

- for large projects, the creation of a community relations manager;
- a preventive and consultative process of impact management;
- an employees' cultural awareness programme;
- an alliance with other institutions;
- a sustainable and market-oriented development programs;
- a volunteering policy among employees; and finally
- the setting of a limit to the company funds in order to share responsibility for the project.

Production stage The environmental dimension is regulated by the following set of laws: the Environmental Management and Adaptation Plans (PAMA), Quality Standards and Maximum Permissible Levels of Liquid Effluents (RM 011-96), Levels of Gas Emissions by Metallurgical Mining Activity (RM 315-96) and the Mining Control Law (Law 27474).

The Environmental Management Adaptation Plan (PAMA) aims to introduce or to elevate the environmental standards of projects already in production. The objective of the PAMA was to prevent, reduce or eliminate emissions in the atmosphere and water bodies and to comply with the maximum permissible levels established by law within an agreed timetable of actions. Current maximum permissible levels (MPLs) for pollutants and quality standards for the mining sector are higher than the standard set by the World Health Organizations (WHO) and Canada, as we can see in Table 18.4.

Table 18.4 Ambient standards for particulate matter

Source	Country	Pollutant	Guideline (ug/m3)	Average time
Env. Canada	Canada	TSP[1]	120–400	24-hour
WHO	For USA	TSP	260	average
Gov. of Peru	Peru	TSP	350	24-hour max. 24-hour average
WHO	For EU	TSP	80	Annual
WHO	For USA	TSP	75	Annual
Env. Canada	Canada	TSP	60	Annual (max desirable)
Env. Canada	Canada	TSP	70	Annual (max acceptable)
Gov. of Peru	Peru	TSP	150	Annual

(*Source*: SENES Consultants Limited, cited in World Bank 2005)
[1] Total suspended particles (TSP) can lead to respiratory diseases and can cause cancer; they can also be corrosive and harmful to vegetation.

As of June 2004, there were 11 mining projects that failed to comply with their PAMA requirements. The smelting operation at La Oroya (by Doe Run Peru) is another symbolic case which shows the limitations in the application of the PAMA. This company has made limited investments to meet emissions standards agreed in the PAMA, and thus a request for extension was filed with MEM to postpone compliance with this agreement to a later date:

> *Many workers, in fear of losing their jobs, began protesting after Doe Run Peru, claiming financial difficulties, threatened with shutting down operations if its PAMA was not extended. Despite high levels of contamination,[11] the communities supported Doe Run's petition to extend the PAMA. In response to the political pressures MEM extended the PAMA's compliance period (World Bank 2005: 27).*

Closure stage Peru is one of the few Latin American countries that have regulated this mining phase. Two laws are relevant: the Mine Closure Law (Law 28090) approved in 2003 and the Law for Environmental Legacies of Mining Activities (Law 28271) in 2004.

Mine closure regulation represented a radical change in the logic of Peruvian environmental legislation. Mine closure is no longer seen as a measure taken at the final stage of the production cycle but as an important component in the design of the project (De la Puente 2005). This plan and the Mining Legacy closure plan have adopted a participative approach. In addition, the provision of financial guarantee throughout the mining life of the project is required.

The Law for Environmental Legacies is another crucial piece of legislation because even with efforts by current mining companies to maintain cleaner operations, these liabilities are a constant reminder of the damage of previous bad mining management. According to this regulation, MEM has the responsibility of identifying the companies responsible for the legacies. For 'orphan' sites, where no former owner or operator can be identified, the government becomes responsible for the cleaning up and rehabilitating, which is estimated to cost around US$800 million (see MEM website).

As this is the last environmental legislation approved by the previous government, it shows a different approach from earlier legislation. Firstly, it includes rules to promote voluntary remediation[12] by NGOs, civil society organizations or companies other than the responsible one, creating conservational areas for tourism, cultural, recreational or sport purposes. Secondly, it promotes citizen participation in remedial, monitoring and control measures. Thirdly, it includes new financial

---

11   La Oroya has been placed fifth in the ranking of the most polluted cities in the world by the Blacksmith Institute (<www.blacksmithinstitute.org>).

12   It is the first time that a piece of mining legislation has include a more incentivizing approach than the traditional command and control approach.

mechanisms for the funding of FONAM,[13] such as issuing social environmental responsibility bonds, and a debt exchange mechanism. Fourthly, it gives roles to other governmental institutions such as PROINVERSIÓN and FONAM.

As a result a non-profit group called Avancemos Juntos, composed of mining businessmen, ex-government officials, and representatives of civil society and NGOs, was formed in May 2004 to address mining liability management. The World Bank believes that this initiative could eventually evolve into a centre of technical expertise for addressing environmental legacies.

Before turning to analyse the legislation regulating the mechanism for transferring resources to the mining areas, it is important to highlight the contrast between the numerous environmental regulations and the few norms regarding the social area.

Canon Minero and Mining Royalty laws

There are two mechanisms for the transfer of taxes from central government to the mining regions: the Canon Minero law (Law 27506) approved in 2001 and the Mining Royalty law passed in 2004.

Canon Minero Fifty per cent of the funds collected through corporate income tax from the extractives industries are transferred by central government to subnational governments. This amount of money from mines' tax is called the Canon Minero. Before 2002, the Canon Minero was 20 per cent of corporate income tax. It was increased as a result of intensive lobbying to members of the congress by mining-affected communities and mining companies (ICMM 2006). The remaining 50 per cent of income taxes and other taxes paid by mining companies are spent according to the central government's priorities. For reasons already explained, mining companies in fact only paid 2 per cent of their exports in taxes in 2002 and 2003. However, in the last three years the Canon Minero has increased spectacularly due to the current high level of exports.

The Canon Minero system for transferring funds to regional and local governments has been criticized by NGOs and companies. First, it takes 18 months for the funds to be allocated after the company pays the taxes. Secondly, the subnational authorities have been unable to present projects with the level of standard set by the Ministry of Finance (SNIP). Thirdly, there have been several projects that show inefficient investment choices. Research by the NGO Ciudadanos al Dia (CAD) shows that with the Canon's funds some municipalities built large buildings for their offices instead of prioritizing investment to address the urgent poverty of those areas. However, CAD also mentions that there are good projects, such as the creation of a rubbish recycling plant created by the district municipality of a town called Carhuaz that receives Canon Minero from Antamina and Pierina mines.

---

13   FONAM is a public institution that promotes public and private investment in environmental programmes.

Mining Royalty law This created a new tax paid by companies according to their size, between 1 per cent and 3 per cent on the value of the concentrate or its equivalent. The total of this payment goes to the regions according to the following scheme: 20 per cent to the district where the mine is located, 20 per cent to the province where the mine is located, 40 per cent to all the other Peruvian municipalities, 15 per cent to regional governments, and 5 per cent to the universities of the region where the mine is located. Thus, Mining Royalty offers a more stable source of revenue than the Canon. Its approval and adoption has been amid much controversy.

Legislation regulating other stakeholders There is a regulation (D.L.892), passed in 1996, that addresses the right of mining employees to participate in 8 per cent of the company's profits. Very recently, this right has been extended to workers under contractors. Another regulation created a Register of Mining Suppliers in 2001.

This section shows that the government has been increasingly regulating diverse areas. Some stakeholders, though, believe that there is still room for improvement. For instance, the preparation of sustainable reports has not been accompanied by reporting guidelines. More importantly, legislation has had a limited role in promoting CSR. A sustainable development approach has been adopted almost a decade after the first laws were passed, as we will see in next section.

An evaluation of CSR's progress in mining

Corporate social responsibility in Peru started as a concept in the late 1990s but it is only since 2002 that CSR has 'taken off' and now many of the big companies – Peruvian and foreign-owned – have embedded the notion into their corporate strategy. Some business leaders see CSR as a way to share the responsibility for the country's development and to help to avoid 'the risk that centralism and state paternalism may take hold again'(quote of Rafael Villegas, Peruvian businessman, in Durand 2005). Others see doing CSR as 'giving up under pressure' and are very keen to point out its voluntary nature (Durand 2005).

Corporate responsibility programmes for the mining companies are heavily influenced by the phases of the projects, their magnitude, their location in a traditional mining zone or in a non-mining area, and the strategy and level of commitment of each company on how to face its community relations and its environmental management system.

Large and medium-sized mining companies have gradually included environmental programmes and community development programmes within their operations during the last six years. Mining companies have made a higher rate of social investment than other sectors. In 2000, it is estimated that the investment in social programmes was US$30 million and US$16 million in development programmes. Yanacocha alone reported US$26 million in rural social programmes between 1993 and 2002 (Polo 2004).

Even though there are still different levels in the integration of sustainable development as the CSR strategy for the sector, community programmes have been changing from a paternalistic approach to one of community development with a sustainable development angle. Moreover, large Peruvian mining companies have been progressively adapting new standards in parallel to the worldwide mining industry. Yanacocha[14] was the first large new mine with a modern approach, as well as Antamina which started production in 2001 and Pierina in 2000. Southern Peru has also recently adopted sustainable development in its strategy.

In order to analyse the content of the CSR programmes within the main Peruvian-based mining companies, Table 18.5 shows comparative information of the CSR programmes of 19 medium and large companies. The table includes the main components of the guideline for EIA's social dimension that were detailed in the previous section of this chapter and are based on information in the public domain[15] provided on their websites and sustainability reports.

The first finding is that CSR is mentioned or implied in at least the communication level in all companies with the exception of Shougang. We can see that Yanacocha and Antamina stand out as the companies with the most comprehensive CSR programme: both have an important Foundation to run their sustainable development programmes. In the case of Antamina, the community relations office manages the areas directly affected by the operation and its foundation works mainly with wider areas of influence (ICMM 2006). Among the modern mines, Pierina mine is the only one that does not have its own website. The information in the table is based on Pierina's information included in the Sustainability Report of the owner of that mine, Canadian Barrick Gold.

However, and as is the case with the worldwide mining industry, among large companies there are still some with little commitment or no commitment at all about the environment and social impacts of their projects based on the information placed on their website. For instance, the American company Doe Run, who attracted much attention because its request for postponing the deadline of the construction of a sulphuric acid plant as a part of its obligations set out by its PAMA, shows incomplete and poor quality information about its social programmes.[16] In fact, there is no information on who the beneficiaries of their programmes are or how much in financial terms it is giving to social or environmental concerns.

Furthermore, only Yanacocha, Antamina, Tintaya, Alto Chicama, Pierina, Southern, Rio Tinto (La Granja) and Xstrata (Las Bambas) – all foreign-owned – have achieved the last step in designing their sustainable development strategy, according to the criteria of Damonte et al. (2003). These authors believe that only if a company has established their social and environmental programmes through a participative/consultative and tri-partnership methods can it be said that they have an sustainable development strategy.

---

14   Started its operation in 1993.
15   Information without an X means that information was not available.
16   <http://www.doerun.com/uploadfile/PeruProgressupdate-social.pdf>

Table 18.5 Comparison of CSR programmes of 19 major companies in Peru

Company	Foundation	Code of Conduct	CSR/community rel. manager	CSR in vision and mission	Governance programme	Integrated to a development plan	Local hire programme	Participative/consultative process	Volunteering programme	Grievance system	Sustainability report	Supplier policy and training	Programme previous land owners	Training on econ. sustainability activities	Infrastructure provisions	Education programme	Health programmes	Local government capacity building	Regional government capacity building	Health and safety programmes	Training for employees	Partnerships (NGOs and gov.)	Environmental certification ISO 14001	Participative monitoring system	Emergency provision	Internal communication systems	Employees' code of conduct with community	External communication system	Employees' training in co. philosophy	Visitor programme	Donations	Information in native language	Commitment to Peru's development
Yanacocha	×	×	×	×	×		×	×	×	×	×	×	×	×	×	×	×	×	×	×	×	×		×		×		×		×	×		
Antamina	×	×	×		×	×	×	×	×	×	×			×		×	×			×	×		×	×	×				×			×	×
Southern	×	×			×	×	×				×	×		×	×	×	×			×	×	×			×			×			×		
Tintaya	×	×					×	×							×	×	×					×		×									
Cerro Verde																							×										
Pierina		×		×			×	×				×		×	×	×	×			×	×		×		×						×		
La Oroya																×	×						×								×		
Alto Chicama																×																	
Milpo		×			×	×	×	×						×	×	×	×			×	×	×	×								×		
Cia. Buenaventura			×	×	×									×	×	×	×				×	×	×		×						×		
Minsur														×	×							×	×										
Volcan										×													×										
Atacocha					×		×								×						×										×		
El Brocal		×	×	×	×	×	×	×			×	×		×	×	×	×				×		×	×							×		
Shougang																																	
Las Bambas		×	×			×	×	×			×	×		×		×	×			×	×	×		×						×		×	
La Granja		×														×	×				×							×	×				
La Poderosa				×											×																		×
MARSA															×	×	×														×		

Regarding the CSR of big Peruvian-owned companies, there are three points worth mentioning. First, they have all received ISO 14001 accreditation in the last three years, while Yanacocha does not have that certification[17] (Instituto de Seguridad Minera 2006). Secondly, while their websites do not include their sustainability reports, they are legally obligated to submit one to the MEM.[18] Thirdly, they include their corporate governance report in their annual report. Corporate governance reports are also a relatively new obligation for companies listed in the Lima Stock Exchange.

The main principles in CSR programmes within the mining industry are: transparency, accountability, proactivity and sustainability. Transparency is an area that needs a lot of improvement in the mining sector in Peru. Even though most of the companies have websites, three large foreign-owned companies already in production stage do not have websites: Cerro Verde, Alto Chicama and Pierina. In addition, as I have already mentioned, many of them do not include their sustainability reports on their website. Cerro Corona, which is at its construction stage, does not have a website.

Gold Fields' 2006 sustainability report announced that next year's report will include this information. However, Xstrata and Antamina appear to be the best of the class in terms of transparency. For instance, Xstrata's project Las Bambas, which as yet is in an exploratory stage, already has a sustainability report on their website. Antamina, on the other hand, always reports voluntarily when the maximum level of pollutions[19] is surpassed.

For the purpose of this article, accountability is as defined by AccountAbility:[20]

> *An organisation can be considered as accountable when it accounts to its stakeholders regarding material issues (transparency), responds to stakeholders regarding these issues (responsiveness) on an ongoing basis, and complies with standards to which it is voluntarily committed, and with rules and regulations that it must comply with for statutory reasons (compliance) (<www.accountability.net>, 10).*

Three of the CSR components included in Table 18.5 show responsiveness: grievance system, participatory monitoring programme and consultative methods. Given the high level of conflict in Peru, instituting a grievance system has become one of the most important recommendations made by ICMM (see ICCM website at <www.icmm.org>) but again, Yanacocha and Antamina are the only companies to have these three programmes. No information is available about such systems in any other company.

---

17 Information on ISO14001 certification was not included on its website.
18 The sustainability reports were not available on the MEM website.
19 Information given by the former CSR Minera Majaz.
20 'AccountAbility promotes accountability innovations that advance responsible business practices, and the broader accountability of civil society and public organizations' (AccountAbility website at <www.accountability21.net>).

Proactivity is probably best evaluated by their day-to-day management; however, emergency programmes, health and safety policy and participative/consultative methods are important ways to prevent problems happening. All the companies that describe their problem-solving method as a consultative/participative one, as we saw before, are foreign-owned.

The concept of sustainability is primarily linked to programmes that will be sustained when the mine closes. This is achieved when programmes increase social and human capital. The main activities that improve sustainability will be: local employment policy, local supplier policy and training, training on other economic sustainable activities, integration with a development plan, local and regional capacity-building programmes, training for employees, environmental certification and work in partnerships. Yanacocha, Antamina, Tintaya, Pierina, Xstrata and Southern have given priority to the two first components of these programmes.[21] For instance, Southern hires more than half of its personnel (52.75 per cent) from the near-by city – Moquegua – which represents 1,952 people. In contrast, Atacocha has decreased its local purchasing by 50 per cent between 2002 and 2004. The same companies have only 385 (17 per cent) direct employees and 1,869 (83 per cent) are employed through contractors.

However, most of the CSR programmes have not necessarily been focused on building social and human capital. Between 1990 and 2000, mining companies invested around US$145 million in infrastructure (Polo 2004). In fact, the majority have supported rehabilitation of roads (93.3 per cent), support to local activities (70 per cent), support to local sports (66.7 per cent), provision of electricity (63.3 per cent), donation of books (60 per cent), among others (Caravedo 1998, cited in World Bank 2005).

Sustainability of the programmes is also shown by the creation of foundations as Yanacocha, Antamina and Tintaya did. Foundations are seen as a way of establishing a long-term commitment to communities: 'by delinking the finances of the corporate foundation from the donor company, the foundation provides guaranteed financial support to communities irrespective of the financial position of the company or mining site' (Warhurst 2000: 13). It also transcends the lifetime of the mine. A foundation has two additional advantages over a company department: it can solicit funds from other sources and it allows the integration of community participation because normally it is represented by members of the board.

Finally, I wanted to evaluate the level of priority given to CSR in the companies' strategy measured by the presence of four items: a Code of Conduct, CSR in its vision and mission, a CSR manager and a governance programme. The results are mixed. A Code of Conduct was present in 9 out of the 19 companies. However, only four companies, Yanacocha, Pierina, Cia. Buenaventura and El Brocal, included CSR in their mission statement and vision. In contrast, only at the Xstrata website was the project's organizational structure found, which shows that the community

---

21 To prioritize local employees and local supplier policies is part of the pledge that all mining companies have to make when they initiate exploration activities. See the section on legislation.

relations manager directly reports to the general manager. There was no information on the level of influence of CSR managers in Milpo and Antamina.

Conclusion

The mining industry has always been one of the most dynamic sectors of the Peruvian economy. Its promotion through privatization and favourable tax rules, combined with high prices in the early 1990s, produced an important improvement in macroeconomic indicators. Nonetheless, this did not translate into a reduction of poverty. Companies, attracted by Peruvian mineral potential and the new rules, have been facing several conflicts.

The government responded with important command and control legislation aiming to improve the economic impact and reduce the negative social and environmental impact. The introduction of a requirement for prioritizing local employment and suppliers, for better participation of communities in the EIAs, for the formulation of mine closing plans, the monitoring of mining environmental impacts, and finally the management of mining liabilities shows a great commitment to addressing the sustainability of mining. However, amid a lack of trust in the institutional framework, these changes have proved to be insufficient for real progress in sustainable development.

In this scenario, the adoption of a CSR angle by Peruvian mining companies has already been an important progress. As this article shows, all companies under analysis except Shougang have included CSR as part of their business strategy.

However, there are still different levels of commitment. Even Yanacocha and Antamina, which have more comprehensive CSR programmes than the rest, show a need for improvement in order to reach worldwide standards in the four basic CSR principles: transparency, accountability, sustainability and proactivity. For instance, 20 per cent of the companies under analysis produced a sustainability report, compared to 59 per cent by international mining companies as a whole (KPMG 2006).

Improving transparency, accountability through participative methods and having a proactive approach to the problems will improve the level of stakeholders' trust, which is much needed in today's highly conflictive situation in the Peruvian mining sector.

In addition, Peruvian mining companies have to raise their commitment to increasing social and human capital through local employment, using local suppliers and training mining area residents in other economically sustainable activities to ensure a more sustainable impact that transcends the lifetime of the mines.

In conclusion, in Peru, as in most of the developing countries with a weak governance framework, corporate social responsibility managers still have a complex and challenging pending task which is greater than that of their colleagues in the developed world. The CSR agenda has been moving forward, but the progress has not yet been enough to remove the risk of backward movement.

References

AccountAbility (2005), *AA1000 Stakeholder Engagement Standard*, London: AccountAbility.

Bastida E. (2005), 'Mining law and policy in Latin America. Historical perspectives and current trends', a presentation made at the conference *Mining in Latin America* at Canning House, London: Canning House.

Bastida, E. (2002), *Integrating Sustainability into Legal Frameworks for Mining in Some Selected Latin American Countries*, MMSD no.120, London: MMSD.

CARE (Christian Action Research and Education) (2006), *Memoria 2005*, Lima: CARE.

CooperAcción (2006), *Boletin Minero No. 90*, Lima (Peru), October, at <www.cooperaccion.org.pe/modulo/boletin/boletin_90.php>.

Damonte G., Leon, C. and Davila, B. (2003), *Estudio Nacional Peruano*, Actividades de Desarrollo Comunitario de Empresas Mineras y de Explotacion de Recursos Naturales en America Latina y el Caribe, Ottawa/New York: IDRC/Ford Foundation.

De Echave, J. and Torres, V. (2005), *Hacia una estimacion de los efectos de la Actividad Minera en los Indices de Pobreza en el Peru*, Lima: CooperAcción.

De la Puente, L. (2005), 'La evaluación ambiental previa: consideraciones' in *Entorno de los proyectos mineros y de hidrocarburos*, Revista de Derecho Minero y Petrólero no. 60, Lima: Instituto de Derecho de Minería, Petróleo y Energía.

Diamond, J. (2005), *Collapse: How Societies Choose to Fail or Succeed*, New York: Viking.

Durand, F. (2005), 'Business and civil society: *grupos* and corporate social responsibility', in C. Sanborn and F. Portocarrero (eds), *Philanthropy and Social Change in Latin America*, Cambridge MA: Harvard University Press, David Rockefeller Centre for Latin American Studies.

Glave, M. and Kuramoto J. (2001), 'Minería, minerales y desarrollo sustentable en Perú', Chapter 8 of *Minería, Minerales y Desarrollo Sustentable en América del Sur*, Lima: MMSD/GRADE. (MMSD, or Mining, Minerals and Sustainable Development, in the research programme of the Global Mining Initiative.)

International Council on Mining and Metals (ICMM) (2006), *Using Mineral Resource Endowment to Foster Sustainable Development: Synthesis Report of Four Country Cases*, London: Instituto de Estudios Peruanos (IEP).

Instituto de Seguridad Minera (2006), *Revista de Seguridad Minera*, no. 48, August, Lima: Institutio de Seguridad Minera.

KPMG (2006), 'Global Mining Reporting Survey', at <www.kpmg>.

Long, N. and Roberts, B.(2001), *Mineros, Campesinos y Empresarios en la Sierra Central del Perú*, Lima: IEP.

Matthews, M., Pearce, R. and Chapman, J. (2004), *Sustainability Reporting by the Mining Industry Compared with the Requirements of the GRI*, London.

Ministry of Energy and Mining, Peru (MEM) (2005), 'Producción minera', in *Anuario minero del Perú 2004*, Lima: MEM.

Oxfam America (2005), 'Peru searches for solutions to mining conflicts', press release, 31 August, Washington DC.

Polo, C. (2004), *'Discurso a los Directores del Banco Mundial del Viceministro Polo'*. February, Lima.

Warhurst, A.(2000), *Private Sector Development Institutions: A Review of Drivers and Practice*, Mining and Energy Research Network, Corporate Citizenship Unit, Warwick Business School, University of Warwick.

World Bank (2005), *Wealth and Sustainability: The Environmental and Social Dimensions of the Mining Sector in Peru*, World Bank Peru Country Management Unit, 33545 v.2.

Taxation and Fiscal Evasion: A Perspective on Corporate Social Responsibility

Fátima David and Rute Abreu[1]

Introduction

The role played by the state in the economy has been object of intense debate, because democracy and popular participation though free and fair elections oblige the government of each country around the world to attempt to accomplish a stable economic policy free from all the phenomena of distortions, corruption, evasion and fraud, while the appropriate legal and practical measures must be taken. Indeed, taxation and fiscal evasion represents a major problem that faces policy-makers (Kaplan et al. 1988).

Thus, governments try to develop and implement taxation policies that represent an efficient national instrument of solidarity in society, with the main objective of economic growth that is sustainable. But these policies are also directly linked to economic changes, technological improvements and social traditions.

In effect, there is no authentic and stable democratic system without social justice and where taxes are not destined, initially, to obtain financial support for the satisfaction of citizens' needs throughout society. They constitute, also, a fundamental vehicle for the redistribution of the wealth and the promotion of equality between citizens. But these citizens, for their part, either individually or collectively, must be recognized, respected and furthered, together as a society.

Also, society demands that individual citizens, firms and intermediate organizations should be effectively protected by law whenever they have rights to be exercised or obligations to be fulfilled. Thus, it is morally wrong that an individual citizen or a firm should receive the benefits of the state without paying taxes or, at worst, if they promote the use and abuse of evasion for not paying taxes.

---

1   The authors are grateful for helpful comments made by David Crowther, and for the financial support of Portugal's Fundação para a Ciência e Tecnologia. The ideas expressed are those of the authors and should not be attributed to any organization.

For example, income tax evasion consists of taxable income that is not reported or that is underreported to the government tax collection authority (Cebula and Saadatmand 2005). Unfortunately, fiscal evasion and fraud have become a current practice for firms to decrease their payments to the state, being caused by different factors which are more immediate:

- politicized (such as the rise in the burden of taxes and social security contributions; and the increase of regulation, especially of labour markets)
- economic (for example, unemployment; and the decline of civic virtue and loyalty towards public institutions)
- psychological (such as the forced reduction of weekly working time and earlier retirement); and
- technical (for example, a lack of checks in the system, or inefficient controls).

Consequently, powerful institutions such as the European Union (EU), the United Nations (UN) and the Organization for Economic Cooperation and Development (OECD) have an enormous potential at levels of public policy to push their approaches on social responsibility by using structures, human resources, legal and voluntary frameworks in accordance with the spirit and letter of the law, and other regulations. Also, at an EU level (CE, 2006: 1), the basic idea is that institutions:

> ... therefore have the duty to guarantee the best use of their money and in particular to fight as effectively as possible against fraud. This is the reason for which the protection of the financial interests of the Community has become one of the major priorities for the European Institutions. This covers activities concerning the detection and monitoring of frauds in the customs field, misappropriation of subsidies and tax evasion, insofar as the Community budget is affected by it, as well as the fight against corruption and any other illegal activity harmful to the financial interests of the Community.

Indeed, the most controversial issue is the fiscal evasion and fraud as a reality that economists, managers and policy-makers are confronted with and that have assumed a growing dimension and new and sophisticated forms (see Pereira 2005).[2] All these dimensions and forms are combined with a decline in of the 'tax moral' and in addition there are some conceptual difficulties with this behaviour.

The struggle against fiscal evasion and fraud is, on one side, a truly private obligation, because those who practise evasion and fraud infringe the fundamental bases of equality, legality, just division of revenue and wealth, loyal competition, social responsibility and fiscal responsibility. As Cooper (2004: 27) states:

> The social impact of organizations is very much influenced by the legal constraints on their activity. Incorporated organizations actually depend upon law for their very existence and all their dealings must take into account

---

2   Among the studies related to this theme, see Schneider and Enste (2000).

the laws … These laws and regulations are socially constructed and therefore an important argument in the business and society field is to consider what role public policy or government regulation has to play.

Following this, the struggle against fiscal evasion and fraud is also a public obligation, because they cause distortion in economic activity, limit the quality of the public services and the social dimension of the state and increase the tax burden supported by those who do pay. In this sense, the combat against evasion and fraud demands an active and permanent position which demands unlimited effectiveness and efficiency (Antunes 2005).

However, in a society in which firms and citizens want to promote the morality of the tax system, that system must be balanced, not demanding overpayment or underpayment of taxes by specific firms or citizens, and equal in its treatment of all. At the same time, it would be reasonable to suppose that firms (in general) and citizens (in particular) pay their respective taxes more because they are motivated by a conscience of civic duty and social responsibility perspective, than properly for fear of the sanction of a non-execution order.

During research of the literature, it was hard to find comprehensive studies that deal with these subjects; or for methodologies that could estimate the loss of a state's budget through these two main problems (evasion and fraud); or empirical analysis about the full evasion by taxpayers; or the nature of the fiscal fraud. The theoretical analysis of tax evasion most often builds on the economics-of-crime model first applied to tax evasion by Allingham and Sandmo (1972). The literature has examined tax and fiscal evasion from the perspective of public economics: there are, certainly, several studies that analyse, for example, income tax evasion (such as Friedland et al. 1978; Feinstein 1991). Despite of these, some authors take a philosophical perspective, such as McGee (2006).

The authors in this research test these models with Portuguese data, but it was not possible to reproduce it, because some of variables used in the models are not available. The complexity and uncertainties inherent in this data did not allow an empirical analysis.

For those reasons, in this research, the authors decided to present a case study about the Portuguese experience of taxation and fiscal evasion and fraud, after an European contextualization, because it demonstrates this particular point more effectively: they find that the prevention, exposure and investigation of this case study is one way to show a bad example that will not provide any basis for scientific generalization. Somehow, good behaviour of citizens and firms is not always easy to find in corporate financial reports.

Thus, this chapter discusses the concept of evasion and fraud. Subsequently, it presents an understanding of the role of ethics and discusses the importance and effects of the code of ethics. The European and the Portuguese fight against fiscal evasion and fraud is presented and argued. The chapter concludes that the research was undertaken to assess the level of taxation and fiscal evasion, as well as measures or precautions against evasion and fraud in the European and the Portuguese approaches.

The concept of evasion and fraud

This research presents dual theoretical frameworks for the analysis of evasion and fraud in fiscal perspective. The first theoretical framework is based on law, taxation, a code of ethics, accounting and social responsibility theory and disclosure information, providing explanations for economic and social decisions (see Gray et al. 1994; Tilt 1994). The second theoretical framework has its origins in organizational and sociological theory (see Rahaman et al. 2004) that will assure the link of social responsibility as a fundamental objective to influence taxation and fiscal evasion and fraud.

It is vital to ensure that the clearest possible definitions are used, because in the literature there are several concerns about the understanding of fiscal evasion and fraud. This research is about what the literature call aggressive international tax practices. They are significant and economic relevant problems that each state is facing.

Fiscal evasion, typically, involves deliberately ignoring a specific part of the law. For example, when they participate in tax evasion, firms may under-report taxable receipts or claim expenses that are non-deductible or overstated. They might also attempt to evade taxes by wilfully refusing to comply with legislated reporting requirements.

Fiscal avoidance happens when procedures are adopted by firms to minimize tax, while continuing within the letter of the law; those procedures contravene the object and spirit of the law. Another example is when fiscal planning reduces taxes in a way that is inconsistent with the overall spirit of the law.

Fiscal planning is designed to arrange an individual's and an firm's affairs in order to maximize after-tax returns and must be exercised in an atmosphere of integrity of procedures adopted, mutual trust and good ethical behaviour (Stainer et al. 1997). So, effective fiscal planning occurs when the results of these procedures are consistent with the letter of the law and the reputation, principles and actions of the firm.

Several studies detail the tax haven that is described as a jurisdiction with no taxes or a very low rate of tax, a lack of transparency in the operation of its tax system, a lack of effective exchange of information with other countries and, usually, strict bank secrecy laws: they often have little or no economic activity of any other type.

Thus, fiscal avoidance, fiscal evasion and fiscal planning procedures and schemes are controversial matters, especially when they involve tax reduction arrangements that may meet the specificity of the law. Another aspect that must be noted is the abuse of tax havens as a growing concern for all countries participating in the global economy. However, standards and laws are different from country to country and in diverse languages that enlarge the complexity of its analyses.

By other perspective, the severest form of an irregularity is fraud. This definition is used in auditing standards. The International Federation of Accountants issued in 1982 the *International Statement of Auditing* [ISA] *no. 11: Fraud and Error*, and explains that the characteristic which differentiates fraud from error is intent.

Errors result from unintentional mistakes (Colbert 2000) while fraud occurs due to intentional act (Spathis 2002). ISA 11 refers to irregularities which incorporate the fraudulent financial reports presented by firms as well as accountancy and auditing departments' embezzlement or defalcation. Kaminski et al. (2004: 15) state that: 'Such fraudulent reporting is a critical problem for external auditors, both because of the potential legal liability for failure to detect false financial statements and because of the damage to professional reputation that results from public dissatisfaction about undetected fraud.' For example, Nieschwietz et al. (2000) provide a review of the empirical research on external auditors' detection of financial statement fraud.

Prosser (1971) describes the elements of fraud as follows:

- false representation of a material fact;
- the representation is made with knowledge of its falsity;
- a person acts upon the representation; and
- the person acting is damaged by his/her reliance upon that representation.

Related to the taxpayer's conduct, as Brackney (2005: 304) specifies, the courts look for certain 'badges of fraud' such as:

1. understatement of income
2. inadequate records
3. failure to file tax returns
4. implausible or inconsistent explanation of behaviour
5. concealment of assets
6. failure to cooperate with tax authorities.

Evasion and fraud are defined as an irregularity committed deliberately.[3] Fiscal evasion and fraud involves a deliberate act with the intention of obtaining an unauthorized benefit. In the review literature, it has been presented in several ways, but may include:

- making or altering documents
- purposely inaccurate financial reporting
- improper handling or reporting of money transactions
- authorizing or receiving compensation for goods not received or services not performed.

This happens because fiscal evasion and fraud is, indirectly, consented to by governments when they systematically treat any information, especially if it is fiscal, as secret or not open to scientific investigation. For example, bank secrecy is widely recognized as playing a legitimate role in protecting the confidentiality

---

3 See the definition in Article 1 of the Convention of 26 July 1995 on the protection of the Communities' financial interests, which came into force on 17 October 2002 (EC 1995).

of the financial affairs of individuals and legal entities (OECD 2000). However, the law usually specifies that the information is originally regarded as secret, but that it shall be disclosed to persons or authorities (including courts and administrative bodies) involved in the assessment or collection of taxes, or the enforcements or prosecutions related to taxes, or the determination of appeals in relation to taxes. The extent of tax evasion may be related to a country's economic and institutional development (Gërxhani 2004).

The authors have limited their focus to the concept of the fiscal evasion and fraud which relates primarily to intentional behaviour and misrepresentation of the laws and rules or to the omission of ethics. Effectively, this last can justify the financial success or failure of firms.

The role of ethics

Fiscal evasion and fraud, corruption and disrespect for the environment are some of the ethical problems that exist in society, as a consequence of profound political, social and economic transformations. However, at the same time and paradoxically, the authors confirmed the increase of an ethical sense; that is to say, that society and firms, as well the citizens, increasingly recognize the importance and the value of ethical and socially responsible behaviours, as well as the risks and costs that the deviations from the ethical ideal involve.

The process of ethical decision-making requires that behaviours be assessed against standards or norms of acceptability. Velasquez et al. (1983) presented a schematic for ethical decision-making that focuses on whether an action or decision meets three ethical criteria: utility, rights and justice. *Utility* judges behaviour in terms of its effects on the welfare of everyone. *Rights* expresses the requirements of ethics from the standpoint of individuals (in other words, ethical decisions must project the individual's legal and moral entitlements) (Gatewood and Carroll 1991). *Justice* is essentially a condition characterized by an equitable distribution of the benefits and burdens of working together, requiring that all citizens be guided by fairness, equity, and impartiality.

These principles are proposed as the normative principles that should be used to anchor organizational and professional ethical standard-setting. However, each of the criteria utilizes different moral concepts, and each one emphasizes aspects of ethical behaviour that are not emphasized by the others. Ethics influence the corporate social responsibility (CSR) assumed by an organizations, elevating the previously acceptable minimum above that fixed by the organization's groups of interests. These values form part of the organizational culture and they should be incorporated in an explicit way in the corporate objectives through the definition of the corporate mission.

Probably, CSR has gained an important position due to the great impact on society of numerous financial scandals involving important firms such as Enron and WorldCom.[4] Armstrong (1987) described the atmosphere in recent years as a crisis of confidence and credibility for the accounting community.[5] For example, anecdotal evidence suggests that mailing firms may be motivated to engage in fraudulent financial reporting to conceal their distress (Rosner 2003). These examples will have left an indelible impression among people that all is not well with the corporate world and that there are problems which need to be addressed (Crowther and Rayman-Bacchus 2004a). Indeed, these recent examples in the business world illustrate the magnitude of the impact that poor ethical behaviour can make in organizations. As Cleek and Leonard (1998: 619) state: '... unethical decisions and activities frequently undermine the performance and abilities of many organizations'. However, the authors agree with Peñalva (2002) who suggests that it is sometimes necessary that a great cataclysm must happen to alter the status quo.

The European Union, and specifically its Commission in its *Green Paper – Promoting a European Framework for Corporate Social Responsibility* (CE 2001: 8), understands the CSR as:

> *... a concept whereby companies integrate social and environmental concerns in their business operations and in their interaction with their stakeholders on a voluntary basis. Being socially responsible means not only fulfilling legal expectations, but also going beyond compliance and investing 'more' into human capital, the environment and the relations with stakeholders.*

Actually, many factors justify the evolution of corporate social responsibility, such as the new concerns and expectations from citizens, consumers, public authorities and investors in the context of globalization and large-scale industrial change; social criteria are increasingly influencing the investment decisions of individuals and institutions both as consumers and as investors; there is increased concern about the damage caused by economic activity to the environment; and increased transparency of business activities has been brought about by the media and modern information and communication technologies, for example with a view to fighting against fiscal evasion and fraud.

The increase of informative transparency has been developing in consequence of the financial scandals that, from 2001, shook the American and European finance markets (Bonsón et al. 2004). Effectively, the transparency and the obligation to diffuse the true and fair view constitute an upward move in corporate social responsibility (Rivero 2003). In this sense, the main objective of information on sustainability is that it allows the evaluation of CSR behaviour, its commitment to sustainable development and its effectiveness in the execution of its economic,

---

4   See Carcello and Nagy (2004), who examine the effects that client size has on the relationship between industry-specialist auditors and fraudulent financial reporting.

5   See Douglas et al. (2001) whose study investigated the effects of personal values and other factors on accountants' judgements of the ethical dilemmas typical of those encountered in practice.

social and environmental functions, as well as the capacity of the firms to generate social externalities that satisfy the needs of the different interested parties (AECA 2005).

CSR should be treated as an investment, not a cost. In the fight against fiscal evasion and fraud, the authors encourage the development of innovative practices, to bring greater transparency and to increase the reliability of evaluation and validation of firms' practices. Transparency and accountability two of CSR's main principles. Specifically, Crowther and Rayman-Bacchus (2004b: 240) consider that accountability:

> ... is concerned with an organisation recognising that its actions affect the external environment, and therefore assuming responsibility for the effects of its actions. This concept therefore implies a quantification of the effects of actions taken, both internal to the organisation and externally. More specifically the concept implies a reporting of those quantifications to all parties affected by those actions.

However, a gap persists between accounting discourse, accounting knowledge and accounting practices relating to CSR because of two factors: a shortage of formative approaches that would simultaneously and reciprocally connect the codified knowledge to concrete experimentation; and a shortage of peer exchange forums in which accountants could confidently and actively test new understandings in a social context marked by professional insecurity. It suggests an approach based on the deepening of partnerships in which all actors have an active role to play. Thus, the true CSR is to stay in harmony with the local environment and with the context of the global economy.

On 31 January 1999 the United Nations (UN), with Kofi Annan's Global Compact Initiative, analysed the CSR in a context of globalization. This initiative of sustainable development would bring organizations together with UN agencies, labour and civil society to support universal environmental and social principles. The UN Global Compact is a purely voluntary initiative (designed to stimulate change and to promote good corporate citizenship and encourage innovative solutions and partnerships) with two objectives: to mainstream its ten principles in business activities around the world (including a tenth principle about fighting against corruption); and to catalyse actions in support of UN goals.[6] The Global Compact's ten principles in the areas of human rights (two principles), labour standards (four principles), the environment (three principles) and anti-corruption (one principle) enjoy universal consensus.

Related to transparency and anti-corruption, principle 10 – 'Businesses should work against corruption in all its forms, including extortion and bribery' – of the UN Global Compact demonstrated a new willingness in the business community to play its part in the fight against corruption, and specifically against fiscal evasion and fraud. Following this, in Portugal it is necessary to increase transparency,

---

6   Available online at <www.unglobalcompact.org/AboutTheGC>.

because in 2005 Portugal occupied 26th place in the *Corruption Perceptions Index*, published by Transparency International, ranking above Greece and Italy, as well as some of the new European Member States.

The UN Global Compact argues that corruption[7] is a major hindrance to sustainable development, since it has a disproportionate impact on poor communities and is corrosive on the very fabric of society. The impact on the private sector is also considerable, because it impedes economic growth, distorts competition and represents serious legal and reputational risks for firms (see UN 2004). There are obvious *legal risks* because, independently of what form a corrupt transaction may take, there are risks involved which necessitate the international enforcement of anti-corruption legislation. There are *reputational risks* in the sense that it is of critical importance for an organization to be able to quickly quash any unfounded allegations by demonstrating that it acts in a transparent manner and has in place policies and procedures designed to prevent corruption. Proof of the relevance of the *reputation* variable is the disappearance of Arthur Andersen in the US (Galán 2002).

So, organizations must focus on anti-corruption measures as part of their mechanisms to protect their reputations and the interests of their shareholders. The reality, that the laws making corrupt practices criminal may not always be enforced, is no justification for accepting those corrupt practices (see UN 2004). Corruption undermines the world's social, economic and environmental development; for that the corporate community can and should play its part in making corruption unacceptable once the corruption diverts resources from their proper use and distorts competition and creates gross inefficiencies in the public and private sectors.

Following this, fiscal evasion and fraud is seen as a violation against the accepted moral norms and values for social, financial and administrative behaviour. The moral nature of these values refers to what is judged as right, just or good (conduct), because ethics absence implies corruption. Thus, the corporate code of ethics has increased greatly, as strategic management nowadays needs more and more business ethics in order to compete in a global market.

Codes of ethics

Ethics governance programmes, including codes of ethics, ostensibly are developed as tools for bringing some degree of uniformity and propriety to peoples' performance of organizational roles (see Gatewood and Carroll 1991).[8] For Weaver (1995), codes symbolize to employees an organization's values or ideology, and how that symbolic role affects peoples' perceptions of and responses to firms and institutions. In this sense, business ethics research appears to conceptualize the

---

7   The UN (2004: 5) defined corruption as 'the abuse of entrusted power for private gain'.
8   The study by Weaver (1995) contributes to our understanding of codes of ethics by focusing on the relationship between such codes' design and recipients' responses.

codes of ethics as distinct and formal documents specifying self-consciously ethical constraints on the conduct of organizational life (Weaver 1993; Schwartz 2001). Research in this domain is characterized by several terms, among which stands out the influence of codes of ethics on employee behaviour in organizations.

In this approach, Weller (1988) said that a code of ethics is a statement of rules to guide present and future action. Subsequently, Weaver (1995: 368) considers that codes of ethics: '… explicitly set standards for the quality of relationships among organization members, and between the organization as whole and specific members. Codes assign responsibilities, benefits, and burdens in organizations, and often establish procedural rules for the evaluation of members' actions.' The code of ethics (or code of conduct, code of practice, corporate credo, mission statement or values statement)[9] is an organization's policy statement and defines ethical standards for sound corporate governance. This code not only establishes the organization's values, but also spells out essential practices, behaviour, ethics and business standards for all employees' firms. Employees are the most important stakeholders in the perspective of the resource-based view (Barney 1991; 2001a; 2001b). According to this perspective, firms can obtain competitive advantages (sustainable)[10] in facing their competitors if they have, simultaneously, four topics: the valuable, rare, imperfectly imitable and non-substitutable resource of a firm (Barney 1991). With a *valuable* and same time *rare* item, as well as *imperfectly imitable* and *non-substitutable resource* of firms, we have the ethics.

The authors agree with Schwartz's (2004) opinion that firms should be required to expend resources to develop and implement a code of ethics in order to reduce the chance of improper conduct by their members. The code of ethics intends to be an instrument that facilitates the recognition and the eventual resolution of ethical problems, and each firm adopts rules in agreement with its own characteristics (activity, objectives and environment). Somers (2001: 194) argues that:

> *… there were clear differences between firms with and without ethical codes on three dimensions: a focus on profitability, use of discretionary funds for charitable contributions and the importance of behaving morally and ethically. In all three cases, employees of firms with ethical codes of conduct felt that these three value-based objectives were more important than did employees in firms without ethical codes.*

---

9   The Green Paper defined 'code of conduct' as 'a formal statement of the values and business practices of a firm and sometimes its suppliers. A code is a statement of minimum standards together with a pledge by the company to observe them and to require its contractors, subcontractors, suppliers and licensees to observe them. It may be a sophisticated document, which requires compliance with articulated standards and have a complicated enforcement mechanism.'

10 Barney (1991: 102) states that 'a firm is said to have a sustained competitive advantage when it is implementing a value-creating strategy not simultaneously being implemented by any current or potential competitors and when these other firms are unable to duplicate the benefits of this strategy.'

Looking at the codes of ethics, Langlois and Schlegelmilch (1990) consider that three basic formats can be distinguished. Firstly, there are regulatory documents giving staff specific advice on behaviour and conduct which include sanctions (termination of employment and/or reimbursement of damages). Secondly, there are short and more widely phrased creeds including statements of aims, objectives, philosophy or values. Specific guidance on employee behaviour or sanctions is not stated in these types of documents. Thirdly, there are elaborate corporate codes of ethics covering social responsibility to a set of stakeholders and a wide range of other topics.

Brooks (1989) states that there is a heightened interest in corporate social performance which is evidenced in six factors, specifically:

- the crisis of confidence about corporate activity;
- the increasing emphasis on quality of life – our health, our leisure time, our working conditions, our fresh air and water, are all in jeopardy from acid rain, radiation and other forms of pollution;
- the growing expectation that, if caught, a corporation and its executives will be penalized heavily rather than let off lightly;
- the growing power of special interest groups (stakeholders);
- the increasing level of publicity of non-ethical behaviours; and
- the change in the objectives which control business, particularly those which reduce the emphasis on the maximization of short-term profit as the only goal.

Considering all these aspects, a code of ethics, to be effective and to be more than a simple written document, should be inherent in the practices and behaviours of an organization, mainly in those of its managers, and in addition, it should correspond to a widespread sense of the duty of everybody in a global society. To summarize, Cleek and Leonard (1998: 620) consider that: '… the interactionist model of ethical behaviour consist on (1) individual factors, (2) ethical philosophy, (3) ethical decision ideologies, (4) external factors, and (5) organizational factors. When these sections are combined into an interactionist model they describe those factors that impact upon ethical decision-making behaviour in organizations.'

Also Ford and Richardson (1994) agree that ethical behaviour can be influenced by *individual* factors, such as gender, nationality/culture, age, religion, type of education, type of employment, years of employment, and personality, beliefs and values, as well as *situational* factors, such as peer group influence, top management influence, rewards and sanctions, type of ethical decision, organization size and industry type.

According to this, Watson (2003: 41) argues that: '… the idea that some people view fraud differently may not be a simple case of "ignorance of the law is no excuse". Rather, it may be the result of something ingrained in the social nature of human interaction, particularly when cultural heritage is introduced into the equation.' Similar parallelism was made by Glover and Aono (1995: 8) that defend

'... the premises that corporate culture and industry traits significantly influence the likelihood for fraud to occur.'[11]

This method cannot ensure 100 per cent detection of all fraud. Behrman (2001) considers that it is not clear that the codes have been as resoundingly successful in changing corporate behaviour, particularly in terms of corruption, as have national government requirements imposed on foreign firms and their own officials. But it offers an advantage over traditional risks models since it focuses on the underlying causes for fraud, which should assist the auditor in both prevention and detection of fraud by identifying early warning signs (Glover and Aono 1995). Following that debate, the Council of the EU and the representatives of the governments of the Member States, meeting within the Council, agreed in 1997 to the resolution on a code of conduct for business taxation (CEU 1998).

The European fight against evasion and fraud

The fight against fiscal evasion and fraud is important to increase fiscal justness, to increase fiscal revenue and, simultaneously, to decrease the tax burden, to eliminate distortion factors in terms of managerial competitiveness and to avoid the dilapidation of the patrimony of the state. As Hillison et al. (1999) state, no industry is immune to fraud losses. For this, the fiscal administration should have the necessary powers to obtain the elements on which it can base its decisions relative to a taxpaying citizen (Sanches 2000). In any case, there is considerable evidence that taxpayers misreport some sources of income more intensively than others (Patterson and Noel 2003; Martinez-Vazquez and Rider 2005). The taxpayers expect to benefit from the misrepresentation, and exploit loopholes in their roles in order to present a deliberately misleading (normally, flattering) impression of a firm's financial position or results (Alexander and Archer 2001).

Studying fiscal evasion and fraud creates an opportunity to discuss the decision-making process related to the 'shadow economy'. This concept refers to a broad phenomenon that, usually, includes tax evasion, activities against government regulation, illegal activities and hidden employment. As Schneider (2005: 598) concludes:

> *The average size of the shadow economy as a proportion of official GDP in 1999–2000 in developing countries was 41%, in transition countries 38%, and in OECD countries 17%. An increasing burden of taxation and social security contributions underlies the shadow economy. If the shadow economy increases by 1%, the growth rate of the 'official' GDP of developing countries decreases by 0.6%.*

---

11   Abbott et al. (2000) examine whether two key audit committee characteristics, activity and independence, in combination, reduce the likelihood of fraudulent or aggressive financial statements actions. Following this, Kneer et al. (1996) consider that the auditor needs to be mindful of appearances, *ex post*.

However, in the OECD countries substantial progress has been made in advancing the goals of harmful tax practices, because these countries seek to establish standards that encourage an environment in which fair competition can take place (OECD 2004).

In order to reduce the shadow economy, it was necessary for governments and intermediate institutions to intensify the action against fiscal evasion and fraud. For example, the EU in 1999 decided to take all possible actions, because it was the 'horrifying year' in the history of the EU. This classification is related to the mass resignation of the Santer Commission, following a series of scandals (culminating in a nepotism row involving the former French prime minister and then EU Commissioner, Edith Cresson). So, the new European Commission acted quickly to create the European Anti-Fraud Office, which adopted its French acronym – Office de Lute Antifraude (OLAF) – and which took over the duties (after 1988) of the Unit for the Coordination of Fraud Protection (UCLAF).

This organization reinforces the fight against fraud, corruption and other illegal activity affecting the financial interests of the European Community. According to the Commission of the European Communities (CE 2006: 5), the OLAF '... is rather the legal instrument for administrative investigation with which the European Union has been equipped by the Commission, to guarantee better protection of Community interests and compliance with the law against attacks from organised crime and fraudsters.'

In the last five years, to satisfy the objectives of a global strategy in a longer-term context, the Community and the Member States have acted with determination and have planned their efforts in a multi-annual strategy (2001 to 2005) around four challenges (CE 2000: 6):

- *an overall legislative anti-fraud policy (the development of the regulatory system towards more effectiveness and coherence);*
- *a new culture of operational cooperation (full participation and concerted commitment of the national and Community authorities on the ground);*
- *an inter-institutional approach to prevent and combat corruption (the strengthening of the credibility of the European institutions);*
- *enhancement of the penal judicial dimension (adaptation of national criminal prosecutions to the new obligations of the Treaty).*

In agreement with OLAF, a *new legislative anti-fraud policy* is necessary to develop a culture that includes prevention, detection and cooperation by integrating all the sectors where fraud and corruption may take place. So:

- *Prevention* denotes the quality of acting in accordance within clear legislation, easily applicable and including provisions likely to strengthen sound financial management and effective control of Community and national policies.
- *Detection* presupposes a sound application of Community and national principles, values and norms as well as sound management of Community policies and funds.

- *Cooperation* is related to the progressive development of administrative cooperation rules between the European Commission and the national authorities which allow for a better application of economic and financial rules.

However, it is important to remember that there may be gaps in the rules and places where the rules are vague or even incomplete. Of equal, if not greater significance is the fact that taxpayers may develop schemes which fulfil the letter of the rules but undermine their spirit (Shah 1996). Taking advantage of gaps or ambiguities in the rules or specifically in accounting standards to present a biased picture of financial performance can be understood as creative accounting (Shah 1998). The authors reinforce that it does not breach the letter of the law, but may breach its spirit.

In relationship to the *new culture of operational cooperation*, the European Commission and the national authorities intended to bring the resources together to encourage a more proactive orientation of action on the ground. Effective action against evasion and fraud inside several countries presupposes the best possible knowledge of their social, economic and criminal environment. In this, the technology and the technical means for gathering, storing and exploiting information must be developed in the light of best social practice.

Additionally, an *inter-institutional approach to prevent and combat corruption* is needed.[12] OLAF will have to cooperate closely and regularly with the Community institutions, bodies and agencies and contribute to training actions. Furthermore, it must encourage transparency and the duty to communicate. The European Commission will develop norms and rules[13] on ethics and conflicts of interests oriented for transparency and security to avoid Community decisions being affected by irregular influences. As the Commission of the European Communities states (CE 2000: 15): 'The objective is to have a working environment where every official at every level is in a position to be aware of his responsibilities, in particular with regard to the obligation of loyalty to the institutions and the obligation to cooperate to prevent irregularities.'

The fourth, and last, challenge is related to *the enhancement of the penal judicial dimension*. The inclusion in the Treaty of Amsterdam of Article 280,[14] the regulations

---

12 For a critical perspective of professional associations, governmental agencies and international accounting and auditing bodies in promulgating standards to deter and detect fraud, domestically and abroad, see Vanasco (1998).

13 The findings of Wenzel's (2004) study are overall consistent with the theoretical predictions concerning the relevance of norms for the deterring effects of legal sanctions against tax evasion.

14 See EC (2002). Article 280 of the European Community (EC) Treaty sets an objective of effective and equivalent protection throughout the Community. It requires all the responsible authorities in the Member States to organize close and regular cooperation with the Commission. It introduces a new legal base to allow the European Parliament and the Council to adopt (by co-decision procedure) the measures to prevent and combat attacks on the Communities' financial interests. Article 280 of the EC Treaty

adopted in May 1999 under the co-decision procedure, the inter-institutional agreement and the establishment of OLAF brings about in a tangible manner the integration of the national judicial dimension in the fight against fraud and corruption (see CE 2000).

In doing this, the four strategic guidelines will allocate the Community to improve in a significant way the level of protection of the Community's financial interests. The implementation of these strategic orientations will allow the control provisions and the audit capacity of the Commission departments to be strengthened overall with a triple aim of effectiveness, transparency and ethical behaviour. The institutions and Member States must adopt the measures necessary to ensure an equivalent high level of protection of financial interests throughout the Community and to fight evasion and fraud unrelentingly and with the utmost vigour.

In this way, the Member States adopted very wide-ranging measures aimed at improving the protection against fraud, among other measures to counter money-laundering and corruption, national anti-fraud strategies, improvements in financial controls and procedures for the processing of data held on computers. For example, in Portugal external audits should be conducted henceforth at least once every eight years on the expenses of bodies that manage public expenditure (in particular European funds). The audits must assess the body's function and aims and whether its expenses meet criteria of economy, efficiency and effectiveness (see CE 2005).

Table 20.1 shows results for the overall index of globalization for the period 1975–2000 as well as the three sub-indices: economic, political and social integration in 2000. The index was developed by Dreher (2003)[15] for 123 countries and is based on 23 variables that relate to different dimensions of globalization.

High globalization indexes are shown for Belgium in 1975, 1980 and 1990, Luxembourg in 1985 and 1995 and Sweden in 2000. Portugal shows the lowest value for its globalization index during the period 1975 to 1990, but this value increases. These encourage us to review Portuguese behaviour and note that in the years of 1995 and 2000 the country generated a surprising higher value of globalization index – more significant than Spain and Greece although lower than other countries. As Dreher (2006: 183) concludes: '... globalization increased average effective tax rates on capital and did not influence the other policy instruments analyzed in this study. When adjusted statutory tax rates on capital are employed, the results show that increasing globalization reduces taxes.'

---

calls finally for a policy of permanent evaluation and transparency which must be implemented on the basis of the Commission's annual report drawn up in cooperation with the Member States (see CE 2000).

15   In Dreher (2003), 'Does globalization affect growth? Empirical evidence from a new index', unpublished paper, University of Mannheim. See under Dreher (2006) for published version.

Table 20.1 Globalization indexes of the EU's 15 countries

Country	Globalization (index year)						Political	Social	Economic
	1975	1980	1985	1990	1995	2000	2000	2000	2000
Austria	4.44	4.54	4.15	4.31	4.47	5.10	6.75	3.61	5.39
Belgium	6.30	5.33	5.40	5.43	5.24	5.48	7.33	3.49	6.18
Denmark	5.28	4.63	4.38	4.23	4.55	5.69	7.26	4.60	5.63
Finland	4.32	4.25	4.15	4.12	4.75	5.71	6.79	4.97	5.67
France	4.24	4.15	4.15	4.14	4.61	5.36	8.58	3.17	5.19
Germany	4.26	4.04	4.57	4.27	4.36	5.20	6.99	3.70	5.38
Greece	3.01	2.90	2.69	2.73	2.90	3.70	4.30	2.27	4.76
Ireland	3.59	3.63	3.62	3.85	4.04	4.95	4.92	3.30	6.75
Italy	4.14	3.83	3.82	3.80	3.90	4.50	7.05	2.05	5.11
Luxembourg	5.45	4.97	5.46	5.34	5.37	5.61	2.21	5.10	8.84
Netherlands	5.31	4.69	4.47	4.42	4.77	5.31	5.52	4.08	6.46
Portugal	2.23	2.49	2.30	2.63	3.10	4.10	4.88	2.12	5.61
Spain	2.85	2.85	2.84	3.13	3.65	3.95	5.31	1.96	5.01
Sweden	5.18	4.53	4.56	5.00	5.36	6.00	7.85	5.00	5.62
UK	5.04	4.73	4.68	4.74	4.64	5.44	7.04	3.73	6.01

(*Source*: Dreher 2006: 182)

Thus, access to bank information can greatly improve the ability of tax authorities to effectively administer the tax laws enacted by their governments, because bank secrecy toward tax authorities may enable taxpayers to hide illegal activities and to escape tax (OECD 2000). The effective administration and enforcement of many tax laws and regulations require access to financial transactions. On one side, the OECD (2000: 32) states that: 'If tax administrations cannot obtain information from banks (whether through specific requests for information or through automatic reporting), taxpayers' compliance costs may be increased and additional reporting requirements may be imposed on taxpayers.' On the other side, the OECD (2000: 33) considers that: '...lack of access to bank information for tax purposes may contribute to the distortion of capital and financial flows that result from harmful tax competition.'

But the lack of access to bank information may result not just from formal secrecy laws but from administrative policies or practices that impede exchange of information.

Most European Member countries require banks to automatically report information to tax authorities: this is the case in Austria, Denmark, Finland, France, Greece, Ireland, Italy, Netherlands (according to Code of Conduct), Portugal,

Spain, Sweden and the UK. Banks are *not* required to do so in Belgium, Germany and Luxembourg (OECD 2000). Table 20.2 presents the types of information automatically reported by banks to tax authorities.

Table 20.2 Types of information reported by banks to tax authorities

Country	Opening/closing of accounts	Interest paid and to whom it is paid	Account balance at year end	Other
Austria				X
Belgium				X
Denmark	X	X	X	X
Finland		X		X
France	X	X		Must report all income from capital
Germany				X
Greece	X			X
Ireland		X		
Italy				X
Luxemburg				X
Netherlands		Paid to residents		
Portugal				Use of household savings for other purpose
Spain		X		X
Sweden		X	X	Interest on loans
UK		X		

(*Source*: OECD 2000: 69)

There was widespread concern that fraud increased dramatically after EU enlargement in 2004, but that impression of malpractice undermines public support for the EU and the relations between the Member States. For this reason, the European Commission in 2004 approved a communication that provide a holistic approach on law to reduce the risk of corporate and financial malpractice covering also taxation and law enforcement (see CE 2004). However, the EU itself cannot bear all of the blame for evasion, fraud and corruption of the EU budget, because each Member State adopts specific programmes approved by the European Commission and spends the budget in accordance with that.

The Portuguese fight against evasion and fraud

Effectively, fiscal evasion and fraud can be combated through the use of preventive measures and fiscal policies, thus reducing the level of bank secrecy, making professional confidentiality more flexible, increasing the exchange of information between the various investigating authorities, and enabling proceedings to be quicker (see Antunes 2005). Brackney (2005: 307) considers that: 'To ameliorate the tax consequences of their criminal activity, taxpayers should attempt to negotiate an order of restitution instead of an order to forfeiture or voluntarily make restitutions before sentencing.' Firms with core restatements have higher frequencies of intentional misstatements (fraud) and subsequently bankruptcy or delisting (Palmrose and Scholz 2004) and the fiscal evasion and fraud could be connected with accounting manipulation. Feinstein (1995: 53) says that: 'An accounting manipulation arises when a firm shifts line-item entries in its accounting statements to misrepresent the relative contributions of different activities to overall profits.'

The manipulation of accounting statements by their preparers can be designated as creative accounting. The authors understand that the concept does not have a full definition, but in essence it will involve fraudulent financial reporting with intentional misstatements or omissions of amounts or disclosures. In the point of view of Naser (1993), creative accounting can be identified as the process of manipulating accounting figures by taking advantage of the loopholes in accounting rules and the choices of measurement and disclosure practices in them, to then transform financial statements from what they should be to what the preparers would prefer to see reported.

On one side Mulford and Comiskey (2002: 3) say that creative accounting is any and all of the steps used to play the financial numbers game, including the aggressive choice (done in an effort to achieve desired results) and application of accounting principles, fraudulent financial reporting (intentional misstatements or omissions of amounts or disclosures), and any steps taken toward earnings management (the active manipulation of earnings toward a predetermined target) or income smoothing (a form of earnings management design to remove peaks and troughs from a normal series). However, other authors, such as Archer (1996), argue that the concept of creative accounting is used to describe a widespread and accepted practice and is neither illegal nor a breach of accounting standards.

Accounting standards are based on the same common principles of taxation, such as that equal firms should be treated equally, providing there is some guidance on issues of fairness. So, the increase, for example, of Portuguese taxation employees presented in Figure 20.1 is connected with reduction of fiscal evasion and fraud and indirectly linked with large budget deficits and the need for increased revenues. The Portuguese government promotes the fiscal policy by investing in physical inventory (such as new buildings, offices), assets acquisition (such as computers, software) and new employees in the Ministry of Finance. This tendency shows progress and promotes the fair treatment of all Portuguese taxpayers, but increases the costs of tax administration (Sandmo 2005).

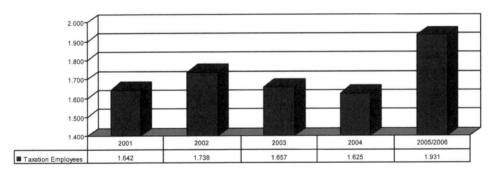

	2001	2002	2003	2004	2005/2006
■ Taxation Employees	1.642	1.738	1.657	1.625	1.931

Figure 20.1 Number of taxation employees in Portugal
(*Source*: MFAP 2006)

The success of these measures by the taxation services depends on the level of modern information and communication technologies. In this context, the progressive computerization of tax services remains a priority for the government, because low automation levels limit the efficiency of the execution of tax payments, of tax audits and the fight against fiscal evasion and fraud.

The fight against fiscal evasion and fraud is always the responsibility of the administrative authorities, the police and other preliminary investigation authorities such as, in the Portuguese case, the Ministério Público or Policia Judiciária. The prevention of fraud is primarily effected by the law and regulation adopted by the government.

Such authorities in Portugal may obtain bank information only if a criminal proceeding is pending or if an enforcement order is issued by a court at the request of the tax administration and also in cases where fiscal benefits are provided through bank accounts (for example, special treatment of retirement savings). Several countries (such as Czech Republic, Denmark, Finland, France, Italy, Norway and Spain) can obtain bank information for tax administration purposes without limitation (OECD 2000).

The level of information and documentation required to open accounts, other than anonymous and numbered accounts, varies from country to country. Most countries require banks to verify the name and address of the client by some type of official documentation (such as passport, identity card, driver's licence) and others require also tax identification numbers (TINs) to open an account, but only ten countries (notably Denmark, Finland, Iceland, Norway, Poland, Portugal, Spain and Sweden) require the customer to provide documentary evidence of the TIN (OECD 2000).

In Portugal, to obtain information from a bank about a third person is permitted only in criminal cases where a judge can decree the lifting of bank secrecy; such information may not include anything about the family of the person about whom the request is made. Most countries can obtain information from a bank about a person who is not suspected of tax fraud but who has had economic transactions with a specified person suspected of tax fraud (OECD 2000: 36). In addition, in

Portugal as in other countries, banks obtain information about the account holder's economic situation and business activities for creditworthiness purposes.

In Portugal, an analysis based on the *Report of the Fight Against Fiscal Evasion and Fraud* produced by the Minister of Finance allows us to conclude that bank secrecy increased significantly in the period 2003–05 (an increase by 769 per cent in the number of court decisions). Table 20.3 shows the high percentage of taxpaying citizens' voluntary authorizations in the last three years (71.6 per cent in 2003, 57.8 per cent in 2004 and 60.7 per cent in 2005) and the low number of judicial participations (6.8 per cent in 2003, 2.6 per cent in 2004 and 7.9 per cent in 2005).

Table 20.3 Processes (court cases) concerning bank secrecy in Portugal

Situation	2003	variation		2004	variation		2005	Total
		value	%		value	%		
Established processes	74	464	627.0	538	105	19.5	643	1.255
Technical analysis	16	197	1231.3	213	-11	-5.2	202	431
Voluntary resolution	53	258	486.8	311	79	25.4	390	754
Judicial participations	5	9	180.0	14	37	264.3	51	70

(*Source*: MFAP 2006)

The previous evidence is based on a Portuguese case study of the Banco Espírito Santo (BES). In Table 20.4, the authors trace the development from 2002 to 2004 of the fraud processes and in Table 20.5 of the money-laundering process in BES.

Table 20.4 Processes (court cases) of fraud in the BES (Portugal)

Fraud	2002	variation		2003	variation		2004	Total
		value	%		value	%		
Technical analysis	61	36	59.0	97	-31	-32.0	66	224
Judicial participations	21	-9	-42.9	12	15	125.0	27	60
Inquired processes	43	-5	-11.6	38	-11	-28.9	27	108

(*Source*: BES 2005)

This research shows the surprising increase in the incidents related to money-laundering, mainly in 2004 (145,000 more technical analyses than in 2002). This reality confirms the reflections of Schneider and Enste (2000) that evasion is a fact of life around the world, and that are strong indications that it is increasing.[16]

Table 20.5 Processes (court cases) of money-laundering in the BES (Portugal)

Money laundering	2002	variation		2003	variation		2004	Total
		value	%		value	%		
Technical analysis	222	46.917	21.133.8	47,139	98.247	208.4	145,386	192,747
Judicial participations	10	46	460.0	56	48	85.7	104	170
Inquired processes	0	0	-	0	0	-	0	0

(*Source*: BES 2005)

Sometimes, the aim of fiscal evasion and fraud is to transfer the capital thus obtained to tax havens. The high-taxing governments wrap themselves up in a cloak of morality, but the fact is that they are suppliers of services, enjoying local monopolies, and financed by their taxpayers under compulsion (Fildes 2002). Thus, the governments should change their approach to taxation law to avoid the taxpayer being reduced to fiscal evasion. The European process of automatic information exchange is one such measure, which should be extended internationally. Portugal has as its fiscal paradise the Madeira International Business Centre (subdivided into the Industrial Free Trade, International Service Centre, Offshore Financial Centre and International Shipping Registry);[17] the firms located there are exempt from corporate taxation (David and Abreu 2005).

Following this, there is urgent need of legislative restrictions. In Portugal, on 27 March 2004, a new prevention and repression regime relatively to the money laundering was launched by means of the Lei no. 11/2004 (AR 2004), which reinforced the internal juridical order Directive 2001/97/EC (EC 2001) on prevention of the use of the financial system for the purpose of money-laundering. However, the Directive 2001/97/EC (EC 2001: 76) states that it '... should not only reflect best

---

16   Obtaining precise statistics about the allocation of a country's resources in the shadow economy is important for making effective economic policy decisions (Schneider and Enste 2000) with the objective of fighting against evasion and fraud.

17   The Madeira International Business Centre was legally created by Decreto-Lei no. 500/80 of 20 October (MFP 1980), Decreto-Lei no. 165/86 of 26 June (MF 1986), Decreto-Lei no. 215/89 of 1 July (MF 1989), as amended by Decreto-Lei no. 198/2001 of 3 July (MF 2001). Other legislation about fiscal benefits included: Decreto-Lei no. 84/93 of 18 March (MF 1993), Decreto-Lei no. 37/94 of 8 February (MF 1994), Decreto-Lei no. 25/98 of 10 February (MF 1998) and Lei no. 30-F/2000 of 29 December (AR 2000).

international practice in this area but should also continue to set a high standard in protecting the financial sector and other vulnerable activities from the harmful effects of the proceeds of crime.'

This new legal regime should be contemplated in the internal regulation control of firms and institutions public and private. For Haugen and Selin (1999) an internal control system has four broad objectives:

- to safeguard assets of the firm
- to ensure the accuracy and reliability of accounting records and information
- to promote efficiency in the firm's operations
- to measure compliance with management's prescribed policies and procedures.

The emphasis on internal control systems and internal audit functions is the result of the globalization of business, technological advancements, increasing business failures and the wide publicizing of fraud (Rezaee 1995).

Directors and all levels of management are responsible for preventing and detecting situations of fiscal evasion and fraud and for establishing and maintaining formal internal controls that, inside of a sphere of social responsibility and functional segregation, provide security for the resources of their firms. However, detecting fraud is a difficult task for auditors, in part because most have never experienced fraud in their careers (Montgomery et al. 2002; Pany and Whittington 2001). Although rare in occurrence, financial statement fraud can result in devastating losses to investors, creditors and auditors (Payne and Ramsay 2005). Thus, directors and management must recognize risks and exposures inherent in their responsibility area, and must be particularly attentive to fiscal evasion and fraud indicators.

Discussion

News methodologies are needed to measure fiscal evasion and fraud and connect them with economic changes, technological improvements and social traditions as dimensions of social responsibility and more specifically with financial performance. Thus, the requirements for firms to be sustainable must be connected with successive positive actions, with correct, fair and good behaviour, as well as with ethical behaviours that slow down the development of the shadow economy.

Indeed, global businesses should promote sustainable development, and governments must be constantly vigilant to avoid being associated with corrupt practices. For example, the Enron business model was unsustainable as a model and this led directly to the demise of Enron Corporation (Baker 2003). This firm had reported rapidly growing revenues, with a corresponding increase in stock prices. Unfortunately, this picture of growth was inaccurate. Instead, this firm was found to have applied generally accepted accounting principles (GAAP) inappropriately, resulting in a massive overstatement of income (Makkawi and Schick 2003). In this case as in others, the firm did not understand the limitations of the options allowed by GAAP and made misinterpretations, with very important effects of sanction severity.

It is urgently that governments reinforce the fight against fiscal evasion and fraud by firms to provide increased revenues through the implementation of formal internal preventative measures. This aim involves, on one side, the effectiveness of the struggle against fiscal evasion and fraud and, on the other side, the social responsibility perspective of the citizens and the generalization of their ethical behaviour. Also, the auditors are important researchers in the discovery of fraudulent financial reporting, for which they should be sensitive enough (see Moyes and Hasan 1996; Abdolmohammadi and Owhoso 2000; Jayalakshmy et al. 2005; McKee 2006). Smith (1998) recognizes differences between auditors, relative to their tolerance of accounting manipulations with an income impact. However, as Humphrey et al. (1993) state, it may be that development in auditors' responsibilities for the detection of fraud will only be forthcoming though further legislation.

International bodies such as International Accounting Standards Board, Financial Accounting Standards Board and International Federation of Accountants may provide new standards that promote the principles of transparency, equality and effective exchange of information between all firms that must follow these regulations. Unfortunately, some countries, like Portugal, attempt to control fiscal evasion and fraud through various punitive measures, rather than through reforms of the tax and social security systems which could improve the dynamics of the official economy.

The authors' proposals in the struggle against fiscal evasion and fraud are concentrated on better access to bank information for tax purposes. At the same time, the Ministry of Finance must implement and promote for all taxpayers a transparency information policy and must establish an effective exchange of information mechanism, allowing the open system to be controlled for each person who pays tax.

Governments must recognize the importance of permitting scientific investigations promoted by researchers that will access fiscal information generated from certain law enforcement purposes. So, more and more progress, partnerships, collaboration and teamwork between the government (through the Ministry of Finance) and researchers will allow a development of new perspectives on taxation and a basis for new fights related to evasion and fraud in the Portuguese situation.

In summary, social responsibility is an essential need of the society; full, open and disclosure of information will permit better fiscal policies to be promoted by the policy-makers. Evasion and fraud should be fought with all available weapons – tools, actions and procedures – by everybody involved in the effort to decrease the range and power of this particular human bad behaviour.

References

Abbott, L., Park, Y. and Parker, S. (2000), 'The effects of audit committee activity and independence on corporate fraud', *Managerial Finance*, 26 (11), 55–66.

Abdolmohammadi, M. and Owhoso, V. (2000), 'Auditors' ethical sensitivity and the assessment of the likelihood of fraud', *Managerial Finance*, 26 (1), 21–32.

Alexander, D. and Archer, S. (2001), 'On economic reality, representational faithfulness and the "true and fair override"', *Accounting & Business Research*, 33 (1), 3–14.

Allingham, M. and Sandmo, A. (1972), 'Income tax evasion: a theoretical analysis', *Journal of Public Economics*, 1 (3/4), 323–38.

Antunes, F. (2005), *A evasão fiscal e o crime de fraude fiscal no sistema legal português*, Lisboa: Verbo Jurídico.

Archer, S. (1996), 'The ethics of creative accounting', *Science and Engineering Ethics*, 2 (1), 55–70.

Armstrong, M.B. (1987), 'Moral development and accounting education', *Journal of Accounting Education*, 5 (1), 27–43.

Asociación Española de Contabilidad y Administración de Empresas (AECA) (2005), *Límites de la información de sostenibilidad: entidad devengo y materialidad* (Responsabilidad Social Corporativa 2), Madrid: Asociación Española de Contabilidad y Administración de Empresas.

Assembleia da República (AR) (2004), Lei no. 11/2004 – Estabelece o regime de prevenção e repressão do branqueamento de vantagens de proveniência ilícita e procede à 16a alteração ao Código Penal e à 11a alteração ao Decreto-Lei no. 15/93, de 22 de Janeiro. *Diário da República*, 74, I Série-A, 27 de Março: 1980–89.

Assembleia da República (AR) (2000), Lei no. 30-F/2000 – Altera o Estatuto dos Benefícios Fiscais aprovado pelo Decreto-Lei no. 215/89, de 1 de Junho no tocante ao regime aplicável à Zona Franca da Madeira e à Zona Franca da Ilha de Santa Maria. *Diário da República*, 299, I Série-A, 3rd Supplement, December 29: 7492(653)-7492(693).

Baker, C.R. (2003), 'Investigation Enron as a public private partnership', *Accounting, Auditing & Accountability Journal*, 16 (3), 446–66.

Banco Espírito Santo (BES) (2005), *Relatório de Responsabilidade Social 2004*, Lisboa: Grupo BES.

Barney, J. (2001a), 'Resource-based theories of competitive advantage: a ten-year retrospective on the resource-based view', *Journal of Management*, 27 (6), 643–50.

Barney, J. (2001b), 'Is the resource-based "view" a useful perspective for strategic management research? Yes', *Academy of Management Review*, 26 (1), 41–56.

Barney, J. (1991), 'Firm resources and sustained competitive advantage', *Journal of Management*, 17 (1), 99–120.

Behrman, J.N. (2001), 'Adequacy of international codes of behavior', *Journal of Business Ethics*, 31 (1), 51–64.

Bonsón, E., Escobar, T. and Gandía, J. (2004), 'Del Código de Buenas Prácticas de AECA a la Ley de Transparencia', *Boletín AECA*, 66, 46–50.

Brackney, M. (2005), 'When crime doesn't pay: the tax consequences of criminal conduct', *Journal of Taxation*, 103 (5), November, 303–7.

Brooks, L. (1989), 'Corporate codes of ethics', *Journal of Business Ethics*, 8 (2/3), 117–129.

Carcello, J.V. and Nagy, A.L. (2004), 'Client size, auditor specialization and fraudulent financial reporting', *Managerial Auditing Journal*, 19 (5), 651–68.

Cebula, R.J. and Saadatmand, Y. (2005), 'Income tax evasion determinants: new evidence', *Journal of American Academy of Business*, 7 (2), 124–7.

Cleek, M. and Leonard, S.L. (1998), 'Can corporate codes of ethics influence behavior?', *Journal of Business Ethics*, 17 (6), 619–630.

Colbert, J.L. (2000), 'International and US standards: error and fraud', *Managerial Auditing Journal*, 15 (3), 97–107.

Commission of the European Communities (CE) (2006), *The Fight Against Fraud*, Brussels: European Anti-Fraud Office (OLAF).

Commission of the European Communities (CE) (2005), *COM (2005) 323 final, July 19, Report from the Commission to the Council and the European Parliament – Protection of the Financial Interests of the Communities – Fight against Fraud – Commission's Annual Report 2004 (SEC(2005)973) (SEC(2005)974)*, Brussels: Commission of the European Communities.

Commission of the European Communities (CE) (2004), *COM (2004) 611 final, September 27, Communication from the Commission to the Council and the European Parliament – Protection and Combating Corporate and Financial Malpractice*, Brussels: Commission of the European Communities.

Commission of the European Communities (CE) (2001), *Green Paper – Promoting a European Framework for Corporate Social Responsibility, COM (2001) 366 final*, Brussels: Official Publications of the European Commission, 18 July.

Commission of the European Communities (CE) (2000), *COM (2000) 358 final, June 28, Communication from the Commission – Protection of the Communities' Financial Interests – The Fight against Fraud – For an Overall Strategic Approach*, Brussels: Commission of the European Communities.

Cooper, S. (2004), *Corporate Social Performance: A Stakeholder Approach*, Aldershot: Ashgate.

Council of the European Union (CEU) (1998), 'Conclusions of the ECOFIN Council meeting on 1 December of 1997 concerning taxation policy', *Official Journal of the European Communities*, C 2, January 6, 1–6.

Crowther, D. and Rayman-Bacchus, L. (2004a), 'Perspectives on corporate social responsibility', in D. Crowther and L. Rayman-Bacchus (eds), *Perspectives on Corporate Social Responsibility*, Aldershot: Ashgate, pp 1–17.

Crowther, D. and Rayman-Bacchus, L. (2004b), 'The future of corporate social responsibility', in D. Crowther and L. Rayman-Bacchus (eds), *Perspectives on Corporate Social Responsibility*, Aldershot: Ashgate, pp 229–49.

David, F. and Abreu, R. (2005), 'Portuguese corporate income tax: an exploratory model', *Contabilidade e Gestão*, 1 (1), 113–135.

Douglas, P.C., Davidson, R.A. and Schwartz, B.N. (2001), 'The effect of organizational culture and ethical orientation on accountants' ethical judgments', *Journal of Business Ethics*, 34 (2), 101–21.

Dreher, A. (2006), 'The influence of globalization on taxes and social policy: an empirical analysis for OECD countries', *European Journal of Political Economy*, 22, 179–201. (Originally a paper entitled 'Does globalization affect growth? Empirical evidence from a new index', University of Mannheim.)

European Community (EC) (2002), Consolidated Version of the Treaty Establishing the European Community, *Official Journal of the European Communities*, L 325, 24 December, 33–184.

European Community (EC) (2001), Directive 2001/97/EC of the European Parliament and of the Council of 4 December 2001 amending Council Directive 91/308/EEC on prevention of the use of the financial system for the purpose of money laundering, *Official Journal of the European Communities*, L 344, 28 December, 76–81.

European Community (EC) (1995), Convention drawn up on the basis of Article K.3 of the Treaty on European Union, on the protection of the European Communities' financial interests, *Official Journal of the European Communities*, C 316, 27 November, 49–57.

Feinstein, J. (1995), 'Asymmetric information, accounting manipulations, and partnerships', *Journal of Economic Behavior and Organization*, 26 (1), 49–73.

Feinstein, J. (1991), 'An econometric analysis of income tax evasion and its detection', *Rand Journal of Economics*, 22 (1), 14–35.

Fildes, C. (2002), 'Fiscal paradise', *The Spectator*, 26 January.

Ford, R.C. and Richardson, W.D. (1994), 'Ethical decision making: a review of the empirical literature', *Journal of Business Ethics*, 13 (3), 205–21.

Friedland, N., Maital, S. and Rutenberg, A. (1978), 'A simulation study of income tax evasion', *Journal of Public Economics*, 10, 107–116.

Galán, J. (2002), 'La reforma del Código de Buenas Prácticas. Lecciones del Caso Enron', *Boletín AECA*, 59, 3–5.

Gatewood, R. and Carroll, A. (1991), 'Assessment of ethical performance of organization members: a conceptual framework', *Academy of Management Review*, 16 (4), 667–90.

Gërxhani, K. (2004), 'The informal sector in developed and less developed countries: a literature survey', *Public Choice*, 120 (3/4), 267–300.

Glover, H. and Aono, J. (1995), 'Changing the model for prevention and detection of fraud', *Managerial Auditing Journal*, 10 (5), 3–9.

Gray, R., Kouhy, R. and Lavers, S. (1994), 'Constructing a research database of social and environmental reporting by UK companies', *Accounting, Auditing & Accountability Journal*, 8 (2), 78–101.

Haugen, S. and Selin, J. (1999), 'Identifying and controlling computer crime and employee fraud', *Industrial Management & Data Systems*, 99 (8), 340–344.

Hillison, W., Pacini, C. and Sinason, D. (1999), 'The internal auditor as fraud-buster', *Managerial Auditing Journal*, 14 (7), 351–62.

Humphrey, C., Turley, S. and Moizer, P. (1993), 'Protecting against detection: the case of auditors and fraud', *Accounting, Auditing & Accountability Journal*, 6 (1), 39–62.

Jayalakshmy, R., Seetharaman, A. and Khong, T. (2005), 'The changing role of the auditors', *Managerial Auditing Journal*, 20 (3), 249–71.

Kaminski, K.A., Wetzel, T.S. and Gaun, L. (2004), 'Can financial ratios detect fraudulent financial reporting?', *Managerial Auditing Journal*, 19 (1), 15–28.

Kaplan, S.E., Reckers, P.M.J. and Roark, S.J. (1988), 'An attribution theory analysis of tax evasion related judgments', *Accounting, Organizations & Society*, 13 (4), 371–9.

Kneer, D., Reckers, P. and Jennings, M. (1996), 'An empirical examination of the influence of the "new" US audit report and fraud red-flags on perceptions of auditor culpability', *Managerial Auditing Journal*, 11 (6), 18–30.

Langlois, C. and Schlegelmilch, B. (1990), 'Do corporate codes of ethics reflect national character? Evidence from Europe and the United States', *Journal of International Business Studies*, 21 (4), 519–539.

McGee, R. (2006), 'Three views on the ethics of tax evasion', *Journal of Business Ethics*, 67, 15–35.

McKee, T. (2006), 'Increase your fraud auditing effectiveness by being unpredictable', *Managerial Auditing Journal*, 21 (2), 224–31.

Makkawi, B. and Schick, A. (2003), 'Are auditors sensitive enough to fraud?', *Managerial Auditing Journal*, 18 (6/7), 591–8.

Martinez-Vazquez, J. and Rider, M. (2005), 'Multiple models of tax evasion: theory and evidence', *National Tax Journal*, 58 (1), 51–77.

Ministério das Finanças (MF) (2001), Decreto-Lei no. 198/2001, *Diário da República*, 152, I Série-A, 3 July: 3923–4012.

Ministério das Finanças (MF) (1998), Decreto-Lei no. 25/98, *Diário da República*, 34, I Série-A, 10 February: 530–534.

Ministério das Finanças (MF) (1994), Decreto-Lei no. 37/94, *Diário da República*, 32, I Série, 8 February: 617.

Ministério das Finanças (MF) (1993), Decreto-Lei no. 84/93, *Diário da República*, 65, I Série, 18 March: 1313–1315.

Ministério das Finanças (MF) (1989), Decreto-Lei no. 215/89, *Diário da República*, 149, I Série, 1 July: 2578–91.

Ministério das Finanças (MF) (1986), Decreto-Lei no. 165/86, *Diário da República*, 144, I Série, 26 June: 1513–1514.

Ministério das Finanças e da Administração Pública (MFAP) (2006), *Combate à fraude e evasão fiscais*, Lisboa: MFAP.

Ministério das Finanças e do Plano (MFP) (1980), Decreto-Lei no. 500/80, *Diário da República*, 243, I Série, 20 October: 3493.

Montgomery, D.D., Beasley, M.S., Menelaides, S.L. and Palmrose, Z.V. (2002), 'Auditors' new procedures for detecting fraud', *Journal of Accountancy*, 193 (5), 63–6.

Moyes, G. and Hasan, I. (1996), 'An empirical analysis of fraud detecting likelihood', *Managerial Auditing Journal*, 11 (3), 41–6.

Mulford, C. and Comiskey, E. (2002), *The Financial Numbers Game: Detecting Creative Accounting Practices*, New York: Wiley.

Naser, K. (1993), *Creative Financial Accounting: Its Nature and Use*, London: Prentice Hall Europe.

Nieschwietz, R., Schultz, J. and Zimbelman, M. (2000), 'Empirical research on external auditors' detection of financial statement fraud', *Journal of Accounting Literature*, 19, 190–246.

Organization for Economic Cooperation and Development (OECD) (2004), *The OECD's Project on Harmful Tax Practices: the 2004 Progress Report*, Paris: OECD.

Organization for Economic Cooperation and Development (OECD) (2000), *Improving Access to Bank Information for Tax Purposes*, Paris: OECD.

Palmrose, Z-V. and Scholz, S. (2004), 'The circumstances and legal consequences of non-GAAP reporting: evidence from restatements', *Contemporary Accounting Research*, 21 (1), 139–80.

Pany, K.J. and Whittington, O.R. (2001), 'Research implications of the Auditing Standard Board's Current Agenda', *Accounting Horizons*, 15 (4), 401–11.

Patterson, E. and Noel, J. (2003), 'Audit strategies and multiple fraud opportunities of misreporting and defalcation', *Contemporary Accounting Research*, 20 (3), 519–549.

Payne, E.A. and Ramsay, R.J. (2005), 'Fraud risk assessments and auditors' professional skepticism', *Managerial Auditing Journal*, 20 (3), 321–30.

Peñalva, F. (2002), 'Por qué ha caído Enron y por qué va a desaparecer Andersen EE.UU', *Boletín AECA*, 59, 6–8.

Pereira, M. (2005), *Fiscalidade*, Coimbra: Almedina.

Prosser, W. (1971), *Handbook of the Law of Torts*, 4th edn, St Paul: West Publishing.

Rahaman, A., Lawrence, S. and Roper, J. (2004), 'Social and environmental reporting at the VRA: institutionalised legitimacy or legitimation crisis?', *Critical Perspectives on Accounting*, 15, 35–56.

Rezaee, Z. (1995), 'What the COSO report means for internal auditors', *Managerial Auditing Journal*, 10 (6), 5–9.

Rivero, P. (2003), 'Responsabilidad social corporativa. Un nuevo modelo de gestión y medición para la empresa, *Boletín AECA*, 64, 35–7.

Rosner, R. (2003), 'Earnings manipulation in failing firms', *Contemporary Accounting Research*, 20 (2), 361–408.

Sanches, J. (2000), 'O combate à fraude fiscal e a defesa do contribuinte: dois objectivos inconciliáveis?', *Revisores & Empresas*, 3 (10), Julho/Setembro, 46–55.

Sandmo. A. (2005), 'The theory of tax evasion: a retrospective view', *National Tax Journal*, 58 (4), 643–63.

Schneider, F. (2005), 'Shadow economies around the world: what do we really know?', *European Journal of Political Economy*, 21 (3), 598–642.

Schneider, F. and Enste, D. (2000), 'Shadow economics: size, causes and consequences', *Journal of Economic Literature*, 37 (1), 77–114.

Schwartz, M. (2004), 'Effective corporate codes of ethics: perceptions of code users', *Journal of Business Ethics*, 55 (3), 323–43.

Schwartz, M. (2001), 'The nature of the relationship between corporate codes of ethics and behaviour', *Journal of Business Ethics*, 32 (3), 247–62.

Shah, A. (1998), 'Exploring the influences and constraints on creative accounting in the United Kingdom', *The European Accounting Review*, 7 (1), 83–104.

Shah, A. (1996), 'Creative compliance in financial reporting', *Accounting, Organizations and Society*, 21 (1), 23–39.

Smith, M. (1998), 'Creative accounting: the auditor effect', *Managerial Auditing Journal*, 13 (3), 155–8.

Somers, M.J. (2001), 'Ethical codes of conduct and organizational context: a study of the relationship between codes of conduct, employee behavior and organizational values', *Journal of Business Ethics*, 30 (2), 185–95.

Spathis, C.T. (2002), 'Detecting false financial statements using published data: some evidence from Greece', *Managerial Auditing Journal*, 17 (4), 179–91.

Stainer, A., Stainer, L. and Segal, A. (1997), 'The ethics of tax planning', *Journal of Business Ethics*, 6 (4), 213–219.

Tilt, C. (1994), 'The influence of external pressure groups on corporate social disclosure', *Accounting, Auditing & Accountability Journal*, 7 (4), 47–72.

United Nations (UN) (2004), *Guidance Document: Implementation of the 10th Principle against Corruption*, Geneva: United Nations.

Vanasco, R.R. (1998), 'Fraud auditing', *Managerial Auditing Journal*, 13 (1), 4–71.

Velasquez, M., Moberg, D. and Cavanagh, G. (1983), 'Organizational statesmanship and dirty politics: ethical guidelines for the organizational politician', *Organizational Dynamics*, 12 (2): 65–80.

Watson, D. (2003), 'Cultural dynamics of corporate fraud', *Cross Cultural Management*, 10 (1), 40–54.

Weaver, G. (1995), 'Does ethics code design matter? Effects of ethics code rationales and sanctions on recipients' justice perceptions and content recall', *Journal of Business Ethics*, 14 (5), 367–78.

Weaver, G. (1993), 'Corporate codes of ethics: purpose, process and content issues', *Business and Society*, 32 (1), 44–58.

Weller, S. (1988), 'The effectiveness of corporate codes of ethics', *Journal of Business Ethics*, 7 (5), 389–95.

Wenzel, M. (2004), 'The social side of sanctions: personal and social norms as moderators of deterrence', *Law and Human Behavior*, 28 (5), 547–67.

Cause-Related Marketing: Doing Good for your Company and your Cause

Ioanna Papasolomou

Introduction

Many businesses are attempting to align their social responsibility agendas with their business motivations. This trend has been driven by society's heightened expectations and by increased criticism by several interest groups such as environmental activists, human rights groups and consumer associations. The effort is placed on 'marrying' the corporate strategy of community involvement with social issues related to their business. Cause-related marketing (CRM) is a prime example of the partnership formed between corporations and charities to raise both money and brand awareness and to demonstrate a corporation's socially responsible behaviour.

CRM is referred to by many names, such as 'social marketing, charity marketing, corporate/strategic philanthropy, social investment, social marketing, responsible marketing … cause branding, sponsorship, PR and simply marketing' (Adkins 2005: 9–10). CRM is a marketing activity which encompasses (for example) marketing, public relations, advertising, direct marketing, sales promotion and sponsorship, as related to a cause. 'Causes' include good causes, charities, and other not-for-profit organizations. The range of these charitable causes is endless; for example, health improvement, helping homeless people and children, environmental issues, the arts and education. Marketing activities and approaches are equally vast, which leads us to potentially endless CRM types and methods.

The chapter aims to discuss societal marketing and relate it to the concept of CRM, to explore the concepts of corporate 'image' and corporate 'identity', and to discuss CRM and corporate reputation by giving examples of how CRM contributes in building and enhancing corporate reputation.

Societal marketing

Marketing has been with mankind since the beginning of civilization, when people used to exchange goods and services for survival. Over the years it has evolved, adapting to the developments and changes in the marketing environment. The 19th century marked the Industrial Revolution that was characterised by mass production, improved transportation and more efficient technology. These developments led to the evolution of the 'production era' in which consumers no longer had to produce goods in order to satisfy their needs. Many needs could now be satisfied through purchases from manufacturing and service organisations. Gradually this period was followed by the 'product era', an orientation that was based on the assumption that consumers will favour those products that offer the best quality, best performance and other features. Over time, companies realised that there was a need to maximise production and supply. Businesses began to make use of different tools to stimulate consumers to buy more; for example, aggressive advertising. Thus, the 'sales era' was introduced, in which companies had to implement aggressive selling and promotion efforts. The 'marketing orientation' was the fourth orientation that emerged. It recognises that in order for companies to achieve goals, they must first determine the needs and wants of target markets, and deliver the desired satisfactions more effectively and efficiently than competitors. However, in the last couple of decades many corporations have adopted the societal marketing concept that holds that businesses should then deliver superior value to customers in a way that maintains or improves the well-being of customers and society. This orientation questions whether the pure marketing concept is adequate in an age of environmental problems, resource shortages, rapid population growth, worldwide economic problems and neglected social services. Many businesses have adopted the societal concept – businesses such as Coca Cola, McDonald's, Esso, The Body Shop, and Johnson & Johnson.

CRM can be used by businesses to achieve their marketing objectives whilst addressing the long-term interests of society. Today businesses operate in a highly competitive and hostile environment dominated by many gatekeeper groups which can hinder their efforts in gaining access to markets or achieving their marketing objectives. Consumer associations, trade unions, environmental groups, human rights groups, local communities, government agencies and the media act as gatekeepers, due to their power and role as watchdogs for the many groups of people whose interests they promote and protect. If a business can actively demonstrate that it acknowledges the concerns and even criticisms raised by these stakeholder groups by, for example, adapting its business practices and launching community involvement programmes, it can enhance its corporate reputation – the picture that different stakeholder groups have about the organisation.

CRM focuses on partnerships/relationships between businesses and non-profit organisations, charities and charitable causes. These partnerships have the potential to instil trust, develop positive attitudes and perceptions towards the business and subsequently strengthen the corporate image.

Cause-related marketing

CRM has been used by businesses for many centuries but the exact phrase was coined in 1983 by American Express. Pringle and Thompson (1999) claim that the earliest CRM campaign was launched by Austin Martin in 1942. The company developed a CRM campaign which made donations to various non-profit organisations as part of the San Francisco Arts Festival. Every time the card was used in an area, a 2 per cent donation was made to a charity, and every time a new member applied for a card a larger contribution was made. Some $108,000 were raised for the charity whilst the company achieved its business objective – increased use of the card. Between 1981 and 1984 American Express supported more than 45 causes including the restoration of the Statue of Liberty, which cost $4 million. This case was the first example of a coordinated CRM effort. Since then American Express has launched 90 programmes in 17 different countries.

Pringle and Thompson (1999: 3) define CRM as 'a strategic positioning and marketing tool which links a company or brand to a relevant social cause or issue for mutual benefit'. Adkins (2005: 11) describes CRM as 'a commercial activity by which businesses and charities or causes form a partnership with each other to market an image, product or service for mutual benefit'. Based on this definition, CRM is not philanthropy or altruism; it is a commercial partnership which leads to mutual benefit and a return on investment. All parties come together in order to achieve their corporate objectives, such as enhancement of their corporate image, an increase in their customer base, a gain in publicity or an increase in turnover. Mutual benefit is actually the desired outcome and the underlying principle of the CRM partnership. There is no doubt that all that the parties enter into the relationship because they have something to gain. The business can generate higher sales and strengthen its corporate reputation and the charity or cause can generate funds and gain publicity. So, CRM provides a commercial advantage for all the parties in the relationship, and this is actually the key reason why partners come together in the first place. In essence, CRM is any activity that has been developed to market an image, product or service for the mutual benefit of a charity/cause and a business. The concept has raised criticism in terms of whether it is manipulative or exploitative. However, the results of the Business in the Community's Game Plan research published in 1997 revealed that consumers do not believe that this is the case.

CRM is a high-profile activity that helps businesses to demonstrate and communicate their social responsibility towards the whole range of their stakeholder groups.

It is expected to increase in importance as more and more firms recognise its role in enabling them to achieve their marketing and business objectives whilst demonstrating a concern towards social problems/issues and creating awareness towards the company's values. Communicating this corporate social responsibility and being seen as actively involved as a corporate citizen has direct benefits towards the company's reputation, which in turn has benefits in terms of stakeholder perceptions, attitudes and behaviour towards the organisation.

After all, the ways organisations that behave, are talked about, and are reported and perceived by their publics, influence greatly the management of their reputation. The existent literature indicates that many successful and profitable organisations spend significant amounts of money in fulfilling their social responsibilities. The rationale could be purely commercial; by raising their profile and improving their reputation through being associated with 'good deeds' they can generate higher profits. However, their actions may be motivated by an understanding that what is good for society is also good for the organisation, or they may be motivated by pure altruism. Irrespective of their motives, the end result is improved corporate reputation. This provides ample rationale for the adoption of CRM which can help a business demonstrate its socially responsible corporate values and behaviour. 'Cause-related marketing enables a corporation to demonstrate its values whilst adding value to these values. It is based on mutual benefit and plays directly into the lifestyle of today's consumer' (Adkins 2005).

In today's 'intrusive' and highly critical society, organisations are not only judged on their achievements but on their behaviour too. This is in fact an opportunity for corporations if they see CSR and CRM as essential business strategies. Why? Because brand value and reputation are widely accepted as a company's most valuable assets, and CRM can instil trust and brand loyalty by highlighting the positive impact responsible business operations and activities have in the marketplace, the workplace, the environment or in the community.

Corporate identity and corporate image

'Corporate image' can be described as the picture that people have of a company, whereas 'corporate identity' refers to all the forms of expression that a business uses to offer an insight into its nature (van Riel 1992: 27). Van Rekom et al. (1991) define corporate identity as 'the cues or signals which it offers via its behaviour, communication and symbolism'. According to Margulies (2004: 68), 'identity means the sum of all the ways a company chooses to identify itself to all its publics – the community, customers, employees, the press, the present and potential stockholders, security analysis, and investment bankers.' Olins (1989) suggests that 'corporate identity is the tangible manifestation of the personality of a company. It is the identity which reflects and projects the real personality of the company.' Corporate image on the other hand is 'a set of meanings by which an object is known and through which people describe, remember and relate to it. That is, the net result of the interaction of a person's beliefs, ideas, feelings, and impressions about an object' (Dowling 1986). Margulies (2004: 68) states: 'image is the perception of the company by its publics'. The corporate image reflects the corporate identity. The corporate image/reputation is based on the signals that the organisation gives about its nature. It is based on how the company conducts or is perceived as conducting its business. When corporate reputation is secure, a flow of positive and tangible benefits accrues to the organisation; for example, strong brand awareness, high customer loyalty, strong credibility and trust, high market share and a strong market position.

However, irrespective of how honest and open these signals are, they may not result in a positive image in the minds of stakeholder groups. This is due to the fact that the stakeholder perceptions and attitudes depend on how the corporation and its employees are seen to behave, what the stakeholders have seen or heard in the media, and their experiences with the organisation and its products. Hence, gaining and maintaining a good corporate reputation is a difficult process which requires strategic planning, management and continuous assessment. It is in fact a long-term investment which is essential as the external environment is characterised by turbulence, instability, hostile circumstances and rapid change.

Birkigt and Stadler (1986) have identified three ways in which an organisation can express its 'personality':

- Behaviour: corporate behaviour is one of the most powerful ways in which an organisation can present its identity. Stakeholder groups judge a business by its actions and organisational activities. Organisations can highlight certain aspects of corporate behaviour through corporate and marketing communications and/or symbols.
- Communication: it is one of the most flexible corporate identity tools as it can be adapted to transmit any message (verbal, visual) the organisation wishes to communicate to its target publics.
- Symbolism: symbols enable an organisation to convey what it stands for or what it wishes to stand for.

Based on this model, corporate identity/personality can be crystallised in the behaviour, communication and symbolism of an organisation. These are the core forms of corporate self-expression. However, this model ignores the fact that image does not always reflect corporate identity. The corporate image is influenced by several factors such as the competitive environment, the market trends and social developments. Nevertheless, businesses cannot afford to leave their corporate image to chance. They should carefully invest in the corporate identity tools discussed as well as in good corporate citizenship, strong stakeholder relationships and cause-related marketing. These are some of the activities which can potentially instil positive perceptions and attitudes towards the organisation among key stakeholder groups and help build a strong corporate image. Therefore, externally managers need to explore the brand's reputation among stakeholders to ensure the brand's identity is communicated effectively and has contributed to developing favourable perceptions towards the organisation. Fombrun (1996) suggests that corporate reputation is regarded as the company's ability to meet the expectations of all stakeholders.

Freeman (1984: 46) defines a stakeholder as 'any group or individual who can affect or is affected by the achievement of the organisation's objectives'. The supporters of the 'stakeholder model' argue that corporate managers must balance the interests of all the different groups who have a 'stake' in the company. This model is founded on the principle of the corporation accepting its social responsibilities and developing corporate policy on the basis of protecting, nurturing and strengthening their relationships with all stakeholders who can impact on corporate performance. The key reason is the pressing need to build the corporate brand/identity in order to sustain corporate reputation.

Bernstein (1986) developed the Cobweb method which holds that the management assesses how the general public rates the corporation on each of eight values: integrity, value for money, technical innovation, social responsibility, service, reliability, imagination and quality. This method measures the picture that the management has about their company but it is not necessarily the same as the one held by the key stakeholder groups. In addition, building a strong corporate reputation is a long-term process which requires effort and investment of resources and human capital. However, it takes only a few moments to be destroyed, and re-instilling trust and confidence in an organisation may never be achieved. Positive interaction with stakeholder groups is a key component that goes towards building and sustaining corporate reputation.

Nurturing, developing and communicating a company's reputation is not an easy task. It requires careful planning and management. Marketing plays a vital role in the external communication of the company's reputation through the effective integration of marketing communication tools. However, this alone is not enough as companies need to demonstrate a commitment to corporate social responsibility codes, as well as to invest in community programmes and CRM strategies. Corporate reputation can be affected positively by corporate activities demonstrating social concern, awareness and involvement. The challenge is to ensure a consistency of approach and practice and a clear communication strategy to ensure that the benefits and positive impacts of an organisation are well understood by all stakeholder groups. CSR and CRM can be regarded and used as 'signals' for building corporate identity and, hence, helping to build corporate reputation. Stakeholder groups are concerned about an organisation's corporate social responsibility, and their perceptions of it (or lack of it), that is, the corporate reputation, will influence their decisions and actions.

CRM and corporate reputation

Adkins (2005) claims that through the implementation of CRM a company promotes its image and products/services whilst it supports a good cause, and raises money for the cause, resulting in enhanced corporate reputation, demonstration of corporate values, enhanced customer loyalty and sales. Building the corporate reputation is dependent on the consistent delivery of quality and customer service but beyond these, corporate reputation depends on the fundamental benefits of a business as well as the perceptions held by stakeholders towards the organisation and its practices. The literature reviewed revealed a plethora of positive evidence to support the adoption and implementation of CRM by corporations.

The Business in the Community Brand Benefits (2003) research, a study exploring the perceptions of 6,000 consumers in the UK and the US in order to investigate the impact of CRM on actual consumer perception, loyalty and buying behaviour, showed that during Persil's partnership with Comic Relief, the sales of the brand rose 13 per cent, and there was a 3 per cent increase in Persil's market share over the partnership's duration. Business in the Community awards companies and programmes/partnerships that have achieved excellence in the field of responsible business practice. These CRM programmes have generated a number of benefits for businesses, one of which is enhanced corporate image.

The Ford Motor Company and their 'Drive Towards a Cure' programme won the CRM Excellence Award in 2004. The initiative was formed in 1999 between Ford Motor Company and Breakthrough Breast Cancer. The key objective of the campaign was to raise £1.25 million over five years. The impact of the campaign was the following:

- It enhanced Ford's corporate reputation.
- Sales and market share growth exceeded expectations. In fact Ford's sales growth in the female market since 2001 has exceeded sales of major competitors.
- Since 2001, 'Drive Towards a Cure' has generated £621,995 for Breakthrough.
- Since the campaign the Breakthrough charity has attracted new supporters in the form of Ford customers, dealers and employees (see <http://www.bitc.org.uk/resources/case_studies/crmforddrivecure.html>).

The 'Am I Listening?' campaign by BT and ChildLine was launched in October 2002, aimed at ensuring that the voice of every young person in the UK is heard. In early 2006 ChildLine merged with the NSPCC and ever since the company has been working with both partners. The CRM initiative has produced the following benefits:

- improvement in BT's reputation
- an increase in employee motivation and perceptions
- the raising of over £4 million for ChildLine since April 2002
- the awareness of 47 per cent of BT customers of the campaign (MORI) (see <http://www.bitc.org.uk/resources/case_studies/afe_crm_04_bt.html>).

BT designed and developed a programme to support citizenship education, taught in UK schools with an emphasis on communication skills. The programme has resulted in a measurable improvement in the reputation of BT with customers and its workforce. Another campaign launched by BT is 'Communicating for a Better World'. This programme focuses on issues that are perceived as important by stakeholders; for example, carrying on business in a responsible and caring way, giving back to the society, community involvement, and campaigning on issues that are of concern to society. Their CRM campaign has raised awareness of BT's credentials in relation to environmental performance, business ethics, supplier policy and human rights. It has also enabled them to attract new business and the company is rated highly by customers and employees.

For the fourth year running, Debenhams, the department store, has worked in partnership with the 'Breast Cancer Campaign' over a four-week period in September and October. The CRM campaign focused on heightening awareness of breast cancer and its symptoms by providing timely information through a variety of forums. The campaign has provided Debenhams with the following benefits:

- a competitive advantage over its rival firms
- improved relationships with key suppliers and new commercial agreements
- extensive media coverage
- enhanced communication and teamwork throughout the organization (see <http://www.bitc.org.uk/resources/case_studies/afe_crm_04_debenhams. html>).

Tesco's 'Computers for Schools' is one of the UK's most well-known CRM campaigns. It has been implemented since 1992 to help schools to improve their IT equipment, and has resulted in more than £100 million worth of ICT equipment arriving in schools in Britain. The scheme has received wide media coverage and positive word-of-mouth communication (see <http://www.bitc.org.uk/resources/case_studies/afe_crm_04_bt.html>).

An investigation of the CRM literature revealed that CRM programmes can help suppliers differentiate themselves from competitors. A study carried out by Smith and Alcorn (1991) showed that 45 per cent of their sample would be likely to switch brands to support a business that donated to charitable causes. This finding was supported by the 1997 Cone Communication CRM study, which revealed that that 76 per cent of consumers would be likely to switch retailers, assuming that quality and price were equal, based on whether one of them supported a cause (Waugh 1997).

A MORI research carried out in July/August 1998 indicated that, when developing an opinion about a company, 77 per cent of the sample of the adult population claimed that it was very or fairly important for them to understand the activities of corporations in society and also 77 per cent of the sample also stated the same about a product (Adkins 2005). Business in the Community (2003) revealed the following:

- 48 per cent of consumers showed an actual change in behaviour, saying that they switched brands, increased usage, or tried or enquired about new products.
- 7 out of 10 consumers who were involved in a CRM programme reported a positive impact on their buying behaviour or perceptions.
- Awareness of CRM means consumers consistently rate the appropriate organisations higher on brand affinity, statements of trust, innovation, endorsement and bonding.

Kotler and Lee (2005) suggest that the majority of corporate benefits from CRM campaigns are marketing-related and include the aim of attracting new customers, reaching niche markets, increasing product sales and creating positive brand identity. Sir Dominic Cadbury suggests that CRM should become an integral part of corporate practice because it can effectively contribute to enhancing corporate image, achieving differentiation, building customer loyalty and sales. Of course the challenge is for corporations to form appropriate partnerships and then implement and communicate them effectively (Adkins 2005) in a way that will enhance corporate reputation.

Conclusion

CRM can become a competitive advantage for those businesses that can exploit it properly. It has the potential to help an organisation to shape its corporate values and, hence, its corporate identity through a focus on CSR. It has the power to enable corporations to communicate these values to external and internal audiences. CRM is a process by which businesses support worthwhile causes whilst pursuing commercial objectives. Through forming partnerships with charities or causes an organisation markets its image and brands. CRM provides the means for forming and managing their relationships with a variety of key stakeholders. By acknowledging and responding to stakeholder concerns and interests towards society and by demonstrating this through an investment in CRM programmes, corporations can demonstrate their values and enhance their corporate reputation.

The literature reviewed suggests that a corporate image refers to the meanings by which an organisation is known and which people use to describe or remember it. It is the outcome of peoples' beliefs, experiences, perceptions and feelings about an organisation. A strong corporate reputation is the foundation for building successful commercial relationships with different target publics since it generates trust and goodwill between the business and its stakeholder groups. It is important to acknowledge that no company can afford to ignore corporate reputation. The impression it creates either at an unconscious or conscious level inevitably affects stakeholders' feelings and attitudes towards the organisation.

Corporate reputation is shaped to a considerable degree by the signals it gives about its nature. Such signals are subsequently received by different target audiences and are used to form perceptions and feelings about an organisation. CRM can undoubtedly be one of these signals or cues, which an organisation can offer as a form of expression and as a tool for enhancing its corporate reputation.

References

Adkins, S. (2005), *Cause Related Marketing: Who cares Wins*, Oxford: Elsevier Butterworth-Heinemann.

Bernstein, D. (1986), *Company Image and Reality: A Critique of Corporate Communications*, Eastbourne: Holt, Rinehart and Winston.

Birkigt, K. and Stadler, M.M. (1986), *Corporate Identity, Grundlagen, Funktionen und Beispielen*, Landsberg an Lech: Verlag Modern Industrie.

Business in the Community (2003), *Cause-Related Marketing Impact = Celebration – A Celebration of Best Practice and Impact of Cause-Related Marketing Programmes in the UK Discovered through the Cause-Related Marketing Tracker 2003*, published by Business in the Community, printing donated by Tesco.

Business in the Community (2003), *Brand Benefits*, a publication reporting the findings from a research study supported by Research International, Dunnhumby and Lightspeed.

Dowling, G.R. (1986), 'Managing your corporate image', *Industrial Marketing Management*, 15, 109–115.

Fombrun, C.J. (1996), *Reputation: Realizing Value from the Corporate Image*, Boston MA: Harvard Business School Press.

Freeman, R.E. (1984), *Strategic Management: A Stakeholder Approach*, Boston MA: Pitman Publishing.

Handy, C. (1997), 'Will your company become a democracy?', in *The World in 1997*, cited in S. Adkins (2005), *Cause-Related Marketing: Who Cares Wins*, Oxford: Elsevier Butterworth-Heinemann.

Kotler, P. and Lee, N. (2005), *Corporate Social Responsibility: Doing the Most Good for your Company and your Cause*, Hoboken NJ: Wiley.

Margulies, W. (2004), 'Make the most of your corporate identity', in J.M.T. Balmer and S.A. Greyser, *Revealing the Corporation*, London: Routledge: London.

Olins, W. (1989), *Corporate Identity: Making Business Strategy Visible through Design*, London: Thames & Hudson.

Pringle, H. and Thompson, M. (1999), How Cause-Related Marketing Builds Brands, Chichester: Wiley.

Rekom, J. van, Riel, C.B.M. van, and Wierenga, B. (1991), *Corporate Identity. Van aag concept naar hard feiten materiaal*, working paper, Rotterdam: Erasmus University, Corporate Communication Centre.

Riel, C.B.M van (1992), *Principles of Corporate Communication*, Harlow: Pearson Education.

Smith, S.M. and Alcorn, D.S. (1991), 'Cause marketing: a new direction in marketing of corporate responsibility', *The Journal of Consumer Marketing*, 8 (3), 19–35.

Waugh, L. (1997), 'Cause-related marketing more accepted than ever', *Philanthropy Journal*, 3 November, available at <http:// www.philanthropy journal.org/corp/causerelated1097.htm>.

<http://www.bitc.org.uk/resources/case_studies/afe_crm_04_bt.html>, accessed 18 April 2007.

<http://www.bitc.org.uk/resources/case_studies/afe_crm_04_debenhams.html>, accessed 16 April 2007.
<http://www.bitc.org.uk/resources/case_studies/crmforddrivecure.html>, accessed 22 September 2005.

Index